An Inconvenient Black History of British Musical Theatre

ABOUT THE AUTHORS

Sean Mayes is a New York music director active in both New York City and Toronto, with a background in London and the UK. He is an active member of the Broadway music community as a vocal coach, accompanist, orchestrator-arranger and pit musician. He is a part-time professor in Musical Theatre at Sheridan College, Canada, and has published on the history of music directing and the role of Black music directors on Broadway.

Sarah K. Whitfield is a senior lecturer in Musical Theatre at the University of Wolverhampton, UK. Her research focuses on exploring the historiography of musical theatre and recovering the work that women and minoritized groups have done through archival research and digital humanities. She has published widely on collaborative practice in musical theatre, film musicals and in Queer fan studies. Her most recent book is the edited collection *Reframing the Musical: Race, Culture and Identity* (2019).

An Inconvenient Black History of British Musical Theatre

1900–1950

*Sean Mayes and
Sarah K. Whitfield*

methuen | drama

LONDON · NEW YORK · OXFORD · NEW DELHI · SYDNEY

METHUEN DRAMA
Bloomsbury Publishing Plc
50 Bedford Square, London, WC1B 3DP, UK
1385 Broadway, New York, NY 10018, USA
29 Earlsfort Terrace, Dublin 2, Ireland

BLOOMSBURY, METHUEN DRAMA and the Methuen Drama logo are
trademarks of Bloomsbury Publishing Plc

First published in Great Britain 2022

Cover design by Charlotte Daniels
Cover image: Roman Sigaev / Alamy Stock Photo

A catalogue record for this book is available from the British Library.

A catalog record for this book is available from the Library of Congress.

ISBN: HB: 978-1-3501-1963-5
         PB: 978-1-3502-3268-6
       ePDF: 978-1-3501-1964-2
      eBook: 978-1-3501-1965-9

Typeset by Integra Software Services Pvt. Ltd.
Printed and bound in Great Britain

To find out more about our authors and books visit www.bloomsbury.com
and sign up for our newsletters.

The book is dedicated to the memory of the Black performers, practitioners and creatives whose names we speak: Rest in Power.

CONTENTS

KEY FIGURES

MUSIC FIGURES

IMAGES

TABLES

PREFACE

Sean
1 June 2020, New York City

I sit writing these words as the incessant sounds of police sirens roam the streets of New York outside my home. The blades of helicopters chop the air as a constant reminder from police presence that too much dissent may result in another unjustified and stinging death at the hands of law enforcement. Despite inferred intentions of keeping the streets safe, these sounds are a reminder of the presence of nearby uniformed officers, not unlike the ones who actively and implicitly killed 45-year-old Black father, brother, lover, son, US citizen and fellow soul of this earth George Floyd only a week earlier. Three months earlier (13 March 2020), Breonna Taylor was shot eight times by the police officers who were raiding her apartment in Louisville, Kentucky.

Protests continue, multiple cities are on nightly watch and a recently imposed curfew acts to quell potential new acts of resistance to an already unjust system. Voices of Colour, either through vocalization or silence, express their fatigue. White voices express their personal emotional disarray, their rage and their willingness (or not) to step up and make a difference. Voices pollute the airwaves, in the streets, on social media and in unrelenting emails that affirm that '*this* is the moment; *this* is the Black body that made the difference; *this* is the wonderment for the Black race that we needed to make the step to change systemic racism once and for all'. What particularly interests me in this moment as a theatre practitioner is how theatre companies across the globe are responding in this moment. Almost all affirming how wrong what has happened is, with most claiming that once we enter a post-Covid-19 landscape, where theatres can once again be open, things will look different structurally. And yet, I wonder.

I am Black: and I wonder because I am Black, and will remain Black until the day I die. I wonder because I know my own journey – being a Black theatre practitioner and scholar has required a great deal of resilience, education, resilience, experience, resilience – most often in that order. Arguably, being a theatre practitioner and a scholar have both required a more precise harness of these aforementioned attributes than some of my white colleagues, as at each step of the ladder, I have witnessed colleagues with less education and experience than myself move past me up the ladder faster. As a result, the journey to climb the ladder has taken longer, and it is at certain points where one must wonder how to not get tired when climbing with double the hardiness, and yet being further back. And so, we reach another rung of fatigue in the witnessing of the murder of George Floyd.

To use graphic imagery not lightly, the system has, in a less literal fashion, always had its knee on the necks of Black artists, and artists of Colour alike. We feel the pressure to breathe constantly. The measured and minimal success that we witness and achieve within our own community compared with the seemingly limitless bounty of artistic opportunity from our white colleagues gives us the strength to keep going, keep creating, keep believing. We are given just the right number of opportunities to present and work on stories of Colour amongst a palette of shows focused on people who do not resemble us. As an artist and scholar of Colour, I have never benefited from a privilege of my skin colour – with the rare exception of when it has checked a box for diversity on a grant application or a workplace requirement for a company for which I have laboured. When I was first introduced to the art form that would become my life, I never sat in rehearsals with a majority of performers that looked like me; never learned about shows that were written by composers and lyricists that looked like me; never performed in shows with characters that didn't require a complete conversion of my culture, or were directed by people who looked like me, nor performed for an audience of people who looked like me. I am, and was, the exception, as many of us Black artists are. And so, when I further pursued study amongst overwhelmingly white colleagues, and dove further into scholarly work in a field that is not only overwhelmingly white but in fallacy believes it is not racist even when dispelling truths about Black influence in musical theatre, my eyes slowly opened more and more to the need of the work of *recovery* in the musical.

When Sarah first approached me to write a chapter for the *Reframing the Musical: Race, Culture and Identity* collection in 2017, there was initially no impetus on my behalf to write about the intersection of music direction in musical theatre and race. Why would there be? Even though I am Black, there was never a need for me to encounter my Blackness in any of the work I did, and so, what implications could that have on the rest of the art? However, with Sarah's encouragement, I was opened up to a world of new discoveries, which, embarrassingly, revealed to me that there were in fact many Black practitioners and practitioners of Colour that I had never even heard of. For years, I had been an implicit, active participant in performing and bearing witness to the work of Black artists whose faces I could not pull out of a line-up if required to under duress. And so, the work started and continues today to these pages which you read ahead of you.

You are reading these words because of some interest and solidarity in what lies ahead. As a fellow discoverer on this journey of *recovery*, I can affirm with you that I did not know my relevance to this work even at a reasonable point in my career. I affirm further that the work that lies ahead is truly remarkable and will convince you of the need to press forward in learning about what *recovery* is left to be done. This is my relevance to this work: as a Black practitioner active on Broadway and across Canada and the world in musical theatre, I come to scholarship with a genuine curiosity – and further a *duty* – to reveal the names of the people who worked with monumental capacity to open the doorways to where I stand today. Sarah and I continue to find names of people – people whose names were previously names unremembered, unspoken. And regrettably, we also see how quickly through time erasure becomes *passive* – an act of not *actively* knowing a name, or not *actively* knowing whose land you stand on, or not *actively* knowing a true history turns into an actively *passive* form of erasure. Despite their labour being the backbone of our industry up to, and including, today, you will likely know few of them, as we did when we started this journey. It is in this work, the work of *recovery*, that this proves relevant *right now*.

This book should not be relevant. And yet it is. Now more than ever. As these words are written, our industry is actively undergoing a punishing self-examination of its wrongs and shortfalls, with the sole aim to finally do better. It is not simply up to the ones at the top to find this higher path; it is through our collective education and awareness that we find the stories that have been buried to affirm, yes, for us to be relevant to the issues of erasure and recovery related to race today, we need to understand what has been done before. The history of musical theatre is a complex one, and many of us know it as an unchallenged tale largely written by a private club of white men. British musical theatre is even more complex; it is a system of numerous forms of theatre and art, all curated by amazing musicians who laid the groundwork for an entire industry before legislation outlawing racial discrimination even existed.

In an early chapter, you'll read of the resistance work of the revolutionary musical *In Dahomey*, of which scholar Theresa Saxon claims that, though it 'was formulated with an uplift agenda, to challenge, subtly, racial prejudice, the show's potential resistance to racialised stereotyping was, ultimately, eroded in England's auditoria.'[1] The work we have done looks to challenge this idea of erosion of Black resistance. We aim to redistribute the names of these practitioners into present and fresh minds. We aim to redistribute their stories to more voices so they can be retold and remain alive. We aim to redistribute the responsibility of who gets to claim that their voices were not ones of resistance. We aim to redistribute the notion of who their stories were for, and who was meant to truly consume them. And with all of this comes an empowerment. That these voices and people are about to be read and witnessed by one more interested reader is no small task in a system designed by virtue to keep them hidden. The journey of active recovery is a long one, and we are aware the work here will take years, as has its erosion. It will take all of us, leaders and allies alike, to invest the time it takes to expose, stop and listen to what has been laid down in the past so we can acknowledge doing better in the future. And it starts here.

Sarah
Birmingham, UK

The Black Lives Matter movement (#Blacklivesmatter) uses Floyd's last words: 'I can't breathe.' Protestors chant them across hundreds of cities in the United States and then the world. The names of people killed by police brutality, by structural indifference, names of people whose families have never had justice – protestors speak their names too as they demand change. As the United States moves to use the military to stamp down on protests, on 1 June 2020, the US Defense Secretary Mark T. Esper says they will 'mass and dominate the battlespace'. That same day, to enable President Trump to walk to church and hold a photo op with a Bible, police officers deploy tear gas and flashbangs on protestors.

In the days that follow, theatres and arts organizations issue renewed statements about their commitment to Black lives, and to doing *better* on inclusive practice and supporting their Black staff. The Black Lives Matter movement started in 2013, after the acquittal of the police officer involved in the shooting of Trayvon Martin. Through the work of organizers and activists Opal Tometi, Alicia Garza and Patrisse Cullors maintained an active presence in the intervening period. In this moment though, something shifts. Production companies and Broadway musicals (all on a Covid-19-enforced pause) issue statements. Drama schools do similar, and Black students share their experiences of racist language and of white supremacist structures that have inflicted trauma and shaped their training. Black performers and writers share their experiences of the traumas that structural racism and white supremacy, that white people, have inflicted on them.

I am white, white privilege materially benefits me, and gives me access to social and cultural capital over and again. When I was at university, everyone who taught me had the same skin colour as me. Everyone on the syllabus had the same skin colour as me. Race was never part of it because it was always part of it. I am a university lecturer who teaches musical theatre, and my focus is often the history of the form. I have worked in many all-white departments in universities where most of the academic staff are white. My entire education as a white person has trained me to take up space and occupy room: I have shelves full of books about the musical that largely tell white histories.

During the process of editing *Reframing the Musical: Race, Culture and Identity*, which brought together the contributions of twelve emerging academics and practitioners in the field in challenging scholarship around the musical, Sean and I had started to wonder where the thread of the faulty history of the musical would lead us. We wondered if the history of British musical theatre that we had encountered, where Black performers and practitioners were on the periphery until 1948 and the arrival of the HMT *Empire Windrush*, could possibly be accurate. It was not. My services to this project are as a historian and researcher. It is a privilege to be able to work on the history of Black performers, and to be able to use my skills in finding material to develop on established histories and to attempt to restore where they have been lost. As Sean and I started work, we turned to established findings of scholars like Daphne Brooks, Marva Carter, Rainer Lotz and Stephen Bourne. Arianne Johnson Quinn suggested that we look in regional British newspapers for more information about the scope of what we were dealing with. Then information started tumbling out. We began a database of performances, finding the work of hundreds of Black performers and practitioners from 1900 onwards. Every single time we looked, we found more – more Black performers and endless shows and revues, revusicals and musicals across the UK. We found 1,000 performances in British theatre before we stopped compiling more data; there is much more to be done. There is so much information; it becomes increasingly difficult to see anything other than a wilful insistence that Black performance practice could not have been present in the history of the musical in 1950. It is. Everywhere, widely, extensively, in every aspect of British musical theatre life, from variety to musicals, to ballet, from Blackpool to Brighton, from the West End to Dundee.

Our book is *an* inconvenient Black history of performance practice, but it is not *the* definitive one. It points at the scale of what we are dealing with and acts, we hope, as an urgent call for you as the reader to carry it on, to find the history of another performer. Even as we stop looking for new people to talk about, and we start writing about those we already have decided to focus on, we keep finding more. We had planned visits to finish writing the book together during 2020, but it became clear neither of us were going anywhere. Instead, we co-ordinate time zones and talk on video calls about the work we are doing and the people we are encountering and the progress we are making. We work through reports of how People of Colour are experiencing higher mortality rates because of Covid-19: in the UK, Black people die at a far higher rate.[2] As a curfew operates on the streets of New York, we talk again, and Sean speaks to the heart of the issue: this book should not be relevant.

ACKNOWLEDGEMENTS

Many academics and researchers have supported us in this work and taken time to give their expertise and advice on our queries. We are deeply grateful to the following people: Stephanie Batiste; Marva Carter; Arianne Johnson Quinn, for her expertise in British musical theatre in this period; Mat Dalgleish, for his expertise in audio technology developments; Nathan James; Abbie Cobden, who supported some of the newspaper research on Buddy Bradley; Clare Chandler; Juliet and Richard Gunn; John Cowley; Bill Egan; Paula Seniors; Rainer Lotz; and Catherine Tackley.

This book builds on the remarkable study and approaches of several key scholars, without whom the work would not have been possible, not least David Olusoga, Thomas L. Riis, Stephen Bourne, Rainer Lotz, Jeffrey Green and Peter Fryer. There are many researchers who, like Bourne, have interviewed key figures and secured their work for future generations; these include Marshall and Jean Sterne's interviews with key dance figures, including Buddy Bradley; and the valuable Oral History of Jazz in Britain interviews carried out largely by Val Wilmer. We have been deeply humbled to talk to the families of some of the people in this book, and our thanks go to John Schuman and Camille Campbell. We are grateful to the Mabel Mercer Foundation.

In supporting and presenting the data which underpin this book, we are particularly grateful to the advice and support of Martin Eve, Derek Miller and Lorna Robinson. We have relied on the support and expertise of research librarians at several archives, including Doug Reside at the Billy Rose Theater Division at the New York Public Library for the Performing Arts; the Schomburg Center for Research in Black Culture; the Victoria and Albert Museum Theatre Archives; and the Rare Books and Manuscripts Division at the British Library. Part of this work was presented in conference papers at the International Federation for Theatre Research (IFTR) and Digital Humanities in Theatre. We are grateful for the vision and support of Methuen Bloomsbury editors Anna Brewer and Dominic O'Hanlon, and to our anonymous peer reviewers who have helped us communicate this work more clearly and precisely. It is a better book because of their help and contribution.

We note with gratitude that the University of Wolverhampton helped to fund a portion of the research for this book.

We are appreciative of the patience and support of our families in what has been a substantial undertaking: Meghan, and Jakob, Emmy and Ada.

ABBREVIATIONS

BBC	British Broadcasting Corporation
BNA	British Newspaper Archive
CAA	Council of African Affairs
FBV	Faux-black vernacular (songs) (see 'Note on language')
ISDN	*Illustrated Sporting and Dramatic News*
LCP	League of Coloured Peoples
LPE	*London and Provincial Entr'acte*
MHTR	*Music Hall and Theatre Review*
NAACP	National Association for the Advancement of Colored People
NYT	*New York Times*
ODJB	Original Dixieland Jazz Band
ODNB	*Oxford Dictionary of National Biography*
PAA	Pan African Association
UNIA	Universal Negro Improvement Association
USO	United Service Organizations

NOTE ON LANGUAGE

We have made a conscious decision not to replicate racial slurs in the book; slurs do damage and remove power from Black people both historically and in the present moment. We have noted racialized and racist intents behind their usage. This is a subjective approach, but we feel it is necessary to support future Black students for whom these words continue to remove power in the classroom.

We have tried to consistently redact racial slurs – where they feature in quotations, we have noted them as [*racial slur*] or, if necessary, we paraphrase in brackets. Some of the meaning behind particular words has changed over time – where words have been used to reclaim power or through activism, we have made this clear when relevant. It is important to note that some words were originally used as demonstrating racial pride and identity – for example, Negro. This is not a word that would be used now but is an important term in the Harlem Renaissance period to reclaim Black identity and power.

Sometimes slurs are in the title of a show written or produced by Black writers. In this scenario, we refer *once* to the full title in the endnotes at the first point of usage. This is particularly an issue with a slur which music studies has continued to reprint to refer to an early genre of popular music which attempted to parody Black dialect and expression,[3] songs which were popular around the turn of the twentieth century. We suggest that the word as a genre does not need to be reprinted, as it perpetuates racial violence. We have suggested faux-black vernacular (FBV) songs and use this throughout. Our decision is not born from squeamishness, or over-sensitive reactionary responses; the word was *already* a slur at the point of use. It is also true that some performers of African descent wrote in this song form as active forms of resistance and performed within it, and that our solution may only be a temporary one.

We believe we can point to and elucidate this resistance without repeating the violence against which they struggled. At some point, we have to say *enough*.

Introduction

This book should not be relevant. The substantial presence of Black practitioners in British musical theatre from 1900 to 1950 should not be news, and it should not be surprising. The diligent work of many Black scholars and archivists, in building and maintaining the histories of the way in which the African diaspora has shaped popular musical theatre, has made this information accessible for a very long time. Black scholars and scholars of Colour have extensively demonstrated how Black theatre performers, musicians and practitioners worked internationally from 1900 to 1950. Such work has been supported by significant scholarship elsewhere from early twentieth-century recording histories and popular music histories. Yet, despite this, the historiography of British musical theatre has avoided incorporating this story. Peter Fryer notes that 'white historians, almost without exception, have done their best to deprive black people of their history [...] they have consistently belittled or wiped out the black past'.[1]

Where British musical theatre histories have acknowledged Black performance practice during the first half of the twentieth century, they have almost without exception focused on the US experience. One recent history notes that 'the London stage [...] embraced musical comedies that drew on, or configured, the African-American experience, leading to a strong sense of cross-cultural encounter'.[2] Such histories problematically, and falsely, remove people of African descent born in Britain from the narrative, as well as the many other people from across the African diaspora who shaped the form of the musical in the UK. Our archival research, and in particular our work with recently digitized newspapers, theatrical periodicals and international travel records, has made the sheer scale of the presence of Black theatre and music practitioners much clearer. Many of these practitioners were born in the UK, and many others, as a result of British colonialism had British subject status (and therefore a British passport). In the twentieth century, the presence of Black practitioners in the UK is part of a remarkable fluidity of global movement that sees Black theatre and music practitioners arrive in the UK from the Caribbean, for example, as early as the 1900s. We note the revolutionary potential in Black British historian David Olusoga's call to 'see what new stories and approaches emerge if Black British history is envisaged as a global history and – perhaps more controversially – as a history of more than just the black experience itself'.[3] The presence of Black practitioners in British musical theatre is not a subset of the main history; it is the history of the form.

   We start with a potentially radical suggestion: the history of British musical theatre is not the story of a series of important white men writing a series of important musicals, and it is hardly even a story of *musicals*. Existing ways of knowing and understanding the history of the musical in Britain have overemphasized divisions along the lines of genre, forms and geography that simply do not hold out in the face of the evidence. Most crucially, Black performance practice was a vital and significant part of British musical theatre's history between 1900 and 1950. The development of the musical is a complex story of extraordinary interweaving performance industries, industries consistently led by Black creative producers who work in all areas of the expanded definition of the musical theatre industry we propose. We position this performance practice as a resistant one, led by hundreds if not thousands of practitioners of African descent, whose backgrounds reflect the breadth of the African diaspora, from North America, Britain and Europe, the Caribbean, and Africa. Kofi Agawu, in his study *The African Imagination in Music*, notes that 'the potency of black music lies in responsible and unyielding guardianship; it suggests a principled and committed custodianship of a shared heritage'.[4] Custodians of this shared Black heritage are a substantial part of the British musical theatre industry; the failure to address the form's reliance on Black cultural practice has led to misguided histories that overemphasize and assume whiteness.

Challenging established approaches in musical theatre studies

Specific histories of British musical theatre in the period 1900–1950 are somewhat thin on the ground; indeed, the period has until recently been covered only as part of the context of editions focused on post-war musicals. These histories have tended to limit the involvement of Black practitioners and theatre professionals until after 1948 and wider migration, and as a result, we focus our work as a result on the years 1900–1950. The emphasis on whiteness in twentieth-century British musical theatre history has largely operated through a persistent focus on individual white-led achievement, key composers and lyricists who become a shorthand for Britishness in the creative work they produce. There has been a concurrent emphasis on inaccurate ideas that suggest racial diversity only entered the musical with the occasional visit of African Americans and after the 'arrival point' of HMT *Empire Windrush* on 21 June 1948. The additional question of what being British means is a thorny one, particularly at a time when Britain's rampant desire for empire grabbing extended British subject status to people thousands of miles away from the UK itself. In our context, we consider musicals that are performed in the UK as part of British musical theatre history. This is an area which has been addressed but without a stable understanding of the long contribution and important presence of people of African descent in Britain.

Ben Macpherson, in his 2018 unpicking of cultural identity in British musicals between 1890 and 1939, questions Britishness as a coherent entity and addresses important contradictions around social class. Yet the identity he explores here is assumed as *white* Britishness. Although Macpherson quite rightly acknowledges the representation of South Asian, and Southeast Asian identities in the period he is focusing on, his work does not address the full role people of African descent played, perhaps because of the perceived difficulty in accessing this information. In a footnote, he observes: 'it has to be noted that – considering their relative positions in the Empire – there is a distinct absence of material relating to Caribbean or African influences/representations in musical comedy.'[5] Elsewhere, Stephen Banfield does consider the presence of Black music in the early twentieth century but does so only through the perspective of white audiences – considering the popularity of the turn to syncopation as building on an existing turn to Black music as an apparent 'twentieth-century salve to the Anglo-Saxon conscience already long exploited in minstrelsy', that is, liking Black music might make white people feel better.[6] The point of Black music is not what white people did with it.

Black musical theatre in the UK has been addressed elsewhere by Macpherson, in his chapter on Black and South Asian work in the *Oxford Handbook to British Musicals*, under the subsection '"The Art of the Possible": Alternative Approaches to Musical Theatre Aesthetics'. Again, we would highlight the word 'alternative', which subtly positions it as to the side of the main *white* event. In his chapter, Macpherson reports the minimal presence of people of African descent in the UK, suggesting that some 'black performers from America' and 'black Caribbean musicians' were present, but as we have suggested seems to be a prevalent view, he asserts that it was not until post-Windrush that Black people had any real presence in British musical life:

> The growth in immigration to Britain in the decades following the 1948 British Nationality Act that affected these changes of citizenship can in many ways be seen as the beginnings of what might be called an 'indigenous' black British and Anglo-Asian cultural presence.[7]

This inaccurate idea is echoed by other academics: Robert Gordon argues that jazz 'was not a mode with which British composers felt comfortable until the late 1950s [and as] much as it may have been enjoyed by West End audiences of Broadway musical comedies in the 1920s and 1930s, was never part of the British musical theatre vocabulary'.[8] In this context – that is, what is British musical theatre vocabulary? – does it mean musical theatre written in Britain for British theatres? What about the work, say, the African American composer Noble Sissle (see Chapter 5) was creating in London during the 1920s for British revues?

Another way of speaking about post-Windrush immigration has been through the lens of 'multiculturalism'. Here, Millie Taylor suggests that this cultural force only really changed British musicals after post-Windrush immigration:

> Partly influenced by British popular forms and in response to decades of immigration which began to alter the ethnic character of British cities and by second- and third-generation British minority ethnic communities who wanted to represent their own experiences of living in Britain, new companies and new types of performance began to merge alongside the mainstream musical world.[9]

Taylor goes on to suggest it was not until after 1975 that 'black writers and performers have begun to move from the fringe into the British theatrical mainstream'.[10] Such progress narratives also appear in the work of Macpherson; he suggests that only in the contemporary moment 'the pluralities of postcolonial British popular culture are increasing, and the vital signs are looking more robust than at any time in the nation's past'.[11] The study of the history of musicals in the UK would do well to heed Peter Fryer's position that 'British history cannot be written honestly without taking into account the contribution that black people have made to it',[12] however inconvenient that taking into account might be.

All these assumptions about the history of British musical theatre during the years 1900–1950 have been enabled by problematic assertions which have asserted singularity of form and location; in this story, the musical is something which happens in Britain primarily in London's West End theatre district. But this does not represent even the geographical reality of London as a city – and the many theatres it had during this period that catered to different kinds of performance practices. Theatre in London did not take place in one area only but had many variety theatres in and around the West End and throughout its suburbs. (Variety theatre originated from the music hall but slowly shifted to more unified revues and even revusicals, which loosely threaded plot or character between acts. This kind of theatre is generally called vaudeville in the United States.) As cinema became more established, some theatres were adapted or even newly built to be cine-variety theatres where short films would be played alongside variety acts. These theatres were not small affairs; they often had seat capacities in the thousands. London's West End itself had many variety theatres, including the Pavilion, the Coliseum, and the Leicester Square Theatre, and all of these had capacities of more than 2,000 people each. In addition, musicians, performers and acts might pass from variety theatre to musical theatre to nightclubs – without any sense of progression or career development (or, perhaps as importantly, demotion). Regional theatre played an important part in the musical theatre industry during the period 1900–1950 (and continues to do so). Musicals and variety theatre relied on touring; just because a musical never arrived in London does not make it any less a part of the fabric of British musical theatre history.

If theatre location or type is not stable in this period, then any definition of what a musical actually contained is slippery; while multiple terms were in circulation throughout the period, in this book we propose an expanded definition. It is of course possible to provide a working definition of a musical as a dramatic form, usually of entertainment, that uses a series of scenes with related songs and usually dance that tell a story or idea to an audience. This is by no means a universal descriptor and securing any such definitions for the contemporaneous differences between operettas, musical comedies, musicals, musical revue or even the revusical in Britain is tenuous at best. Johnson Quinn's work in unpicking the implied anti-US sentiments that such naming practices implied reveals that these distinctions were never purely factual dramatic distinctions but rather laden with cultural value and nationalistic intention.[13] Cultural industries in Britain in this period were interlinked rather than separate from one another: producers have always disseminated musicals across any means possible to maximize profit. From sheet music to early forms of recording; then radio and television; the film industry; regional and provincial tours; and disparate forms of theatrical entertainment – British musical theatre is not just a limited number of theatres in a few streets of London's West End.

This privileging of West End theatres as historically *the* most financially and artistically significant space, at the expense of other kinds of British musical theatre, does not represent any contemporaneous networks of performance during this period. The industry is also a global one: Christopher Balme's work in uncovering early twentieth-century touring circuits and the Bandmann Circuit from 1900 to 1920 draws attention to the expansive scale of performance. Balme reveals how theatrical touring began to be 'organized on an industrial scale', allowing theatrical transfers of Anglo-American works while at the same time encouraging 'movement in other directions', noting transfers of Japanese, Chinese and Parsi theatre during this very early period.[14] Similarly, the importance of regional performance to British musical theatre, not only in terms of a place for trying out expensive musical theatre but to train and develop performers and to disseminate popular song and dance styles, was vital to the overall survival of individual performers and of the industry as a whole. In 1909,

Lily of Bermuda, described as 'colonial [musical] comedy',[15] opened at the Theatre Royal, Manchester. It was written by Ernest Trimmingham (born in Bermuda) and Dusé Mohamed Ali (born in Egypt), with a collection of other white contributors. The musical, which starred Trimmingham, was a gentle satire of British colonialism in Bermuda. It played only one other venue, and no music survives from the piece.[16] It is still part of the history of British musical theatre; and while Colin Chamber's 2011 history of Black and Asian theatre notes Trimmingham's presence, he is little noted in histories of the musical.[17] There is little left of the musical itself (a script lodged in the British Library, but no score) – but the importance of Dusé Mohamed Ali, a key pan-African and anti-colonial activist, being involved with the form of a musical is striking. Through Trimmingham's writing and performance, *Lily of Bermuda* satirizes British colonialism in the Caribbean.

Releasing contained insurgent Black labour and resistant practices

The fluidity and indistinct nature of musical theatre during this period lead to blurriness between concepts that may now feel more secure; frankly, dealing with the professional versatility at work during this period starts to make your head hurt. Following an individual practitioner's career reveals that concepts like high or light music are not strictly delineated during a person's working week, never mind their working life. Following and writing about the history of British musical theatre during the period 1900–1950 is inconveniently blurry. When this blurriness is combined with white assumptions that have assumed there could not have been a serious presence or contribution of People of Colour, then vital reassessment is needed. Ryuko Kubota has addressed how epistemological racism works, suggesting it operates as 'epistemological hegemony, compelling non-Euro-American people of color to adopt these white assumptions as legitimate knowledge'.[18] The assumptions that make musical theatre in the years 1900–1950 *white* have become, erroneously, legitimized knowledge. We note Peter Fryer here in restating that 'There has been a continuous black presence in Britain for approximately 500 years.'[19]

We need to challenge the assumption that there was only a limited contribution from a certain few Black practitioners. Obviously, this is difficult in a book which is, by its nature, finite, but you will notice we have tended to use historical periods and interweaving stories wherever is possible. Even the title of this book risks continuing to perpetuate a separation between Black performance practice and British musical theatre. Musicals produced by people of African descent tend to be named as such in general histories – defining 'African American musical theatre' or 'Black British musical theatre'; musicals written by white people are just 'musical theatre'.

Notice the immense difference between our actual book title and an apparently close variant: *An Inconvenient History of Black British Musical Theatre*. In the former, Black is situated at the context of the history: the history is Black, and its creation and locality are Black-centred. But in the latter, Black British Musical Theatre becomes a clear subset of the main (e.g., white) British event. This is where we suggest that established notions need repositioning; but in order to make our case we risk reiterating separation because we are pointing out its difference from the usual story – assumed to be a white one.

Packing Black narratives into boxes allows selective unpacking; these certain musicals become part of a system of privileged convenience. Some narratives are useful in collective (often, white) consciousness, because they tell the stories we want to or that white histories propound need to be told. When Black histories exist in these white boxes, they are regulated, distantly comprehensible, controlled: *In Dahomey* goes there, tap dance goes there, Florence Mills in that one, and Paul Robeson there. This 'boxing' is a settler colonial historiographical practice. It tidies away the mess of anti-racist, activist Black labour, which is messy, complicated and requires challenging what we think we know. To assume the best intentions in distinctions between Black musical theatre and the assumed but unspoken 'white musical theatre', white historians, perhaps, have considered 'Black musical theatre' as a way of giving credit where credit is due, outlining the 'contributions' that Black practitioners have made *to* (white) musical theatre. But the reality is far more complicated – Black practitioners clearly work within many kinds of musical theatre event, sometimes for shows which are positioned as 'Black' (whether they chose that distinction or not), but far more frequently they are just working in musical theatre.

We must also challenge the assumption that Black performance practice in the UK could only really have begun with the arrival of the HMT *Empire Windrush* in June 1948. Such views suggest that Black people only make any real 'impact' in British cultural life, and specifically musical theatre, *after* the beginnings of mass migration of Black British 'subjects' from Caribbean countries after 1948. Tackling this period means understanding Black performance practice is a product of the African diaspora and is not a singular type or kind of product, made by people with a singular experience. Doing this work means dispelling the privilege of living in a place of comfort where there are singular answers that come easily. So often, in tracing this practice, we are left with inconclusiveness and with the feeling of more questions than we started with. Sometimes a person's name is the only thing that appears to survive of a Black practitioner's practice; where possible we have made the decision to say the name. Perhaps the biggest questions that emerge are around identity and a frustrating sense of wanting to know what the experiences we discuss were like. What were individual experiences of identity like for Black performers who had been born in the UK? So little material currently survives that we may now be posing many more questions than we can answer.

In her exploration of Depression-era African American presence in US theatre history, Stephanie Batiste powerfully challenges the concept that 'disempowerment resultant from racial oppression keeps people from imagining, or more important, enacting themselves as empowered subjects'.[20] She considers 'African American imaginations of empowerment through their participation in discourses of imperialism'.[21] We call on Batiste's exploration of the agency of performers working within racist performance structures, and her consideration that Black practitioners enact empowerment *while* consuming white consumption. bell hooks, in her crucial work outlining the concept of 'eating the other', notes that white consumption and commodification of other cultures is successful as a strategy because it offers 'a new delight, more intense, more satisfying than normal ways of doing and feeling. Within commodity culture, ethnicity becomes spice, seasoning that can liven up the dull dish that is mainstream white culture'.[22] Clearly, within the period we are considering many white audiences consumed Black performance practice and culture through their encounters with performances which added spice to the 'dull dish' of mainstream white culture.

We note that, while white audiences were consuming Black experience, Black performers were enacting resistant strategies and, at times, actively consuming white consumption. If histories of the British musical are prepared to admit the possibility of Black practitioners at all, they have not been prepared to engage with this kind of insurgency. Priyamvada Gopal's key 2019 text *Insurgent Empire* considers how the people Britain had enslaved and made their colonial subjects were agents of their own liberation. She notes how that dissent changed Britain; viewing dissent not as marginal or rare but positioned as such *only* in the discourse, dissent 'emerges as (often, constitutively) marginal*ized* discourse which must articulate itself against the grain of the dominant'.[23] In responding to Gopal, we read Black performance practice as an insurgent presence in British culture, actively consuming white consumption. Clearly, there are many other stories that need to be readdressed during this period – other minoritised practitioners who also contributed to the development of musical theatre and whose contributions need urgent reassessment. In addition, the influence of Black practitioners does not stop after this period.

Ifeoma Kiddoe Nwankwo's path-breaking work on 'Black cosmopolitanism' establishes the broader definitions of cosmopolitanism as 'the definition of oneself through the world beyond one's origins' and as a strategy taken up as an active decision by Black people to reclaim personhood and subjective identity in the face of white supremacy:

> [Cosmopolitanism is] one of the master's tools (Blackness being another) that people of African descent tested for its possible usefulness in attempting to at least get into the master's house, if not to destroy it.[24]

Black cosmopolitanism as a practice has been explored in relation to performance practice: most notably in Bennetta Jules-Rosette's work on Josephine Baker and Jo A. Tanner's work on Black performers working in Russia (including Laura Bowman, see 'The 1900s in context').[25] It provides a way of understanding the complex organization and sophisticated management of extensive performance networks of travel, management and entrepreneurship across Europe, the Americas and even into Russia from the 1900s onwards. These professional networks led to an expanded dissemination of Black performance and creative practice through West End theatres, regional theatres and in variety and revue formats; nightclubs and bands, those in central London; early radio, television and film industries; and concerts and public programming. It also informed the building of musical repertoire through which Black performers and practitioners established and expanded repertoires of song, music and dance that led to the introduction of many kinds of 'new' music into British cultural life.

Our focus is on understanding resistant practices rather than finding scripts; much of the material evidence of the products of Black practitioners' talent is lost, missing or incomplete. Many resistant practices are led by the formation of Black community spaces, where Black practitioners were able to be housed and fed in safe areas, through community building that established family-like networks outside of white gaze and consumption. While these spaces may have sometimes been interracial, and white allies may have been invited in, they also operated as defensive and protective mechanisms to support Black spiritual and personal well-being. They also became centres for anti-colonialism and for resisting racism, through direct invention and in fundraising for legal campaigns, as well as supporting the extended Black community through charity. Attending to these practices raises questions that cannot easily be answered; it is particularly difficult to attend to questions of identity and how various practitioners felt about their own work and experience. At the moment, we simply do not have enough information to always articulate the answers that this work so often raises, but that does not mean we should stop telling the stories.

Why is this an inconvenient history?

What does it truly mean to deal with an uncomfortable, inconvenient history? It means addressing that what we have previously understood as 'right' may not be. It means speaking and recovering names – and acknowledging the violence of their removal from how the story has hitherto been remembered. We note the related discomfort of speaking names of those identities buried in deeper tragedies such as societal violence against People of Colour; a full consciousness of their names opens an unavoidable understanding that their contributions not only were underlying but had to be somehow, in some measure, packed away from sight. The book lays out the stories of individual practitioners of African descent and their professional practice in British musical theatre life during this period, in a roughly chronological order (there are overlaps). We use a series of contexts for each decade we deal with, to point to the wider picture. This should help the reader assess the enormity of what is at stake – since our book represents only a few of the *hundreds* of Black practitioners we have noted working in the UK during the years 1900–1950. There will be hundreds more still to uncover. By focusing in on several key practitioners, we can reveal how Black practitioners were able to enact resistance practice *within* contemporaneous racist structures that racialized Black performance in order to perpetuate white supremacy. Crucially, Black performers and practitioners were able to resist the white consumption of Black performance practices through complex and oftentimes surreptitious professional, personal and performative strategies. Black performance practice was not just for the consumption of white audiences; something bigger is at work.

Michael Omi and Howard Winnant's later reflection on their foundational text *Racial Formation in the United States* notes: 'We live in racial history. Structural racism is not a fixed feature of United States society. It can be named; it can be challenged; it can be reduced.'[26] As we imagine the future, in which you, the reader, are accessing this text, we perceive two choices for how the musical theatre industry and field of scholarship around it might move forward in attempting to include Black practitioners, Black lives and Black history. The first option, diversity, relies on continuing to commoditize Blackness as a by-product of 'white' theatre, as something auxiliary to the main history. This requires seeing musical theatre as slowly improving, in a progress narrative where things seem to get 'less racist' and 'more diverse' over time. Tania Canas, in her work on arts in Australia, writes diversity is a 'white word', noting that this kind of inclusion 'is conditional on predefined, palatable criteria; a means to frame, describe and ultimately prescribe diversity through constructed visibilities'.[27] Diversity allows gestures of inclusion – the performance of inclusion does not change the underpinning white structure. Sara Ahmed positions this as the 'non-performative' work of diversity within institutions (she is discussing university structures but her work clearly applies to both the musical theatre industry and the scholarship around it):

> We might wish to examine how institutions become white through the positing of some bodies rather than others as the subjects of the institutions (querying for example, who the institution is shaped for and who it is shaped by). Racism would not be evident in what we fail to do, but what we have already done, where 'we' is an effect of the doing.[28]

The history of British musical theatre *is an effect of the doing*.

This may be uncomfortable for white people to challenge the assumed knowledge of this period. In his work on white emotionality and 'white discomfort' – that is to say, white people's shock at feeling bad when confronted with whiteness – Michalinos Zembylas suggests that discourse which focuses on a space to feel those 'discomforting feelings' risks not interrogating 'the wider structures and practices of race, racism and whiteness that trigger such feelings in the first place'.[29] It is essential to unpick the 'structures and practices' that have placed us in this situation in the first place; the reason most of us could not imagine a book called *The Inconvenient White History of British Musical Theatre* is, in claiming not to see race, the 'white' has always been assumed. To call back to Ahmed, 'the positing of some bodies rather than others' has led us to this point; and it is time to stop.

So, we are led to the second option: we resituate and retell the story. We acknowledge that these histories have coexisted simultaneously, or even radically, that Black performance histories are the precursors of others. Option 1 is white-centred because it focuses on diversity; Option 2 is anti-racist, inclusive and receptive to reframing established notions. The work of Option 2 is messy and complicated and means challenging what we are prepared to accept. There is established literature that considers Black performance practice in the United States, and occasionally in reference to earlier periods in the UK, but never specifically in musical theatre in the UK. In jazz studies, the influence of Black musicians in theatre has been underestimated: one introduction to a collection published in 2014 erroneously suggests that during the 1920s jazz 'moved out of the theatres and into London nightclubs'.[30] But it enriched and maintained a presence in British theatre – despite this apparent transition.

There is a fine, fine line between acknowledgement and othering. Identifying something as Black automatically situates Black as a descriptor, unless you invest extra labour into maintaining that it truly belongs *within*. Paul Gilroy establishes the Black Atlantic as a site of 'movement, translation and relocation'.[31] Annalisa Oboe and Anna Scacchi, in the introduction to their collection *Recharting the Black Atlantic* (a response to Gilroy's foundational text), define their use of Black as a:

> loosely defined, adaptive signifier, disconnected from essentialized notions of 'race,' African diaspora, or African American culture: it is a useful label to be negotiated and opportunely filled in a variety of ways, so as to include marginal subjects.[32]

Stuart Hall defines Black popular culture as a 'contradictory space. It is a site of strategic contestation'.[33] He notes that popular culture is 'where we discover and play with the identifications of ourselves, where we are imagined, where we are represented, not only to the audiences out there who do not get the message, but to ourselves for the first time'.[34] Clearly the Black history we are discussing makes identification paramount; but it also calls for understanding what is at stake. Gilroy's powerful work on Black music notes that its 'obstinate and consistent commitment to the idea of a better future is a puzzle'.[35] He explores the moral character of Black music, noting that 'by posing the world as it is against the world as the racially subordinated would like it to be, this musical culture supplies a great deal of the courage required to go on living in the present'.[36]

We cannot ignore these histories as being Black, as doing so provides problematic further erasure. It is tricky. Perhaps in a radically different space we would be able to say 'musical theatre' and not need to further maintain where whiteness ends and Blackness begins. But, in this moment of racial history, that is simply not the case. The phrase 'Black musical theatre' must be used with proper conditioning, as we risk othering and further fractioning the narrative when we do so. Fred Moten's work on the philosophy of Black music notes that 'black performance has always been the ongoing improvisation of a kind of lyricism of the surplus – imagination, rupture, collision, augmentation'.[37] Moten positions Black music as a rupture, but one that enacts insurrection:

> The West is an insane asylum, a conscious and premeditated receptacle of black magic. Every disappearance is a recording. That's what resurrection is. Insurrection. Scat black magic, but to scat or scatter is not to admit formlessness. The aftersound is more than a bridge. It ruptures interpretation even as the trauma it records disappears.[38]

We propose a standpoint that reads Black performance practice as an act of insurrection against white supremacist structures, insurrection that ruptures interpretation. Matthew Morrison's critical positioning of Blacksound allows us to understand much of what is happening here in the performance processes we encounter. He establishes the term as an analytical frame to:

> consider how quotidian and spectacular performance of self and community in contemporary popular culture are embedded within a racially audible past that resonates in low, less perceptible frequencies. Blacksound amplifies these low frequencies by directing attention to how the sonic and material histories of race continue to resonate through the practices embedded in the development of popular music, style, and entertainment at large.[39]

Clearly, there is much more work to be done in exploring how Black performers worked within – and at times against – Morrison's concept of Blacksound, work which we hope this book will support.

It is also important to acknowledge the complex racial history that these performers are operating in. Paula Seniors, in her work on early Black musical theatre on Broadway, notes that figures such as Bob Cole, J. Rosamond Johnson and James Weldon Johnson are often dismissed as conformists that replicated white hegemony. She counters that 'they used the very tools of hegemony to create a distinctly black theater informed by black politics, history, and culture'.[40] She reads their work – despite what at times can be read as a complex negotiation of racist structures which seem at times to reiterate them – as 'an inclusionary form of uplift'.[41]

Reframing the narrative: Expanding the focus

As much as we may wish to disrupt tidy answers, clearly writing a book about these complex stories risks the same issue by putting people into 'boxes' of chapters – and you will notice that there are purposeful blurs around the edges. There are no single stories here: but stories that belong to a complex bigger picture. Black theatre histories *are* theatre histories: and ultimately, are uncontainable. In this book then we unpack these stories while pointing towards their full impact – and acknowledging where this work will need to continue to restore the impact of the practitioners we name. The book has three parts, which are broadly chronological but with necessary overlaps.

'Part One: Black practitioners and international performance networks' looks at the period roughly from 1900 to 1919. Chapter 1 considers the work of Will Marion Cook and his turn to the audience in the London auditorium of *In Dahomey* – a precise moment of resistance which protects Black performers while challenging white spectators. Chapter 2 looks at three extraordinary Black women, Belle Davis, Laura Steer and Cassie Walmer; three women whose extensive travels reveal global performance practice – activating creative resistance through commercial aptitude and skill. In Chapter 3, we consider Black performance practice in a single year in the life of British theatre, 1916. Chapter 4 considers how the performer, producer and musician William Garland was part of a Black community in London, and actively worked against racist structures in his theatrical practice by presenting powerful images of Africa.

'Part Two: Black networks of production' looks at the period from 1920 into the 1930s. Chapter 5 focuses on a much smaller time period and looks at a previously hardly addressed charity concert on a Sunday afternoon in January 1928. The concert, nominally to raise money for a Flood appeal, was an unofficial Florence Mills memorial concert and provided an opportunity for the Black community to mourn and celebrate the tragic loss of Mills. The chapter explores how the concert changed the casting of the London production of *Show Boat*. Chapter 6 explores the careers of two women who performed at the concert and in *Show Boat* (1928): British-born Mabel Mercer and blues singer Alberta Hunter. Both women used their work in Britain to different ends. Hunter was able to build a European performance practice while asserting her own agency and creativity. Mercer began her long career with Will Garland, and while her work in the UK has been thought to be of minimal importance to her later work as a cabaret singer, Mercer also conducted a tour of one of Garland's many shows. Chapter 7 addresses two choreographers whose work in the UK is little known: Clarence 'Buddy' Bradley and Clarence Robinson. Bradley established the aesthetic and practice of dance throughout the 1930s, but he also worked alongside key ballet choreographer, and founder of the Royal Ballet Company, Frederick Ashton. Robinson, best known for his work at the Cotton Club, ran a theatre in London but transported revues from the UK back to Harlem. This aspect of his work has been overlooked in previous approaches.

Chronologically, there is a slight overlap from Part Two into Part Three; 'Part Three: Anti-racism and anti-imperialism theatre practices', focuses on the 1930s to the end of our focus period, 1950. Chapter 8 addresses the work of the Caribbean community in London focused around Amy Ashwood Garvey and Sam Manning in the mid-1930s, and the founding of the Florence Mills Social Parlour Manning produced and toured a show in 1934 called *Harlem Nightbirds*, and this chapter explores this production in full. In Chapter 9, we consider the work of Ken 'Snakehips' Johnson who drew on Cab Calloway's performance for his act and persona. Calloway also had a performance career in Britain, which clearly impacted sound and visual aesthetics. In Chapter 10, we follow the way Caribbean performers in the UK, including Edric Connor and Berto Pasuka, can be read as performer activists in staging Black music, culture and experience, and the formation of key Black theatre and performance groups.

We have made the difficult decision to avoid retelling some of the stories of those few important Black practitioners whose stories are already well known or have significant material about their travels in the UK, purely to make space for the many people who have not been fully recognized. For example, though Paul Robeson (Paul Leroy Robeson) (1898–1976) obviously appears in many of the 'contexts' sections, we have not covered his work in specific depth here. We have tried to prioritize the many stories which have not previously been told, and names which have been discursively under-spoken. Once these practitioners are conscious knowledge, it is not enough to simply *know* their names: we must dig to understand why these narratives have not been part of existing histories. You will read of moments of practitioners' lives in this book that will make it incontestable that their influence can be traced to others you are familiar with – the path of unknown to known. The transformation of this history we put forth is up to us, the discoverers, to digest, appraise, disseminate and, most importantly, affirm that these histories will never be buried again. As consumers and protectors of this art, this is our *duty*; and as conscious sharers of its history, it is our *duty* that no Black musical theatre student, creator or spectator ever sees a history of the form that doesn't have them included, or says they weren't, again.

PART ONE

Black practitioners and international performance networks

The 1900s in context

During the 1900s, pioneers of Black performance practice were consistently among the first to engage with new forms of technology, in particular the early music recording and film industries. The further development of international travel and communication networks, and the affordability of such travel, served to support international theatrical touring in ways which, more than 100 years later, are startling in their geographical scope. In 1907, the *Mauretania* broke the speed record for a transatlantic crossing in four and a half days, though five to six days was more usual.

When making Atlantic crossings for performances and productions, African American performers were not unaware of its history; their crossings assert resistance to the continuing impact of slavery in US life. Saidiya Hartman positions the Atlantic as an essential part of Black history: 'The sea is history ... the sea has nothing to give but a well excavated grave.'[1] During the Middle Passage alone, chattel slavery led to the deaths of more than 2 million enslaved Black people; slave traders threw the bodies of enslaved people into the Atlantic Ocean.[2] To speak of transatlantic performance travel requires noting which ocean is being crossed.

Black practitioners were able to move across the world, performing in front of all social classes through extensive performance opportunities. In the UK, Black performers worked across regional theatres of all sizes and locations, and even in front of the Royal Family in the case of *In Dahomey*. Though there was already an existing presence in the UK of Black performers, the arrival of Will Marion Cook's *In Dahomey* in May 1903, fresh from its success on Broadway, helped establish a network of Black British and African American as well as Caribbean and African performers (see Key Figure 1).

Black practitioners seem to seamlessly move between small British theatres to major London variety houses, into Europe and beyond, even on to Australia. Some performers move freely between centres of performance like London, Paris, Berlin, Amsterdam, Chicago, New York and New Orleans. Performance practice in this first decade clearly emerged from the minstrel traditions of the nineteenth century: minstrel companies and amateur minstrel performances form a great deal of British theatre.

The breadth and legacy of their work in this decade may be surprising to our modern eyes, purely in geography alone. Three key Black performers during this period point to the extent of this work. Four African American members of the second company of *In Dahomey* established the Darktown Entertainers: Pete (George) Hampton (b. 1871, Kentucky; d. 1916, New York City), a baritone singer, banjo player and actor; Hampton's wife Laura Bowman (alt. Bauman) (b. 1881, Quincy, IL; d. 1957), a singer and performer; Fred Douglas (dates unknown); and William 'Will' Garland (b. 1875, Iowa; d. 1938, London; for more, see Chapter 4). Will Garland, like many practitioners, drew on his professional experience of transcontinental touring in the United States. There, he had worked alongside W. C. (William Christopher) Handy, now regarded as the father of the blues, in a minstrel show, where he worked as a musician, performer and vocal director. Will Garland, along with other cast members of the production, brought his knowledge of touring theatre to establishing companies that toured the UK and beyond for the following thirty years (see Chapter 4).

Extensive professional versatility frequently occurs during this period. It is possible that performers may appear as a performer and comedian, singer or dancer, and instrumental musicians, as well as operating as a producer, agent and even as choreographers and teachers. This versatility demonstrates practitioners' savvy business sense, for example in cashing in on named recognition of hit shows. Until the middle of the 1910s, Garland's early revues namechecked *In Dahomey* in their advertising to assure audiences they would like his new work.

Social and political context

Britain's quest to colonize African regions continued throughout this decade (and throughout the next). Britain had already seized control of many African regions, including what is now Kenya (1888); Ghana (1821, known as the Gold Coast for what Britain was able to export out of it); Malawi (1907); the Republic of The Gambia (1821, then the Gambia), Somaliland (c.1884), areas of Sierra Leone (1896), and regions of southern Africa, including parts of Zambia (1900). Driven by competition with other European nations, Britain continued to push to colonize more of Africa.

This was justified through the promise of Africa's rich material resources as well as what David Olusoga calls 'rapidly evolving forms of racism',[3] which placed white people in a position of moral, intellectual and, above all, evolutionary superiority to people of African descent. Olusoga argues that the contemporaneous idea that Africans were 'overgrown infants with the same predilections, weaknesses and irrationality' had first emerged through the slave trade,[4] and now Britain once again employed the concept to justify its actions in 'the civilising mission in Africa'.[5]

In 1900, Britain took control of the 'Northern Nigerian Protectorate' (a region of northern Nigeria); in 1903, Eswatini became a 'British protectorate' (then known as Swaziland); in 1910, the Union of South Africa became a self-governing country within the British Empire with policies that would later serve to formalize racial segregation. Britain's actions in committing human rights atrocities in pursuit of these goals remain rarely discussed or acknowledged 120 years later. During the Second Boer War (1899–1902) – a British campaign for control for what is now part of South Africa – Lord Kitchener placed women and children in concentration camps, an action which led to 'perhaps up to 45,000 deaths, approximately 25,000 Boers [largely white Dutch settlers] and 14,000 to 20,000 Africans' due to the despicable conditions.[6]

As a response to aggressive and destructive European colonialism, Black activists and intellectuals such as Henry Sylvester Williams (c.1867–1911), a Trinidadian lawyer, developed the Pan-African movement through the 1890s, building on W. E. B. Du Bois' earlier concept of Pan-Negroism. William Edward Burghardt Du Bois (1868–1963) was a key African American writer and activist; he published *The Souls of Black Folk* in 1903 and was one of the founding members of the National Association for the Advancement of Colored People (NAACP) in 1909.

London became a meeting point for Pan-Africanism, a movement which was formalized after the first Pan-African conference in the city in 1900, when the Pan African Association (PAA) was formed. The PAA's aims included 'to secure to Africans throughout the world true civil and political rights' and 'to ameliorate the condition of our brothers on the continent of Africa, America and other parts of the world'.[7]

On stage

Many of the artists of African descent who toured the UK during this decade played across different sorts of British theatre, including variety theatres and music halls. Vocalists like Morcashani (Laura Steer), Cassie Walmer (for details on both, see Chapter 2) and the currently unknown, possibly African American performer Bessie Lee.

A broad range of practices are represented in touring Black performers' work and output during this period. Choirs included Abbie Mitchell's Tennessee Students who toured the UK. Abriea 'Abbie' Mitchell Cook (1884–1960) was Will Marion Cook's wife and an important performer in her own right. The Jamaican Choir also toured, with their members Louis Drysdale, Carlton Bryan and Frank Weaver (the choir also featured dancing)[8] and the pianist Henry 'Harry' Nation.[9] Drysdale (b. 1883, Jamaica; d. 1933,

London) became a music teacher from his home in Forest Hill, London, and became an important part of the Black community in London. Frank Weaver later performed with Will Garland, but very little is currently known about him.

Dance groups included Belle Davis and her company of children (see Chapter 2), as well as all-round entertainers like Jasper White (no further details emerge) and the prolific Garland himself. Dance styles during this period focused on early tap styles, sand dancing and buck and wing dancing, though it is very difficult to identify dancers in this period as individuals are unnamed or hard to trace.

Music styles reflect the ongoing popularity of banjo music, with the continued touring of the African Canadian George Bohee (1857–?) and the African American Silas Seth Weeks (1868–1953), a composer and banjo player who performed a banjo concert at St James's Hall, Piccadilly before touring extensively across the UK.[10] There was a declining presence of minstrel troupes in this decade, though they had a lasting presence in British theatre. The white cast of the Moore and Burgess Minstrel troupe (which ran for more than forty years at the St James's Hall venue) closed in 1904. Many white artists continued to perform in blackface during this decade as a particular 'black' character, reinforcing racist tropes and ideas that were common at the time.

In 1909, the African American double act Harry Scott and Eddie [Peter] Whaley arrived in the UK from the United States for a nine-week tour and stayed for the rest of their lives. Scott (1879–1947) and Whaley (1877–1960) were a comedian and singer who played across West End revues and variety theatres across the UK.[11] Scott married Belle Davis in 1929.[12]

Many of the Black performers in the UK in this period must have faced extremely challenging circumstances in operating in a theatre industry which had such pervasive expectations of minstrel performance. Key African American composers and activists J. (John) Rosamond Johnson (1873–1954), James Weldon Johnson (1871–1938) and Bob (Robert Allen) Cole (1868–1911) performed in British variety theatre; coverage at the time reflected on their musical accomplishments in the United States.[13]

1

Will Marion Cook and
In Dahomey (1903)

W ill (William) Marion Cook (b. 1869, Washington, DC; d. 1944, New York City) was an American composer of theatre and other musical works. He was a leading Black composer of early American music in the 1890s and 1900s. In this early period, Marion Cook worked with a range of key figures in Black history, not least the writer Paul Laurence Dunbar (b. 1872, Ohio; d. 1906, Ohio) who wrote the lyrics for *In Dahomey* (1903). The book was written by Jesse A. (Allison) Shipp (1864–1934), an important Black actor and director. His influence is not only in establishing Black musical theatre on Broadway but also in his production of professional networks of Black creative producers. He later established the Southern Syncopated Orchestra and became a key figure in the dissemination of jazz music.

Cook and his *In Dahomey* contemporaries defied artistic norms through their use and creation of Black musical theatre – both in *In Dahomey* and through their other works, created within and supported by a transatlantic network of performers that resisted and dispelled stereotypes of the day through Broadway, West End and touring stages.

In the process of spawning Black musical theater from Black minstrelsy, a remarkable cluster of Black performers, choreographers, and writers [...] – Bob Cole, Bert Williams, George Walker, Aida Overton Walker, James Weldon Johnson and his brother J. Rosamond Johnson, Will Marion Cook, and Paul Laurence Dunbar – perfected a host of Black resistance gestures for display before largely white audiences. Acutely race conscious, this group recovered and invented much of the moral and conceptual vocabulary and the sly oppositional stratagems which would sluice Black resistance into public entertainment.

Cedric Robinson[1]

Marva Carter's biography of Will Marion Cook recounts an incident that allows us to understand the composer and his work and frames Cook's importance to the musical as a form. In 1899, Cook had already debuted on Broadway when he was commissioned to write the score for the musical *Casino Girl* (1899). *Casino Girl* is now merely a footnote to theatrical history, but his experiences reveal the complexities he and other Black artists faced. After writing the score, the musical director 'asked Cook to modify his score, since the orchestral players found his writing too intricate and not commercial enough to be popular'.[2] He insisted that stepping in himself as conductor would solve this. He was informed that to conduct it himself as a Black man would 'jeopardize its success'; instead, he was told to 'write in the style of the white composers who were successful'.[3] After opening night, Cook stormed into the pit and destroyed all his music in frustration; a white composer replaced him and only one of his songs remained in the show. The musical's producer George Lederer referenced this moment, and others like it, in characterizing Cook as 'the greatest constructive and the greatest destructive genius in the American theatre'.[4]

Lederer's remark, perhaps unwittingly, allows us to glimpse at who Cook truly was: a sophisticated musician and composer, a patriarch of unprecedented networking abilities who helped cultivate British and American theatre communities alike, despite being an undervalued Black artist in white circles. Yes, this imagery attempts to evokes the trope of an angry Black man, finding a fitting outlet for his rage in destroying his sensitive art in a fit of barbarism. To consider this moment outside of white codified histories reveals something different. Cook's ownership in a bout of frustration resisted the racist frameworks surrounding him at the time, reclaiming (even physically) the work that was his while instating his confidence in the value of the music. Cook's *destructive genius* in exposing and resisting racism sits alongside his *constructive genius* in creating musical shapes and structures and working practices at the heart of musical theatre. Cook's genius (constructive) and resistance (destructive) would not only create a network of what is resolutely the bones of musical theatre but also clarify his position as one of the leading forebears of the theatrical form. But this influence was not limited to the United States, and his significance in developing musical theatre in the UK has not been fully acknowledged.

In deconstructing previous narratives, this chapter will explore Will Marion Cook's work in London, building upon the theoretical work of Daphne Brooks in understanding performance as a site of occupation and resistance in reconceiving key moments of *In Dahomey*.[5] This has previously been erroneously read as 'an enactment of otherness rather than a political commentary on race issues'.[6] As we noted in the Preface, Theresa Saxon argues that, though '*In Dahomey* was formulated with an uplift agenda, to challenge, subtly, racial prejudice, the show's potential resistance to racialised stereotyping was, ultimately, eroded in England's auditoria'.[7] This chapter disputes this, suggesting that pieces such as 'Swing Along' and 'Emancipation Day' can be read as an act of resistance. This reframes the musical as returning the colonial gaze through a performance of Black virtuosity, responding to Daphne Brooks' idea that the song 'metatextually signifies on the exigencies facing black performers in a crossover musical production' by considering the context of its writing and performance on a London stage.[8] We consider how Cook resists through several intersections, as lyricist, composer and as a performer – since he conducted the performance in clear sight of the audience. The way in which performers, musicians and creative producers racialized as Black in British musical theatrical life are currently understood is too narrow for the complex and virtuosic realities they faced. It is no mere coincidence that W. E. B. Du Bois's work on Sorrow Songs was published in the same year as *In Dahomey*; recognizing Sorrow Songs as containers of histories of oppression and struggle, 'there breathes a hope – a faith in the ultimate justice of things'.[9]

In Dahomey is frequently referenced in histories of the musical as 'the first all-black show to open on Broadway'.[10] It starred Bert (Egbert Austin) Williams (b. 1874, Bahamas; d. 1922, New York City) and George Walker (b. *c.* 1872, Kansas; d. 1911, Kansas). The musical was choreographed by Walker's wife, Ada (Aida) Overton Walker (b. 1880, Virginia; d. 1914, New York City), who was a central figure in the Black community and in early dance history.

When *In Dahomey* opened in February 1903, the *New York Times*' review ran under the headline 'The Negroes in the Audience Were in Heaven'.[11] The Black audience was certainly segregated from the white audience – the musical director 'and the boys who peddled water in the aisles were the only persons of color on the [ground] floor'.[12] The *New York Tribune* noted that Bert Williams and George Walker had 'vindicated their right to appear on Broadway'.[13]

In Dahomey opened at the Shaftesbury Theatre, in the West End, starring Bert Williams, George Walker and Aida Overton Walker, with a performance at Buckingham Palace. It played around 200 performances in the West End; 360,000 people could potentially have seen the show during that run (see Appendix A). Williams and Walker then toured in the UK; more than 500,000 people in total could have potentially seen their performances during the first tour.

KEY FIGURE 1 In Dahomey *(1903) and beyond.*

In Dahomey from Broadway to London

Historical narratives that have seen *In Dahomey* as exceptional have often minimized the musical's influence. In white theatre histories, the piece has existed as a convenient placeholder, less resembling of 'success' and more of Blackness against an otherwise claimed white industry that affirms only that Black people and pieces had existed but not that they were fundamental to musical theatre's narrative. The plot of the music parodies the 'Back to Africa' movement, which sought to 'return' former enslaved people. The Dahomey of the title refers to Benin. The importance of the musical to theatre history has never been about the piece itself; rather, its underdiscussed success and competitive performance practice situate it and its creators as part of a nucleus of Black music and theatrical practice of its time. As true of 1903 as of the next fifty years to come, it was a demonstration of Black artists acutely aware of their worth and artistry who were able to view themselves situated in prejudiced constructs of their audiences and still situate their active resistance and protest within their work.

After the show closed on Broadway, the entire team of the show prepared for a six-week run in London's West End. The quick transfer is intriguing – and suggests an awareness of the commercial potential in the show. The run of the show at the Shaftesbury Theatre signifies its success; it opened in mid-May 1903 and it lasted until the start of January 1904 before embarking on the first of two regional tours. Cook, as conductor of the show, would have been a connective tissue as the conductor of any musical is – laying the foundation as the ancillary of what was deepening as the nucleus of Black performance practice in England. Members of the original Broadway cast who made it to London include Cook's collaborative partners George Walker and Bert Williams, Alexander (Alex) Rogers, Aida Overton Walker, Lottie Williams, J. Leubrie Hill, George Catlin, Jesse A. Shipp (playwright and director), Richard Connors, Theodore Pankey and, notably, the eighteen-year-old Abriea 'Abbie' Mitchell (Cook), Cook's wife and mother of their two young children, Marion Abigail (1900) and the infant Will Mercer (1903). Numbers indicate that around 200 performances of *In Dahomey* were enjoyed by London audiences; we do not know how many tickets were sold, but the capacity of the theatre would have allowed 360,000 people to have seen the show in the West End during its run (see Appendix A). The musical was widely disseminated; even if the theatre was running at a lower occupancy rate, it must have retained a reasonable level to justify the show's continuation.

Saxon argues that the response to the show was due to its confusing representations of race:

> Surprise certainly featured in reviews of the opening night, and bewilderment as well, but, overall, *In Dahomey* became quickly 'assimilated' into the cultural economy of performative racialisation as British audiences latched onto racialised characterisations based on

interpretations of the stage 'negro' as an ethnologised and essentialised song and dance figure.[14]

As the run came to a close, press reports begin to speculate as to what the company would do next in British theatre. Given the phenomenal success of the show, it is no surprise that some assumed the performers would continue to work in British theatre. One gossip column wonders, 'The last weeks of "*In Dahomey*" are announced. Shall we see the principals at the halls for a season? More than likely.'[15] In fact, a regional tour had already been reported only days earlier: 'On January 25th [they] will begin a suburban and provincial tour lasting till May 23.'[16] Existing literature on *In Dahomey* has tended to focus on the New York and London productions rather than any subsequent suburban and provincial tours. This is perhaps unsurprising given the immense difficulty of tracing regional newspapers to ascertain tour dates, pre-digitization. Work which has addressed the regional tours tends to focus on national newspaper coverage for evidence of the public discourses around the show at the time (for a breakdown of tour dates, see Appendix A).

In revisiting Saxon's position, it could be, perhaps, what happened further *outside* of England's auditoria that may start to point to not only the influence that *In Dahomey* was having in Britain at the time but also how the entire team of *Dahomey*, including Cook, were laying the groundwork of resistance. One of the most stunning moments of the show's journey lies in a special guest appearance at Buckingham Palace, by request of the Royal Family. The entire company was invited 'by command of the King' to perform on 23 June 1903 in commemoration of Edward, Prince of Wales' birthday (later, if briefly, Edward VIII).[17] What is most notable about this event is the extent to which the detail of the company's involvement demonstrates the fullest interest of their inviters; the performance, conducted by Cook, was equipped with intricacies of 'scenery, sets, props, musical instruments, and costumes'.[18] Cook conducted; the *Greenock Telegraph* notes, 'it is nearly a quarter of a century since a theatrical entertainment has been witnessed by a Sovereign at the palace',[19] clearly this was an event that was rare by virtue of infrequency. This marked event would not solely delight the Royal Family but also exemplified the sentiment that was felt across receiving white consumptionist circles at the time: *Dahomey* and the show's Black practitioners were desirable. This is not an unproblematic desire.

Regardless of how one reads the material being presented in the show, existing solely for white pleasure or subverting Black stereotyping, Cook and the *Dahomey* family had literally entered the walls of aristocracy and, while there, existed among white bodies as physical manifestations of Black culture. Cook would not have been alone as resistor; David Krasner's uncovering of Aida Overton Walker's choreography as 'a double-voiced parody' of whiteness is reframed in the context of a British audience.[20] Cedric Robinson, in *Forgeries of Memory and Meaning*, further affirms that others in the company would have also been aware of their positions and not simply unconscious pawns of white consumption:

> Like Cook and Cole, Aida Overton Walker, George Walker (her husband), and Bert Williams shared a deep resentment towards the dominant representation of blackness in American popular culture and entertainment. Another similarity between these artists was that they all possessed the inventiveness and resolve to appropriate minstrelsy for their own ends.[21]

In entering the palace, Cook and the company's resistance was furthering its stance and reach as resistors – not just simply within popular circles but intramurally among the most upper class of England's societal structures.

By May 1904, Williams and Walker are reported to have left the UK, but the show continued with the original cast for a further month. By late June, the whole cast is reported to have left the country.[22] This is clearly in preparation for a US tour, with a brief return to Broadway in August and September 1904 before the tour commenced. Yet, back in the UK, in July 1904 Will Marion Cook is reported as rehearsing for a second British tour, with Williams and Walker replaced by Charles Avery and Dan Hart (this company would eventually feature William Garland; see Chapter 4). The *Sporting Times* reported that Cook had arrived 'to conduct the rehearsals' in July 1904.[23] He seems to have then conducted at least some of the earliest dates in this tour, as the *Hull Daily Mail* reports in August:

> There is something strangely bizarre about the wild strains and extraordinary harmonies of Mr W. Marion Cook. Perhaps much of the effect of last night's adequate presentation of the music was due to the fact that Mr Cook himself conducted.[24]

Swinging along, 'Emancipation Day' and Cook's double consciousness

Reconstructionist approaches in theatre obsess with the focus on 'finding the old work so we can do the work again' – a focus on remounting or reviving and looking at what was done on stage as a way of getting it back on stage to truly understand it. We are less interested here on the work itself than in thinking about the working processes its key practitioners and, in particular, Cook, are doing. Understanding Cook's performance practice *is* an important work of recovery.

In understanding him further, numerous histories of Cook provide evidence of his life and career being one of complex intersections of identity. He is consistently depicted in this light: being a man of complexity in both personality and craft. Carter notes, 'the personal peculiarities and eccentricities of Will Marion Cook [spawn] many apocryphal stories that have taken on a life of their own'.[25] Numerous accounts of his life reveal a duplexity: as a child of early Reconstruction America, born and raised in Washington, DC to an upper-middle-class family, Cook shaped music and theatre and had a direct influence on Black composers and musicians, including Duke Ellington, Eubie Blake, James Reese Europe and W. C. Handy as well as the white composer Harold Arlen.[26] His musical training exemplifies a pull between worlds as well: Cook was equally adept in the American world of newer popular song with the advent of ragtime and jazz idioms and where these intersected with theatre as much as he was admired for his contribution as an 'academy' or what we might now think of as a classical composer. Cook's time spent studying with such European establishments and musicians as Joseph Joachim and Antonín Dvořák signifies the weight of his connection to the greater music world outside of Black circles. This educational grounding and his catalogue of works indicate an ability to drift effortlessly between a realm of classical grounding and a contemporaneous mode of popular song.

We understand this further when considering his works and the context that surrounds them. The musicologist Thomas Riis, who compiled the *The Music and Scripts of 'In Dahomey'*, notes, 'Cook, the principal composer created stirring operatic effects in his choruses and evoked tender feelings [...], but he also contributed songs of a more conventional character'.[27] A pressing need to recontextualize and reclaim exactly what Cook was doing at the time emerges – dually intersecting with convention, yet discordantly pushing back against expectation to create works that affirm the truest nature of resistance to established bias at the time. In *Bodies in Dissent*, Daphne Brooks describes what Cook was up against as a composer in the eyes of critics who were predisposed to consume Black culture: 'white critics and audiences alike often clung to an agenda that wilfully assigned regressive, caricatured meanings to black performers'[28] – sonically as well as visually. Cook's identity is undoubtedly what enabled him to weave between identities: uniquely a Black artist, while possessing the skills of the alternative camp in composition using techniques more familiar and arguably subversively comforting to white consumers. Brooks notes the troubling assumption that 'the (black) body will always persevere as the fundamental plot for the white spectator'.[29] Cook's compositional nature confidently presents the ability of Blackness in *In Dahomey* to navigate white consumption without preserving preconceived musical notions of what the *Times'* critics insisted was a show where one could, as a spectator, just 'simply look and listen'.[30]

The interchange of the switching of one's 'mask' is ardently prodded by Paul Laurence Dunbar, the leading African American poet and writer of the early twentieth century and Cook's lyric collaborator on the show. Ray Sapirstein explores Dunbar's intersection between song and poetry: 'Like the European artists and intellectuals who pioneered artistic Modernism, Dunbar's lyric poetry responded to the nascent popularity of African American vernacular forms, music, and dance, appropriating its oppositional stance and formal construction.'[31] Dunbar's second stanza exemplifies the notion that a higher philosophical level is founded in W. E. B. Du Bois's thoughts on double consciousness, as in 'We Wear the Mask' in 1896, when he writes:

> Why should the world be over-wise,
> In counting all our tears and sighs?
> Nay, let them only see us, while
> We wear the mask.[32]

It is continually Cook's performance practices, both as composer and as performer, that situate him as an active resistor, challenging Saxon's argument that he was unable to resist racialized stereotyping.

This is evident earlier than *Dahomey*: in navigating the realm of articulating Black experience among white consumption, Cook is noted in earlier collaborations as waging 'a struggle to balance blackface consumption with classical experimentation'.[33] In the case of *Dahomey* and its controversial cakewalk, previous historians have made note of how this final number in the show was reinserted for English audiences, attempting to situate it further in the notion of being just another example of how the Black creators and cast of *Dahomey* lost additional agency over their resistance. In fleshing out Du Bois's notion of how Black practitioners were constantly navigating their 'twoness' as a constant double negative – possessing a voice of power opposed to being given a voice of agency in setting forth works that displayed their likeness while displaying complexly problematic notions of Blackness – Dunbar and Cook are actively fusing forces among other Black practitioners at the moment the piece is not only being developed but gaining momentum. Consider James E. Smethurst's further ideas surrounding these complexities:

> How does one represent and/or recreate his or her culture without being (contaminated) by minstrelsy, 'c—n songs,' and plantation literature, by popular and so-called 'high' culture appropriation or misappropriation? How does one deal with the doubleness of popular culture as seen in minstrelsy, the Cakewalk, the 'c—n song,' ragtime, and the ambivalence of African American minstrel-influenced vaudeville?[34]

A compelling exploration of this question is found again in evidence of the performance practice within the show's Overture. In *The Evolution of Jazz in Britain, 1880–1935*, musicologist Catherine Parsonage addresses *In Dahomey*. As in other cases, the text problematically simplifies the production's historical consideration down to being a predictably consumable version of 'the expected features and stereotypes of [B]lack entertainment that had been delineated on British stages for several decades' prior to its presentation.[35] Parsonage then moves on to include a quote from a review in *The Times* from 18 May 1903, two days after opening night, which concludes that Cook 'apparently conducted the Overture facing the audience and singing along' and that the 'freedom of this unusual style was noted':

> the composer conducted with much vigour, singing most of the tunes with his band with a kind of untrammelled spontaneity that finds expression in the whole action of the piece, and more particularly in the dancing, which seems the natural expression of a racial instinct, not the laboriously acquired art of schools.[36]

In embracing this 'unusual style', it is worth dissecting to consider *why* Cook would actually be participating in the performance practice of this moment in this fashion. Was Cook, an artist of rigorously focused technical training in his musical skills (one could say, *laboriously* attained), simply reduced to a 'racial instinct', as the *Times*' reviewer would have its reader conclude? Is the history of this performance practice simply an uncontrolled moment of tribal instinct, as some white frameworks may guide us to contend with? Or did Cook, a trained musician, capable performer and active resistor, purposefully utilize this moment as one to push back against the expectations of his audience – right in front of their faces? Cook's 'untrammelled' expression of the music and words that would have, by some percentage, been penned by himself is more compelling to be viewed as a resistance versus an uncontrolled act of ignorance. Considering his thoughts as an artist, he made no reservations of his stance on where Black artists stood, the resultant inequities and how things would need to change moving forward. His cognizance of his fluidity between these two worlds was no mystery. Consider his words when interviewed in the London *Tatler* at the start of Shaftesbury's *In Dahomey*:

> 'The terrible difficulty that composers of my race have to deal with,' said Mr. Cook, 'is the refusal of American people to accept serious things from us. That prejudice will be educated away one day I hope. Our people who have studied music prove by results that they are capable of appreciating to the full the benefit of a musical education.'[37]

He is unmistakeably clear in the interview, and the interviewer remarks: 'No excitement could be traced in his manner of speaking about the question. On the contrary he took it very quietly, being convinced that someday the negro would not lag behind the white man in the world of music.'[38]

To willingly abide by words that a white audience would sing along to in entertained delight and bigotry is uncomfortably difficult to fathom at base principle. Further, the performative act itself, all complexities removed, begs further exploration. As the conductor in a proposed repressed narrative, Cook could surely have held more agency in simply keeping his back turned to the audience. This becomes a renewed act of embraced exposure in this simple movement – turning outward, away from a playing group of

MUSIC FIGURE 1 *First statement of 'On Emancipation Day', in 2.*

MUSIC FIGURE 2 *Later in first statement of 'On Emancipation Day', in 2.*

MUSIC FIGURE 3 *Return of 'On Emancipation Day' theme, in heavy 4.*

musicians, to enfold the audience and invite them into the moment even further. We revisit the music and lyrics of 'On Emancipation Day', which in its numerous iterations in the Overture was the tune Cook was likely activating in this moment and undoubtedly was the iconic archetypal song that all paying audience members would have been anticipatedly waiting to hear. Further to the evidence that this was a common tune of the show, this theme features prominently three times through the Overture: appearing first in jaunty duple metre, it is the second main theme of the show stated musically (see Music Figures 1 and 2) and returns at the end, first as a recapitulation of the earlier theme, followed by a massive, rousing final presentation in a solid even four beat (Music Figure 3).

In both these examples, the lyrical exertion of the song is potent: 'On Emancipation Day, all you white folks clear the way' and 'When they hear them ragtime tunes, white folks try to pass for c—ns, on Emancipation Day' speak to the ironically weighted nature of the show's spectatorship. The lyrics of 'Emancipation Day' have been further explored by Brooks; she maintains that this ragtime number specifically '[envisions] parodic inversions of identity which clear a space for renegotiating "black" [...] identity in the spirit of the cakewalk'.[39] Singing this, Cook is turning to the consuming audience, wearing the mask of 'polite' performer while spitting Dunbar's acerbic words back in their faces for their consideration of who was *really* in charge. Marva Griffin further confirms: 'Here was a clear, perhaps even prophetic statement about the appropriation of [Black] culture.'[40] Singing this, Cook is turning to the consuming audience, singing words that are unmistakably not intended for them and bestowing them with confidence – confidence in the agency he and the rest of the cast and creators held as Black artists over the moment.

Plainly, there is something going on here. The numerous intersections of resistance that Cook embodies are too weighty to ignore. An unfortunate underwriting and oversight of constructed histories makes this an easy moment to camouflage, but even in this, the denial of Cook's artistry, his skill, his theatrical acumen, his candidness in speaking about the shortcomings of societal equality as well as the matched sympathies of his contemporaries, is not just historically incorrect but categorically short-sighted. Cook's embodiment of resistance is the profound manoeuvring of wearing the mask that all practitioners in this book have done; where Cook is exceptionally profound is that he did this both directly and indirectly, through his art and elsewhere. In considering our own role as spectators of his legacy, we consider where we can be both *destructive* and *constructive* to give light to the expectation of hope of *In Dahomey*'s performers and creators. Carter ends her biography thus: 'Cook launched an important challenge to the deeply rooted practices of segregation, forcing many to confront racism. He displayed a courageous agitated demeanour. His memoirs reveal that his ultimate challenge was "to destroy wrongs, and at the same time write beautiful music".'[41]

2

Belle Davis, Laura Steer
and Cassie Walmer

This chapter traces the resistant practices of three extraordinary Black women who worked variously as singers, performers and dancers: Belle Davis, Laura Steer (who was known professionally as Morcashani) and Cassie Walmer. Each of the women challenge preconceptions about what might be possible in the first decade of the twentieth century.

Davis (b. 1874, Chicago; d. *c*.1938) was an African American singer, dancer, choreographer and co-ordinator of an early dance troupe that featured Black children. She toured extensively across the UK and Europe and was professionally active between *c*.1885 and 1936.[1] Davis married Eddie Whaley (of Scott and Whaley) in 1924. Though Davis's professional work has been discussed in 'The 1900s in context', we uncover new aspects of her professional career in the UK for the first time. Walmer (b. 1888, Camden, London; d. 1980) worked professionally for more than four decades in theatre in the UK, New Zealand and Australia. She took on an additional performance name of Janice Hart later in her career to adopt a Josephine Baker-like Parisian aesthetic. Morcashani (b. 1870, Islington, London; d. 1929), born Laura Fanny Josephine Steer, toured music halls and variety theatres as a baritone singer. She performed extensively in London, the wider UK, Europe and even South America.

Davis, Walmer and Steer enacted resistant practices through their performance presence, global touring and, in particular, transatlantic crossing; through monetizing white tastes for exoticism; and by making connections with other activist artists and sportspeople. This chapter points to the phenomenal scale of their work.

There were numerous Black women theatre professionals at work in the UK during the first decade of the twentieth century as part of global networks of performance, and there were many women touring: African American singers, dancers and actors like Inez Clough (1873–1933); and operatic singers like Abriea 'Abbie' Mitchell Cook (married to the composer Will Marion Cook; see Chapter 1) and Arabella Fields (1879–1931). Several of these women's global working practices have been explored in the literature, revealing the ways in which Black women's work informs and establishes modernism. Contributions include Paula Seniors' consideration of the choreographer and performer Ada (Aida) Overton Walker and Abbie Mitchell's relationship to the 'Gibson Girl' ideal and Jo A. Tanner's work on Laura Bowman's international touring practices.[2] Thomas Riis notes: 'the presence of genuine black entertainers without minstrel getup on the British stage in the late nineteenth and early twentieth centuries allowed Britons to see acts similar to those Americans saw in vaudeville.'[3] Given that many of these performers also had a European and even global performance presence, Black women were therefore at the forefront of shaping international performance industries. This chapter focuses on three women: the African American Belle Davis and the Black British performers Laura Steer (Morcashani) and Cassie Walmer, who embraced global touring practices.

Variety theatre was still the predominant form of popular entertainment in Britain during this period – often mixed with early film bioscopes (sometimes called cinevariety). The popularity of faux-black vernacular (FBV) songs continued through this period, though the popularity of syncopation and ragtime rose as minstrel troupes became less dominant. It should be noted that the minstrel form had an astonishing longevity in the UK not only into the 1930s and 1940s (on television and on radio) but also in amateur theatre groups and on television as late as 1978. Michael Pickering has considered minstrel performance in the UK at length and traces the processes by which individual performers (white and Black) moved out of minstrel performance and into the music hall.[4] Pickering assesses the performance qualities of the minstrel show as 'vibrant and compelling in structure and style' and the ways in which its structure led to later vaudeville and productions.[5] Many individual Black performers operated within these racist practices: Cedric Robinson reminds us that 'Black performers infused the form [of minstrelsy] with their talent'.[6] Robinson demands that we attend to the potential, and realized, consequences of their 'skills', performance practices and professional networks. In this chapter, we focus on three women working within racist frameworks, who often adjusted and subtly resisted these frameworks throughout their careers. In the chapter, we build on the work of Annemarie Bean, who has established the resistance present within Black minstrel performance and Black music revues and vaudeville, arguing 'what [performers] created was a new form of theater based in the skills of the performers, not in their ability to conform to stereotypes'.[7]

Belle Davis: 'Yours [everywhere] in ragtime'[8]

Unusually for many of the people discussed in this book, and particularly for women practitioners, Davis already features in the existing literature on Black performance in Europe; she even has an entry in the *Oxford Dictionary of National Biography* (*ODNB*).[9] This is largely due to the recovery work of Rainer Lotz, who mentions that Davis was the 'first black American woman to record on flat disc records'.[10] Lotz notes that Davis was particularly important because of her vocal practice, as she performed across the transition from operatic and concert sounds to ragtime and became a fully fledged 'vocalist of the new rag art'.[11] Lotz and Jeffrey Green's *ODNB* entry for Davis draws attention to her remarkable travels in the 1900s across the UK, as well as engagements in 'Berlin, The Hague, Paris, Vienna, St Petersburg, and Brussels'.[12] Lotz has recovered the music she recorded in 1902, and even an early film recording in Germany in 1906.[13] Davis toured with her company throughout the 1900s and 1910s, training key choreographers, such as Louis Douglas,[14] before working as a choreographer in the Casino de Paris in the mid-1920s.

Previous approaches to researching Davis have split her career into three stages: first, before her permanent arrival in the UK and Europe in 1901; second, the touring career that followed; and third, her return to the United States in later life. It turns out that there was still much more to discover; while Davis did work predominantly in the UK, she made frequent trips back to the United States, crossing the Atlantic many times and continuing to perform there professionally as well in Europe. The reality of her working practices disrupts our expectations of the limitations of travel during this period. We may find it hard to imagine crossing the Atlantic (which meant at least ten days' travel) for a two-week variety booking, but Davis did this, maintaining family links and accessing professional networks. She demonstrates the flimsiness of our assumed separation of popular theatrical and musical cultures in this period. Moreover, she reveals how white consumption works in practice, not least through her performance but also in the training and development of Black performers. Finally, her career demonstrates an unmistakeable resistant practice through the command over Atlantic travel; and this reveals how Davis was able to respond to and disseminate emerging trends in popular theatre, music and dance.

Working within faux-black vernacular (FBV) styles

Davis's early career included joining the white producer John W. Isham's touring company. His company, *The Octoroons*, toured US circuits and made two separate visits to the UK, in July to September 1897 and again in March 1898 (with a largely different cast).[15] Isham's company featured traditional elements, such as operatic numbers, alongside FBV songs and cakewalk sequences (complicated by the fact that performers of African descent were performing this material).[16] One review of the tour, in St Helens, Merseyside, calls out Davis's 'mezzo-soprano voice of much sweetness'.[17] The tour introduced many Black performers to the UK who would stay in or return to British theatre, including Jasper White and Inez Clough.[18] After Davis returned to the United States, her fame clearly grew, and reviews referred to her in terms like 'The Wizard of [FBV] songs'.[19] Davis's early career demonstrates the close relationship between FBV songs and ragtime, songs with titles like 'Ma Blushin' Rosie' or 'The Honeysuckle and the Bee' – which astonishingly survives as a recording.[20] The clearly syncopated chorus and the stride piano accompaniment demonstrate the infusion of this sound into her early repertoire: she was singing 'You've Got to Play Ragtime' in 1902.[21] Davis achieved some serious success in the United States before she left for London. One report in September 1898 notes that she performed in three separate theatres in New York on the same night:

> [She] opens the olio with the Octoroons at the Bowery Theatre, works in the olio as a third number at the Casino Roof Garden and closes the show at Koster and Bial's in her new success 'Ma Rag-Time Gal.'[22]

At this time of transition out of minstrel performance and into variety, Davis's songs were synonymous with ragtime; the advertisement cards she placed in British stage newspapers in the early 1900s are frequently signed with the note 'Yours in Ragtime'.[23] Ray Sapirstein notes that the ragtime of Paul Laurence Dunbar's period (concurrent with Davis) is 'palpably the first popular iteration of contemporary musical forms, such as dub and hiphop sampling, to reconfigure appropriated elements parodically and with virtuoso ingenuity'.[24] Davis's act included vocal imitations which double down on this appropriation, notably of the white FBV singer and comedian May Irwin (1862–1938).[25] Born in Canada, Irwin had been an early proponent of FBV songs, or 'shouting' as this style came to be known.[26]

Arriving in the UK in June 1901, the traces of Davis's early months show shifting language around her identity, revealing the complex experience of being Black *and* American in the UK.[27] While much of the coverage suggests implied contemporaneous meanings now lost to us, it is possible to read a double estrangement that reveals British ways of seeing as both racialized and nationalized. Comments about her act reveal both racialized and racist responses to Davis, but these are more focused on the Black children in her act. One *Music Hall and Theatre Review* (*MHTR*) review records Davis as 'indubitably the genuine article' because of her features and movements; that same review goes on to speak of the children, Williams and Jones, in explicitly racialized terms.[28] The *Era* describes the children's 'ways as odd' and notes their 'grimacing'.[29] Non-theatrical and regional newspapers reflect another kind of response: a fascination with Davis as authentically *American* and curiosity about the strangeness of her national identity rather than a more specific focus on her racial identity. The *Islington Gazette* notes she has the 'true American flavour about her – lively and musical – while her little assistants well second her in harmony and comedy'.[30] Her American accent is frequently commented on as 'distinct, though charming';[31] the *Sheffield Daily Telegraph* tells their readers: 'she is an American – yankee [*sic*] in her talk and every action [...] The lady sings well and the lads are full of fun and dance.'[32]

Davis's troupe were known under a clearly racialized name (a racial slur for Black children); and her earliest engagements in the UK were advertised with this word in full.[33] At Collins' music hall in Islington, she was billed as 'America's Greatest [racial slur] Cantatrice'.[34] By September, her advertising card described her as 'the feature of fashionable vaudeville of America'.[35] By October, she was styled as 'The American Comedienne'.[36] Since performers and their managers controlled the publicity material supplied to theatres in advance of their attendance, it is possible to imagine she was able to take some sort of control over the press around her bookings. She certainly gained a level of fame; by January 1902, she was appearing at two of London's largest variety houses (the London and the Middlesex) on the same nights, echoing her previous success in New York.[37]

Training children in 'strategies of freedom'

Jeanne Klein has critically explored the performance practice of Davis and the children in her act in the United States, alongside other key women practitioners working at this time, including Ada (Aida) Overton Walker and Ollie Burgoyne.[38] Klein's work reveals how these set-ups created performance training opportunities. Davis's act developed aspects of her work with Isham's company, continuing the format of her working with Black children who would dance and sing. Klein notes that such work with children afforded them 'their first performative steps and pursued multiple strategies of freedom and survival during the oppressive Jim Crow era of segregation'.[39] She notes that Belle Davis, along with others such as Stella Wiley, Bert Williams, George Walker and Aida Overton Walker, 'mentored innumerable girls and young women as they shifted African American musical theatre away from its racist roots in minstrelsy'.[40]

Presumably, Davis's act developed out of her performances with Isham's company but with a better chance of seeing the income from her success. In 1899, she was reported as earning $200 a week in variety.[41] When Davis arrived in the UK, she was the de facto guardian of two children in her care as part of her act: Irving 'Sneeze' Williams (age nine) and Fernandez 'Sonny' Jones (age seven).[42] Most of the children Davis worked with are unnamed, though this work clearly had a long influence on Black performance practice. Louis Douglas appeared in her act until he was twenty; he became a key figure in the development of Black dance and cabaret in Paris as well as on Broadway, where he choreographed *Africana* (1927). Douglas married Will Marion Cook's daughter, Marion Douglas Cook.[43]

Careful crossings (controlling the transatlantic)

Belle Davis did not travel unaware of the history of the Atlantic; we suggest that we should recognize her repeated crossings as part of a resistant practice. Davis deploys international travel and cosmopolitanism, and this is part of her resistant strategies. During her childhood, the Middle Passage was still within living memory (see 'The 1900s in context'). Davis was able to build a successful career in both the United States and the UK (and Europe) simultaneously. In 1905, one variety columnist in Berlin noted that 'Belle Davis has enough offers to fill her date book on this side of the water for a few years' (i.e., in Europe).[44] In 1907, Davis is found performing in Illinois;[45] the following year, from January to May 1908, she played Brooklyn, Chicago and Marengo, Illinois.[46] She returned to the United States for a two-week tour in 1909.[47] Between January and July 1910, she toured across a remarkable geographical reach (sometimes, but not always, on the Orpheum Circuit), playing theatres in San Francisco; Long Beach, California; Utah; Nebraska; Battle Creek, Michigan; St Louis; Chicago; Philadelphia; Detroit; Buffalo, NY; and Philadelphia.[48] Her return to the United States was written about in African American newspapers: 'However, we can see why Miss Davis and her Crackerjacks remained in Europe so long – for no other reason than that the act pleased all because it is headed by one of America's foremost comediennes, who has always held her own through her remarkable ability.'[49] By 15 September 1910, she had returned to Paris, again performing with unnamed children.[50]

Davis returned to the United States for visits in 1912 and 1913.[51] She continued to travel during the First World War, at a time when the British had declared the North Sea a war zone (to the dismay of the Americans) but just before Germany responded with its own declaration of unrestricted submarine warfare on 4 February 1915, which led to the sinking of the Atlantic liner RMS *Lusitania* in May of that year.[52] The *Ashwood* reported that Davis was visiting the United States to tend to her ailing mother and that she intended to return to London within the month; she applied for a new passport on 24 February 1915 in Chicago.[53] In March 1915, her choreography was shown in the 'aquatic revue' *The Lovely Limit*, notable for the presence of the white musical director Percival MacKey. This is potentially ground-breaking but no more is currently known of the project,[54] and Davis was performing in variety by the end of March.[55] Black performers like Davis were sharing emerging musical styles in a period before the mass dissemination of recorded music.

Green and Lotz suggest Davis's 'last known performance in Britain was in 1918'.[56] She was still touring in 1919, and she performed in variety in Paris in 1920.[57] From the early 1920s onwards, she ceased to perform and focused on choreography. She managed a troupe of dancers, 'Belle Davis's Magnolia Blossoms', in 1928,[58] arranging the dances for the 1930 London and touring variety revue *The Casino de Paris Revue*.[59] She continued to have a European presence, making visits for casting from Paris in 1926,[60] and for Berlin in 1929.[61] Casino de Paris revues toured the UK in 1930.[62] The last reference to Davis's work appears in Belgium in 1937, where she was recruiting dancers from the UK.[63] Between 1897 and 1920, Davis made at least twenty return crossings of the Atlantic – bringing with her music, dance styles and working practices that must have informed theatre in both the United States and the UK and Europe.

Laura Steer (Morcashani)

The glamorously named Morcashani was born as Laura Fanny Josephine Steer in Islington, London. She married the African American performer Joseph Highsmith in 1891.[64] Highsmith had remained in the UK and become part of the Southern Syncopated Orchestra in 1917.[65] Steer never presented her own identity in any connection with Britain, first working in a Black American company and then adopting the 'creole' identity that connected her with New Orleans, the Caribbean and Europe. She presented herself variously as American, Creole (suggesting a French Louisianan background), Native American and even Australian. Her fantastically styled performance identities hint at her shrewd assessment of how to advertise herself in different countries. Steer was at the forefront of early technologies: Rainer Lotz notes that she recorded a now lost sound film in Germany in 1908 but that 'neither her films nor the discs that went with them have been found'.[66]

Steer first appeared in a touring production of *Uncle Tom's Cabin*, alongside the 'Louisiana Troubadour Quartette' and her husband, Highsmith. The performers were repeatedly advertised as 'real [Black] performers' – alongside the Louisiana signifier and the text at hand, all working to communicate their status as authentically American.[67] Reviews called out Steer's performance: '[she] possesses a splendid contralto voice, which she used with good effect.'[68] She cannot be found again under that name in the UK until her return to British theatre with the new name, Morcashani. While there is no way of knowing why she reinvented herself, apart from the obvious 'exotic' allure of the new moniker, it may well have been due to distancing herself from an upsetting event and its ensuing press coverage. In 1902, lurid press reports of a coroner's case recount that Steer had separated from her husband three years previously on the Continent. She had written to her husband (clearly they had not divorced) from abroad, and Highsmith's current partner had intercepted a letter from Steer, had feared the possibility of their reunion and had killed herself.[69] Steer took up the name 'Mademoiselle Morcashani' for the rest of her working life – perhaps to remove herself from the scandal.

Morcashani effectively rebranded herself and created a performance history that placed her in France. She could have fabricated this, but she did have the backing of music publishers, so it is entirely plausible that records of her in Paris have not yet been found. In January 1903, Wittmark and Sons announced their new sheet music line-up: 'the pet of Paris [Morcashani] repeats her Parisian triumphs with "I'll be Your Honey in the Springtime".'[70] Her publicity material specifically announces Mlle Morcashani's *return* from a two-month engagement at the Casino de Paris, but there is no mention of Morcashani in the UK (yet) before 1903.[71] The theatrical press did not question any discrepancy. Gossip in *The Stage* in January of that year notes her return to the Tivoli, 'where a few months ago, she made a successful appearance'.[72] Accounts of this performance call her 'the famed Creole baritone eccentric who has created the greatest furore known for years on the variety stage'.[73] Like Davis, she performed FBV songs, but her style was clearly different: one review of her on the same bill as Davis notes Morcashani's 'powerful, almost masculine voice, and a striking appearance'.[74]

A clipping from 1905 demonstrates the complicated identities she was working within; billed as 'Mdm Morcashani', her travels to Germany as 'La Belle Creole' are noted. 'On her return to England she will introduce a beautiful Spanish number, written and composed by Joseph Highsmith, entitled "The Picador's Serenade".'[75] The reappearance of her erstwhile husband in proceedings perhaps confirms our guesses at her name change: the emphasis on the Spanish song sits with her advertised Creole identity. Later, she even employed the plausibly French *'chanteuse eccentrique'*.[76] The publicity material continued to emphasize European credentials: 'the never-to-be-forgotten creole baritone eccentric, returns direct from the Continent.'[77] Steer toured both independently and under the auspices of producer Thomas Barrasford (around 1905); as an independent performer, she would have been expected to send 'all billing matter' two weeks before her arrival at a venue for circulation in the local press.[78] This raises the possibility that she was sometimes able to have direct control over the advertising copy announcing her performances.

The mysteriousness of her early transformation into Morcashani aside, she really did frequently travel widely across Europe and even further afield. In February 1908, she played an engagement in Berlin at the Folies-Bergère cabaret as an 'Australian Excentric [*sic*]' – though limited information exists on any relationship between this and its Parisian namesake.[79] Jeff Bowersox notes that, in Germany, performers like Morcashani 'performed versions of American Blackness and played with audiences' racialized expectations'.[80] But she also made use of these expectations in building a truly international career. Lotz suggests that Steer 'criss-crossed Europe from Dublin to Lisbon, from Bordeaux to St. Petersburg' and even raises the possibility of her appearance in Latin America in 1909.[81] Recently digitized Brazilian newspapers confirm Lotz's suspicion: 'Miss Morcashani: *cantora americana*' plays the Moulin Rouge in San Paulo in July 1909.[82] Steer's last performances in the UK appear to have been in around 1913.[83]

Cassie Walmer

Cassie Walmer's parents were Stephanie, born in France, and George C. Walmer. She worked professionally for more than four decades in theatre in the UK, New Zealand and Australia. She had appeared in a production of *Uncle Tom's Cabin* aged only three with her father and mother; this broke child labour laws at the time, and the resulting coverage of the court case noted her parents were both Black.[84] Walmer began her professional career in variety at age twelve, initially billed in explicitly racialized terms,[85] before being styled as 'the black princess and songstress'.[86] Walmer's act was originally dancing and singing, before she developed the comedy aspect of her act as a singing impressionist or, as it was then known, a 'mimetic vocalist'.[87] Cassie toured across the UK, continuing to mix sand dancing with singing FBV songs, as audiences would have presumably expected.[88] The scale of this touring across the UK is documented in newspaper reviews and theatrical listings across the 1900s. Table 1 lays out 1905 as a single year of her bookings, demonstrating the geographical reach of her performance and the returns to London within it.

TABLE 1 *Cassie Walmer's bookings in 1905.*

	1905 Bookings
January	Panto in Oldham and then Hull[89]
February	Bury, Rochdale, Liverpool[90]
March	Bolton, London's Shoreditch, the Canterbury and Euston[91]
April	London's Paragon and Manchester's Palace[92]
May	Hull, South Shields, Leeds City Varieties[93]
June	Birmingham's Gaiety; London's Collins's, Balham, Poplar, New Bedford Palace of Varieties; Manchester's Tivoli[94]
July	London's Metropolitan, Eastbourne, Hastings[95]
August	Margate[96]
September	Portsmouth, Bradford, Blackpool[97]
October	North Shields, Stockton[98]
November	West Hartlepool, Oldham, Dundee[99]
December	Dundee, Aberdeen, Leeds[100]

Cassie Walmer's persona clearly responded to the audience's desire for exoticism; though she herself was only fifteen, someone (perhaps her mother?) was managing her career.[101] Her early successes caught the attention of Harry Rickards, a British variety theatre producer who ran a touring circuit and theatre in Australia. She arrived there, aged only eighteen, in June 1906, together with her mother Stephanie. Bill Egan notes that 'despite her English birth, she was widely regarded in the Australian press as being American, a status she was legally entitled to in view of her father being a US citizen'.[102]

Egan's study of African American performers in Australia lays out details of Walmer's multiple lengthy visits to the country and to New Zealand, where she was extremely popular. This is particularly notable given the contemporaneous White Australia policy; one wonders how Walmer and Rickards were able to circumnavigate such legal obstacles to her visit. The boxer Jack Johnson secured an exemption for his later visits. In fact, Walmer and Jackson actually met in March 1907, as part of a party held by the Coloured Progressive Association in Australia. This group brought together mostly sailors from different communities, including the Worimi activist Fred Maynard, other Aboriginal men, and African, Caribbean and African American men.[103] Jackson's engagement with early activist groups and his outspoken comments that its greatness came from 'Aboriginal culture rather than the so-called "civilization" of its recent white immigrants' unsurprisingly caused some consternation.[104] Walmer must have been aware of the political nature of Jackson's presence.

Walmer returned to the UK in 1907, and the 1911 census documents her living in Brixton with her mother. Walmer continued to perform in the UK but made a further trip to Australia in 1913.[105] She used the name Walmer until at least 1920,[106] before beginning a remarkable transformation of professional identity. In 1921, performing together with her Australian husband Frank O'Brian, she took on the name Janice Hart, presumably in response to the shifting demands for performances inspired by Josephine Baker. Initially Hart and O'Brian presented a mini revue billed as a comedy sketch where Hart/Walmer plays an alluring judge and which featured song, sketch and dance.[107] One newspaper account of their billing in 1923 is presented in Table 2.[108] This reflects the lasting reality of anti-black racism on British stages that Walmer, and other Black performers, worked alongside.

There is no mention of the connection between Walmer and her previous identity until she is billed under both names in 1924.[109] Bill Egan notes the same happened when she toured Australian variety circuits in 1928: 'The local media either failed to realize that Janice was actually Cassie or chose to ignore it.'[110] As variety shifted towards revues, Walmer and her husband began a remarkable business venture, a revue that began in the UK in 1931 before moving to Australia in 1935. They created a fictionalized version of a Josephine Baker revue which had itself never existed. They gave the show an English and French title *Birds of the Night* (*Oiseaux de la Nuit*), which was 'declared to be their version of a long running Casino de Paris revue, with Janice allegedly playing the roles originated by Josephine Baker'.[111] While it is perhaps understandable that the Australian press did not question the claims, given the distance, the British press gladly presented the exciting

TABLE 2 *Billing at the Stratford Empire, 11 April 1923.*

Act	Details
Grock and Partner	Grock was a clown, real name Adrien Wettach (1880–1959)
May Henderson 'the original Duskey [*sic*] Comedy Queen'	Sings 'Virginia Shore' and 'Troubles of Drowning Her Dog'. Henderson was a white performer who wore blackface
Adam Tomlinson	Comic stories about cooking
Frank Benson	'Jolly Jack Tar', a 'screamingly funny Egyptian song'
Janice Hart and Frank O'Brian	Sings 'Floating Down to Cotton Town' and 'The Italian Song'
Inez and Dolly St Vincent	A sister act who presented a 'variety of songs dances and dresses'; they performed jazz dance, classical dancing and toe dancing (possibly *en pointe* tap dance)
Maximo	Listed as a Cuban tightrope walker

news to their readers. In what must have been an almost direct reprint of the couple's publicity material, the *West Middlesex Gazette* reported on the 'spectacular revue':

> In the role Josephine Baker played in Paris, Janice Hart has achieved a great personal triumph, her vitality, vivacity and versatility having never been revealed to such advantage. This attractive star of a score of revue successes is one of the most talented artistes on the stage today – singing, dancing or acting, her magnetism and personality hold her audience enthralled.[112]

In the months that followed, Hart became described increasingly as an 'international star'.[113] She was still touring in 1942 in a new revue 'Victory Vanities',[114] and throughout the 1940s she performed regularly on BBC radio, making her last appearance in 1952.[115] When Hart retired, she had worked professionally in British theatre for more than fifty years, finding ways to extend her career across an extraordinary geographical and chronological span. In fact, each of the women reviewed in this chapter can be read as actively consuming the white consumption of Black performance; if we understand the work in this way, it allows a way into understanding and reading Black experience in the UK as an insurgent act of resistance.

In this chapter, then, we have explored Belle Davis's transatlantic touring practices which complicated existing overviews of her work. Though the engagement with FBV songs is complex, the prevalence of vocal imitation in Davis's and Morcashani's practice is particularly intriguing and deserves future work. The significance of Davis's work with children has been noted by Klein as an active strategy in moving 'African American musical theatre away from its racist roots in minstrelsy'.[116] This practice was truly international. Laura Steer as Morcashani demonstrates a complex engagement with racial identities, deploying identities to support her creative work. Though we are unable to know how Steer felt or experienced that identity, her practice became an intercontinental performance career and starts to reveal how women might be able to control their own advertising copy to position their work. Cassie Walmer's work is particularly striking; she reinvented a second persona to extend her creative life. She engaged with key resistant Black practitioners, such as Jack Johnson, and was able to work across Europe and into Australia. Nadine George-Graves notes, specifically focusing on dancers during the early twentieth century, that Black women dancers were trying out owning their own bodies: 'Always already a commodity, the uses (and abuses) of the Black body shift significantly at this time and the stakes of performance were far more critical than the perhaps nominal wages earned.'[117] The stakes of these practices establish networks of performance which were necessary for the rise in Black-led revues through the following decade, and in continuing to subvert the hold of minstrelsy on British stages.

The 1910s in context

In 1910, George V became king of the United Kingdom and emperor of India. The decade saw continued British colonialism and, in particular, British political ambitions to control Africa and its precious resources. In 1910, the Union of South Africa became a self-governing dominion of the British Empire, but such decisions were not the norm; in 1914 alone, Britain declared Egypt a British protectorate and merged North Nigeria with the southern region to form 'the largest British colony in Africa'.[1] In the UK itself, the early part of the decade was marked by workers' strikes over miserable pay and conditions. In Ireland, the revolutionary period emerged to overthrow Britain's colonial control of the country (the Irish War of Independence took place from 1919 to 1921).

The 1910s saw the collapse of stability in central Europe in the First World War (28 July 1914 to 11 November 1919). Industrialized warfare spread across the continent and drew in countries far beyond the main regions of conflict. Partly as a result of German naval submarine warfare in the Atlantic Ocean and attacks on American ships, the United States joined the war on 6 April 1917.

The British Army relied on recruits from countries it had colonized during the war; around 8.5 million people from across the Empire joined the services. The war also helped expand the British Empire. Britain captured German colonies (later formalized in post-war peace treaties), taking control of Cameroon and parts of Togo. Britain continued its violent policies of control. In 1919, British troops killed 379 Indians at a religious festival, known as the Jallianwala Bagh (Amritsar) massacre.

The Treaty of Versailles encouraged nations' rights for self-determination and government, and Britain reluctantly began to shift its policy. After events such as Belfast's Bloody Sunday (1921), Ireland was partitioned in the same year into two separate regions, with the South only gaining the full status of a republic in 1940.

US developments and anti-colonial activism

During the 1910s, the Great Northward Migration (also known as the Great Migration) saw 6 million African Americans move away from Southern US states to Northern urban centres like New York and Chicago. Many Pan-Africanist literary and cultural movements began to formalize, particularly in New York, London and Paris, alongside the emergence of a transatlantic periodical (literary magazine) culture.[2] These networks laid the ground for sharing ideas and, in particular, anti-racist, anti-colonial and anti-imperialist thought; and prepared the way for the Harlem Renaissance.

In the United States, the NAACP (established in 1909) launched its important magazine *The Crisis* in 1910. In 1911, the First Universal Races Congress was held in London; the many guests included one of the NAACP's founder members, W. E. B. Du Bois, and Dusé Mohamed Ali, co-writer of the British musical *Lily of Bermuda* (1909). Mohammed Ali co-founded the *African and Oriental Review* in 1912 with John Eldred Jones; the anti-imperialist, pan-African and pan-Asian journal was banned in the British colonies during the war. Marcus Garvey (1887–1940), the Jamaican activist and Black nationalist, founded the United Negro Improvement Association (UNIA) in July 1914, in Kingston, Jamaica (then a Crown colony of Britain). Garvey founded the New York Branch in 1918, with a further periodical *The Negro World*.

Black people's experiences in the UK: 1919 racist attacks

As well as the many Black troops from countries colonized by Britain, many Black people in Britain played a vital role in the war effort in Britain.[3]

> The outbreak of war in 1914 brought dramatic changes for black workers in Britain. Now there was well-paid work for them to do. Their help was needed for the war effort. [...] By the end of the war there were about 20,000 black people in Britain.[4]

After the war, the political climate shifted and anti-Black racism surged, fuelled by police racism and inefficiency; racist press reporting; and government action which forbid Black troops from taking part in the victory parades, including 'the much trumpeted Peace march on July 1919'.[5]

In 1919, racially motivated attacks and murders took place across the UK; they were reported as race riots, driven by unemployment rates but fuelled by racism: 'Isolated attacks soon became widespread and there were extremely violent riots in major towns and cities between January and August 1919: Barry, Glasgow, Liverpool, London's East End and South

Shields. The most violent outbreaks took place in South Wales (Newport and Cardiff).'[6] In Cardiff, three men were killed, with dozens more injured. In Liverpool, anti-Black violence turned into mobs, going house to house to remove Black families from their homes and setting some on fire, as well as robbing and attacking individuals.[7] A 24-year-old Black Bermudian man, Charles Wotten (alt. Wootton), was chased into the River Mersey, where he was hit with stones until he died.

Fryer notes: 'the lessons of the riots were etched into the consciousness of an entire generation [of Britain's Black community].'[8] Black communities in the United States were also the target of racialized violence and white supremacist violence in 1919, through an eight-month period of violence known as 'Red Summer'.

The Jamaican poet Claude McKay (1889–1948) published the poem 'If We Must Die' (1919), it became a key rallying cry of resistance:

O kinsmen! We must meet the common foe!
Though far outnumbered let us show us brave,
And for their thousand blows death-blow!
What though before us lies the open grave?
Like men we'll face the murderous, cowardly pack,
Pressed to the wall, dying, but fighting back!

On stage: Revues, ragtime and early jazz

When African American troupe divisions were mobilized to fight in Europe the movement of Black military bands further disseminated the popularity of Black musical styles. Susan Cook notes: 'the American military provided a new conduit for the transnational sharing of popular culture.'[9] Jim (James) Reese Europe's band were by far the most significant of these early jazz pioneers; they were part of the 369th Infantry Regiment, the 'Harlem Hellfighters'. (The US Army was racially segregated throughout both world wars).

Reese Europe (b. 1881, Alabama; d. 1919, Boston) had been a principal figure in the professionalization of Black musicians in New York. He formed the Clef Club in 1910, which operated as a social and community space, an employment exchange and a concert venue. The Club's influence was quickly felt in the UK, amplified by pre-existing networks around Chicago's Black musical theatre and music industries. Musicians who were part of the Club, like Joe (Joseph Taylor) Jordan (b. 1882, Ohio; d. 1971 Tacoma) and later Dan Kildare (b. 1879, Jamaica; d. 1920, London) brought bands with new musical styles and line-ups (see Chapter 3) to the UK. Both Jordan and Kildare, and their musicians, quickly performed in a variety of venues including nightclubs and theatres.

Ragtime's early hold on popular music shifted through the decade, as jazz became established at the end of the decade as *the* popular musical style. The steady development of recording and communications technology, in particular the music recording industry and early filmmaking, led to expanded ways of hearing popular music. Though film was silent, it featured the presence of a pianist or, at the larger venues, full orchestras. The British Board of Film Classification began in 1913.

Jazz and early recording studies have traced how these musical cultures and working practices transition, but it is essential to note the groundwork for the jazz age was already established in the 1910s. The year 1919 has been seen as the start of jazz, when 'The first actual American jazz bands to arrive in Britain were the Original Dixieland Jazz Band and Will Marion Cook's Southern Syncopation Orchestra'.[10] In fact, music influenced by the New Orleans and Chicago music industry was being heard in British theatres throughout the 1910s. The extent to whether it was jazz or ragtime is incidental to the substantial presence of Black musicians working in British entertainment industries.

J. (John) Rosamond Johnson co-composed and conducted the West End revue *Come Over Here* (1912–13) with the white composer Louis Hirsh. Joe Jordan (for a biography, see Key Figure 2) toured British theatres with various bands and revues as early as 1910–11. In 1912, the white British producer Sir Alfred Butt hired the Black group of singers, the Royal Poinciana Quartette, presumably because they had been part of James Reese Europe's Carnegie Hall concert earlier that year.[11] Louis Mitchell's jazz band was in 'residence in London' by 1914;[12] by 1917, his band the Seven Spades were touring in variety theatre.[13] Black musicians from Dan Kildare's Ciro's orchestra also went into variety and revues. Kildare's drummer, Hughes Pollard, toured from May 1915 onwards and was reported as the 'extraordinary ragtime trap drummer in the latest Yankee revue catch'.[14] Pollard (?–1926) was the brother of Fritz (Frederick Douglass) Pollard, the National Football League Hall of Fame coach. Dan Kildare wrote two songs for the revue *Hullo America!* (1918), and the cast appears to have been white. In 1915, Ernest Trimmingham (see 'The 1900s in context') co-wrote the West End revue *A Revue of Their Own*.[15]

Many white musicians and bandleaders attempted to cash in on the new sounds and rhythms. The touring show *Ragtime Revue* (1913), for example, presumably white given the absence of other information in the advertising, showed 'The Evolution of Ragtime from the cotton fields before the War to the present day craze'; it specifically featured a plantation and Mississippi number.[16] The resurgence of white-performed minstrel shows in the early 1910s also seems to reinstate ragtime as Black music, albeit through racist tropes and structures. In 1913, Moss Empires ran their own show featuring an 'excellent banjo band'; while the show followed the format of the older minstrel shows, the final act was 'a well arranged selection of all the rag-time [*sic*] tunes of the day'.[17]

During this period, many important Jewish American composers like Irving Berlin and George Gershwin helped to popularize both ragtime and jazz within popular music and in musicals themselves, demonstrating the complex processes of interpolation and reuse across marginalized US groups.

In classical music, the death of the Black composer Samuel Coleridge Taylor (b. 1875, London; d. 1912, Surrey) was widely marked in concert hall programming.

Variety theatre and the revue form

Popular variety theatre shifted increasingly towards embracing the revue form as the main form of entertainment. The revue had previously acted as a smaller section of variety bills and later became the full evening's entertainment. Through this change, revues showcasing Black performers were a steady presence (see Chapter 3).

Individual acts sometimes made this transition: Harry Scott and Eddie Whaley began to appear more frequently in revues written around their act (see Chapter 3); Will Garland continued touring across the UK, Europe and into Russia; and performers like Louis Douglas moved from variety theatre into starring in revues (see Chapter 3). Individual performers continue to tour widely: singers and dancers such as Frank Weaver and Kidd Love (buck and wing, sand dancing). Walter Bentley is named as a Black conductor working in variety in 1913 (little more is known about him).[18]

In 1919, Will Marion Cook brought his Southern Syncopated Orchestra to the UK; they first performed at the Philharmonic Hall, Great Portland Street. The orchestra's residency at the Philharmonic Hall in London was managed by the African American producer and impresario George Lattimore. During that year, they played in front of the King and Queen's Garden Party – an annual event for the servants at Buckingham Palace – as well as at free concerts as London's East End theatre, the People's Palace. The African American clarinettist and composer Sidney Bechet also played with the company.

In 1919, the bandleader W. H. (William 'Billy') Dorsey (c.1880–1920),[19] reported living in 'a handsome flat' in an 'exclusive West End section of London', told the *Los Angeles Herald*:

> I've come over here to show these London people the real jazz music. There are a lot of cheap imitators [...] who don't know anything more about our real American jazz music than a rabbit. To hear jaz [*sic*] music played by an English trap artist is like witnessing a performance of Ibsen by the Georgia minstrels.[20]

The article notes that Dorsey's musicians were making $25 a day, with engagements from 4 p.m. to 4 a.m. the following morning. Jazz was widely seen as a Black cultural form; when Jim Europe died, one British headline read: 'Jazz inventor dead.'[21]

3

Following a year of Black performance in the UK: 1916

This chapter traces some of the expanse of Black performance practice taking place in the UK during 1916, when Britain was in the midst of the First World War (the United States did not join the war until 1917).

Though the chapter addresses a twelve-month period, rather than an individual, key figures do emerge. The unlikely presence of the Black boxing hero Jack Johnson throughout this period challenges existing ideas about who was part of the British musical theatre landscape. Johnson (John Arthur Johnson) (b. 1878, Galveston, Texas; d. 1946) was the first Black heavyweight boxing champion, turned theatrical showman. Johnson collaborated with key figures like the composer Joe Jordan (b. 1882, Cincinnati, Ohio; d. 1971) in producing the boxing themed revue *Seconds Out*. The producer, performer, composer and musician William 'Will' Garland (b. 1875, Keokuk, Iowa; d. 1938 London) also appears. Garland was becoming an increasingly important figure in developing the popularity of the revue form in British theatre. Gordon Stretton (William Masters) (b. 1887, Liverpool; d. 1983, Buenos Aires) was a Black British jazz musician, theatre producer and performer. Stretton performed with the Jamaican Choir and visited Jamaica with them. He later moved to Argentina where he helped popularized jazz.

Black performers and practitioners during this period countered racist ideology and dialogue through their international presence. The development and popularity of the revue form, still part of an overall evening of entertainment rather than a show in itself, demonstrate the increasing popularity and reliance on Black theatrical production in this period.

During 1916, working- and middle-class audiences were able to encounter Black performance practice in regional theatres and variety theatres through individual acts and ensemble revues across the UK. In London's West End, upper-class clientele could see Black practitioners at work in glamorous West End revues or Black musicians in exclusive nightclubs like Ciro's. Many of these practitioners were African American, including the boxer turned showman Jack Johnson, the composer and music director Joe Jordan and the prolific theatre practitioner Will Garland (see Chapter 4). This widespread presence of an international Black musical and performance practice in British theatrical life demonstrates a particular connection between Chicago and New York as creative centres of the Great Northward Migration (see 'The 1910s in context') and British theatrical life. From the Chicago theatre and music scene, W. H. Dorsey and Joe Jordan, a prolific composer and orchestrator, and even Jack Johnson, though better known as the first Black heavyweight boxer, were a significant part of Chicago's early 1910s nightlife. Other Black practitioners were born in the UK, most notably the producer and performer Gordon Stretton. By following a particular year, it is possible to see the geographical reach of this performance and its prevalence in British theatrical life.

January 1916: *Seconds Out*, an unlikely musical journey from Chicago to Dundee

Now fourteen months into the First World War, Dundee's long-standing nickname of 'Juteopolis' accurately described a city busy making the raw materials for sandbags for trench warfare 650 miles away. For factory workers in need of some distraction, tickets were available for *Seconds Out*, with the chance to see the champion Black boxer Jack Johnson in person. One Dundee local newspaper assured its readers that 'record-breaking business is assured during the week'.[1] *Seconds Out* was billed as a revusical and advertised as 'a beautifully staged musical comedy, in five seductive scenes [...] with elaborate electrical effects, and furnished with tune and attractive music'.[2] The revue had toured since August 1915, playing various theatres, including in suburban London and venues around London and the South East, the North East (Yorkshire, Northumberland and County Durham) and the Midlands. Johnson recalled that he had 'engaged the best stage talent available in London', before taking the show on a national tour 'receiving everywhere a welcome and patronage that was gratifying and profitable'.[3] As was the norm for revues, it played alongside some variety acts and short film reels (bioscopes) which told audiences at home of the latest news from the front. It was one of the earliest touring Black shows to be explicitly called a revue rather than an act, and it featured Johnson prominently. As odd as it might seem, boxing was an established part of music hall and variety theatre billings, in both the UK and the United States.[4]

Johnson was a boxing legend, the first African American to hold the world heavyweight boxing title (from 1908 to 1915), and was still billed as the 'World's Greatest Fighter'[5] even though he no longer held the championship. In Dundee, 'a great crowd congregated in front of the King's Theatre awaiting the arrival of the "white racing car"'.[6] In the revue, Johnson showed his boxing skills while also speaking and presenting a song.[7] In Dundee, he delivered a speech on the ethics of boxing because his ill health had prevented him from singing, though this did not make much of a difference to the crowd, who wanted to see their boxing hero. Three soldiers and a sailor stepped up to fight with Johnson, though he ensured the men, and their egos, went unhurt.[8] Johnson's success as a Black athlete had provoked international fear and racist violence, particularly after the so-called 'Fight of the Century', in which he defeated the white fighter James J. Jeffries in July 1910. Racist riots broke out across the United States, leading to the deaths of multiple African Americans. In the UK, film footage of the fight was also shown in variety theatres. One report notes that, on the night of the match itself, two music hall artists of African descent had been violently assaulted in London's Leicester Square 'because Johnson had won'.[9]

The historian Paula Seniors makes clear that, as a boxer and activist, Johnson 'challenged the discourse of white male superiority [...] his very presence challenged the attempt to subjugate black men by defying the discourse that defined the black male body as unmasculine and weak'.[10] In 1911, when Johnson appeared in variety at the London Palladium, the *MHTR* published a deeply racist complaint.[11] *Seconds Out* toured after Johnson had lost his title in April 1915 to the white fighter Jess Willard (and was perhaps perceived as less of a threat); footage of the fight continued to circulate. In April 1916, one British regional newspaper highlighted an upcoming showing, proudly and erroneously assuring its reader that, since then, no other Black fighter 'will ever again be allowed to compete for English championships'.[12]

Perhaps surprisingly, press responses to the revue and Johnson's presence were generally positive; when articles specifically address Johnson as a Black man, it is usually to explicitly criticize US attitudes, something which may indicate prevailing anti-US feeling. During 1916, wider racist anti-Black discourses were perpetuated in the UK by D. W. Griffith's strategically racist and white supremacist film *Birth of a Nation* (1915), which continued to be shown in British cinemas. The film's depiction of the formation of the Ku Klux Klan was described in the *Dundee Courier* as 'an organisation of whites for the correction of negro influence', suggesting that the end of the film shows 'whites are victorious in [the allegorical depiction of] good over evil'.[13] In the face of racist discourse, Johnson's response in Dundee is startling. Henry T. Sampson's sourcebook records the coverage in the *Indianapolis Freeman* (an African American newspaper) in December 1915 of Johnson's work in public campaigns for army recruitment campaigns in Scotland. *Freeman* readers are assured that, in Scotland, Johnson's 'color has nothing against

IMAGE 1 *Jack Johnson driving an automobile in Chicago, Illinois, holding on to the steering wheel, 1910. From the Chicago Daily News collection. (Photo by Chicago History Museum/Getty Images.)*

him'.[14] It obviously did, but it is nearly impossible to unpick the reality or know what the contemporary experience of a Black person born in Dundee would have been during this period compared to Johnson's experience as a beloved celebrity. Johnson's mistreatment in the United States was certainly sensationally covered in the UK. He had recently been forced to flee the United States as a result of his marriage to a white woman, Lucille Cameron (who performed in *Seconds Out*). One interview notes that Johnson's marriage 'stirred up the cauldron of persecution that seethed long after he had left the inhospitable shores of "God's own country [i.e., the United States]."'[15]

Seconds Out is not just noteworthy because of Johnson's participation in it. It relied on key Black composers, musical directors and performers from the Chicago theatre scene; it was composed by Joe Jordan and conducted by W. H. Dorsey (any score is lost). Joe Jordan had a prodigious career in Chicago and a long association with the Pekin Theatre (see Key Figure 2). The Pekin Theatre was managed by a Black entrepreneur, Robert Mott, from 1905 to 1911. Despite its short lifespan, the theatre is immensely significant in histories of Black performance practice. Edward Robinson notes that the Pekin 'provided Afro-American theater artists with an opportunity to master theater craft and to contribute significantly to the development of an emerging black theatrical tradition'.[16] Whatever *Seconds Out* actually sounded like, it brought ragtime and blues-influenced Black musicians who had honed their craft in Chicago's Black music and theatrical scene. This very early connection between emergent jazz sounds and the UK has not previously been addressed in histories of British musical theatre. The influence of the Chicago scene was significant: Jack Johnson also ran a nightclub there during 1912 called Café de Champion.[17] Since Jack Johnson was 'a personal friend' of Mott's, it is entirely possible Johnson had seen (or heard) Jordan's earlier work, or at least was introduced to him via Mott.[18] Johnson's connection to key Black musicians is well established. Paula Seniors notes his influence on Bob Cole, James Weldon Johnson and J. Rosamond Johnson.[19]

Joe Jordan (Joseph Zachariah Taylor Jordan) (b. 1882, Ohio; d. 1971, Tacoma, Washington) was a prolific Black composer and bandleader.[20] Jordan composed 'The Pekin Rag' in 1904. He was hired as music director of the Pekin Theatre in Chicago's South Side in 1906, where he was astonishingly prodigious. In sixteen months, he 'composed, arranged and conducted over fifteen musical comedies'.[21]

At the Pekin, Jordan was a contemporary of Will Marion Cook, Will Vodery and J. Rosamond Johnson. These professional relationships led to Jordan's subsequent work in New York and on Broadway. His music featured in Cook's *Bandana Land* in 1908.[22] Jordan wrote with Bob Cole and J. Rosamond Johnson for Broadway operetta *The Red Moon* (1909).

Jordan was also a key figure in early jazz music. He collaborated in New York with James 'Jim' Reese Europe and Cook. He also published 'That Teasin' Rag' in 1909, when the Original Dixieland Jazz Band used its tune without credit in their recording 'Original Dixieland One-Step', often regarded as the first jazz single. He successfully sued them for attribution.[23]

Jordan first toured the UK in 1910–11 with George W. Baker as 'the Emperors of Ragtime'[24] and again in summer 1915 with his Syncopated Band, made up of Black musicians, then described as 'how rag-time should be played'.[25] The band featured trap drummer Hughes Pollard, who was initially part of Dan Kildare's Ciro's orchestra. Jordan then composed Jack Johnson's revue *Seconds Out* (1915–16).

Jordan later returned to the United States, where he worked again for Will Marion Cook and the Southern Syncopated Orchestra. He later performed in the revue *Keep Shufflin'* (1928) and became part of the Federal Theatre Project's Negro Unit Orchestra during the 1930s. He served in the US Army for many years as an entertainer before entering semi-retirement with his family in Tacoma.

KEY FIGURE 2 *Joe Jordan, a short biography.*

Jordan's was not the only musical influence on this entirely forgotten revue, and the role of W. H. Dorsey as a conductor is a significant one. In advertising copy for *Seconds Out*, Dorsey is noted as the supposed only Black conductor 'who has won fame in America'.[26] While there were in fact many Black conductors during this period, not least W. C. (William Christopher) Handy, W. H. ('Billy') Dorsey had also worked extensively in the Chicago theatre scene. Dorsey was explicitly involved in the transition from ragtime to blues; in 1915, he published his arrangement of 'The Long Lost Blues'.[27] This raises the intriguing prospect of a blues-influenced musical director conducting in British theatre in 1916. Dorsey's wife, Lizzie Hart, also starred in the revue. She had also been part of the Chicago theatre scene and had previously performed the work of other Black composers.[28]

Black-produced revues, the work of Gordon Stretton and Will Garland

Seconds Out was by no means the only opportunity in music hall and revue to hear Black music and performance. As a performance style, ragtime's popularity in the early 1910s was well established by this point. Catherine Parsonage notes that the West End revue *Hullo Ragtime* (composed by Louis Hirsch in 1912 and revived in 1913 and 1914) 'was important in defining and popularising ragtime in Britain'.[29] Much of this ragtime syncopated music was written by white composers like Hirsch, but, notably, in 1913 Hirsch collaborated with J. Rosamond Johnson in *Come Over Here* in a 'colossal stage production',[30] which also starred Charles Hart (who toured with the second *In Dahomey* company). Joe Jordan and W. H. Dorsey also collaborated as part of the band for the 1915 revue *Push and Go* written by Albert de Courville.

By 1916, Black-produced Black revues were a significant part of the British theatrical landscape. Two of the most significant figures in this period are Gordon Stretton and William Garland, both polymath producers and performers who created new theatrical material explicitly for the UK. From May 1916, Gordon Stretton's *Dark Town Jingles* was touring the UK, and he went on to write a further show, *Smoke's Up*, later in the same year. Stretton, born William Masters in Liverpool 1887 to an Irish mother and a Jamaican father, is an important figure in early Black musical theatre history. His career has been retraced in a recent publication, *Gordon Stretton, Black British Transoceanic Jazz Pioneer: A New Jazz Chronicle* (2018). Michael Broken and Jeff Daniels trace Stretton's early connections, performing alongside a young Charlie Chaplin in the 'Eight Lancashire Lads' troupe, his work with the Jamaican Choir and his friendship with numerous African American practitioners including Billy Dorsey.[31] Stretton had also travelled to Australia and, like Cassie Walmer, met with Jack Johnson there.[32] Although Stretton did not remain in the UK, and left in 1923 for Paris, he clearly contributed to the popularity of the revue form there.

Jingles was billed as 'A Black and White Revusical Comedy',[33] written by Ed. E. Rylat and Gordon Stretton, with music and lyrics by George Baker and Stretton (Baker was possibly the same Black musician who had toured with Joe Jordan in 1911, but little more is currently known about him) and conducted by W. H. Dorsey (here noted as Mr Dersey) with Lewis (Louis) Michell on drums.[34] Mitchell had come to the UK as part of the Dan Kildare jazz band (see the section 'Nightclubs and theatre music: Ciro's Nightclub, Orange Street, London'). Howard Rye notes that the African American drummer Louis Mitchell's career in theatres 'must have been a major part in spreading the new rhythms across the country'.[35] The revue itself was advertised as 'the modern successor to *In Dahomey*', with 'dancing in every style performed by experts',[36] and 'a plot and originality at last'.[37] While the musical clearly connects with the longer presence of Black performance by referencing *In Dahomey*, it is challenging to deal with since it seems to merge complex racialized tropes and ideas (the 'Dark Town' descriptor was used for parts of cities, such as the South Side of Chicago, which had a large Black population). The show was set around a search-for-talent plot, apparently opening 'at the directors meeting of a variety board' where, with no talent to speak of, the directors visit a Southern (US) plantation and bring 'some of the natives back to England'.[38] The musical finished with a cabaret scene which ends with 'a Creole wedding scene';[39] what this actually meant is difficult to ascertain though it is notable that the dancers in the cast are billed as 'Creole dancing girls'. Though it is unclear what is precisely meant by this in 1916, it is most likely referring to skin tone rather than any Louisiana connection; what exactly the wedding entailed is unclear.

Jingles was produced by Lemus Productions Syndicate (also known as Colonial Amusements) whose offices were based in Holborn, London. The mysterious company only seems to have been in operation from 1916 to 1917 and worked consistently on Black cast shows. In one year alone, they produced multiple horribly named productions. In one November 1916 issue of the *Era*, they pitched three separate revues.[40] *Jingles* appears to have been the most successful; it was possibly rebranded as *Dusky Revels* (Brocken and Daniels suggest it was the same piece).[41] *Revels* was also conducted by Dorsey, with an augmented orchestra, though it is unspecified with what – perhaps drums, given Louis Mitchell's earlier connection.[42] *Jingles* also 'opened in a plantation scene'[43] and included topical wartime songs like 'Taffy got his Jennie in Glamorgan' and generic love songs such as 'Loving Old Moon' and 'When You're Away from Home'.[44] During 1916, Lemus also produced *In Sunny Tennessee* (1916) and *Hullo! Dixie!* (1916); there was clearly a connection to earlier minstrel tropes. *Tennessee* was advertised as a nostalgic return to minstrel show material; one review noted: 'there is a good old-time flavour about the entertainment, added to the characteristics of the modern revue.'[45] *Hullo! Dixie!* (1916), billed as a musical comedy revue, had a cast of thirty established Black variety performers and a playing time of seventy-five minutes.[46] The form of the revue was clearly becoming established entertainment in itself.

Over the course of 1916, Stretton seems to have moved away from Lemus Productions, producing *Smoke Up* (1916) by himself – with the line 'A fragrant revue in three whiffs'.[47] The show was written and composed by Stretton and starred Eddie Emmerson, a Black British comedian who played a significant part in the work of William 'Will' Garland. It was described as a 'brilliant show with good comedy, catchy music and effective dances'[48] – notably, it was the entire evening's entertainment, with no other acts 'filling' the variety billing.[49] Shorter revues still persisted for some time; during 1916, Belle Davis was still a significant part of British theatre, touring with her company of children in the short review *Southern Pastimes*.[50]

Will Garland was one of the most significant Black practitioners during the period this book covers. Garland was more than a producer and performer; he was a theatrical polymath. He first worked in the UK during a tour of *In Dahomey* in 1904 (see Chapter 4). During 1916, he was a comedian in solo and double acts, as well as a vocalist, a solo musician (pianist, trombone and tuba) and a tenor, actor and choral performer. Off stage, he played in pit orchestras and worked as vocal director and, perhaps most significantly, led troupes as a producer and director of revues. His later work is discussed in Chapter 4, but for now it is useful to see what he was doing during this single year. During 1916, he was performing in a revue called *Coloured Society*, initially produced by a Manchester-based producer and agent, George Sax. Sax was presumably white, since no mention is made of his ethnicity at any point and given the tone of much of the coverage of the revue it likely would have done.[51] The title of the revue is clearly essentialized around the racial identity of its cast – something which is particularly an issue since Garland did not initiate it and was hired by Sax as a performer. The title endured, however, since versions of it toured for the next six years; although at some points the production seems to have been known interchangeably as *All Black*.[52] By November 1917, Garland had taken control of the production as sole producer and star.

In its early incarnation, the revue spent around a month with weekly bookings in theatres on the fringes of Manchester, in suburban variety theatres, perhaps as to presumably be accessible to Sax's eagle eyes. In 1916 alone, after its Manchester engagements, the show toured Newcastle, Liverpool, Aston (Birmingham), Salford, Derby, Dundee, Edinburgh, Cowdenbeath, Motherwell, Greenock, once more to Manchester, Ashton-under-Lyne, Preston, Jarrow, returned to Newcastle, Birkenhead, Chesterfield, Peterborough, Colchester, Runcorn, Blackburn and once more to Salford. In its earliest incarnations, the revue was a series of scenes on a regular variety bill. In April 1916, when playing Birmingham, the company shared the bill with Belle Davis's *Southern Pastimes*.[53]

In March 1916, the show was playing at Newcastle Pavilion; its reviews reveal racialized responses which, while not always explicitly negative, clearly contain essentialized views of race. The unusual nature of the production (whether true or not) is frequently mentioned in responses: 'an all black revue must be voted something of a novelty';[54] elsewhere as 'a new variety of this type of production.'[55] The reviews also reiterate racist ideas about a 'natural connection' between Black performers and song and dance, noting the company's 'characteristic ragtime exuberance'.[56] This idea of authentic Blackness as opposed to white performance of blackface is also used to praise the performance. One review notes that those who see the show at the Newcastle Pavilion 'will agree it possesses some elements which have not been approached by its white competitors'.[57] While there is no surviving paperwork around the production, word-for-word similarities in *Society*'s reviews suggest there must have been some kind of press release or information sheet that almost certainly contained the word novelty – again, note that the production had a white producer. Similar coverage at Preston, Lancashire, in August 1916 reiterates: 'We are all in search of novelty in these days of stress, and a real novelty is provided at the Hippodrome [...] which is claimed to be the only show of its kind on the halls performed by [people of African descent].'[58]

The revue was loosely structured around five scenes and could incorporate up-to-date material and changing cast members. Walter Dixon was part of the company; he had been part of the second *In Dahomey* tour. Dixon had gone on to record with the Four Black Diamonds.[59] He had also performed in two Broadway productions: the Cole and Johnson brothers' production of *A Trip to C—ntown* (1898) and Marion Cook's *The Southerners* (1904). But, despite the glamour of such a connection to Broadway, it is the emphasis on London that is positioned in the newspapers; in June 1916, it is advertised as 'London's latest novelty revue'.[60]

Coloured Society presents people of African descent far beyond the imagined 'Southern America' (i.e., the Southern US states and their plantations) and merges racial identities in ways which are difficult to unpick or even fully understand. As we will address in Chapter 4, when Garland was fully producing revues the imagery was complicated in ways which explicitly invoke resistance against white supremacy. But while the show was Sax's production, the show is subverted largely through the skill of the Black performers within it. The show presented a Zulu scene, which reflected a continuing British fascination with Zulu warriors as a way of re-celebrating the British victory in the Boer War. As late as 1915, a touring spectacle drama *Kaleema: A Zulu Queen* was billed as having 'a company of real Zulu warriors'.[61] Garland played the Zulu Chief, with a song called 'The Zulu Queen', accompanied by Frank Weaver (the Jamaican pianist who had been in the UK since the early 1900s).[62] But Africa, in this case South

Africa, was conflated with imaginings of other apparently interchangeable acts: the representation of Polynesian peoples and the inclusion of 'a very pretty' Hawaiian dance.[63] The dance sequences were clearly important: 'some marvellously clever and quick steps are introduced which never fail to secure the heartiest applause.'[64] There was also topical patriotic content. One sequence of dance-based impressions included 'a German doing the goose-step, and, as he describes it, the way he limps back after the British have finished with him'.[65]

As a revue, it is important primarily because of Garland's involvement and eventual takeover of the revue. In the only surviving interview, which is in fact the only trace of Garland's own words that currently exists, Garland claimed to have invented the form.[66] Though this was not quite true – the form was established in France in the 1840s – he certainly helped transform it into a permanent part of British theatre. Garland toured with revues from as early as 1907, with his own version of *A Trip to C—ntown* from 1907. This was less than ten years after one of the very earliest revues, *Pot-Pourri* (1899) seen by the *Era* as a 'novel entertainment [...] unfamiliar in this country to the large majority of theatre goers'.[67] Though there were occasional appearances of the form – *The Revue* (1902), featuring white music hall stars Marie Lloyd and Little Tich; and George Grossmith's *The Bugle Call* (1905) and *Venus* (1906) – it was not until the 1910s that the revue form became a major part of British musical theatrical life. The work of Garland and Stretton played a major role in its dissemination.

Nightclubs and theatre music: Ciro's Nightclub, Orange Street, London

Nightclubs provided another space where Black band leaders and musicians could be heard in Britain during 1916. They are important in a theatrical context because there was a fluidity between provincial touring networks and major West End houses. A musician in a nightclub band may clearly also play within a theatrical pit bands market. If a new sensation, like the syncopated beats of jazz, became commercially successful in one arena, it would quickly be employed across others. One nightclub was particularly important: Ciro's, a nightclub better known for its later incarnation during the 1920s and 1930s, though it also operated between 1915 and 1917, until it was closed for breaking licensing laws. During 1916, Ciro's became the site of heated newspaper debate about the upper classes enjoying the high life, while ordinary working people made wartime sacrifices. But it was also an important place for the development of Black music in the UK and demonstrates connections between professional Black music in New York and the British theatrical scene. From April 1915, Ciro's had employed Dan Kildare and his six-piece jazz band as the Clef Club Orchestra. The band's influence quickly moved to theatre. Kildare's band (piano, cello, three banjos, drums/vocal, bass violin) included the trap drummer Louis Mitchell, who, as we have seen, was part of the theatrical touring circuit in 1916.

Kildare was an established part of the New York Black music scene. He was born in Jamaica in 1879 and had moved to the United States in the early 1900s; he worked there as a touring musical director with a minstrel company before taking up residency in Harlem.[68] He became vice president and then president of James Reese Europe's Clef Club, a booking agency for Black performers. The Clef Club was a regular feature of the emerging musical scene in Harlem. Gilbert notes that it 'forged new labor relations between black musicians and white clients – whether restaurant managers or private hosts – and introduced a new type of black professional musician to New York City'.[69] The Club had an extraordinary roster of musicians. In 1914, Kildare took part in the Clef Club Symphony Orchestra's concert at the Manhattan Casino in Harlem. The extraordinary line-up featured among others 'Forty-six mandolins and bandorins [sic ...] five traps, two bass violins and thirty pianists' (including Kildare); the assistant conductor and chorus master was Will Marion Cook.[70]

Kildare's main influence is in broadening established networks of Black musicians in the UK. Like Joe Jordan, he had professional connections with Reese Europe in New York. Kildare's band's activities in London have been painstakingly traced by Tim Brooks, who notes their early recordings were often of white composed music,[71] for example songs from Jerome Kern's 1915 musical *Very Good Eddie* (a show which had not yet opened in the UK), though Kildare also recorded music by Reese Europe. But the coverage of Kildare's work at the Clef Club reveals racist attitudes to jazz and to Black musicians. In December 1916, British newspapers sensationally reported the attempt to prosecute the owners of Ciro's for breaching Sunday licensing laws in a debate which led to Kildare and jazz music becoming the centre of debates about the morality of jazz music. During the trial, the police inspector suggested the club's music was 'of a rather crude and riotous character' and that there was no sheet music on their stands – 'the musicians evidently struck the notes on their own accord'.[72] In defending the nature of the music of the nightclub, Bodkin noted that 'the music was ordinary ragtime music [...] played by the very best band that can be obtained – at a cost of £100 a week'.[73]

The court case, and the discussion of Kildare's band, led to some of the most explicitly racist coverage of Black music during 1916. While there is very little use of the n-word during 1916 in the British press in connection to Black musicians, coverage of this court case and broader high-society coverage of the band frequently reverts to this slur.[74] Black musicians in nightclubs had been the subject of complaint and control. Johnson's nightclub in the South Side of Chicago was hugely popular, and its open admittance to white and Black patrons attracted the attention of the police's ongoing 'vice purge' in the city, partly because of their fear of racial mixing. Amy Absher notes that policing of night-time venues meant that 'Black music – and, by extension, the Black musician – were seen as the accomplice of vice'.[75] Such racist views also pervaded British responses to 'mixed' nightclubs in London. In later years, Kildare did not experience prolonged commercial success. His final years were very grim; he murdered several people, including his wife, before killing himself in 1920.

The music and musicians in these bands clearly influenced theatre. Drummer Hughes Pollard, who had been part of Joe Jordan's 1915 line-up, played in central London revues and regional theatres, often as a speciality act in various white-produced revues. Pollard performed in *Watch Your Step* (1915 tour) under the famous white jazz conductor Jack (Jackson) Hylton, which, in June 1916, returned to a central London venue, the Alhambra.[76] Puzzled newspapers tried to convey to their readers the effect of the sound Pollard could create: '[he is] a host in himself and master of the mysteries of true syncopation – ragtime at its best [...] When really busy Pollard, who works with both hands, both feet and his mouth, can touch of his sixty effects per minute.'[77] The overture of the *Watch Your Step* seems to have been written to showcase Pollard. One uncertain critic in Birmingham described the 'wonderful design in tropical ragtime', while calling the overall effect 'hard work and noise'.[78] Pollard seems to have worked continuously in the UK throughout 1916; in addition to *Watch Your Step* he is also listed in *Special Mixtures* and *Any Complaints*.[79] It is notable that his skin colour is frequently unmentioned, and the obviously problematic 'Black Lightning' moniker is not consistently associated with his performance. Instead, the most frequent response to Pollard's work is grasping for vocabulary to describe his virtuosity. One response to Pollard describes Hylton as only a 'competent musical director' but Pollard as 'something of a musical sensation'.[80]

Other kinds of theatre performance

Clearly, there was an incredible range of Black performance practice during 1916, as Table 3 demonstrates. The comedians Scott and Whaley had numerous revues written around them in 1916 alone: *Introduce Me*,[81] *Don't You Push Me No More* and *Friend*.[82] The double act appeared in several films, including *The Kentucky Minstrels* (1934), usually performing their onstage act.[83] They toured British theatre extensively for three decades, as well as across Europe and even Australia in variety and in revues written around their onstage personas.[84] In 1928, they said in an interview that 'they would like to make pictures, so that they could have the chance to see themselves at work'.[85] They ended their professional partnership in 1946.[86]

TABLE 3 *Black performers working in British theatre during 1916.*

Types of Act	Names
Actors	J. Bessima Kofie, Black South African; [87] Joseph Bruce and Napoleon Florent – both extras in *Chu Chin Chow*, a musical; Florent's daughter noted: 'He didn't have speaking roles. He was an exotic extra.'[88]
Singers and dancers	A. W. Scott[89] Burt Russell – in *Coloured Society*
Acts featuring children	Belle Davis (see Chapter 2)
Singers	Cassie Walmer (see Chapter 2) Dorothy St. Elmo 'the West Indian Nightingale (of the Follies Bergere, Paris)'[90] Smith & Johnson – a comedy/singing duo[91]
Comedians	Jack Woods[92] Jasper Snowball[93] Sam Henry Andy Clark Harry Brown[94]
Dancers	Buck and Sand Kidd Love – who danced 'on an elec. [*sic*] illuminated table'[95] Willie Robbins The Two Daniels – comedians and dancers with a speciality act of 'plantation clog dancing'[96] Dollie White Richard Winn – 'Expert American Buck & Wing Dancer'[97] Hilda Dawson and Lewis Hardcastle – *Coloured Society* company Rastus and Banks[98]
Entertainers (or acts unknown)	Scott and Whaley Flournoy Miller and Aubrey Lyles[99] Jasper and Eva Caldwell[100] Martinette and Wallace – 'comedy musical artists'[101] The Delroys – 'strong singing, dancing and comedy speciality [...] British subjects'[102] The Four Black Diamonds (featuring Gene Abbott) – 'eccentric vocalism and dancing'[103] Frank Weaver [Jamaican?] – 'entertainer with his own compositions' appears in billings across the country for some years previously, appearing as a sand-dancer in 1910;[104] usually noted as a 'talented dancer'[105]

	Harry Jeanette and Oscar Logan – of the Dark Town Comedy Trio[106]
	Ella Moore – male impersonator[107]
	Arthur Crawford, Nora Dawson, Carl Thomas, Pete Spriggs, Lulu Smith and Lillie Day – *Coloured Society* company[108]
	Emmie Austin – 'humorist and pianist'[109]
Writers and producers	Gordon Stretton – composer, performer, writer, producer
	William Garland (see Chapter 3)

This single year shows us the geographical reach and scale of Black performance. Here, presence is resistant practice. Individual acts are harder to trace but appear to have been regularly performing throughout 1916. In the West End, Lewis (Louis) Douglas also appeared in shows like *Honi Soit* in a beautiful ice-skating sequence.[110] Douglas was an actor, dancer and choreographer. As a child, he had trained and toured with Belle Davis; this is a clear example of her profound influence. In general, it is important to note that individual performers' racial heritages are not noted in every performance listing or review, which suggests that the appearance of Black performers in variety revues and music hall billings was not especially surprising.

During 1916, another production of *Uncle Tom's Cabin* toured, led by a white producer, Charles Harrington, which advertised 'a full chorus of real Negroes'.[111] Uncle Tom was played by the Black South African performer Mr J. Bessima Kofie.[112] The production featured a 'grand plantation festival [...] Hymns, songs, dances, tambourines, bones, and banjo solos, all added to the realism of this particular part of the performance'.[113] The deeply racist way in which reviews frame this production reveal racialized expectations of character: 'Eva, the little white angel on earth, and her faithful "Uncle Tom," under whose black skin beat a heart of purest white.'[114] Again, though it is absent in other descriptions of Black performance practice, the n-word is often used in relation to this production in its description of the 'plantation festival' to specifically refer to enslaved people.[115]

Nadine George-Graves has a particularly clear way of understanding how a singular Black performer (in her case study, Jeni Le Gon) can operate within racist structures of an entertainment industry focused on the consumption of Black performers. George-Graves proposes the concept of will not only understood as controlling personal events and individual feeling but also 'will in the sense of willing a career by mastering control over her oppressive, racist encounters'.[116] For George-Graves, 'will' instigates 'dynamic performative presences, despite inequitable realities [...] that were neither ignored nor accepted'.[117] This means understanding that performance practices in 1916 were taking place within the context of oppressive and racist structures, while also attending to what she calls the persistent 'dynamic performative presence'. It is also crucial to note that this was by no means an exceptional year, and that the many performers we have noted do not represent a complete list. Furthermore, this single year points to the scale of Will Garland's professional work, whose career we pick up in Chapter 4.

4

Will Garland: Black cultural production on a national stage

This chapter traces the significant work and output of Will (William) Garland. Garland was a musician (tuba, trombone), singer, comedian, actor, theatre producer and writer. He has been little discussed in established histories of musical theatre. Locating Garland's work in Britain is essential to understanding British musical theatre's reliance on Black music and performance, partly because it follows key musical and dance transitions from ragtime to jazz and swing. His extensive activities in the UK are revealed here, much of which for the first time. Perhaps the best known of his collaborators is with Mabel Mercer. She began her career with Garland in revue shows but also conducted several performances and worked as their musical director.

In a period before most people would think of leaving their own country, William 'Will' Garland was a global theatre maker. His career is impressively international for an artist working even a century later. In the Americas, Garland toured across the United States on both coasts and extensively in Southern states and performed in Cuba. In Europe, he performed across the UK and Ireland, as well as in France (Paris and Bordeaux) and across modern-day Germany, Switzerland and Austria, Finland, Denmark, Poland, Latvia, Estonia, the Czech Republic, the Ukraine, the Netherlands and Belgium. In Russia, he went as far east as Oblast and Yekaterinburg. In all likelihood, Garland toured more venues and locations than can be currently traced. Our research has substantially expanded what had already been painstakingly traced by revealing his return visits to the United States, a more complete chronology and clearer details of what Garland was performing.

In Chapter 3, we met Garland during 1916 as he was establishing himself as a central figure in British touring theatrical life. In this chapter, we address the implications of Garland's work by addressing how he maintained international Black performance networks while simultaneously working within and actively resisting pervasive racist structures. Our research builds on, and owes much to, the work of scholars of early recording histories, who have recovered much of Garland's audio work and placed it in context. Researchers of Black performance have also diligently enabled an understanding of Garland's working practices: in particular, the scholars Rainer Lotz, Jeffrey Green and Howard Rye.[1] Lotz has been the principal researcher on Garland's work for the last forty years and, as part of his wider research on Black performers in Europe, has pieced together an expansive chronology for Garland's professional output across the United States and Europe and into Russia.

William 'Will' Garland (b. 1875, Keokuk, Iowa; d. 1938, London) arrived in the UK with the second tour company of *In Dahomey* in around 1904. He was based in the UK until his death in 1938.

Garland was married twice. His first wife was the trombonist Nettie Goff, who was also in the *In Dahomey* company. It would appear she returned to the United States in around September 1906, and the couple divorced, that is if they had ever been legally married. His second wife was a white British citizen, Rosie Schumann, the multilingual daughter of a nineteenth-century German immigrant.

Garland began his career in the late 1890s, touring with several minstrel companies in the United States. He worked for Mahara's Minstrels company, and worked alongside his then wife, Goff, as well as key Black performers Avery and Hart George Catlin and the troupe's musical director, W. C. (William Christopher) Handy, better known as 'the father of the blues'. When they toured Havana, Cuba, the *Freeman* reported that 'Prof William Handy [...] and his military band are discoursing sweet music to the delight of all'. Nettie Goff's trombone playing was reported as 'causing the people to stand in open-mouth wonder at her brilliancy'.[2]

With Pete Hampton and Laura Bowman (alt. Bauman), he started the Darktown Entertainers, before establishing a small revue called *In Dahomey: A Trip to C—ntown* (1904 onwards). This is not the same musical as the Cole and Johnson production; Garland's show borrowed the title for a UK-based revue that traded on the popularity of *In Dahomey*, and the content of the revue clearly shifted over time.

Over his thirty-five years in the UK, Garland toured nineteen separate revues in the UK (for the full list of titles, see Appendix A) and performed in at least two others. He also made return visits to the United States that allowed him to maintain professional connections with a huge range of practitioners of African descent, as well as visiting many centres of Black production practice such as Paris and Harlem. He maintained a US address in Iowa until at least 1917.[3] He toured across Europe and into Russia. He challenged white producers profiteering in shows presenting Black casts by producing shows with extremely similar titles or which explicitly reoccupied Black culture (e.g., *Rhapsody in Black*). Garland died in London, 1938, and his name is on the memorial to variety theatre performers in London's Streatham Park Cemetery Variety Artistes Memorial.

KEY FIGURE 3 *William 'Will' Garland, a short biography.*

Cedric Robinson's discussion of the ways in which early Black US performers and practitioners is particularly relevant here. He considers how the establishment of Black musical theatre out of minstrel shows through the perfection of 'Black resistance gestures for display before largely white audiences [and, in addition, this group] recovered and invented much of the moral and conceptual vocabulary and the sly oppositional stratagems which would sluice Black resistance into public entertainment.'[4] Garland's shows employed hundreds of performers and musicians, many of whom were British citizens and British subjects – the complicated rules governing who was 'allowed' to be British shifted during his working life. Rye and Green note that his revues 'gave employment to black performers and introduced new audiences to black music and dance'.[5] We have recovered a single surviving interview with Garland from 1927; it offers a frustratingly short glimpse into his career and is currently the only preserved words of his that are known to exist. Garland reports that the Black women in his shows were 'born in the British Isles and amongst other cities and towns represented are London, Dublin, Birmingham, Manchester, Liverpool, Hull and Cardiff'.[6] The interviewer informs the reader that 'of the other members of the company, three are Americans and the rest British, with representatives from Jamaica and the West Indies'.[7]

Garland's most prolific onstage collaborator was the Black British comedian and singer Eddie Emmerson (discussed in Chapter 3 in connection with one of Gordon Stretton's revues), born in Birmingham in the West Midlands. Garland also worked with the cabaret star Mabel Mercer at the very beginning of her career. Mercer (see Chapter 6) was born in Staffordshire in the Midlands and began her professional career in one of Garland's revues, not only as a singer but also as their conductor and as musical director. Though this is unusual for a Black woman in the UK, it is not unique (see the notes on Valaida Snow in 1934 and her sister Lavaida in 'The 1930s in context'). Paul Oliver notes that 'Garland's success through multiple shows demonstrates his formula [...] readily appealed to British theatre-goers'.[8] Howard Rye and Jeffrey Green have suggested that Garland's work (and other British Black touring shows) 'drew on the ideas of *Shuffle Along* and *Blackbirds*' and was significant for giving employment to Black performers but primarily influenced other practitioners, such as Fela Sowande, who 'in turn influenced Americans'.[9] While this is no doubt true, Garland's performance career in the UK pre-empted both of these shows by at least fifteen years. Garland's significance is far greater, not least because of the ways in which his work also models resistant strategies within the shows he was producing.

Garland's work relied on 'sly oppositional stratagems' that resisted white supremacism and racism.[10] First, in consuming white consumption, by directly reclaiming white appropriated Black culture through commercially occupying titles and jazz music standards, and then successfully disseminating that across theatres in the UK and beyond. Second, he created and maintained work for Black performers and practitioners over a long period, as well as contributing to offstage Black spaces that allowed community and healing outside of white consumption. Third, Garland established spaces of interracial possibility through integrated companies, in breaking the love story taboo through performing love songs, and through casting practices. Fourth, although representations of Africa in Garland's work are not straightforward and sometimes appear to reinstate minstrel tropes, the surviving evidence demonstrates moments in which they directly defy British colonialist narratives.

Consuming white consumption and subverting white-produced revues

Following Garland's career reveals the way in which his musical revues frequently take ownership of performance practices and musical styles that white producers had appropriated. He was clearly able to spot a commercial property; he performed under many changing names of revues and performances, some of which appear to reference earlier Black shows (see Appendix B) but had no apparent connection. Importantly, Garland repeatedly took ownership of white-produced shows like George Sax's *Coloured Society* (1916) – perhaps buying the rights to produce it. Some of Garland's show titles seem to allude to white versions of Black music and culture: Garland's 1929 *Swanee River* (1929) arguably references Gershwin's global hit song 'Swanee' (1920); his *Rhapsody in Black* (1933) certainly references Gershwin's 'Rhapsody in Blue' (1925). The reoccupation of white consumption moves to actively consuming it; Garland effectively consumes white consumption in his musical theatre output. Garland traded on established 'brand recognition' of white-produced revues by launching competitor versions with similar names. When the white producer Lew Leslie's *Blackbirds of 1927* was playing at Newcastle Empire Theatre, Garland's *Brown Birds* was playing at Nottingham Empire (and both were touring the same circuit, the Moss Empire network).[11]

Leslie must have been aware of Garland's actions. In fact, in 1936 Garland appeared in the touring company of *Blackbirds*, alongside the dancer Peg-Leg Bates, Fela Sowande and Lavaida Carter (occasionally known as Lavada or Lavaida Snow, and who conducted *Rhapsody in Blue*) and Mildred Marshall, the American soprano.[12] The African American dancer Peg-Leg Bates was one of the most important tap dancers of the 1920s. Lavaida Carter was the sister of Valada/Valaida Snow, the jazz singer and trumpeter. Valaida had performed and conducted in Lew Leslie's 1931 Broadway production *Rhapsody in Black*, and had conducted Pike Davis and his Continental Orchestra.[13] She also conducted in the 1934 *Blackbirds*. (There were several Black women conductors during this period; recovering their performance practice in full is an urgent task yet to be completed.)

Shortly before his death, Garland went back to producing his own *Brown Birds* in 1937, though perhaps, since he was close to retirement, it was co-produced with the Black dancer, Louis Hardcastle.[14] He died in 1938 in London. No obituaries have been found.

Creating and maintaining Black professional networks

Garland's way of working brought him into contact with a wide range of practitioners, which means some reflections on his work have survived. Garland's second wife was Rosie Elise Schuman; they married in January 1923. Her surviving family explained that her father was from the Alsace region and came to the UK during the Franco-Prussian War, and her mother was German. Schuman was born in London and lived in the East End. How she met Garland or became part of his touring shows is something of a mystery. It is possible she began touring with him in 1917 as a Rosie Parker is listed as part of the company; after around 1923, only Rosie Schuman is present. Her family told us that she spoke multiple languages (French, German, Russian and English),[15] so it seems likely she was able to negotiate and intervene on Garland's behalf. His marriage to a British citizen explains why Garland was able to work in the UK throughout periods of restriction on US performers that forced many of his friends and colleagues to leave the country. Leslie Thompson, a Black trumpet player from Trinidad who appeared briefly in one of Garland's shows, recalled one of the ways Garland was able to navigate British theatrical life:

> Will was an enormous fellow, a great big fellow. A wonderful tenor voice, and a fine singer, and he had a nice wife who sort of [...] she was the boss, she was the one who, and quite rightly too, because, she was able to do the bookings, go into the places and do everything for him, all the difference ... because she was white and he was black.[16]

Garland's work in Britain was widely reported on across Black newspapers as well as British and US theatrical presses. *Billboard*, for example, noted in 1922 that his revue of thirty cast members was booked 'in the Moss and Stoll houses on a two-year contract to alternate between the London Music Hall and the Boulevard Capucan in Paris'.[17] Ivan H. Browning (a performer and journalist; see Key Figure 7) also regularly updated readers on Garland's plans, in November 1928 writing that he was 'planning a trip to America in early summer to get new ideas for his new revue next season'.[18] Garland worked alongside performers of African descent from across the globe, but he was part of the Black theatre community in London. He worked directly with other African Americans in London; for example, he co-produced a revue with John C. Payne in 1933 (though it only played two venues, it is notable for the inclusion of Connie Smith). It was noted that 'John Payne's Jubilee Singers supply typical deliveries of some of the most tuneful Southern melodies'.[19]

John C. (Clarence or Charles) Payne (b. 1872; d. 1952) had been in the UK since 1920 as Will Marion Cook's Southern Syncopated Orchestra's choral director. He had slowly built on the success of his vocal group (initially a quartet) which had changed members several times. The group featured at least two Black British performers: Evelyn Dove (b. 1902, London; d. 1987) sang with the group before Mabel Mercer joined later. Just before Mercer joined, the Southern Trio toured with Lew Leslie's *Blackbirds*.[20] The company were involved in other publicity events, and there are reports of Payne, Mercer, Clinton Rosemond, Connie Smith (for a biography, see Key Figure 3) and Noble Sissle laying a wreath at Abraham Lincoln's statue in London on the anniversary of Lincoln's birth.[21] He was close friends with Lady Cook, a white aristocrat, who seemed to support him and his network of performers. During the war he moved to her Cornish estate and remained there after her death.[22]

KEY FIGURE 4 *John C. Payne, a short biography.*

During the 1920s and 1930s, there were several key London hubs that nurtured the Black community, providing training, housing and social support. Established Black theatre practitioners were able to maintain home bases in London, even as their professional work dispersed Black practitioners across the UK. But many practitioners worked alone within all- or majority-white variety bills – being able to return to the Black community is a vital part of surviving white spaces. Perhaps the most important homes were those of Jennie Haston and John C. Payne, though Will and Rosie Garland also hosted events 'at their pretty home in Paddington'.[23] We know about these events because of Browning's letters for the *Chicago Defender*, in which he detailed Jennie Haston's Thanksgiving party guests, who included Eubie and Avis Blake, Noble and Harriet Sissle, Will and Rosie Garland and Ike Hatch and Lewis Carpenter.[24] Fannie Cotton wrote in the *Philadelphia Tribune* in 1929 that, 'While over here I met Mrs Jennie Haston, […] who has been here nineteen years. Her husband is one of the Versatile Trio. I am stopping at her home now.'[25] John C. Payne's home at 17 Regent's Park Road was a vital centre of the Black theatrical community and hosted many parties with important Black guests, including Ira Aldridge's daughter, Miss Ira Aldridge (a pianist and composer),[26] Marion Anderson, Paul Robeson and Laurence Brown.[27] The Payne house provided lodgings for visiting performers, which, given the racism many Black people endured trying to get hotel rooms in London, was a far safer environment. They housed several African American practitioners, including the opera singer and soprano Marian Anderson (1897–1993), a contralto singer later known for performing at the Lincoln Memorial steps in 1939;[28] the conductor and composer Will Vodery (1885–1951);[29] the performer Zaidee Jackson (1898–1970);[30] and Alberta Hunter (1895–1984; see Chapter 6).

These community hubs offered professional networking opportunities and interracial possibility. Payne was particularly close to Lady Cook and spent the last years of his life living on her country estate. Lady Cook was the wife of Sir Herbert Cook, a British art historian and philanthropist (he was a great buyer of paintings), and she presumably had considerable access to finances herself. She was involved in John C. Payne's London's home, though any further details are unclear, and was clearly a patron kind of figure for some Black musicians (see Chapter 5). Payne's parties brought together leading actors and creative practitioners. One party in honour of Marion Anderson included guests such as Lady Peel (the actor Beatrice Lilly); the ballet dancer Anton Dolin; the Cuban pianist Marino Barreto; Mabel Mercer; Alberta Hunter; various counts and countesses; and the head of BBC popular programming, E. J. King Bull.[31] Professor Louis Drysdale, who had been a friend of Samuel Coleridge Taylor, offered vocal tuition from his home in suburban Forest Hill and wrote about his technique in Black US newspapers.[32] Drysdale coached Anderson, as well as Florence Mills. In 1928, one of Browning's columns notes that Drysdale was busy not only with his regular pupils but also with 'teaching three or four West End musical comedy stars'.[33] The benefits of the Black spaces that Garland contributed to bestowed networking opportunities, community generosity and housing, as well as training and development opportunities. Perhaps most crucially of all, they must have offered experience and advice for surviving in the UK; Garland must have appreciated the vital links he was able to maintain.

Understanding Garland's work relies on understanding his position as a cosmopolitan Black creative producer. Rachel Gillett has noted the importance of the Black diaspora in jazz music, suggesting that their 'loosely knit diaspora' built community and camaraderie: 'If a cosmopolitan is a member of diasporic network that both reflects a local identity and yet connects many locales [...] then black jazz performers clearly qualify.'[34] Garland's touring shows in Europe connected him with other key centres of performance practice, such as Paris, Vienna, Berlin and Amsterdam. But, like many of the US practitioners in the UK, we have encountered so far, Garland also returned home; he travelled back to the United States twice during 1914, in April and after Britain was at war in October 1914, via the *Lusitania* (the passenger ship later sunk by a German U-boat in 1915).[35] Garland performed at the Lafayette Theatre in Harlem in January 1915, reforming the long since disbanded Bowman trio; and despite the decade they had been apart, they were a success: 'a pronounced singing hit [...] their work stamped them as artists of ability'.[36]

While commercial imperatives were the motivation for Garland's naming practices, especially as his revues transitioned from a short set within a variety bill to the entire bill, it is possible to examine the choices he was able to make in how he positioned his work and see recurrent themes. Garland advertised his first touring revue, *A Trip to C—ntown* (1905–15), both in Europe and in the UK initially as 'a grand musical production'.[37] By 1908, the production was being advertised more explicitly as 'a Negro Operetta, including real [Black] Americans'[38] – though Lotz has suggested this has little to do with the 'type or style of the performance' but rather the number of people on stage in what was 'a song and dance ensemble'.[39] Despite titles that are challenging to deal with, Garland *never* used minstrel as a description of his work, something which is noteworthy in the context of his extensive background in US minstrel shows (and their continuous presence in British theatre). Coverage of the piece instead recognizes the skill of its performers. One 1915 review notes: 'it is an artistic and refined performance, introducing all the latest Transatlantic [*racial slur*] songs and dances, beautifully harmonised choruses, and some clever and quaint comedy.'[40] The revue form was fully established for British audiences by 1915, at which point the show was advertised as a 'musical melange revue'.[41]

Representing Africa: Defying British colonialism

Because his shows toured so extensively, there are many regional newspapers (often several for the same city) which together provide detailed accounts of what was in each of Garland's production. The same sentences and phrases are repeated, which suggests that local newspapers were provided with some kind of press release about the show that was then augmented by the reviewer's responses. Critics were rarely named; their anonymous reviews appeared early in show's week-long run at a particular venue, generating perhaps two or three reviews a week for shows that were touring most weeks of the year. While the Lord Chamberlain's collection at the British Library preserves some but not all of Garland's revue scripts, they are largely short or descriptive scenes that only hint at the total experience of the overall song and dance show. Newspaper reviews demonstrate how white spectatorship 'read' the company's work in sometimes confusing and contradictory ways; different reviews describe the same show as both 'a merry South African revue'[42] and 'a South American revue'.[43] Reviewers clearly responded to the perceived exoticism of the musical. Reviews of *Creole Carols* (1927) particularly praised 'the exotic Honolulu episode'.[44] Garland's work performed aspects of US identity. *Swanee River* featured 'the Negro spiritual scene', 'the silver Hawaiian scene' and 'the Dixie Derby Scene'.[45] The Hawaiian scene was called one of 'the spectacular features of the revue', with a 'picturesque background to the Ukelele dance by Miss Hilda Brown and song by Mr. Bert Seeley'.[46]

The blurring of geographical and racial identities is hard to unpick; indeed Howard Rye notes: 'Garland's shows evidently reflected popular expectations about black culture with eclectic abandon'.[47] Clearly, British audience expectations of Black music and culture, or more broadly culture which just was 'not white', were very blurry. In 1928, one review highlights the spectacle nature of the production: 'Dancing is a feature of the show and although the setting may be in Shanghai, in Africa, or in the East, the steps are those which hail from somewhere south of the Mason-Dixon line.'[48] But despite their connection to the US, Garland's musicals staged things that would have been unthinkable in American theatre. In one letter to US readers, Browning noted his surprise at seeing a scene accepted by a British audience, which featured a white actor 'made up a real light brown' singing a love song to a Black woman. Browning notes: 'it was plain to see that he was white. I wonder just what would happen if this revue was in America and presented as it is here.'[49] The presence of an interracial kiss in 1927 is particularly striking.

Newspapers described the performers in Garland's revues in varying ways. It is difficult to know for sure what led to this. Whether it was driven by the (presumably white) reviewers' racialized curiosity or added to by the press releases that must have coexisted with the shows, individual racial identities are the subject of considerable interest. As we have seen elsewhere, there is an underpinning blurriness about which was more newsworthy, that the performers were American or that they were of African descent. British reviewers were quick to note Empire connections: 'the Company is a collection from all parts of Empire'.[50] In Garland's surviving interview with the *Derby Daily Telegraph*, he says that all of the women in his cast were 'born in the British Isles and amongst other cities and towns represented are

London, Dublin, Birmingham, Manchester, Liverpool, Hull and Cardiff'.[51] The interview also notes that Eddie Emmerson (1894–?) was born in Birmingham, UK. Despite the actual identities of Garland's cast, reviews often read cast members as coming from the United States. One 1929 reviewer of *Swanee River* remarked: 'fifteen or twenty [black women] from the Southern States showed us how we should sing [spirituals]; with great expression, perhaps; even with a hint of sadness; but also with the fire and enthusiasm of a hopeful race.'[52]

Amid a wave of enthusiasm for theatre productions about the US Southern states, Brian Ward notes the rarity of Garland's revue *Down South* (1922), since it was written 'by an African American writer.[53] Ward notes that the desire for pastoral and plantation stories simultaneously evoked straightforward order, while at the same time offering 'decidedly modern, flamboyant, risqué and transgressive alternatives to the nostalgia for rural living, fixed racial identities, timeless values, and traditional social hierarchies'.[54] The music and dancing in Garland's shows clearly presented the 'decidedly modern' alternatives that Ward suggests. By 1927, named dances were being highlighted, with audiences reassured that 'The Charleston, the Black Bottom and other American dances [which] will figure prominently'.[55] The music similarly shifted. One revue of *Swanee River* notes: 'the whole production throbs with jazz [...] the performers in the whitest cotton drill suits show what jazz is really capable of in the hands of experts.'[56] Garland's revues used the existing theatre orchestra until the mid-1920s, when jazz bands featured. *Coloured Lights* (1925) had seven on stage: 'Triny Mendez, saxophone; Jeanette, trumpet; Archie Palmley, clarionet [*sic*]; Andy Clarke drums; Alex Loftus, piano, Will Garland, trombone, and Jackson, banjo.'[57] By 1929, 'even the regular orchestra is changed for the occasion';[58] musical standards had clearly shifted in terms of what would be adequate. Garland gave the bands various authentic sounding titles, like the Cabaret Jazz Band or the Chicago Jazz Hounds.[59] Garland himself could play 'the saxophone, trombone, tubular bells, Hawaiin [*sic*] guitar, piano'.

Garland's shows also explicitly staged Africa. Mabel Mercer recalled a scene set in Dahomey (Benin) with 'a big fellow from Africa with a gorgeous bass'; she remembered:

> we were all Zulus, running around and saying 'Woo, woo, woo.' Then we'd each do our different things, and we'd wind up, believe it or not, singing the sextet from *Lucia*. It was so unexpected – all those Zulus singing *Lucia*. I loved it. I never realized the incongruity of it until I was grown and looked back and wondered what must people have thought![60]

Renee Lapp Norris has noted that the practice of burlesques of opera within minstrel performances dates back to the 1840s and 1850s and that it 'relied on the recontextualization of the original and an unpredictable mingling of sources and subjects'.[61] In this case, it is perhaps less Donizetti's Scottish opera being burlesqued here (it is never mentioned in any of the reviews) than it is the apparent, racist, shock of Africans singing it – though note the lack of specificity about places in Africa (Mercer points to both Benin and South Africa). This was not the only kind of reference to Africa in Garland's revues.

One frustratingly short revue of *Brown Birds* (1928) mentions an aspect which has previously gone undiscussed: 'one scene shows King Prempeh on his golden stool in the famed city of Coomassie [Kumasi].'[62] Another review of the production at Shepherd's Bush Empire notes, in far more racist terms: 'one scene of barbaric splendour will remind us of a picture of childhood days showing King Prempeh on his golden stool in the far-famed city of Coomassie [Kumasi].'[63] The picture that is being referred to is presumably a drawing which portrays the moment Prempeh I, the Asantehene (King) of the Asante people, knelt before a British general. Though he was seeking to maintain the independence of his people, Prempeh would not surrender the Golden Stool, and so the British exiled him to the Seychelles in 1896 and brought his throne back to Britain. Two years later, Frederick Hodgson, the British governor-general of the Gold Coast, demanded that he should have been brought the Golden Stool to sit on as the new leader. The Stool has sacred properties for the Asante people, who believe their 'strength and unity' depend on the object which descended from heaven, and Hodgson's arrogance infuriated them.[64] As a result, Yaa Asantewaa, the queen mother of Ejisu, led the War of the Golden Stool against British colonialism, and the British never captured the Stool. Though Yaa Asantewaa was later exiled, heavy British losses during this war shifted the British approach in the area, later known as Ghana. Prempeh was allowed to return to Kumasi in 1924 and was reinstalled as a Kumasihene (a lesser title) in 1926. In 1935, the British instated the Asante Confederacy.[65] Garland's performance of an exiled African leader as King on a sacred object in 1928 can clearly be read as an act of resistance against British colonialism: the kind of 'sly oppositional stratagem' that Robinson primes us to recognize in Black performance practice.[66]

PART TWO

Black networks of production

The 1920s in context

The Jazz Age and the Harlem Renaissance

The Harlem Renaissance was a period of Black political, intellectual, artistic and cultural growth and revival that took place during the 1920s. As a movement, it quickly had international implications. It originated out of Harlem, a neighbourhood in upper Manhattan which, due to the Great Northward Migration (see 'The 1910s in context'), had become a largely Black population.

The Harlem Renaissance was led by the work of many key Black figures who came from across the African diaspora, in particular from the United States and the Caribbean. The African American philosopher Alain Locke published his important anthology, *The New Negro*, in 1925. This brought together the work of key writers such as Zora Neale Hurston and Langston Hughes and helped formalize Black self-expression in literature.

On Broadway, the popularity of Black theatre reached a new sensation with the opening of *Shuffle Along* (1921), a key milestone in Black performance practice. The musical about a mayoral election at a time when many Black people were unable to vote in the United States was one of the first to feature a serious love song between two Black characters. *Shuffle Along* was written by four Black creatives: the composer and performer duo Noble Sissle and Eubie (James Hubert) Blake; and the performers Flournoy Miller and Aubrey Lyles. It provided early professional opportunities for numerous Black practitioners, performers like Florence Mills, Josephine Baker and Paul Robeson, and musicians including William Grant Still (1895–1978, an important composer).

Black creative practitioners worked across multiple creative industries, in centres of Black cultural practice such as Chicago, New York, London, Paris and Berlin. This movement between place and medium was fuelled by the growth of recording technology, which sped up the wider dissemination of Black performance practice across the UK in homes, theatres and in cinemas. The British Broadcasting Company was founded in 1922 as a semi-commercial radio company. It was later replaced by the non-commercial and Crown-owned British Broadcasting Corporation (BBC) in 1927. The increased fidelity of magnetic tape, invented in 1927, enabled pre-recorded as well as live broadcasts and created new possibilities to be heard.

The visibility of the Black nationalist and civil rights movements

In August 1920, the Jamaican political activist and civil rights campaigner Marcus Garvey arranged a parade from the UNIA's headquarters down Fifth Avenue in New York: 'Garvey's dramatic impact, especially manifested in his parade down Fifth Avenue and his visceral rhetoric, was the galvanizing element that captured the imagination of the black working class.'[1]

The campaign for Black rights was carried out internationally. The history of Black travel and cosmopolitanism during this period has repercussions on popular music. Rye and Green note: 'False history has obscured the global black involvement in the spread of American music outside the United States in the Jazz Age.'[2] In reality, many Black artists and performers travelled the world. Paris was a particularly important centre for the Black diaspora. Babacar M'Baye notes that Langston Hughes' time in the city offered him the ability to 'flow in and draw on the "Circumatlantic" space and expand the Pan-Africanism, transnationalism, and cosmopolitanism that were already sowed in his consciousness during the Harlem Renaissance'.[3]

Black literature of the Harlem Renaissance was published in the UK, regional newspapers wrote about campaigns for Black rights and specialist literary periodicals reprinted key works. *Outward Bound* magazine, for example, published Clarence Cameron White's essay 'The Music of the American Negro' in 1921.[4] Langston Hughes' novel and poetry was written about;[5] and Claude McKay's essay 'Socialism and the Negro' was published in the *Workers' Dreadnought* in 1920, a socialist periodical edited by Sylvia Pankhurst. (Pankhurst became involved with Haile Selassie's campaign against the Italian invasion in the 1930s, and she eventually moved to Ethiopia after Selassie returned as emperor.) McKay used the *Dreadnought* to address racist media coverage. Other left-wing periodicals like *The Clarion* published essays by key figures such as the writer Eric Walrond (b. 1898, Guyana; d. 1966, London).[6]

Social and political contexts

In the aftermath of the 1919 race riots, racism and colonialism continued in Britain. When particularly egregious exclusions occurred, the British media liked to appear liberal and 'fair' – above all, not American. When

Paul Robeson was prevented from eating at the Savoy in 1929, the matter was raised in parliament.[7]

After the First World War, the UK began to move slowly towards accepting changing international opinions of its empire. The UK reluctantly permitted self-rule in some of its larger (and whiter) colonies, with the caveat of maintaining British interests. Nonetheless, the British Empire reached its largest point in 1920, when its reach was supposed to have been a quarter of the land mass of the world. In the 'redistribution' of Germany's and Austria's colonies, Britain expanded its control of African regions and resources.

The Pan-African Conference had sessions in London in 1921. Those present included Jessie Walmisley, Samuel Coleridge Taylor's widow; and the African American musician Roland Hayes (b. 1887, Georgia; d. 1977, Boston), who was a concert singer and a composer. The conference saw 'forthright criticism of British colonial rule' in an officially adopted document called the 'London Manifesto'.[8] In 1923, further sessions were held, and the demand for home rule from British-occupied African countries became more strident.[9]

In 1921, the partition of Ireland created Northern Ireland, and the Irish Free State in 1922 (which did not become the Irish Republic until 1937). In 1922, Egypt became an independent kingdom but Britain retained control of the Suez Canal area. In 1924, Britain took over Northern Rhodesia (now Zambia). In 1925, the Nigerian political activist Ladipo Solanke (1886–1958), with the support of Amy Ashwood Garvey (1897–1969; see Chapter 8), formed the West African Students Union, an important campaigning group.[10] By 1926, the UK agreed the Balfour Declaration, which made Canada, Australia, New Zealand and South Africa independent – although still part of the British Commonwealth. Marcus Garvey visited the West London Mission in 1928.[11]

Black music in the Jazz Age

Jazz became the most popular style of music in the UK, particularly for the upper classes, though it was often mediated through white performers. The Prince of Wales, who would go on to become the ill-fated Edward VIII, was now a little older than when the *In Dahomey* cast had accompanied his childhood birthday party in 1903. But he continued his fascination with Black music and his fondness for jazz was well known in the press, even as a player.[12] In 1927, The Southern Trio (John C. Payne, Mabel Mercer and C. C. Rosemond) performed for a party in his honour (for more on Mercer, see Chapter 6).[13] Several Black jazz performers also enjoyed celebrity status: Leslie 'Hutch' Hutchinson (Leslie Arthur Julien Hutchinson) (b. 1900, Guyana; d. 1969, London) was a singer and musician who became particularly famous during the 1930s as a central part of British high society. In 1928, he played in the pit at the London Pavilion for Cochran's *Graces of 1928* before going straight to a nightclub for a second show.[14]

Some African American performers of spirituals and other Black folk music also experienced fame in Britain. J. Rosamond Johnson and (Emmanuel) Taylor Gordon performed spirituals at Wigmore Hall in 1927,[15] as well as radio broadcasts of variety bills and at 'many smart parties'.[16] As this musical style became prominent, many key venues programmed the talents of Black vocalists like Roland Hayes, Paul Robeson, John C. Payne and Marian Anderson (for biographies of Payne, see Chapter 4). Hayes performed at several key venues with the pianist Lawrence Brown (1893–1972) in 1920, including the Æolian Concert Hall, which led to a command performance at Buckingham Palace for King George V and Queen Mary.[17] He had a unique connection with Wigmore Hall, establishing a repertoire of spirituals alongside songs and *lieder*, particularly that by the white British composer Roger Quilter. Hayes also performed with Samuel Coleridge Taylor's daughter, Gwendolen, suggesting a continuation of Coleridge Taylor's esteem in British culture.[18] Brown was a pianist and arranger who is best known for popularizing classical arrangements of spirituals, many of which Paul Robeson later performed and recorded. Marian Anderson also performed at Wigmore Hall in August 1928, accompanied by Roger Quilter; this led to her appearance at the Proms featured Marian Anderson performing Henry Thacker Burleigh's spirituals (arranged by Brown).[19] Brown also accompanied Robeson's special performance of Black music in Drury Lane in 1929, and Payne's own Wigmore Hall concert.[20] Samuel Floyd notes that, for Black composers during this period: 'the idea was to produce extended forms such as symphonies and operas from the raw material of spirituals, ragtime, blues and other folk genres.'[21] They clearly did this from the stages of theatres and concert halls alike and, in particular, Wigmore Hall.

Many Black practitioners felt a responsibility to educate younger Black performers, including Amanda Aldridge (b. 1866, London; d. 1956, London) who trained Marian Anderson and was the daughter of the African American Shakespearean actor Ira Aldridge (1807–67). Louis Drysdale (who had come to the UK with the Jamaican Choir) offered several scholarships for Jamaican students to study with him in London.[22] Drysdale later trained the African American singers Ethel Waters (1896–1977) and Florence Mills (c.1895–1927).[23]

On stage

As part of the popularity of jazz, many white producers continued to capitalize on the expertise and skills of Black performers. The white US director and producer Lew Leslie directed numerous jazz revues, some of which revolved around being an all-Black cast, including *The Plantation Revue* (1922) in New York, or *The Blackbirds of 1926*, which starred Florence Mills, Johnny Hudgins and tap dancers Johnny Nit and U. S.

IMAGE 2 *Cast members of* Blackbirds of 1926, *on the roof of the London Pavilion, 1926. Front row (left to right): Florence Mills, Johnny Hudgins and Edith Wilson. The other performers are members of the chorus. (Photo by General Photographic Agency/Hulton Archive/Getty Images.)*

Thompson. The show travelled to the UK. The 1927 edition of *Blackbirds* again starred Mills; the comedians in the show still used blackface makeup.[24] Others made a point of having all-white casts: *White Birds* (1927), for which the African American Will Vodery (1885–1951) orchestrated songs and was musical director; and for another set of shows which presented a 'white' first half against a second that featured Black musicians and performers. David Linton and Len Platt have suggested that *Dover Street to Dixie* (1923) 'was specifically arranged as a display of blackness made safe, a different kind of consumer product characterised not by strength and sexuality, but by a further set of stereotypes and their associated markers'.[25] *Dover Street* brought both Florence Mills to fame in the UK and to a lesser extent Will Vodery with his 'Plantation Orchestra'. While audiences were plainly impressed, contemporary public discourse in the early 1920s tended towards racialized understandings based on primitivism, responses which naturalized the skill of performers. One music critic wrote: 'There is no technique here. Technique is the very antithesis of their performances.'[26] The Prince of Wales attended multiple times, along with Lord and Lady Mountbatten. The revue gained the approval of the high society magazine, *The Sketch*, who reported: 'All our prejudices against these cafe-au-lait entertainers melt when Florence Mills begins to sing [...] she turned the voice of protest into acclamation.'[27]

A huge number of Black artists and creators performed in variety theatre: J. Rosamond Johnson;[28] double acts like Scott and Whaley, Louis Douglas and Sonny Jones (both trained as children with Belle Davis); Zaidee Jackson; dancers like Ritchie Winn; and Lewis Hardcastle's band for whom 'jazz music is a feature'.[29] In 1924, *The Chicago Defender* reported:

> For the first time in the history of variety, four American acts, with all Race casts, are headlining in the largest West end theaters here. They are all acts of the highest class and are drawing unusual crowds. They are: At the Holborn Empire, Billy Robinson; at the Alhambra, The Four Harmony Kings; at the Coliseum, Layton and Johnstone, and at the Victoria Palace, Jones and Jones.[30]

Sissle and Blake (see Chapter 5) left the United States to perform in London's Metropole Club in 1925.[31] Their financial success was so great that the *Afro-American* reported the pair's wives were able to take flights across to Paris for shopping trips.[32] They became an ongoing presence in British theatre.[33] Charles B. Cochran's use of their song 'Lady of the Moon' in *Still Dancing* (1927) was widely noted, along with details that Cochran had repeatedly tried to bring *Shuffle Along* to the UK. The *Pittsburgh Courier* reported 'negotiations are on again'.[34] Sissle and Blake's music was also performed in variety.[35]

There were several Black-produced revues during this period, largely down to Will Garland's prodigious output (see Chapter 4). By 1927, the success of these revues was starting to worry white producers and theatre professionals. The *Era* reported that the Variety Artistes' Federation were planning to 'stop the introduction to England of companies of […] theatrical and variety performers'.[36] Though they apparently did not object to Black double acts or individuals, they suggest 'many British turns of talent are without engagement' – the fact that many of the performers who were in these groups were actually British subjects reveals the racism at work.[37] British musical unions resisted the arrival of further non-white players: Lew Leslie's *Blackbirds of 1927* was forced to hire a white orchestra to sit silently and play the overture in the interval, under the order of the Ministry of Labour.

Oscar Hammerstein and Jerome Kern's musical *Show Boat* opened at Drury Lane Theatre in 1928 starring Paul Robeson and Alberta Hunter (see Key Figure 9), along with a chorus of Black dancers. Mabel Mercer understudied Hunter's role. John C. Payne conducted the vocal ensemble. On Sundays, Robeson gave concerts of spirituals at the theatre that were said to take as much as £750 per concert, well over £130,000 in today's money.[38] Paul Robeson had performed in Britain throughout the 1920s, playing the lead in a 1925 revival of *The Emperor Jones*, which developed his reputation as an actor as well as a singer, and in *Show Boat* (1928).

On radio

The growth and formalizing of radio as a domestic form of entertainment expanded the presence of Black music in the UK into British homes. There were regular broadcasts of Black variety stars.[39] Music by Black composers was regularly broadcast on the radio: Sissle and Blake's music in the mid-1920s, and the John C. Payne's Southern Trio broadcast in 1925 for a special Independence Day broadcast.[40] J. Rosamond Johnson also broadcast spirituals and jazz music.

On film

The first feature-length sound film, Al Jolson's *The Jazz Singer* (1927), explicitly staged blackface and appropriated jazz music, through the story of a Jewish cantor's son embracing theatrical performance rather than the religious life his family desired. Other sound films quickly followed it: the white director King Vidor's *Hallelujah* (1929) brought together elements of jazz and gospel music in telling a story of a rural Black community. The film starred Nina Mae McKinney (1912–67) who would later come to the UK as a theatrical performer; she also featured in several television specials in the 1930s before returning to the United States.

5

The secret Florence Mills
Memorial Concert: January 1928

This chapter explores a concert which brought together some of the most influential Black practitioners of the decade, from Paris, London and across the UK. If you were in possession of a time machine and nowhere to take it, might we suggest setting it to 29 January 1928, for an afternoon of jazz at the London Pavilion. Though if you wouldn't mind, we'd quite like to come with you. The concert, advertised as a charitable flood relief concert, was in fact the Florence Mills Memorial concert – held under a slightly different guise. Officially, the three-and-a-half-hour spectacular was a concert to raise money for flood relief funds for those Londoners impacted by storm damage, and 'proceeds amounted to $5,000'.[1] But, as well as this philanthropic act, the concert also acted as a Florence Mills Memorial for the Black community and in turn celebrated the importance she placed on charity. The concert was organized by the African American composer, conductor and lyricist Noble Sissle and enabled the Black community in Britain to mourn Mills' tragic death at the age of only thirty-one. The event provides a window into the sheer breadth of Black performance practice at work in British theatre and the networks of Black musicians and performers who were shaping British theatre at the time.

London Pavilion
Sunday, January 29th, at 3 o'clock
Doors Open at 2.30
Special
Benefit Matinee Performance
in aid of
Mayor of Westminster's Flood Relief Fund
Under the Patronage of

The Right Hon. Lord Jessel, C. B.C.M.G	Viscount Falmouth, L.C.C.
Otho Nicholson, Esq. M.P. Frank G. Rye, Esq. M.P. The Mayor and Mayoress of the City of Westminster (Councillor and Mrs. Jacques Abady).	Admiral Sir Henry Bruce, K.C.B, M.V.O. Samuel Gluckstein, Esq. The Aldermen and councillors of.

Personal appearance of MISS MADGE FRANCKEISS,
the heroine of the Thames Flood

| Scott and Whaley (by the courtesy of their respective managements) Williams and Taylor Russel and Vivian Three Eddies Four Harmony Kings Hatch and Carpenter Alberta Hunter Noble Sissle 'South Before the War' Co. (By permission of the European Motion Picture Co., Ltd) Eddie Emerson | Josephine Baker Jackson and Blake George Garner Southern Trio Southern Serenaders George Minott Jim and Jack William Garland Leslie Hutchinson Leon Abbey's Jazz Band (by Courtesy of Bertram Mills) Bruce James Heatie King-Reavis |

James B. Lowe (the Uncle Tom of Uncle Tom's Cabin)
(by permission of the European Motion Picture Co., Ltd)[2]

KEY FIGURE 5 *Replica program for the Florence Mills Memorial Concert.*

The *New York Amsterdam News* reported the event, under the headline 'London Taken by Storm by Our Own', noting that, though there had been many benefits for the flood victims, 'when our performers saw fit to stage an "all black" benefit England went wild'.[3] Little survives of the concert as far as we know; there is no full program, only a list of some of the performers (which we have reprinted in Key Figure 5). The traces of the event that we have uncovered, many of which are presented here for the first time, also demonstrate the cultural importance of jazz. Theorist George McKay positions jazz as 'the musical culture or legacy of the triangulation, a music of modernity, the sonicity of the black Atlantic'.[4] This points to the ways in which jazz-as-modernity was, as McKay notes, driven by Black practitioners, and which led to the reshaping of the sonicity of musical theatre. It demonstrates London's West End relationships with Parisian nightlife and theatre, just as commercial air travel had emerged and shortened the time of travel between the two cities. The concert was Josephine Baker's 'first time in in England' performing live.[5] Media coverage highlighted Baker's glamorous arrival; she had been booked into another show in Paris but was able to appear because the organizers 'chartered a special airplane [...] with orders to bring Miss Baker back at all costs'.[6] Baker was not the only performer to travel: 'Alberta Hunter came all the way from Monte Carlo to sing the blues.'[7] Crucially, the concert demonstrates just how important Noble Sissle was to British musical theatre, something which has rarely been acknowledged. Sissle, Blake, Miller and Lyle's *Shuffle Along* (1921) instigated a long running professional network, which helped to popularize jazz in Britain, something which has also been underexplored. The concert also sheds light on the British production of *Show Boat*, which opened in London in May 1928.

The influence of *Shuffle Along*
on British theatre

Though *Shuffle Along* never transferred to the UK, throughout the 1920s British newspapers often touted the possibility of it transferring to London, sometimes with the white producer C. B. (Charles Blake) Cochran at the helm.[8] While *Shuffle Along* never played in London, its songs did; 'I'm Just Wild about Harry' was widely played in variety theatres across the UK, and the publisher Feldman's offered it as a way to 'solve all pantomime problems'.[9] HMV released this song and 'In Honeysuckle Time' from the musical as 'Eubie Blake and his *Shuffle Along* orchestra' in December 1921.[10] Given the popularity of *Shuffle Along* in New York, it was unsurprising that British producers would take an interest in Sissle and Blake's work as composers and as performers.

As composers and writers, Sissle and Blake were booked to write material for multiple British revues, adding songs for Noël Coward's revue *London Calling* (1923) produced by André Charlot, which starred Coward himself and Gertrude Lawrence, for whom they wrote 'You Were Meant for Me'. Sissle and Blake also contributed songs for *Still Dancing* (1925) at the London Pavilion, with songs by 'Novello, Sissle and Blake, and Irving Berlin'.[11] They also composed for *Cochran's Revue of 1926* (1926). Sissle's substantial professional contribution to British musical theatrical life has been almost totally overlooked, though Arianne Johnson Quinn has gone some way to remedying this with her discussions on Sissle and Blake in the context of Cole Porter's British work.[12] In January 1927, Sissle testified in a US court that he earned $20,000 a year, something equivalent to around $1.5 million per year in today's money.[13]

As performers, Sissle and Blake played a long booking in the West End, before moving into other London variety theatres from November 1925, after which they toured in the UK until March 1926 as 'America's ambassadors of syncopation'.[14] Sissle was evidently hired to write at least one essay explaining the appeal of jazz. He argued that the form only became popular after the (First World) War because before then, white people 'could not understand the sufferings of the colored man. They might sympathize in the same facile way as a rich man will fling a beggar a penny, but that was all'.[15] When Sissle and Blake closed at the Piccadilly, they had a party with guests including Jack Hylton, the white jazz bandleader, and many important Black musicians and performers including Layton and Johnson, Scott and Whaley, and Hatch and Carpenter.[16]

When Sissle and Blake formally ended their partnership in September 1927, Sissle returned to the UK and worked carefully to make his career a success on both sides of the Atlantic.[17] Sissle hired Harold Tillotson as a personal representative, to manage his affairs in the press and to report how well he was doing after his split from Blake.[18] In November, the *Afro-American* ran with 'Reports from Paris say that Noble Sissle and his representative [...] are making preparations to bring from Europe a flashy revue to be played in one of the local cabarets.'[19] *Billboard* had noted earlier that month that the plan was for 'a mammoth revue' that would draw Black performers from across Europe.[20] In December 1927, reports of Sissle's act in London variety theatre reached *Variety*, who noted his opening 'at the Coliseum in a song cycle, mostly comprising his own compositions. He scored nicely despite an early spot'.[21] UK coverage explained Sissle was more than a jazz singer and that he 'extracts every ounce of effect from the lyrics, [he] gives something like half a dozen numbers, but this does not appear to be enough for his admirers'.[22] Sissle maintained US news coverage about his activities in Europe and in Black newspapers and in entertainment trade presses. *Billboard* reported Sissle was becoming 'a star composer in England [...] and ought to be able to bring back plenty of English crowns'.[23]

Other members of *Shuffle Along*'s cast also influenced British musical theatre; the show had kick-started an astonishing number of careers. Many of the show's Broadway cast went on to work in Britain, including Josephine Baker, Florence Mills (see Key Figure 6), Paul Robeson, Adelaide Hall and Ivan H. Browning with his Harmony Kings (see Key Figure 7).[24] During the 1920s, Josephine Baker's work in Paris was widely reported in the British press – albeit with sexualized and racialized overtones.[25] In the UK, Baker's performance style was seen through film releases and in imitation performances by performers like Janice Hart (aka Cassie Walmer, see Chapter 2).

Florence Mills (b. *c.*1895, Washington, DC; d. 1927) was born Florence Winfrey to Nellie and John Winfrey who had been enslaved.[26] Mills started her stage career at age seven, first as Baby Florence Mills and then with her sisters as 'The Mills Sisters'. She later performed with Ada Smith (later 'Bricktop' Smith of Paris fame) in 1915. Touring in vaudeville, she met Ulysses Thompson, who she married in 1921. He was a tap dancer and performer in his own right and the two often performed together.

Mills appeared in only three Broadway shows and her voice was never recorded; but her legacy was clear from her first performance in *Shuffle Along* (1921), when she stepped into Gertrude Saunders' role. Mills went on to perform in white producer Lew Leslie's *Plantation Revue* (1922). Part of this show came to London as *Dover to Street to Dixie* (1923), before she returned to New York for the counterpart *Dixie to Broadway* (1924–5). This show propelled her to further fame with the song 'I'm Just a Blackbird Looking for a Bluebird'. She returned to London for Leslie's *Blackbirds of 1926* to huge acclaim. Leslie was planning a further revue around her in 1927/8, but Mills tragically died after an appendicitis operation.

Duke Ellington dedicated his song 'Black Beauty' to Mills in 1928.

KEY FIGURE 6 *Florence Mills, a short biography.*

During the 1920s in the UK, Florence Mills was a star. She had first arrived in London with the Cochran production of *Dover Street to Dixie* (1923) at the London Pavilion. She returned to London shortly afterwards for *Blackbirds of 1926*. Zakiya Adair, in her important work on Mills' career, notes that Mills 'challenged multiple and interlocking systems of oppression in early musical and vaudeville theater'.[27] Mills' popularity in the UK has also been assessed. Caroline Bressey and Gemma Romain note that, while in Britain, she 'effectively challenged racial, gender and class boundaries for her fans and colleagues'.[28] While in London, Mills and her husband delivered gifts to hospitals and distributed 'money to those sleeping rough along the river Thames'.[29] After Mills' premature death in November 1927, details of her funeral and the procession, with streets packed with mourners, were widely reported across the UK.[30]

Planning a concert: Celebrating the Black community in the UK

In the months before the concert, multiple plans emerge in British and American newspapers for a revue-style concert that Black performers would lead and star in, though the timeline is slightly complicated to follow. In

October 1927, Ivan H. Browning (see Key Figure 7) reported that Scott and Whaley were making plans, noting he could 'see no reason why it shouldn't be a big success' since they were intended on casting Lottie Gee and that 'Sissle and Blake will be asked to write the music'.[31] Though that event did not come to fruition, it could possibly have morphed into the Mills concert. Sissle was involved in many other charity events both with Black performers and in interracial spaces with white performers.[32] Sissle's work in supporting the theatrical community was a major part of his creative life. He worked to raise money for the family of Black actors – in particular, George Walker's mother (of Williams and Walker fame), who faced serious poverty after the death of her son.[33] Sissle also had a long running connection with the London Pavilion theatre; it is possible it was loaned to them for the charitable concert and the publicity it would raise. At the time, the Pavilion was screening *Uncle Tom's Cabin* (1927), with a specially written live prologue that had been written and staged by Sissle and starred James B. Lowe (who was also in the film).[34] The prologue featured the Southern Trio (John Payne, Mabel Mercer and Crescent Clinton Rosemond) who were themselves playing two venues simultaneously, Sissle's prologue and the Chez Victor nightclub.[35]

Ivan Harold Browning (b. 1891, Texas; d. 1978) had featured roles on Broadway in *Shuffle Along* (1921) and *Chocolate Dandies* (1924), as well as in the Chicago production of Sissle and Blake's *In Bamville* (1924).[36] His recordings with Eubie Blake in 1971 demonstrate the longevity of his association with their partnership; both Sissle and Browning had been part of Jim Europe's military band and served together in the First World War.

As a performer with the Four Harmony Kings, Browning had established an extensive career in the UK broadcasting 'spirituals and lighter numbers' on the radio in December 1925.[37] Alongside Browning (1st tenor), the group was made up of W. H. Berry (2nd tenor), Charles Drayton (baritone) and John S. Crabble (basso). They played variety theatres and church venues – spirituals clearly spoke to religious audiences and allowed the performers to reach a broader public.[38]

While he was touring, Browning maintained columns for the *New York Amsterdam News* and the *Chicago Defender*, detailing how Black performers were doing in the UK and in Europe. His columns also allowed artists to report news and relay family information via them. He was a performer-activist, constantly working for performers of African descent, often by making public interventions in racist discourse. Browning confronted Frederick Hannen Swaffer, a leading British theatre critic, for using the n-word in his column. He explained in his *Chicago Defender* column: 'I would like to know what on earth Negroes have done to him, and if they have done anything to him I am sure he gave them every cause.'[39]

He wrote about his experiences in different parts of the UK, including Lancashire, and reflected on his encounters with local people who were shocked at seeing a Black man: Browning also reported writing to the editor of the local newspaper that 'we were certainly not "c—ns".' He went on to explain his reasons for writing, explaining: 'Like many offensive words used with reference to our people over here, one gets tired and fed up with such and can't help calling attention to shame every once in a while, regardless of their always saying they mean no harm whatever.'[40]

During the 1930s, Browning publicly campaigned against the unfair laws the Ministry of Labour had placed on foreign performers, laws that particularly impacted Black US performers. He publicly protested the treatment of several Black people who were turned away from London hotels, like the editor of the *Chicago Defender* R. S. Abbott and his wife.[41] He also stepped in and housed the Abbotts and hosted meals with other visitors such as the African American bishop John A. Gregg.[42]

Browning's contribution has not fully been assessed. His letters record Black activism against the erasure of Black performer's success in the UK. One of his campaigns focused on *Variety*'s 'prejudicial' coverage 'of our performers in England', which meant that 'you never see a blessed thing about their success in *Variety*'; but Browning also confronted the magazine's British representatives: 'I told [them] that they were absolutely prejudiced. Of course they denied it, but on the other hand it is always the first theatrical magazine over here to publish anything uncomplimentary about the Race performers.'[43]

KEY FIGURE 7   *Ivan H. Browning, a short biography.*

Remembering Florence Mills:
Gathering the Black community

The Black community in the UK also organized to mark Florence Mills' death. Ivan H. Browning reported that he was in touch with the (white) Lady Mary Cook, who was trying to arrange a benefit concert, and mentions Robeson, Sissle, Browning and Baker in the original plans.[44] Though this never materialized, the concert in February brought together many of the same people. Lady Cook's letter to Browning notes Mills' importance as a performer and as an activist; in London, 'many people had heard of the NAACP from Florence herself'.[45] Priyamvada Gopal's methodology considers how it is possible to 're-vision colonial subjects as agents whose actual resistance put critical transformative pressure on British claims to cherishing freedom, and on those Britains who spoke and campaigned in its cause'.[46] Lady Cook's letter can be read as evidencing the ways in which Black performers like Mills were able to work as activists exerting critical transformative pressure.

Frederick Hannen Swaffer, the white major theatre critic for London in the 1920s and 1930s, whose racism drew the attention of Ivan H. Browning, was also clearly influenced by Mills. In 1939, he wrote a long article about the performer, recalling a speech Mills had given at a Piccadilly cabaret about the Black experience and racism and her own hardship in starting work as a child. He recalled: 'No one wrote it down, so there is no record left.'[47] He reflected on Mills' connection with Lady Cook, she had arranged for Mills to speak about her experiences, and noted Mills' comment: 'I feel our visit here has done a lot of good. No one has complained about us. Some people have been to see our show, not only two or three times, but 20 or 30 times. This must surely have helped.'[48] Hannen Swaffer's article also reveals that the Thames concert was a Florence Mills memorial in disguise: 'in spite of the altered announcement. [...] It went on hour after hour, and they all made speeches, and some of them could scarcely be induced to leave the stage. Even then, they talked about Florence Mills.'[49]

Sissle's arranging of the concert clearly drew on both his London and his *Shuffle Along* connections, though Josephine Baker had established herself independently as a star of some means in the intervening years. In a society round-up of Parisian news, a publicity shot of Baker in *La Sirène des Tropiques* pictured her alongside the note that '[she] is said to be contemplating financing another new film with her own money'.[50] It is possible the costs of her appearance in London were in part paid for by the film company who were producing her next film, *Parisian Pleasures*, which had opened in March that year.[51] Glamourous photos of her leaving for Paris from Croydon Aerodrome show Baker wrapped in furs, posing for photographers; and the trip clearly brought the movie extra publicity. After the concert, photos were printed of Baker alongside the Mayor of London and Miss Frankeiss (the so-called 'heroine of the floods').[52] Baker returned to London several times and broadcast on the BBC in 1933.

The concert demonstrates the breadth of the Black community in the UK. Many of the performers in the concert we have already explored – for example, Scott and Whaley and Will Garland. Others were at the beginning of their careers, and the event played a significant part in allowing them to work in the UK. Alberta Hunter's biographer notes that it was the concert, and Sissle, which provided Hunter with a way into the UK because she was able to 'mention the Lord Mayor's name at passport checkpoint'.[53] While we know very little about how the audience responded to the concert, we do know Jerome Kern and Oscar Hammerstein II attended while preparing for the London production of *Show Boat*. Kern and Hammerstein saw Alberta

IMAGE 3 *The dancer and actress Josephine Baker in the BBC's studio. London, 2 October 1933. (Photo by Imagno/Getty Images.)*

Hunter, accompanied by Leslie Hutchinson, performing 'Just Another Day Wasted Day'. Hunter recalled that she 'tore the place up [...] I put my foot down and went to town'.[54] While no photographs have been found of the actual event, the descriptions hint at the spectacle: 'When Josephine Baker did appear, she sat on a grand piano, in a beautiful rose-pink dress and a bejeweled sort of nightcap with long dazzling earrings and sang.'[55] Many of the practitioners who performed at the concert are little known about or discussed; we have identified many of them in Key Figure 8.

L ittle is known about Russell and Vivian (Shepherd), but the pair may have been from Chicago, and they started touring in the UK from the mid-1920s.[56] They appear to have worked a song and tap dance routine (one review notes that they 'sing and patter successfully'),[57] and they toured British variety extensively until the early 1930s. In 1929, they became known for 'Sleep Baby Sleep' and were pictured on the sheet music cover; that same year they also toured with *Going Some* with Hardcastle and (Amos) Howard.[58]

George Garner was a classic tenor singer and contemporary of Roland Hayes. He was described as 'a revelation in tenors' for his articulation and balance.[59] He broadcast regularly on British radio from 1927, often singing spirituals. He was later engaged by the Samuel Coleridge-Taylor Choral Society as part of the Schubert centenary.[60] He moved to California in the early 1930s where he started 'George Garner's Negro Chorus' and a Black music research centre.[61]

Williams and Taylor had been in the UK since at least 1925, when they appear touring in the London Theatre of Varieties Ltd circuit (which included the Palladium).[62] In 1927, the duo were touring with Lew Leslie's *Blackbirds* – one tour stop review notes: 'they are a success as comedians and dancers.'[63]

Leon Abbey's jazz band was of international importance to the dissemination of jazz music. They had worked widely in the UK and across Europe in the earlier 1920s. Abbey was a bandleader and violinist who had originally played in J. Rosamond Johnson's orchestra earlier in the decade. Abbey and his band broadcast six times around the months of the Flood Charity Concert from Olympia Music Hall,[64] presumably before resuming their European tour.[65] In 1935, Abbey took his band to Mumbai (then Bombay), to the Taj Hotel, as the first Black jazz band ever to play in India.[66]

Hatch and Carpenter (Ike Hatch and Lewis Carpenter) toured extensively in variety in the 1920s and 1930s, and performed regularly on the radio. They recorded numerous records,[67] and would have been well known to audience members. Later, Hatch became best known for his long association with the radio program *Kentucky Minstrels*. He was filmed by Pathé in 1938 singing both 'Lawd You Made the Night Too Long' and 'The Rhythm's O.K. in Harlem'.[68] He went on to work as a nightclub host and remained an important figure in British popular music.

Other acts are much harder to pin down – dancers like George Minnot and Jackson and Blake. Minnot was a 'quick step' artist[69] who toured with Eddie Emmerson in *Going Some* in 1923 and had worked consistently in British variety touring with jazz revues like *Stage Struck*.[70] Jackson and Blake toured with *Blackbirds of 1928* and also performed on British radio.[71]

Some other performers are not directly mentioned in the billing for the concert, but we know they performed. Stephen Bourne notes that Connie Smith was also seen by Jerome Kern and Oscar Hammerstein at the concert and hired in *Show Boat* as Alberta Hunter's understudy.[72] Smith (b. 1875 in Brooklyn; d. 1970, London) also wrote to Black US newspapers, reporting on the state of theatre business and maintaining communication between this dispersed network.[73]

KEY FIGURE 8   *Brief biographies for lesser-known company members who performed at the memorial concert.*

Show Boat comes to town: Staging the imagined Black experience

Hammerstein and Kern's presence at the concert is not the only connection between it and *Show Boat*. Several of those who performed that afternoon also went into its West End company. (Intriguingly, the theatre historian Todd Decker suggests that the white performer Edith Day appeared at the concert, though, if she did, it was not particularly noted in the widespread contemporary coverage.)[74] Payne was himself involved in the production and conducted the Black chorus, the so-called 'Mississippi chorus'.[75] Connie Smith and Mabel Mercer were both part of this ensemble. The show had a touring company; Ivan H. Browning noted they were made up of 'mostly English born and African' performers.[76]

It is notable that, through Alberta Hunter's performance specifically, the role of Queenie was no longer played by white performers. Alberta Hunter was hired for Queenie instead of Maisie Ayling, a white performer. The role of Queenie was performed on Broadway by the white performer Tess Gardella, who was known for her blackface variety performances of 'Aunt Jemima'. Hunter recalled that, having secured the part, she was able to live in London at John C. Payne's house, noting that at the time Marian Anderson was also living there.[77] Though she had not visited until the concert, her music had been played, and her co-composed 'Downhearted Blues' (written with Lovie Austin) was released in the UK in 1923 and was played on the radio.[78] In order to prepare for her British stage work, after the concert, Hunter began working in British variety as well as in London nightclubs, touring with the white pianist Peggy Desmond.[79] Hunter went on to perform in *Show Boat* for eleven months.[80]

The response to the British production of *Show Boat* in the Black community was a complex one, particularly because, despite Paul Robeson's rumoured involvement with the show on Broadway, he did not appear in it until the London production. J. Rogers, a Black journalist, wrote in the *Philadelphia Tribune* about his experience and describes the pain of seeing the repetition of US racist subjugation repeated on the British stage: '*Show Boat* in short is a white man's play, and the colored brothers, as usual, occupied the usual place. Not a bit different from in America.'[81] Rogers asks, without finding any answer, 'why doesn't Robeson withdraw and have his own show instead of being a pawn for the white man?'[82] Rogers notes that, despite Robeson's ability, the part of Joe 'exists more in white man's fancy than in reality'.[83] Rogers specifically attends to Hunter's performance: '[she] was as good in her part as the white leading lady was in hers, yet Miss Hunter was only a maid and played also a very trivial part.'[84] Other reviews from the period call attention to the small parts Robeson and Hunter played. In a review from *The Bystander*, there is a note that Black artists 'must necessarily represent persons of menial status'; it goes on:

> that admirable actress, Miss Alberta Hunter, is no more than the native cook on the Show Boat; while even an actor of the rare quality of Mr Paul Robeson [...] may be nothing more than a Man with a Duster. It is by a nice irony that Mr Robeson takes the house by storm with his first appearance, and from that moment becomes the dominating personality of the show.[85]

Todd Decker erroneously suggests that Hunter was left with 'no musical role whatsoever, perhaps the reason reviewers hardy mentioned her'.[86] But it seems that Hunter's role was progressively cut: Rogers attended in October when he saw Hunter play 'a trivial part'. *The Stage* review, in May, says that the best musical items in the show were Robeson's 'Ol' Man River', 'In Dahomey' and 'C'mon Folks' – Hunter's solo.[87] Hunter recalled in later life that 'Originally she was to sing a number called "C'mon Folks" with the twelve Black chorus girls imported from America for the show. But because it was such a big success early in the show, Edith Day created a fuss and had it removed.'[88] Decker notes Hunter was 'unlikely to have admitted to the reduced size of Queenie's part' in the letters she wrote to Black US newspapers.[89] But the strength of Hunter's performance practice was clearly noted in the press – and the success of her work in the UK is explored in Chapter 6.

Several lines for future enquiry emerge from this period, alongside shifts that now need to take place in how we address the period. Noble Sissle had a considerable influence in the UK in contributing music for a range of revues and as an organizer and producer, as well as in the organization of networks that allowed Black performers to be seen by influential white producers and practitioners. The idea that jazz was not influencing musical theatre during this period entirely negates the contribution Sissle practically made and the certain influence that had; he was not alone. While the ways in which Black US newspapers reported success in Britain might be somewhat, let us say, enthusiastic, there was, however, clearly a professional capital to be had by having success in the UK in order to return back to the United States. Ivan H. Browning's many letters to Black newspapers provide us with important information about his own practice and the ways in which the Black community supported the production of Black art. We have encountered this in other practitioners, though Alberta Hunter is perhaps the most significant example as we will now turn to in more detail.

6

Alberta Hunter and Mabel Mercer

During the 1920s and 1930s, many Black women performers toured extensively in British music theatre, moving from tours to variety and to West End musicals. As we have established, some of the women touring during this period were exceptionally well known, particularly Josephine Baker. Although they have not remained in the wider spotlight in the same way, other Black performers such as Florence Mills, Ethel Waters, Evelyn Dove, Nina Mae McKinney and Elisabeth Welch are recognized for making some contribution. Notably in the case of Dove, McKinney and Welch, Stephen Bourne has written biographies on each of the women to reinstate knowledge of their contribution.[1] To support, rather than to replicate this work, this chapter focuses on two key practitioners: Mabel Mercer and Alberta Hunter. Both women performed at the Florence Mills memorial concert discussed in Chapter 5, and both were part of the production of *Show Boat* (1928) at Drury Lane. Their impact stretches beyond the two decades we are focusing on here, but we explore how they worked within the musical theatre industry during the 1920s and 1930s. We consider how both women challenged limitations placed on their career and can be seen as enacting resistant performance practices through their cosmopolitanism, community building and active resistance of racism.

On her return to New York after *Show Boat*, Hunter told an interviewer that when she saw the Statue of Liberty she cried tears of sadness, not joy. When asked to explain she said: 'Of course I prefer Europe. What Negro with sense doesn't? There I was received with kindness, consideration and appreciation, here I have met with little except unkindness and lack of appreciation.'[2] She was clear that she wanted to return: 'So far as I am concerned I am willing to stay in Europe always.'[3] She spent prolonged periods in later life touring with the United Service Organizations (USO) in Southeast Asia during the 1940s and 1950s. In the UK, she styled a reputation as America's 'foremost' blues singer, a title she could not really claim over Bessie Smith, but she was nonetheless one of the most significant blues singers.[4] During her first period in the UK (1928–9), Hunter quickly became part of extended Black creative networks that brought together people from across the United States, the Caribbean and the UK; as we noted in Chapter 5, she lived in John C. Payne's house for a period and became part of his wider social network. This almost certainly connected her to the Jamaican music teacher and professor Louis Drysdale, with whom she studied voice 'so that I would know how to sing and to discuss my work intelligently'.[5] She also used the cultural capital of Payne's connections with white upper-class society – Noble Sissle recalled that the Duke of Windsor's 'patronage and personal acclaim' helped many Black performers in Britain, including Sissle himself, Roland Hayes, Paul Robeson, the Four Harmony Kings, Cab Calloway and Hunter.[6]

In 1929, Hunter turned to continental Europe. She received 'a fine offer to appear in an edition of the same show which opens in Paris sometime during the New Year. Miss Hunter is studying French at one of the best French schools in London'.[7] Hunter did not appear in the Paris production and went into cabaret instead: 'Clever Miss Alberta Hunter, after a tremendous opening at the new Cotton Club in Paris, has settled down and is now causing much talk and comment in the busy city by her [French] singing of "Chiquita".'[8] Hunter clearly developed her French during this period, left her employment, now at the Casino de Paris, to accept work at the Hotel Carlton, in a glamorous resort in the Netherlands.[9] She eventually returned to the United States, where she continued working in variety theatre, but clearly her ambition was to return to Europe.

Alberta Hunter (1895–1984) was a singer, dancer, composer, lyricist, actor, activist and community builder. She was significant for her early work as a blues performer and for her comeback in her later life. Her performance practice has been considered in terms of representations of race and sexuality.[10] Hunter was a lesbian, and although she had to hide her sexuality throughout her life, her songs often contain suggestive lyrics which reject expectations of how women should behave and govern their enjoyment of sexuality.

Born in Memphis, Tennessee, she faced a difficult childhood. Still a child, Hunter ran away from home to Chicago where she began work singing at a brothel called Dago Frank's. Hunter moved on to bars and nightclubs in Chicago, where she performed with Louis Armstrong at venues where celebrity performers like Al Jolson and Sophie Tucker came to watch her. By 1917, she was working at the Dreamland Ballroom, Chicago's 'most prestigious venue for black entertainers'.[11]

In 1921, she recorded with W. C. Handy's short-lived record company Black Swan before signing a recording deal with Paramount as a composer, lyricist and singer; among her early recording work, she is best known for 'Downhearted Blues' (composed with pianist Lovie Austin, also a Black woman) which Bessie Smith released in 1923. Hunter also recorded her own version of the song. Hunter moved to New York and performed in vaudeville and two shows on Broadway, including the musical *How Come* (1923) with Sidney Bechet. She recorded in Chicago with Louis Armstrong and claimed to have copyrighted the Black Bottom dance in 1926.

In 1927, she came to Europe and then to London for eighteen months, touring British variety theatre as 'America's Foremost Blues Singer'.[12] She stayed in John C. Payne's London home (Marian Anderson was also lodging there then).[13] She performed in variety and in cabaret,[14] before starring in the UK production of *Show Boat* (May 1928) as Queenie. When restrictive labour laws threatened her ongoing appearance in *Show Boat*, she successfully mounted an appeal.[15]

During the 1930s, she performed on British radio regularly, including in a radio version of *Show Boat* broadcast in 1934 alongside Ike Hatch.[16] She starred in an early British colour film, *Radio Parade of 1935* (1934). In 1937, Hunter returned to London; she performed with Robinson's Cotton Club Revue at the London Palladium and on British radio. She returned to Broadway with the *Mamba's Daughter* (1940), a play by Du Bose and Dorothy Heyward, with songs by Jerome Kern, which also starred Ethel Waters. During the Second World War (and beyond), Hunter toured the world with the USO.

In 1954, after the death of her mother, she gave up touring and lied about her age to train as a nurse. She said she was fifty; she was in fact sixty. She enjoyed this career until reluctantly retiring in 1977, when she was eighty-two.

Despite this prolonged period away from performing, she restarted her career during the final decade of her life when, bored of retirement, she took up residence as a cabaret performer in a Greenwich Village club, The Cookery. She composed a film score, *Remember My Name* (1978). She also began performing internationally once more, and several of the performances were filmed in full, which preserved her extraordinary live performance skills, and her raucous (and often downright filthy) sense of humour. For Hunter, blues were a kind of spirituality: 'blues is what the spirit is to a minister.'[17]

KEY FIGURE 9 *Alberta Hunter, a short biography.*

Hunter in the UK during the 1930s

Hunter maintained a complex professional presence in Europe during the 1930s, often travelling between France, the UK and beyond for broadcasts and bookings. In May 1933, Hunter returned to Paris to work in cabaret, where she was able to reunite with her friend Mabel Mercer. The *Chicago Defender* (an African American newspaper) reported she had received 'more offers for her services than she can accept'.[18] Though Hunter accepted a contract to replace Josephine Baker in her Paris cabaret act in October 1933,[19] she maintained a British presence in radio and theatre.[20] She performed across an extensive range of venues that engaged with musical theatre repertoire and reprised her role as Queenie on a radio broadcast of *Show Boat*. She also regularly sang with Jack Johnson, who was a white jazz band leader, and his band at the Dorchester Hotel on Park Lane, London, at a time when Duke Ellington's orchestra was struggling to receive permission to enter the UK to work.[21]

In 1934, she recorded with Johnson for HMV, releasing Noël Coward's 'I Travel Alone' and Cole Porter's 'Miss Otis Regrets'.[22] Coward was reportedly a 'regular admirer' of Hunter's.[23] She also broadcast in radio variety programs as well as with Henry Hall's BBC orchestra.[24] Hunter also performed in variety in Aberdeen and Liverpool as well as Hackney Empire where she sang the Sophie Tucker standard 'Some of These Days'.[25] (Tucker, a white performer who was hugely popular in the United States was influenced by Ethel Waters and Bessie Smith.) Hunter performed hit songs from US film musicals like 'I'll String Along With You' from *20 million Sweethearts* (1934) before the film had a UK release.[26] She also performed the Western-style song 'Wagon Wheels' which originated from the Broadway *Ziegfeld Follies of 1934* in British variety.[27] Though she did experience success and glamour in London, her experience could not have been an easy one. She was cast in an all-Black cast pantomime of *Robinson Crusoe* at Lewisham Hippodrome in 1934, in which she starred alongside John C. Payne and played the 'savage Princess'.[28] The performance clearly traded on racialized imagery – Hunter was the Princess of the 'Island of Bangaloo'. This must have been painful; she does not appear to have discussed it subsequently. Hunter had three solos in the show: 'I Long for that Moon Country', a tango 'Isle of Capri' and 'You May Not be an Angel'.[29]

After playing a role which played to racist tropes, she left London to tour again in continental Europe, something particularly notable given the growth in fascism during this period. She performed extensively with a Black pianist, Norma Payne Davis (Hunter's biography has a picture of Payne Davis and Hunter riding camels in front of the Egyptian pyramids).[30] In February 1935, on her return to the United States, she warned other Black performers to not accept contracts in Nazi Germany,[31] making clear the dangers. It is particularly heartbreaking that, by December of the same

IMAGE 4 *Alberta Hunter, studio portrait, Paris, France, 1935. (Photo by Gilles Petard/Redferns.)*

year, when performing in Egypt, she was quoted as making a New Year resolution 'that she will never again sing in America but will spend her time between London, Paris, Monte Carlo and Berlin'.[32]

Hunter returned to London in 1937 to take part in *Cotton Club Revue* and was reported in the US press to be giving a variety of radio and television broadcasts around George VI's coronation in 1937 – though, if she did, she was never credited for them in the UK.[33] In February 1938, it was reported that she had chosen to return to Europe rather than perform in Hollywood.[34] She was still able to reach the United States, performing in a prestigious joint US and UK broadcast in 1938.[35] In November 1938, her mysterious engagement to the British nobleman was announced (reportedly) Baron Sommery Gade (no further trace can be found of the chap), but clearly they were never married.[36]

Community and professional resistance: Securing ownership and credit

Hunter's work can be seen to support the transatlantic Black community. From the early 1940s onwards, Alberta Hunter took up the role of community columnist in her 'Little Notebook' column, taking up Ivan H. Browning's role as community correspondent within the Black musical and theatrical diaspora.[37] She was part of the Black community's social activism. In New York, during the early 1930s, she performed in numerous charity concerts for the NAACP with J. Rosamond Johnson, Duke Ellington, Ethel Waters, Ada Brown and Adelaide Hall.[38] One concert for the NAACP saw her perform alongside George Gershwin, Jimmy Durante, Duke Ellington and Miller and Lyles.[39] She sang with Leon Abbey's band in The Hague in 1938.[40]

Hunter rigorously enforced contracts and challenged unfair practices because of her early experiences as a composer. When recording for Paramount, her pianist and arranger Lovie Austin taught her how to copyright her music, but after she had written 'Downhearted Blues', the producer Jay Mayo 'Ink' Williams sold the recording rights to Columbia – who recorded Bessie Smith singing it, making the song a huge success but only for Williams, who retained Hunter's share of the royalties. She made only $368 for the song; she stopped working for Williams.[41] She later recalled 'Ink Williams robbed me. Not only me, everybody. The people that didn't know how to have their songs copywritten [copyrighted], he took all their music.'[42] After experiencing such crushing unfairness, Hunter was careful to ensure her commercial properties in future. She widely claimed to have copyrighted the Black Bottom dance. Anthea Kraut has explored this claim and the importance of it at length.[43] There were no such provisions for copyright law for dance at this period. Kraut argues: 'the rhetoric of intellectual property rights could attempt to perform work similar to that of the law itself.'[44] She notes that, 'even unsubstantiated, Hunter's copyright claim should thus be seen as a weapon against and check on white hegemony in the theatrical marketplace'.[45] It was certainly well known in the Black community. In 1927, Ivan H. Browning noted that Lew Leslie was 'said to be telling people on this side' that he had created the Black Bottom dance. He notes: 'I hope Alberta Hunter will read these few lines and act accordingly.'[46]

Rather than take a salary cut in *Show Boat* (she had received a telegram from the producer Sir Alfred Butt informing her he would have to cast someone at a lesser salary), she packed her bags to return to the United States; he changed his mind and reinstated her.[47] In 1930, she sued the white producer of the Lafayette Theatre for breaching her contract and trying to trap her into reducing her salary. She challenged this injustice with the full support of Equity.[48] One newspaper reported that 'Miss Hunter told a different story [...] and backed it up with a suit for her full salary through her attorney, Ralph Warrick'.[49] Her legal actions did not prohibit her prospects of securing work either. After she returned to the United States from Paris in 1930, she utilized the reports of her success there and in the UK and secured a tour on the Keith circuit (theatres with largely white audiences).[50] She was also active in fights to see her work permits renewed in the UK in 1935, something which was particularly crucial as the Nazi reach over occupied Europe prevented travel and further work opportunities.[51] She performed across Europe, in Copenhagen and then in Athens, Greece in May 1936.[52] Hunter warned Black performers not to travel to Italy in 1937, informing them of a new ban.[53]

Hunter's songs themselves stage different kinds of resistance, not least in terms of her own sexuality as a lesbian. While Hunter had to professionally be closeted in order to continue working, her blues songs explicitly stage women's sexual enjoyment and pleasure. Angela Davis has explored Hunter's powerful lyrics in 'Downhearted Blues': 'I got the world in a jug / The stopper's in my hand / I'm gonna hold it until you men / Come under my command'. Davis notes the song 'ends with an address to men in general – a bold, perhaps implicitly feminist contestation of patriarchal rule'.[54] Maria Johnson, in her work addressing lesbian blues performers, notes that blues lyrics allow for multiple interpretations and invites us 'to celebrate the provocative possibilities blues performance provided for affirming a range of gender and sexual identities'.[55] Clearly, it is difficult to explore this aspect of Hunter's life in the UK, but it is important to acknowledge it and her experience of having to mask and hide her own identity – within her already minoritized identity as a Black performer.

Hunter's performances explicitly stage Black activism. Her work in *Radio Parade of 1935* (actually 1934) places Black performance practice as the glamorous opening act of an elaborate televised variety bill, which, due to plot-based shenanigans, is being shown in packed parks and city squares. The film gently parodies the BBC, while criticizing an out-of-touch theatre industry ill-equipped to deal with the threat of new technology bringing entertainment into domestic settings. The film shows the fear that radio and television would erode the need for variety theatre. It reveals other fears: as the white jazz orchestra plays, four senior men give the shocked announcements that 'it's unheard of, it's not done, it's not cricket, it's communism, it's Bolshevist'. The musical film features explicitly racist songs like 'Let's Go Wild' (i.e., 'like the heathen or the savage'), a song which mentions Anna Mae Wong's work (a Chinese American actor) and Josephine Baker's dance routines but simultaneously suggests 'let's find Hitler and kick him in the pants'. The film also features a somewhat incongruous protest number, which begins the spectacular colour sequence of the film: Alberta Hunter is accompanied by John Payne's choir singing 'Black Shadows are Haunting Me' (music by Carl Falck and lyrics by James Bunting, but no further information can currently be found). The lyrics explicitly describe anti-Black racism: 'People regard me with hatred [...] All just because of my skin?' Though the song does not offer any solutions, it allows us to spend time with the powerful vocal performance of Hunter along with Payne's chorus in the song. Their performance practice can be read as a demonstration that this suffering is not an inherent part of being Black but is brought about through white racism.

Mabel Mercer: Vocal performance and cultural memory

As a performer, Mabel Mercer's influence on international cabaret performance is reasonably well known, particularly in terms of her unique style of delivering lyrics. David Román describes Mercer as 'perhaps the most influential singer of cabaret performance in the twentieth century'.[56] Román has explored the ways in which cabaret 'becomes an embodied archive of American cultural history, a place where women, especially older women, perform the history of their lives in the theatre and, by extension, the larger culture'.[57] Clearly, it also becomes a place of asserting Black performance practice as a central part of American cultural history. Michael Feinstein notes: 'Mabel Mercer and Bobby Short [a pianist/performer himself and sometime accompanist for Mercer] sang songs throughout the 1940s and '50s that they recognised as classics long before everyone did.'[58] Though the quality of Mercer's voice in later life deteriorated from her original soprano range to an enforced spoken style, she maintained a narrative power in telling a story through song. She herself said: 'People say I can't sing for toffee! I say, I know that, I'm telling a story.'[59] Mercer influenced many kinds of performers, including Frank Sinatra, Barbara Cook and Billie Holliday.[60] Through Mercer's interpretation, Joni Mitchell saw her song 'Both Sides Now' in a radically different light, though Mitchell recalled somewhat insulting Mercer by suggesting to her that it took an older woman to understand its meaning (never assume anyone is happy to be called old).[61] Mercer's repertoire has been 'credited with keeping alive an impressive list of songs that might otherwise have been forgotten'.[62] But Mercer also worked within British musical theatre at the beginning of her career, challenging expectations of what women could do.

Mabel Alice Wadham (later Mercer) (b. 1900, Burton upon Trent, UK; d. 1984) was born to Emily Wadham, a white variety theatre performer and an unnamed father of African descent. Perhaps because her mother was a music hall actor on tour, she was placed in the care of a convent boarding school in Blackley, Manchester (though she is described as an inmate in the 1911 census). Emily Wadham is often described as a teenager; she was in fact twenty or twenty-one when her daughter was born, but this clearly did not make matters any easier. In later life, Mercer recalled loving holidays spent with her grandmother in Liverpool.[63]

In 1914, having reached the end of formal schooling, she began working in variety theatre billings with her aunt, Rhodda King, in a group called the Romany Five. She worked with a minstrel-style show called *Spades and Diamonds* (perhaps around 1917–18), which featured Sam Carter who had also been part of Gordon Stretton's *In Sunny Tennessee*.

In 1918, Mercer joined Will Garland's company (see Chapter 4); she sang and played piano with them as Mabel Wadham. She also worked as their music director, conducting the tour of *Coloured Society* in 1918 and again in 1924. Sam Carter (with whom she presumably worked in her first revue) was also part of the company. In 1920, Mercer took over from Evelyn Dove in touring with the Southern Syncopated Orchestra. The forty members of the group were joined in 1920 by Buddy Gilmore, the drummer. One reviewer noted: 'What he can't do with drums is not worth doing.' Indeed, he quickly went on to performing in variety theatre.[64]

By 1925, she joined John C. Payne's Southern Trio with whom she toured to Paris. She moved to the new name of Mercer from this point onwards, and she performed as a 'singer, dancer and pianist'.[65] Mercer met Florence Mills and understudied her part in *Blackbirds of 1926* and *Silver Rose*.[66] Mercer took over for Mills while *Blackbirds* was touring, and Mills 'stayed with Belle Davis at her home in London'.[67] Payne's Trio were also in demand, playing for the Prince of Wales in 1926.[68] (She played again for them, after his abdication, in the United States in 1941.)[69]

By November 1928, Mercer was working in Paris and in London. She became part of Ada 'Bricktop' Smith's line-up at her eponymous nightclub, Bricktop's. Maya Cantu notes that she was 'drawn to Mercer's alluring poise – complementing her own entrepreneurial hustle – Bricktop took Mercer on as a featured singer and partner'.[70] Cantu also notes Mercer introduced Cole Porter's 'Love for Sale' to Paris (from *The New Yorkers*, 1930).[71] Sharpley Whiting, Bricktop's biographer, notes her importance at the club: 'It was through Bricktop's sheer will and Cole Porter's melodic tunes that Mabel Mercer became a cabaret star in Paris. Her presence at Bricktop's helped solidify the club's stature.'[72] She became part of Louis Douglas's revue *Lisa* in Paris in September 1929, alongside Sonny Jones and Marion Cook (Will Marion Cook's daughter).[73]

In Paris, she carried out the sombre task of supporting and entertaining the mothers of Black soldiers who had died in the First World War. They were called respectfully the Gold Star Mothers; Bricktop and Mabel Mercer were there and 'did some dancing and singing that made the mothers feel like getting up and dancing themselves'.[74]

During the 1930s, Mercer continued to work in Paris, but she also continued to impact the UK through her work on radio with the Black British pianist Reginald Foresythe. She appeared in two movies, *Tropical Trouble* (1935) and *Everything Is Rhythm*. She broadcast Sunday radio shows from Luxembourg (beyond Britain's strict religious broadcasting laws) alongside violinist Eddie South. Mercer left Paris in 1938 for Amsterdam. She was able to settle in the United States in 1941 after a marriage was arranged to Black musician Kelsey Pharr, a gay man, in order to get her a US passport. There, she settled in New York as a fixture in the city's cabaret scene.[75] After her long career in New York, Mercer returned to the UK in 1977 where she appeared at the Playboy Club, a performance which was broadcast on BBC 2 some forty-two years after she had last performed for the broadcasting company. She died in 1984.

KEY FIGURE 10 *Mabel Mercer, a short biography.*

Mercer's professional identities in the UK

Recalling her years in the convent school, Mercer spoke of being unaware that there were other Black people (and recalled no discussion of her identity in her family life) until she worked on the *Spades and Diamonds* revue in 1917: 'I just took for granted that I was one of a kind. And finding these others was like a dream. I was delighted.'[76] Mercer's biographer somewhat blithely recalls the racism she experienced as a child, recounting her cousins 'playfully push[ing] her head under a water tap to see if they could wash the light brown from her skin'.[77] Around this time, while still a teenager, Mercer came to the attention of Nanette Horton Boucher, the mother of James Boucher, 'who took her into her household where she associated for the first time with others of African descent'.[78] Mercer became part of the Black community in the UK; she too worked with John C. Payne in his Southern Trio from 1920 onwards. Mercer certainly faced isolation from her family before finding refuge with the Bouchers and Will Garland's company. Ivan Browning's letters made clear she was 'an English girl with a typical English manner in every way'.[79] In 1941, writing in the *New York Age*, Floyd Snelson described her as 'of British-African extraction'.[80]

Her own identity sometimes perplexed British newspapers in the 1920s, particularly around her work with Payne. When she toured with the Southern Syncopated Orchestra, Mercer was seen as African American. One example in the *Dundee Courier* describes her as a 'sweet singer from Sunny Southern Shores'.[81] Brian Ward notes that 'The British public was encouraged to think of the SSO [Southern Syncopated Orchestra] as a genuine example of rural southern, as well as black, musical heritage.'[82] Touring with the Southern Syncopated Orchestra must have deepened Mercer's knowledge of jazz and strengthened her developing sense of Black community. John C. Payne's work with spirituals and the many concert performances they gave surely deepened her repertoire of concert music too.

Mercer was a pianist, singer and, importantly, music director. While the cigarette card of Mercer in a white tuxedo fits with the grand story Mercer herself told about the conductor going off sick one night, Mercer clearly engaged with conducting on more than one occasion. In her interviews with biographer James Haskins she noted that the situation came about because 'the conductor, who was also the pianist, fell sick with the flu and had to go to the hospital'[83] – during the flu pandemic in 1917–19. Mercer explicitly recalled attempting to 'pass' as a man for the musicians and orchestra.[84] Yet the press coverage from the time straightforwardly presents that Mercer was the music director for the revue. One review notes that the 'musical director [was] a lady – Miss Mabel Mercer'.[85] Mercer actually returned to work with Garland in 1924. Again, a review notes that she was both a conductor and a performer, noting: 'the orchestra music did much for the success of the production.'[86] It is fascinating to consider what lessons she took from the Southern Syncopated Orchestra in conducting practices in UK theatre.

Alberta Hunter only returned to performing when the subject came up at a party with Mercer, still her friend of many years. Hunter returned to performing after her retirement from nursing and was able to preserve her cabaret style in a series of international performances. In her summation of Ada 'Bricktop' Smith's life, Cantu notes that her 'life and work centralize the agency of African American women as not only performers, but enterprising producers and creative catalysts, within a musical theatre historiography that has often marginalized their innovations'.[87] As it happens, Smith, Mercer and Hunter all died in the same year, 1984; and Cantu's words clearly can apply to each of them. As composers, conductors, performers and activists, Hunter's and Mercer's work challenges what we might have previously thought to be possible.

The 1930s in context

The 1930s were a period of rapid social and political change. The global depression that followed the financial crash of 1929 led to a turn to far-right nationalism and fascism as well as growing anti-Semitism across Europe and the United States. Hitler came to power in Germany in 1933, and he revoked the citizenship of German Jewish people in 1935. In the UK, Oswald Mosley founded the British Union of Fascists in 1932 (though a coalition of anti-fascist groups violently protested it in the 1936 Battle of Cable Street), before it was banned in 1940. In the United States, the activities of the Ku Klux Klan continued to incite racial hatred; and in 1939, a Nazi rally took place in Madison Square Garden with more than 20,000 people in attendance. In the face of aggressive German and Italian expansion campaigns in Europe and beyond, Britain's diplomatic position was to engage in a policy of appeasement while simultaneously rearming for a future conflict. When Germany subsequently invaded Poland, the UK and France declared war on 3 September 1939.

War largely paused the emerging technological developments in entertainment, such as the beginning of television broadcasts (1936 in the UK; 1941 in the United States). International telephone communication was possible – making instant communication possible, if ruinously expensive. The rise of commercial flight shortened travel times; and the first regular commercial transatlantic flights began in June 1939, though these became intermittent during the war period.

Social and political contexts

In January 1936, George V died and Edward VIII (the Prince of Wales) briefly succeeded him. Edward VIII abdicated in December 1936 due to scandal over his choice of bride. His brother, George VI, took power as king of the United Kingdom and emperor of India. In this decade of political extremism and continuing British colonialism, political activism was a vital form of resistance against the assumption of British rule. In the fight for Indian independence, Gandhi's success through the Salt Marsh protests (1930) encouraged other anti-imperial protestors. Haile Selassie was crowned emperor of Ethiopia in 1930; the Rastafari movement developed around this (an Afro-centric religion around Selassie and Marcus Garvey's philosophy for the return of Black people to Africa).

In 1935, Italy, under the fascist rule of Mussolini, attempted to extend its African colonies by invading Ethiopia from Eritrea. Amy Ashwood Garvey and the theatrical performer and musician Sam (Samuel L.) Manning (for details, see Chapter 8) became founding members of the activist Pan-Africanist group the International African Friends of Ethiopia. Other founders included C. L. R. (Cyril Lionel Robert) James (1901–89), a Trinidadian historian, playwright, journalist and activist; George Padmore (1903–59), a Trinidadian journalist and key figure in Pan-Africanism and in shaping postcolonial African states, including Kenya; and Jomo Kenyatta (c.1897–1978), the first president of Kenya.[1] In 1936, Haile Selassie was forced into exile after repeatedly pleading Ethiopia's case to the League of Nations in Geneva to little avail; he lived in the UK until 1941.

In 1931, the fate of the 'Scottsboro Boys' (Haywood Patterson, Clarence Norris, Charlie Weems, Andy and Roy Wright, Olin Montgomery, Ozie Powell, Willie Roberson and Eugene Williams) raised wider consciousness of racial injustice and caused an international outcry. In March 1931, these nine Black teenagers, aged twelve to nineteen, were falsely accused of raping two white women. All but the youngest of the men were convicted and sentenced to death in a rushed trial in Scottsboro. Through the help of the NAACP and the Communist Party USA, the defendants appealed. After several retrials and even after one of the women acknowledged on the stand that the accusation was false, five of the defendants were still found guilty. Black creative practitioners used their platforms to campaign: Ada 'Bricktop' Smith (1894–1984) was involved in a petition to President Herbert Hoover.[2] In the UK, 2,000 people marched in protest on the US embassy.[3] Ada Wright, the mother of Roy and Andy, came to Europe and the UK in 1932 as part of a campaign for justice.

Public awareness of anti-Black racism in the United States was renewed by Nancy Cunard's anthology Negro (1934). Cunard, a white heiress and activist, brought together established and newly written work by contributors such as W. C. Handy as well as the vital essay 'Characteristics of Negro Expression' by Zora Neale Hurston.[4] Gopal notes its anti-racist potential which 'enacted solidarity through cross-racial alliances'.[5] (Though Cunard, specifically, has been criticized for engaging in 'a form of romantic and sexual tourism' in her wider work.)[6]

In 1931, Harold Moody (b. 1882, Jamaica; d. 1947, London) formed the League of Coloured Peoples (LCP) in London.[7] Moody, who had qualified in the UK as a doctor in 1912, practised in Peckham, south London, and led the organization from his home. His Peckham house 'functioned alternately as a social club, housing bureau, employment agency, and political pressure group',[8] and figures like Paul Robeson visited. Moody was sometimes criticized for failing to support more radical protest, though the LCP did become 'steadily more active and effective politically' throughout the 1930s.[9]

Racism operated in everyday life in the UK through the unofficially sanctioned colour bar.[10] Black people were prohibited through official and unofficial means from gaining work or employment or from finding housing (whether those people had British passports or not). Moody and the LCP intervened in 1935, when Cardiff police illegally removed the British passports and therefore citizenship of Black sailors, making them official aliens. After the LCP's intervention, many men had their passports restored. The LCP also produced theatre, including Una Marson's play *At What Price* (1934).[11] Marson (b. 1905, Jamaica; d. 1965, Jamaica) was a feminist activist, poet, playwright and performer, as well as an important broadcaster and journalist. She also worked as secretariat for the Ethiopian society in London (she had been Haile Selassie's secretary in his negotiations with the League of Nations).[12]

Nationalism in Britain led to protectionism over who could work in the UK. The *Manchester Guardian* reported at the time on the Ministry of Labour's policy of 'refusing to extend the permits of numbers of foreign concert and music hall artists in this country'.[13] Marc Matera notes that, in 1932, the Musicians' Union 'imposed a virtual ban on jazz musicians from the United States. [...] In effect the Musicians Union's ban introduced imperial preference to the British jazz scene, if not a complete embargo on American imports'.[14] These decisions affected many performers (white and Black). Ivan H. Browning and the Four Harmony Kings (see Key Figure 7) had been in the UK for seven years and had their work permits revoked, causing international outrage and reports in *Variety*, the *New York Times* and across US Black newspapers.[15] The Ministry of Labour eventually restored the Harmony Kings' permits, perhaps bowing to this international pressure.[16] Browning noted that many of the Black artists in the UK 'are safe and have resident papers making them a British subject'.[17] Despite his experiences, Browning wrote that England was 'the land where there is in the main no racial discrimination' and Black performers could make no less than $75 a week and as much as $125.[18]

On stage

The influence of the Harlem Renaissance continued to influence British musical theatre life. The appreciation of Black culture and artwork during this period was a complex one; though sometimes sincere, white people's fetishism and consumption of Black people and cultures certainly underpinned it. Marian Anderson again performed at the Proms and on the radio, performing spirituals.[19]

Like Anderson, many Black practitioners found ways to work within problematic and white supremacist structures. In 1930, the African American playwright Garland Anderson's *Appearances*, about a white woman falsely accusing a Black man, transferred from Broadway to the West End with its original Black cast in the leads.[20] *Appearances* toured the UK and Anderson gave lectures across the country. The white writer Marc Connelly's play, *Green Pastures*, imagined heaven through Black culture. It opened on Broadway to widespread acclaim in 1930, winning the Pulitzer Prize. The Lord Chamberlain's office refused its licence – it represented God on stage (and perhaps more shockingly, as a Black man).[21]

Noël Coward's *Cavalcade* (1931) at Drury Lane featured two Black musicians in its nightclub scene: Jack London and Leslie Thompson.[22] London (b. 1905, Guyana; d. 1966, London), a Guyanese runner who had won silver and bronze medals at the 1928 Olympics, was the first Black British Olympic medallist. After retiring from athletics, London became a professional pianist; he also played in another West End show *Night Club Queen* (1933). Leslie Thompson (b. 1901, Jamaica; d. 1987, London) was a jazz trumpeter and became a key figure in British swing over the course of the 1930s.

Buddy Bradley choreographed a number of musicals and revues, including Rodgers and Hart's *Ever Green* (1930) with Billy Pierce (see Chapter 7). Ernest Trimmingham's *Eldorado* (1930) was co-written with music by George Ruthland Clapham (part of the Southern Syncopated Orchestra) and Gerald Robinson (presumably white, since his identity is always uncommented upon at the time). *Eldorado* ran for ninety-three performances, and excerpts were broadcast on the radio. Elsewhere, Elisabeth Welch had a leading role in the West End musical *Nymph Errant* (1933), Cole Porter's risqué piece on sexual experimentation.

Some of these productions clearly reiterated racist and anti-Black views, while at the same time being used as showcases by Black performers: the Drury Lane musical *The Sun Never Sets* (1938) starred African American performers Todd Duncan and Adelaide Hall. The musical, presumably a spin on the saying 'the sun never sets on the British Empire', told the problematic story of a white British female pilot getting lost 'somewhere' in Africa and meeting 'natives'. Duncan, who had recently originated the role of Porgy on Broadway in *Porgy and Bess* (1935), released two records from the show: 'River God' (by Cole Porter, but all the music in the show was his) and 'Drums'.[23] Hall was a significant musical figure in the Harlem Renaissance and lived in Britain from 1938 until her death in 1993.

Paul Robeson continued to command respect in British cultural life. In 1931, he starred in the BBC's adaptation of James Weldon Johnson's novel *God's Trombones* (1929). He appeared in a number of important stage roles, including *Othello* (1930); and in trade union and anti-racist stage productions at the Unity Theatre, notably as the title role in the 1935 play *Toussaint L'Ouverture*, written by C. L. R. James. Robeson also starred in *Stevedore* alongside John C. Payne and Robert Adams (for more on Adams, see Chapter 10). In 1932, Ivan Browning wrote to the *Pittsburgh Courier* that, 'while the southern crackers are lynching our people down south, all Europe and England are bowing at the feet of Paul Robeson. He's the toast of old Lon'dun town'.[24] In one 1937 concert at the Royal Albert Hall, Robeson changed the lyrics to 'Ol' Man River' from 'tired o' living, feared o' dying' to 'I must keep on struggling until I'm dyin'.[25] The same year, he helped found the organization that became the Council of African Affairs (CAA) in the United States, partly because of his experiences in London.[26]

White-produced all-Black cast revues like *Blackbirds* continued in London and nationally throughout the decade: *Blackbirds of 1934* featured the jazz trumpeter Valaida Carter and De Lloyd McKaye. *Blackbirds of 1936* featured Lavaida Carter (Valaida's sister, sometimes listed as Snow) with the Nicholas Brothers, Peg-Leg Bates, Will Garland and Fela Sowande, who gave 'a remarkably fine' piano performance.[27] The revue featured both 'Rhapsody in Blue' and 'St James's Infirmary'. Garland counter-produced *Brownbirds*

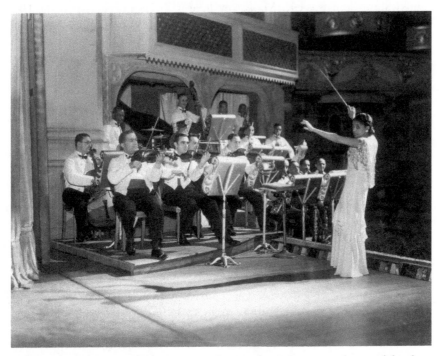

IMAGE 5 *Performer Valaida Snow conducting the orchestra on the set of the show* Blackbirds *at the Coliseum in London, 5 October 1934. (Photo by Sasha/Hulton Archive/Getty Images.)*

shortly after appearing in Leslie's show. Notably, the show's programme featured an essay by James Weldon Johnson on the history of Black folk music.[28] Other Black-produced revues include Clarence Robinson's *Dark Doings* (see Chapter 7) and Sam Manning's *Harlem Nightbirds* (1935–6) (see Chapter 8). The *Cotton Club Revue of 1937* brought exceptional Black musicians and performers to the UK: first to the London Palladium and then to a UK tour.[29]

Many important individual acts were showcased in variety: Black musicians, dancers and performers include those who had performed in revues and others such as the Harmony Kings; Garland Wilson; Evelyn Dove; Adelaide Hall and Fela Sowande;[30] the Dandridge Sisters (Dorothy, Vivian and Etta);[31] Nina Mae McKinney;[32] Ada Brown;[33] and Zaidee Jackson. The important tap dancers Buck and (John) Bubbles performed on stage in variety.[34]

Rudolph Dunbar played extensively in variety theatres in London and across the UK, both with his group the African Polyphonics,[35] as a dance band,[36] and giving clarinet concerts.[37] He also established the Rudolph Dunbar School of Clarinet Playing in London.

This period saw a move away from jazz bands into 'dance' bands with the rise of swing music and the growth of celebrity bandleaders in both the United States and the UK. Many key figures in US music visited the UK during the period: Noble Sissle and his band in 1930–1; Louis Armstrong toured variety and vaudeville theatres across the UK in 1932, 1933 and 1934; Cab Calloway visited in 1934 (see Chapter 9); Fats Waller at the Palladium in August 1938;[38] and Duke Ellington visited the London Palladium in July 1933.[39] Demand for these visits was often fuelled by film releases: Waller had been releasing records in the UK throughout the 1930s and appeared in the movies *The King of Burlesque* (1936) and *Hooray for Love* (1935), before touring the UK again in 1939 where he headed variety theatre line-ups (as opposed to playing individual 'gigs').[40] As swing bandleaders like Ken 'Snakehips' Johnson became celebrities, London's nightlife began to rival that of Paris's.

On radio

The stage was a rich source for broadcasters filling schedules. In what must have been a thrilling broadcast of *Blackbirds* (1934), Valaida Snow conducted De Lloyd McKaye playing Gershwin's *Rhapsody in Blue*.[41] Many Black performers performed on the radio, including Adelaide Hall and Fela Sowande; Leslie Hutchinson; the Kentucky Minstrels, featuring the Black performers Scott and Whaley alongside white variety acts; Ethel Waters; John C. Payne; and even Louis Armstrong, who broadcast live from the theatre in 1934. Ken Johnson presented his own radio program, 'Calypso and Other West Indian Music', from June 1939 (see Chapter 9).

On television

Early television extensively featured the work of Black composers and performers during its brief iteration before the Second World War switch-off. Stephen Bourne explains: 'Pre-war television showcased some of the greatest black personalities then working in Britain.'[42] The first full evening of television broadcasts featured tap dancing stars Buck and Bubbles. Shows like *Dark Sophistication* featured Fela Sowande and Adelaide Hall. Ken 'Snakehips' Johnson broadcast several 'jam sessions'. The radio program *Kentucky Minstrels* also broadcast on TV and featured a number of important Black performers: Scott and Whaley, Ike Hatch and Adelaide Hall.

On film

Paul Robeson starred in a number of films, including the screen adaptation of *Show Boat* (1936); others with music include *The Song of Freedom* (1936) and *Big Fella* (1938) alongside Elisabeth Welch. These were widely distributed across the UK. *Way Down South* (1939), written by African Americans Clarence Muse and Langston Hughes, was released in the UK. *Kentucky Minstrels* (1934) starred Scott and Whaley alongside Nina Mae McKinney.

7

Clarence 'Buddy' Bradley and Clarence Robinson

Boxing Day, 1942. Britain was three years into the Second World War and glamour was pretty thin on the ground. But one newspaper story tried to provide some to its weary readers in its coverage of the glitzy preparations for the London Coliseum's traditional pantomime, *Mother Goose*. The story featured an image that strikes to the heart of how Black musical theatre practitioners have been minimized in histories of musical theatre. The picture shows the choreographer Buddy Bradley in rehearsal with the young white performer Patricia Burke. Burke is dancing and smiling into a mirror – we see her body from behind, and from the reflection facing up, she takes up the majority of the frame. Bradley can only be seen in the mirror as a reflection: Bradley is showing Burke the perfected version of the move that she has clearly not quite yet mastered, given her hand positioning.[1] This black and white image tells us so much about Bradley's role in British musical theatre and the way white musical theatre edged Bradley out of the picture, leaving him rendered barely visible. In this chapter, we consider the role of two choreographers in Britain in the 1930s: Clarence 'Buddy' Bradley and Clarence Robinson. It addresses how this process has made them less visible – even invisible – in histories of the form. It reveals how Black dance practices in Harlem New York shaped dance on British stages and establishes that this was not a one-way process.

Histories of British musicals have rarely included Bradley's work, as a choreographer or as a teacher, a particularly striking omission given his work in British musical theatre for almost four decades. In the UK, Bradley worked as a choreographer for theatre and films, as an instructor, a stage and film performer, and a stage director (for an overview, see Key Figure 11).

Brenda Dixon Gottschild notes that Bradley and other Black choreographers 'were invisible men in the white world (and this was a male-dominated profession). They were not credited for their work but were looked upon as dispensable assistants to the white dance director'.[2] Bradley's extensive contribution has been undervalued – perhaps because of the historical difficulties in tracing his extensive career in the United States and in the UK. In 1998, Dixon Gottschild notes that 'little is recorded of his American work', a problem shared by other Black choreographers such as 'Leonard Harper, Clarence Robinson and Addison Carey'.[3]

However, the advent of digitized and searchable newspapers has made it possible to find fuller details of his rich career. In this chapter, we present a more complete picture of both Bradley's US and UK work than has previously been possible, in order to understand how Bradley influenced and shaped British dance practice. Hill has provided the only in-depth assessment of Bradley's work in London; she notes that the fact he 'ended up staying for 38 years is significant because through him, American vernacular dance was literally transplanted onto the English musical stage'.[4] She argues the dance itself was not white-washed, and by following the names of the musical dance sequences he worked with, including 'Black Magic' and 'A Window in Harlem', she suggests his work demonstrates 'not only the presence but celebration of African-American music and dance traditions in the English musical revue'.[5] Brian Seibert concurs that 'Bradley exercised an influence on British theatrical dancing that was significant and prolonged'.[6]

IMAGE 6 *Buddy Bradley in the musical* Evergreen, *directed by Victor Saville for Gaumont. (Photo by Hulton Archive/Getty Images.)*

Clarence 'Buddy' Bradley (alt. Clarence Bradley Epps) (b. 1905 Epps, Alabama;[7] d. 1972, New York City) was born to Georgia Epps (b. 1883), a restaurant cook, and Robert Epps (b. 1880). He had three siblings: Ernestine, Robert and Aurelius. Bradley was a choreographer, teacher, performer and later stage director. He 'popularized black tap and jazz dancing in the American and English theater'.[8] The legacy of his students is perhaps best remembered through his early mentorship of Henry LeTang,[9] who in turn mentored Gregory Hines, who in turn mentored Savion Glover.

Bradley taught thousands of performers and created a stylistic language of dance in musical theatre. He developed jazz tap and jazz ballet in the UK, developed jazz ballet and was partly responsible (along with Frankie Manning in 1933) for the introduction of the lindyhop to Britain.[10] He trained many key white dancers in London and in New York, including Adele and Fred Astaire, Eleanor Powell and Jessie Matthews. He worked with an extraordinary range of choreographers who had a profound influence on film and stage musicals, including Busby Berkeley, George Balanchine and Agnes de Mille.

As well as his long-running association with Frederick Ashton (who went on to form the Royal Ballet), Bradley worked alongside many key figures in ballet history, such as Anton Dolin, (Eva) Brigitta Hartwig and Andrée Howard. With Ashton, he co-choreographed the jazz ballet *Follow the Sun* (1936). At the long-since relaunched Ciro's nightclub, he choreographed a ballet piece for two members of the Marie Rambert company, Anton Dolin and Brigitta Hartwig, in 'Slow Water Blues'.[11]

In the United States, he was based at Billy Pierce's studios. Together with Pierce, he was a consultant on *Greenwich Follies of 1926* and *1929*, as well as *Show Boat* (1927). As Bradley's popularity grew, he caught the attention of producer Charles B. Cochran, who hired him and Pierce to choreograph Rodgers and Hart's *Ever Green* (1930). He became Cochran's dance director and remained in the UK. There, Bradley choreographed numerous shows, including *Cochran's Revue of 1931* (1931), Noël Coward's *Words and Music* (1932) and Jerome Kern's *The Cat and the Fiddle* (1932). He choreographed two Porter musicals, *Fifty Million Frenchmen* (1931) and *Anything Goes* (1935).[12] Bradley worked with almost all of the major white British composers throughout his career, including Arthur Schwartz (*Nice Goings On*, 1933), Sandy Wilson (*Divorce Me Darling*, 1964), Noel Gay (*Lights Up*)[13] and Vivian Ellis (*It's Foolish But It's Fun*, 1943).

Bradley's career in the UK encompasses movie musicals, popular revues, more recognizable musicals and variety theatre. He was also an important teacher. Bradley quickly set up studios in London, and became closely associated with the career of Jessie Matthews, choreographing many early film musicals, including the adaptation of *Evergreen* (1934), *Brewster's Millions* (1935) and *Gangway* (1937). He also choreographed for early TV, including the pre-wartime show *Burnt Sepia*. His shows often featured Black performers, including Josey Shields and Eddy Williams,[14] as well as Jules Bledsloe.[15]Bradley choreographed dances for the revue *All the Best* (1938) in Blackpool, produced by the white producer Jack Hylton, which starred Elisabeth Welch. He arranged dances for the 1941 play *Room V*, written by white writer Peter Wendy but which featured Ernest Trimmingham.[16] He also taught Ken 'Snakehips' Johnson how to dance (see Chapter 9).

Bradley also danced himself: in a short-form version of Cochran's 1931 revue at the London Palladium;[17] in the out-of-town previews for Cole Porter's *Fifty Million Frenchmen* (1931);[18] and in the 1943 Jack Buchanan show *It's Time to Dance* (Manchester Palace).[19] In the latter, Bradley performed as a dance instructor in the show-within-a-show musical.[20] The musical actually staged Buddy Bradley's School of Dancing.[21] One Black US newspaper wrote Bradley had been 'resurrected from his teaching chores and given the role of co-star along with Buchanan'.[22]

Bradley is remembered for his work with tap, in drawing on elements from contemporaneous street dance and for developing easier versions for white dancers to perform, but he also worked with many other dance forms. He had a significant influence on dance aesthetics in nightclubs and nightlife in London during the 1930s and 1940s. He choreographed and ran numerous acts like Buddy Bradley's Eight Rhythm Girls; Buddy Bradley's Cochran Girls at the Kit Cat Restaurant (1932), one of the Prince of Wales's many haunts;[23] Buddy Bradley's Young Ladies;[24] and Buddy Bradley Rhythm Girls, at venues including the Mayfair Hotel.

Bradley continued to choreograph into the 1950s and 1960s. He assistant produced and choreographed the 1949 revue *Sauce Tatare* at the Cambridge in London, which starred Muriel Smith, the Black US singer and actor;[25] the revue used a Calypso stage band.[26] He choreographed Cecil Landeau's 1950 revue *Sauce Piquante*, which starred Audrey Hepburn.[27] He also had a troupe of dancers who appeared in variety and television in the 1950s, when he choreographed specialist shows around Black performers such as *Black Magic* starring Hilda Simms and Adelaide Hall (1950), or for variety style shows like *Shop Window* (late 1952 to 1953). His troupe continued on television well into the 1960s; he also became a director and produced nostalgia-themed shows like *Blackbirds of 1964*.[28] He returned to the United States in the late 1960s. He was interviewed by Marshall and Jean Stearns for their collection on the history of jazz dance. Dance instructors as far as Australia advertised their skills in the Buddy Bradley method.[29]

Bradley died in 1972. The only surviving known footage of him dancing is a short clip in *Evergreen*; during a Charleston sequence Bradley dances outside the stage door to the delight and astonishment of the kids outside. So little remains of such an extraordinary figure, something that can be explained by a story published in February 1927, back in New York: Marie Saxon – a white dancer – had agreed to perform some routines with her instructor, Bradley, on the radio. Her show overran, and since Buddy was on time, he performed two dances of his own before he continued performing as Miss Saxon – doing a full five routines. He was finishing when she 'put in an appearance, in time to tell the announcer and the listeners-in how much she enjoyed dancing for the radio'.[30]

KEY FIGURE 11 *Clarence 'Buddy' Bradley, a short biography.*

Alongside Bradley, this chapter address a second choreographer, Clarence Robinson, who was best known for his association with the Cotton Club. Robinson's full career in the UK has gone almost entirely unremembered (it was admittedly much shorter than Bradley's). Dixon Gottschild notes both Robinson's and Bradley's work for London revues but suggests that Bradley remained to get the credit he was due and could not receive on Broadway:

He and his colleagues were responsible for taking the vernacular African American dance styles, as well as the rhythmically complex black tap forms, and transforming them into theatrical genres that could be performed by whites.[31]

Though Robinson was only in London for a year, he was running the Leicester Square Theatre for much of this period. Uncovering his work points to a close association with Harlem theatre, the transatlantic nature of dance in the UK and the professional reach of Black practitioners during this time. Even though at the time Robinson was widely credited for his work at the theatre, and that Robinson discussed his own transatlantic practices, the full extent of his contribution in the UK has not entered into histories of the musical.

Buddy Bradley in New York

Bradley worked closely with Charles B. Cochran, the celebrated white theatre producer and impresario, throughout the 1930s. Cochran hired Bradley and his business partner Billy Pierce to come to London in 1930 to choreograph the Rodgers and Hart musical *Ever Green*. Bradley later recalled Cochran insisted he was hired for a new iteration of Lew Leslie's *Blackbirds* because Cochran felt the dance in the show had become 'just a rehash'.[32] Cochran must have been aware of Bradley's work in the late 1920s; and it is quite possible Bradley had been influencing British dance for some time already. As early as January 1930, Ivan H. Browning revealed Bradley's impact on British musical theatre, even from New York, noting that Black dances were making up all the dancing in the three 'all-British musical comedies' he visited, explaining:

> There are at least three dancing producers that go to New York regularly to visit all the Harlem cabarets, and then get Billy Pierce and Buddy Bradley to teach them all that they can't really grasp by observation.[33]

The exact nature and balance of Billy Pierce and Buddy Bradley's working relationship is at times unclear. Pierce seems to have been the director of the school for which Bradley worked, though Pierce sometimes receives choreography credits. The *New York Age* listed Pierce as the dance director in a report of his return back to the United States in November 1930 after the British success of *Ever Green*.[34] Elsewhere, Pierce was described as an agent in the 'musical comedy and floor show field'. In 1924, he is noted for supplying casts for Paris and Berlin revues;[35] by 1925, he is supplying performers for films.[36]

Marshall and Jean Sterns note: 'Pierce was not a dancer himself [but had hired Black dancers before Bradley] to coach white clients without much success.'[37] In the mid-1920s, business changed as Bradley became increasingly well known in the industry. Sterns and Sterns suggest that a producer even asked Bradley to re-choreograph the *Greenwich Village Follies of 1928*, although the name on the program would remain Busby Berkeley.[38] Pierce ended up hiring five instructors, selling routines for $250 and making 'over a thousand dollars a week'.[39] The 'Billy Pierce Studios' were established by the mid-1920s, and by 1927 they were taking up 4,500 square feet of floor space in the Navex Building, West 46th Street, at the heart of New York's theatre district.[40] While Pierce was clearly in charge of the finances in New York, Bradley did well. In 1928, the *Tattler*, an African American newspaper, reported with obvious glee that Bradley had taken delivery of his new La Salle Roadster, 'with a white chauffeur'.[41]

Constance Valis Hill, who has worked to retrieve much of Bradley's career, notes that Bradley's name 'never appeared on any program: it was the custom that as long as the "dance director" who grouped scenes and coached the stars got his pay, there was no need for any credit.'[42] Though Bradley clearly did not receive the credit he deserved, there is also a practical issue here. Sterns and Sterns conducted interviews with Bradley in the 1960s – some of the details are understandably slightly out in exact dates, to be expected given the many years that had passed in the interim. Perhaps these slips have obscured that, while Bradley may have been unknown to the white theatregoing public, his career received extensive news coverage in both African American and theatrical newspapers. In March 1926 (not 1928, as Bradley recalled), *Variety* noted Bradley and Pierce's contribution to *The Greenwich Village Follies*, and their reworking of Irene Delroy's ensemble numbers, and even remarks their success meant that the pair would 'be pretty busy hereafter'.[43] In June 1926, *Variety* also reported that Pierce and Bradley would be staging the dance numbers for Jed Harris's new musical *Bright Lights* and that they would be 'the first [Black] stagers to do numbers for Broadway musicals (white)'.[44] By December 1926, *Variety* reported that Bradley was teaching Elizabeth Hines, who had been cast in *Show Boat* as Magnolia, 'some [Black] dance routines'.[45] Bradley's contribution has not been considered in existing scholarly approaches to *Show Boat*; he is absent in Todd Decker's biography of the musical. In 1927, *Variety* reported on the pair's continuing business success, their new $2,100 floor and their model of charging reasonable prices 'to the profession' and somewhat higher prices to society figures: 'Both Bill and Buddy [say] they know they are from society because they can pay more.'[46] By January 1927, the *Tattler* was running advertisements for Bradley, who was looking for '16 peppy brown skin girls' for a Ziegfeld Production guaranteeing applicants 'long Broadway run assured'. Since the advertisement suggests free dance instructions by Bradley himself, someone was funding their training – presumably Ziegfeld.[47]

In November 1928, *Variety* reported that Pierce and Bradley were staging the dances for Lew Fields' revival of *The High Cost of Living*: 'a clause in the agreement provides that Buddy and Billy shall have credit.'[48] The production became *Hello Daddy*. Despite any initial promises, Bradley received no attribution in the program, with credit going to Busby Berkeley. Though one of Berkeley's biographers suggests Bradley 'shared dancing credits' with Berkeley, there was no coverage in contemporary news coverage, which, as we have seen, was clearly keen to note this kind of activity.[49] Shelley Berg notes that, despite the contemporary masking of Bradley's full contribution, 'His ideas permeated Harlem clubs as well as black and white Broadway and helped shape popular theatrical dance as we know it today.'[50] In July 1930, *Variety* reported that 'Cochran wants [Pierce and Bradley] and [is] likely getting them'.[51]

Bradley in London: Unpicking his influence

Bradley began his career in the UK working as a co-choreographer with his professional partner Billy Pierce on the Cochran-produced Rodgers and Hart musical, *Ever Green* in 1930. Though there are slightly conflicting accounts of their arrival in the UK, Stephen Bourne suggests 'it was Fred Astaire who suggested to Jessie Matthews that she persuade C. B. Cochran to invite Bradley to London to stage the dances'.[52] Pierce publicized his experience via *Variety*, writing:

Our (meaning Buddy Bradley, tap instructor) stay has been pleasant here in Glasgow. It is a rainy cold place, but the natives are nice to us. [...] They don't see many [Black people] here and when you go by the barber shops they all dash out to give you the once over.[53]

After the success of *Ever Green*, Bradley and Pierce were hired again for *Cochran's 1931 revue* (London Pavilion). Cochran announced in January that year's revue would make a feature of dancing because he was employing the two men Pierce and Bradley.[54] Cochran also employed George Balanchine to choreograph the revue's ballet. After the show, Pierce returned to New York; 'commissioned by Cochran to pick up a fast pair of [Black] hoofers for the new revue', he sent Joey Shields and Eddie (Pee Wee) Williams to star in the show.[55] Bradley was held in high esteem. On one occasion in July 1932, Bradley was instructed to go to Noël Coward's studio late at night, with Cochran, to be given a unique premiere by the composer himself of Coward's new work *Words and Music*.[56]

By 1932, Bradley established his own school in London. He clearly attempted to turn the school into the Pierce model. One legal notice placed in the *Era* announced that Clarence Bradley Epps and Coleman Goodman were establishing a 'dancing school and employment agency for Theatrical, Variety, and Film Artists Agency'[57] – but this does not seem to work, as there is currently no more mention of it. Instead, he focused on the school, which clearly was financially successful. In 1937, an interview with Bradley noted that individual dances could be choreographed from upwards of 25 guineas (around £4,470 in today's money).[58] One account in the *Capital Plaindealer* reported that Bradley had spent $8,000 renovating his Somerset Mews apartment that same year (around $697,000 in today's money).[59]

Bradley's influence on British theatre music is significant, both as a disseminator of Black music and because of his choreographic processes. Spike Hughes, the white jazz bandleader, then a musician, played double bass in the pit of this show alongside Leslie Thompson, the Trinidadian trombonist (he also orchestrated some of the music). Hughes recalled the importance of his early work with them both, but particularly Bradley. He recalled Bradley 'provided what proved to be the most important blueprint in our history: a handful of records by Duke Ellington which had not been issued in Britain'.[60] He noted that his friendship with Bradley led 'to innumerable small jobs of orchestration within the Cochran organisation, including some for *Ever Green*'.[61] Hughes composed *High Yellow* (1933), the ballet that Bradley co-choreographed with Frederick Ashton.

Bradley's musicality shaped the sound of the orchestras, as Leslie Thompson later recalled. Thompson suggested that after Cochran had hired Bradley for his revue of 1931 the choreographer visited other productions to get a sense of the theatre in London:

[Bradley] asked [Cochran] what are you doing about music, and Cochran said 'oh well we'll have the usual pit band', you know, and he said, 'like the ones I've been hearing all over town?' 'Yes that's right', so he said, 'those won't do for our Hollywood you know. And I would like a Hollywood orchestra.' [...] A good symphonic dance orchestra that could play everything.[62]

Percival Mackey was hired to form the orchestra through Elsie April, Cochran's music director, which included Thompson. That Bradley's influence establishes an orchestra sound that would plausibly support the onstage choreography is crucial. Bradley's relationship with Spike Hughes is also significant, since Hughes was an important orchestra conductor and bandleader and, to some extent, a white advocate for Black performers through his friendship and activism (for Hughes' connection to the decision to allow Cab Calloway to perform in the UK in 1934, see Chapter 9).

In the Stearns recording of the history of jazz dance, Bradley explained that his process relied on listening to music and then 'translating the accents of improvising jazz soloists into dance patterns that were new to Broadway'.[63] In this way, he used music to create dance routines and movements: 'I had to get a picture in my mind of how a dance should look, and those accents always gave me new ideas.'[64] Catherine Tackley notes that Bradley's approach, 'in which close listening is the basis of the dancing experience, exposes the inextricable links between listening to and dancing to jazz'.[65] Such close listening clearly benefited the musicians: Jill Flanders Crosby and Michèle Moss note that '[jazz] musicians were creatively influenced by the dancers' movements and rhythms'.[66]

Bradley's influence on ballet in the UK is somewhat less noted. Bradley co-instigated the first jazz ballet in the UK, *High Yellow* (1933), in collaboration with Frederick Ashton. Hill notes that their collaboration began with their work on Jerome Kern's *The Cat and the Fiddle* in 1932:

a musical romance between an American jazz composer (played by Peggy Wood) and a Rumanian opera composer. Their union bears fruit when he composes a new operetta blending both styles: what a perfect analogy for Bradley, the show's upbeat jazz choreographer, and Ashton, who was called in to stage a poignant song in the first act finale.[67]

Bradley and Ashton collaborated and the show was produced by the Carmago Society, a society organized to support the development of British ballet. The ballet dancer Alicia Markova later recalled that she had six weeks of private lessons with Ashton and Bradley: 'I used to stay over in the evening, under Sir Fred's direction, to learn how to dance [...] all the snake hips, the rhythms, everything, which I did. Then eventually [Bradley and Ashton] got together and did a ballet called *High Yellow*.'[68] Their collaboration was not an overwhelming critical success: the critic for one right-wing news periodical, *Truth*, described the ballet's music, composed by Spike Hughes, as 'monotonous and boring, and the choreography by Buddy Bradley and Frederick Ashton seems to have very little of the merits of Frederick Ashton in it'. The critic added, dismissively, 'I know nothing of "Buddy's" other choreographic performances'.[69]

Bradley made further contributions to ballet and worked again with Ashton. In November 1932, Bradley choreographed for a performance of a lost Jerome Kern composition 'Desperate Blues' with the Marie Rambert company at the Ballet Club's Mercury Theatre in London.[70] The evening also featured Ashton's choreography. Together the pair choreographed the *After Dark* revue in 1933, though credits carefully differentiated the work of the two: 'ballets arranged by Frederick Ashton, dances and ensembles by Buddy Bradley.'[71] They worked on Cochran's 1936 revue together, *Follow the Sun*, which Cochran had promised would 'be a great dancing show'[72] – this was jointly credited to Bradley and Ashton (in that order) and featured Jeni Le Gon. Bradley and Ashton worked together again in 1937, in the revue/musical *Floodlights*, which previewed at Blackpool's Opera House before coming into London.[73] That musical paired them jointly; one critic noted: 'the dance arrangements and ballets by Buddy Bradley and Frederick Ashton must also be mentioned' (in that order).[74] Benjamin Frankel composed music for that piece. Frankel and Bradley had a continuing professional relationship in a radio series 'Swing Song', which Bradley performed in (tap being one of the few dance mediums that might work on the radio). One 1939 interview explained that Frankel and Bradley 'have been writing ballets together, and, in the words of the conductor, this music is composed "note by step"'.[75] Dancers had other links to the Black community in London. Anton Dolin, for example, attended parties with prominent members of the Black community in the late 1920s (including John C. Payne's party for opera singer Marian Anderson in 1928).[76]

Bradley maintained professional connections in the jazz world. He attended the International Dance Congress of Dancing Masters in New York City in 1934: 'Dalcroze of Paris will present his eurarythmics [*sic*]; Buddy Bradley of London will show his new ballroom tap dances and Carlos of New York city will demonstrate the new tap rhythms.'[77] Bradley choreographed into the 1940s, working with many key performers, including Jack Hulbert, Wendy Toye and Beatrice Appleyard, who were at the beginning of their careers. They all went on to be major choreographers themselves in British musical theatre.

Clarence Robinson's work in London: Unexplored performances

Another of Bradley's many influences was on the Nicholas Brothers (Fayard and Harold), two of the greatest tap dancers of all time. Hill notes that the brothers were influenced by Bradley and George Balanchine: 'both these choreographers reinforced a more vertical and downward drive of rhythm, combined with an inventiveness in playing the body as a percussive instrument.'[78] The Nicholas Brothers also worked closely with another important Black choreographer, whose time in London has not been fully examined until now: Clarence Robinson. The first Black choreographer at Harlem's Cotton Club, Robinson began his career as a dancer and choreographer in nightclubs but little has been previously known about his work in the UK. His working practices reveal a continuing relationship between Harlem and British regional theatre, via London's West End. Robinson's work in Britain clearly developed his practice at the Apollo Theatre in Harlem. Before his first show in London in July 1933, Robinson had worked extensively in US theatre, with extensive professional connections to some of the most important musicians of the decade. As a dancer, he had toured white vaudeville circuits with Fats Waller in the 1920s. On Broadway, Robinson performed in the musicals *Lucky Sambo* (1925) and the *Shuffle Along* (1921) sequel, *Keep Shufflin'* (1928), which he also choreographed. Robinson toured in one of the white jazz producer Irving Mills' stage tours of *Harlem Scandals* (1931) as a dancer on the East Coast of the United States. Mills was a manager and a key figure in the transatlantic careers of many Black jazz musicians, including Duke Ellington. Robinson had managed the Standard Theatre in Philadelphia, where Duke Ellington's band had played in the early 1930s.[79]

Robinson remains best remembered for his association with the Cotton Club as its resident dance director from the autumn 1929 revue onwards.[80] Robinson auditioned Lena Horne (aged only sixteen) for the Cotton Club and was at the heart of Harlem's nightclub scene throughout the 1930s.[81] Robinson choreographed the Cotton Club's show performed around Duke Ellington's *Black Berries of 1930*.[82] The Cotton Club was racially segregated: while the performers and musicians were Black, its patrons were white; and as its name suggests, it was plantation themed. Though Robinson is often known only for his association with the club, he only worked there for a couple of years before he opened his venue, Clarence Robinson's Grill in December 1930, which had an interracial clientele and quickly became a great success.[83] Its regulars included white celebrities such as Broadway stars like Marilyn Miller and Mary Lewis, a curator at the Metropolitan (Alan Priest), Carl Van Vechten and Bessye Bearden (a journalist and activist). It also listed many Black celebrities such as A'Lelia Walker (the millionaire C. J. Walker's daughter), the actor Embry Bonner, Bill Robinson (the great tap star) and the singer Adelaide Hall. In February 1931, the club shut down as part of a police crackdown on clubs apparently leading to, or accepting, homosexuality.[84] Despite this, Clarence Robinson was clearly doing well financially; in October 1931, the *Afro-American* reported that he was too busy to get to drive his new $5,000 Cadillac.[85]

In February 1933, Clarence Robinson was performing in a revival tour of *Shuffle Along*, with many of the original cast, including Sissle and Blake.[86]

He then directed and choreographed the international *Cotton Club Revue of 1933*, a revue-style show which took him to Europe, first to Paris and then to London. In July 1933, his revue *Dark Doings* opened at the Leicester Square Theatre with stars including Alma Smith (one of John C. Payne's singers), Elisabeth Welch, Jubilee Singers, and Brookins and Van.[87] It began a UK tour in August. Robinson's work history was a particular attraction. The production was advertised as 'a worthy successor to *Blackbirds* [...] produced in revue form by Clarence Robinson, the producer of the famous New York Cotton Club shows, and [...] stars from those exotic revellings with be seen here'.[88] The *Era* consistently noted his background in their coverage of the show, noting it was the 'producer from the Cotton Club in New York to whom the *Dark Doings* triumph is very largely due. Lately Mr Robinson has been responsible on Broadway for the production of *Kid Boots* for Eddie Cantor, the *New Yorkers* the 1933 edition of Earl Carroll's *Vanities*, and the dances in the 1933 edition of the Ziegfeld Follies'.[89]

Robinson was not just choreographing in the UK; he managed a major London variety house, the Leicester Square Theatre, for around a year from 1933 to 1934, while also returning to manage the choreography at the Apollo Theatre in Harlem. During this period, Robinson was directly involved in trying out and importing choreography, performance styles and even revues from the UK to the United States. Though the arrangement was fairly brief, Robinson was operating as producer, director, choreographer and talent manager and travelled back and forwards across the Atlantic at least four times. Leicester Square Theatre was a 2,000-seat variety and cinema house in the centre of London, which was demolished in 2015 after many years as a cinema. There were some doubts over Robinson's suitability, but the *Era*'s variety columnist noted that he had settled down to the task, despite doubts that his first presentations were too 'sophisticated [...] for the tastes of a London Variety audience':

> Clarence's presentations last week proved that he has a real versatility of skill and imagination, and those who like colour and romance must have been well satisfied with his *Indian's Paradise*.[90]

Robinson also choreographed several numbers for the Palladium's variety line-up, clearly drawing on jazz themes. Titles include 'Jazz a la Carte' and 'Kiss in the Moonlight'.[91] He returned to *Dark Doings*, relaunching it at Leicester Square, still with some of the original cast including John C. Payne's 12 Jubilee Singers and Brookins and Van,[92] but with the addition of May Downs (reported as singing 'Stormy Weather').[93]

Robinson produced many revues that started at Leicester Square before touring the UK in 1933: in August, *Tennis in Rhythm*; in September, *A Night in Spain*;[94] in October, *The March of Time*;[95] and in November, *Flashing Ahead* with 'Clarence Robinson's Leicester Square Young Ladies'.[96] Astonishingly, there then starts to be direct relationships between his work in British and US theatres. In January 1934, Robinson returned to Harlem, where he produced the revue that reopened the Apollo Theatre, with Benny Carter's orchestra.[97] In February, the *New York Amsterdam News* reported that his revues were much better because 'Clarence Robbins [was] utilizing ideas gained on his trip to Europe'.[98] Back in the UK, in late February 1934, *Mixed Bathing* (produced by Cyril Lawrence) opened, which Robinson had choreographed and directed;[99] and in August 1934, *Your Favourite Players*. He utilized revues from London for Harlem theatres. In April 1934, he brought *A Night in Spain* to the Apollo Theatre. The *New York Amsterdam News* reported that it was 'Robinson's latest creation' and that the 'ballet numbers [were] staged and devised by Impresario Robinson'.[100] He returned to the UK in July 1934 for a few weeks, presumably to choreograph *Your Favourite Players*, which then toured British theatres (also produced by Cyril Lawrence).[101] In September 1934, a Black newspaper reported Robinson had 'a white assistant'.[102] One has to imagine this was as significant, if not more so, than Bradley's white chauffeur.

Robinson next returned to the UK in July 1937 with the *Cotton Club Revue of 1937*, which brought exceptional Black musicians and performers to the UK: first to the London Palladium and then for a UK tour.[103] The show starred Alberta Hunter; Teddy Hill's band 'Whyte's Hopping Maniacs', which included Frankie Manning – one of the founders of the Lindy Hop (Hill later managed Minton's jazz club in New York); Bill Bailey, the tap dancer; and the Nicholas Brothers. One review reveals the racialized responses to the revue and specifically its music. It was entitled 'One D—n [*sic*] noise after another', and it noted 'I do not venture to emphasise the fact that devotion to rhythm, noise, slickness and speed in an entertainment, to the exclusion of every other quality, is barbaric – and a little barbarism goes a long way'.[104] Despite the racist responses in some newspapers, the show was an opportunity to see an astonishing array of performers, and other reviewers applauded it. The Nicholas Brothers were part of the production before going into British variety. The *Era*'s reviewer writes: 'I will willingly concede them the superlative, for their dancing is the most virile, peppy, rapid and altogether enjoyable thing I have seen. And the Cab Calloway songs, which the smaller of the duo gives, are rendered with tremendous skill and effect.'[105]

In 1943, Robinson choreographed *Stormy Weather* (see 'The 1940s in context'). In 1948, there is an intriguing mention of a further London plan in Robinson's career. Adelaide Hall, who had an established British performing career, was said to be working with him as the potential producer for her show: 'The book has been written by an English woman whose reputation is high in the literary world. Spencer Williams has written the music.'[106] Sadly no further reference to this plan can be found – or the English woman. Spencer Williams, a Black jazz musician and composer (of standards like 'Basin Street Blues'), had been part of the Paris scene in the 1920s with Louis Douglas's troupe 'Black People'.[107] By 1947, Williams was giving jazz concerts in the UK: one report of a Birmingham concert noted he would be talking about his early life and the birth of jazz as well as playing the piano.[108] Though the musical never happened, it demonstrates the transatlantic performance practice of Robinson and points to the close relationship between Black performance in Harlem and the UK.

Clarence Robinson was a significant figure in the transfer of Harlem theatre into the UK, through his work as a producer and choreographer. That this work has been entirely overlooked until now should suggest that this is by far not the last Black transatlantic practice to be found: there is still far more work to be done. Bradley's work in the UK was substantial, which has made documenting and revealing it somewhat easier. Clearly, any future consideration of British musical theatre's choreography, and of musical theatre choreography in general, must address his contribution not only to tap but also to ballet. His collaboration with Noël Coward challenges ideas that Black practice was in any way a fringe event in British musical theatre. In ballet, his work for the Marie Rambert company raises intriguing questions and the hope that there is still more to be discovered in documenting his creative practice. He played a significant influence in introducing jazz music, through his demands for a better orchestra, and his ongoing work with Spike Hughes. Bradley may have been to the side of the mirror in the photo that we noted at the start of this chapter, but his influence impacted everything in the frame.

PART THREE

Anti-racism and anti-imperialism in London

8

Sam Manning, Amy Ashwood Garvey and 1930s anti-colonialism

This chapter explores the theatrical work of Sam (Samuel Lawrence) Manning (b. c. 1896/7,[1] Port of Spain, Trinidad; d. 1960, Kumasi, Ghana) and the presence of his partner and activist Amy Ashwood Garvey (b. 1897, Port Antonio, Jamaica; d. 1969, Kingston, Jamaica) in the UK. Ashwood Garvey was often written about in contemporary newspapers as Mrs Marcus Garvey. (She is not to be confused with Amy Jacques Garvey, his second wife.) This chapter reveals the ways in which Harlem theatre practices influenced British theatre, and it explores Manning's close connection to anti-colonial and anti-racist campaigning. His production of *Harlem Nightbirds* in the UK brought together a number of performers from across the African diaspora. Manning, from Trinidad, was a British subject, he was able to navigate international travel and avoid visa restrictions (see 'The 1930s in context'). In his work, Sam Manning brought together political activism with theatrical performance in enacting resistant practices.

Wanted [...] Performers All Lines for a Super [...] Revue. Producing end of September. Those in London apply personally to Mr Sam Manning, Showman's Club, 28 Charing Cross Road, WC2 3p.m. to-day.
The Stage, September 6, 1934[2]

Histories of the musical have neglected Sam Manning's contribution to musical theatre, whether it was in Harlem, in New York or in the UK. Manning was a musician, composer and writer, performer, director and producer, as well as an activist for Black rights. His influence on the dissemination of Calypso music is clear. Donald Hill notes he 'played an instrumental role in taking calypso to England'.[3] John Cowley, who has carefully addressed Manning's contribution to the early recording of Calypso music in New York in the 1920s, notes his:

> virtually unique role in mediating traditionally based black vocal music from the Caribbean, mixed with American jazz, to audiences in the English-speaking West Indies, North America and later Britain paved the way for future crossover performances that began to emerge during the 1930s.[4]

Lara Putnam notes the complexity of Manning's professional identities in assessing his career, noting he 'recorded in both Okeh's "Race" [i.e., African American] and "West Indian" series in the mid-1920s and as a performer, investor and manager decisively shaped the international presence of Trinidad's calypso complex'.[5]

This chapter traces the presence of such an important musical figure and political activist in British musical theatre, particularly in his revue show *The Harlem Nightbirds*. Marc Matera notes Ashwood Garvey's and Manning's importance to people of African descent in London, noting that, through their transnationalism, 'The imperial metropolis became an important node of the circuits travelled by black musicians and black expressive cultures, facilitating musical exchange, the creation of innovative hybrid forms, and expansive visions of the African world'.[6]*Nightbirds* toured across the UK and brought together Manning's influence as well as the presence of Eric Walrond as publicity officer.

Ashwood Garvey and Manning:
Activists and theatre makers

Manning had a decade-long personal and professional partnership with Amy Ashwood Garvey. Together, as activists and campaigners, their careers intertwined with theatre, journalism and Black intellectual life in New York, across the Caribbean and in the UK. Ashwood Garvey and Manning never married but they travelled the world and lived together. They became key figures in campaigns for anti-colonialism, Pan-Africanism and anti-racism and a central part of many Black people's lives, experience and survival in London. They set up the Florence Mills Social Parlour and International Afro-Restaurant below their flat at 62 New Oxford Street, London. Minkah Makalani notes that 'For many black activists and local residents, [these institutions] provided a welcome respite from a damp, strange country'.[7] It was a crucial centre. There, Ashwood Garvey and Manning remained friends with important Black activists and writers who frequented the club, such as Trinidadians C. L. R. James and George Padmore; Kwame Nkrumah, who would become the first president of Ghana; and Jomo Kenyatta, the Kenyan activist who would go on to be the first president of Kenya. The club was 'a famous Pan-Africanist meeting place'.[8] Marc Matera notes C. L. R. James' recollection that the place was 'very important to me, because from those early days to this day, I find English food uneatable'.[9] It provided practical and intellectual sustenance to the Black diasporic community in Britain.

Amy Ashwood was born in Jamaica and grew up in Panama; she was an activist even as a teenager. She became involved in the formation of the UNIA and African Communities League with Marcus Garvey. She moved to New York and the pair married in 1919. Winston James notes that Pan-Caribbean thinkers had a profound influence in Harlem: 'by 1930, almost a quarter of Black Harlem was of Caribbean origin.'[10] James notes many Caribbean migrants to the United States were disposed towards radical politics, noting their experiences from living in majority Black populations; 'majority consciousness', their political and organizational experience and their experience of travelling all combined with their status as British subjects while they were in the United States.[11] Within the growing community of Caribbean immigrants in New York, Ashwood Garvey worked with Garvey for the UNIA and its shipping company, the Black Star Line. Penny Von Eschen explains that Marcus Garvey and his organization 'brought the notion of the links between the black world and Africa to a mass audience, creating a new working-class diaspora consciousness'.[12]

The Garvey marriage was short-lived. Garvey divorced his wife in 1920: 'What followed was a messy and controversial affair including legal proceedings, attempts to stave off bad publicity and threats.'[13] Ashwood Garvey maintained her married name. Rhoda Reddock notes she subsequently developed 'an independent life as a pan-Africanist, politician, cultural activist and feminist'.[14]

Sam Manning was born in Trinidad. One 1929 Jamaican newspaper recounted his various careers as 'one of the most famous jockeys' in the Caribbean and then a motor mechanic, before he joined the Middlesex Regiment and the British West Indies Regiment in Egypt in the First World War.[15] Manning toured the UK after demobilization in 'a minstrel show tour'.[16] After returning to the United States, he was the first Black performer in a Theatre Guild play, *Processional* (1925), playing a Calypso singer. The *Afro-American* reported that his presence helped to 'swell our big representation on the big White Way'[17] – demonstrating the recognition of his achievement across the Black communities in the United States. Around this time, Manning began 'a succession of almost 40 recordings'.[18] Manning performed regularly in Harlem theatres from 1926 onwards, billed explicitly as the 'Columbia and Okeh records star'.[19] John Cowley has carried out the most significant appraisal of these recordings, noting that they included 'a mix of traditional West Indian themes, and songs reflecting on the life of the newly arrived migrant in the U.S.A'.[20] Cowley notes Manning's 'African Blues' explicitly responds to Garveyism and the desire to go to Africa.[21] Manning and Grainger wrote 'Back Home on the Booker T. Washington' (a Garvey-owned ship form the Black Star Line) to be sung at one of the UNIA benefits.[22]

We do not know how Ashwood Garvey met Sam Manning, but he was also active in the UNIA community. He performed at a benefit for the UNIA in 1924 with the African American musician Porter Grainger in New York.[23] However their association began, Manning and Ashwood Garvey commenced the first of their joint ventures in 1926, with the launch of the *West Indian Times and American*. The publication, a weekly magazine, ran for two years and was led by their belief that 'the African American periodicals neglected the 3 million Caribbean people in the United States'.[24] The couple produced and co-wrote at least three musicals in a short period: *Hey! Hey!* (1926), *Brown Sugar* (1927) and *Black Magic* (1927) 'intended to introduce calypso to Harlem audiences'.[25]

The musicals drew on Ashwood Garvey's connections. Cowley notes that *Hey Hey* contained a section on the rise and fall of Marcus Garvey.[26] By this point, Garvey had declared himself President of Africa, and the press was wildly reporting their acrimonious divorce. The *Pittsburgh Courier* noted that Ashwood Garvey might herself appear in the musical, which was explicitly about Garvey's life and 'interesting adaptations of Garvey's ideas';[27] it clearly does not seem to have been entirely a parody. By May 1927, the plot had changed: Henry T. Sampson explains the show as a comedic trip to Africa.[28] *Brown Sugar* (1927) – advertised as 'Mrs Marcus Garvey presents' – presented Manning alongside Fats Waller, with music by Manning and Porter Granger.[29] Contemporary reviews also note Ashwood Garvey even designed the scenery – she clearly played a crucial part in the entire production process.[30] Manning and Ashwood Garvey were producing musicals together, but Rhoda Reddock notes that, 'beyond the literary and journalistic, theatre and performance were also important to these scholar activists'.[31]

Manning's work demonstrates his negotiation of a complex identity as a Black performer in Harlem, whose stage act clearly responded to the apparent strangeness of his dialect and the duality of his Caribbean identity and his simultaneous Britishness in the eyes of US audiences. One Jamaican newspaper wrote that Manning was 'The possessor of a fine voice, with remarkable vision he certainly let his American cousins know that however big that continent was in the West Indies there were talent and culture.'[32] A review of one of Manning's 1928 performances at the Lafayette Theatre notes, 'Sam finds the lure of the "footlights" irresistible and once again he's going to plaster the cork upon his classic features, don his English togs and proceed to make 'em laugh with his natural West Indian dialect.'[33] Manning's most famous character emerged from *Brown Sugar*[34] – Sir Quashi or 'Mr Squashi'.[35] The name comes from a derogatory Jamaican term about uneducated men from the countryside. In Manning's act, Sir Quashi was an 'educated [Black] British West Indian'.[36]

It is very difficult to unpick what was going on here, but it is important to recall his engagement in activism when attempting to reconcile Manning's politics with the performative acceptance of anti-Caribbean racism. Michael Eldridge suggests that his performance of songs 'in exaggerated accents' reinforced contemporary racist tropes.[37] Manning was working in complex environments across different kinds of spaces and audiences; understanding this layering of blackface and this character requires care. Lara Putnam follows the movements of a song Manning recorded, 'Sly Mongoose' (1925), a Jamaican mento from around the 1900s, through incarnations of live performance to its recording on vinyl and to recordings in West Africa, by Charlie Parker and back to Ghana. She argues:

> The travels of this very sly mongoose challenge us to understand Jazz Age music as created simultaneously in, and ricocheting between, sites geographically distant and socially diverse [...] Each rendition drew difference from its performers and context – new rhythms and instrumentation, new lyrics, new take. Yet the sameness mattered, too.[38]

The sly mongoose recalls Cedric Robinson's consideration of 'sly oppositional stratagems',[39] but it is Putman's idea of 'ricocheting between' that is particularly important in helping to understand Manning's work: Manning seems to be doing one thing while something else is consistently at work.

Manning was a major part of Harlem's theatre scene in the late 1920s, both as a performer and as a producer; but his activism work continued to influence his work. He appeared in many revues that staged his identity, such as *Scuffle Along* (1928, note the play on *Shuffle Along*), which featured 'the story of a West Indian and a Harlemite'.[40] He even appeared in *Crazy Quilt Revue* with the boxer Jack Johnson in Harlem in 1929.[41] Manning tried to set up the 'Independent Colored Theatrical Agency' in October 1929 with the white producer B. L. Burt (who had been the manager of the Lafayette Theatre).[42] Their intent was to set up fairer terms for Black performers and producers; it rebranded just three months later as the 'Immense Thespian Agency Inc',[43] but was still unsuccessful.[44] Manning consistently used music for political activism. In 1933, reports of a fundraising event for the Scottsboro National Action Committee held for a Black audience in New Jersey note that 'Sam Manning, a member of the committee, sang his own composition, the "Scottsboro Blues."'[45]

Manning clearly experienced financial difficulties in maintaining his productions. Reports in February 1929 put him on the Musician's Union's 'unfair' list, which meant union members could not work for him. The exact details are unclear, but he failed to pay musicians booked for his tour of Cuba.[46] In 1929, Manning and Ashwood Garvey toured the Caribbean. The Jamaica *Gleaner* reported Manning was visiting Jamaica, Panama, Barbados and Trinidad 'in the interest of the Columbia Gramophone Co., with whom he has got a contract for five years', to find songs to record.[47] He performed in several theatres in Kingston, Jamaica, along with Syd Perrin.[48] One report noted they 'are packing to capacity local theatres, with their latest sensations from Broadway'.[49]

Ashwood Garvey and Manning visited Panama, where Ashwood Garvey had grown up. Manning performed at the Cristobal Silver Clubhouse 'with a heart-breaking crowd. There was not standing room, nor sitting room either'.[50] Manning even wrote 'a column for the *Panama Tribune* on the need for Afro-Caribbean unity in Panama'.[51] During this time, the Garveys' acrimonious divorce led to a public conflict between Marcus Garvey and Manning. Manning launched libel suits against Garvey in Jamaica.[52] He returned to New York in 1929, sailing from Trinidad,[53] but he travelled frequently – records show him arriving again in New York from Hamilton, Bermuda in 1931.[54] In March 1933, Manning was still in New York and took the lease on a theatre in Harlem, turning the Spanish-language theatre San Jose into 'Harlem Fifth Avenue' to host vaudeville and cinema.[55] Financially, difficulties befell the project: only a few weeks later, he ended the project, unable to pay the cast.[56]

By early summer 1934, Sam Manning turned his attention to the UK and the production of *Harlem Nightbirds*. He made a series of records in the UK with Lionel Belasco.[57] Ashwood Garvey had already travelled to London in the early 1930s, and together with Ladipo Solanke set up the Nigerian Progress Union.[58] Though her involvement with British theatre in this period is slightly unclear, Hakim Adi and Marika Sherwood note 'she is reputed to have helped recruit the Black cast for *Stevedore*, a play about racial and trade union conflict in which Paul Robeson had the lead role'.[59] She did not appear to have any public connection with Manning's British revue, but she was presumably present in the UK for an overlapping period.

Harlem Nightbirds: Understanding the show's importance

Thrillingly, one review of the show in London's East End points to the possibility of people of African descent in the audience: 'It was appropriate that the advent should be among such a cosmopolitan crowd.'[60] Manning's *Harlem Nightbirds* (1934–5) has received minimal scholarly attention; Howard Rye explores it as part of early Black British jazz, and John Cowley has considered Manning's participation in it.[61] Rye suggests that it did not emphasize any Caribbean connection:

> It appears from his title and from his hiring of expatriate African Americans as cast members that his intention was rather to show that West Indians could produce as good an African-American show as African Americans. Though the language points to a desire to assert a Caribbean identity, nothing distinctive of Caribbean culture seems to have been envisaged.[62]

This raises some challenging questions about what counts as 'distinctive' and rather overlooks Manning's own connection to Harlem during the 1920s and early 1930s. The musical really was straight 'from the New York stage',[63] since that was Manning's professional experience, and Harlem music culture was not isolated from Caribbean music cultures. The *Gleaner* reported that, in *Nightbirds*, Manning 'uses the "Calypso" or West Indian folk song [...] he makes use of jazz themes and of native African rhythm'.[64]

In fact, the revue's cast brought together people of African descent from the Caribbean, the UK and, potentially, the United States. *Nightbirds* toured across the UK and returned to several London venues, including the large Metropolitan Theatre in Paddington, something which perhaps led to the only slightly exaggerated coverage of the show as 'London's Latest Craze'.[65] Table 4 lays out the full tour.

TABLE 4 Harlem Nightbird's *Tour.*

Date	City	Theatre	Notes
24/09/1934	East London	Poplar Queen's[66]	T. Crowther is music director
03/11/1934	South London	Brixton Empress	
08/10/1934	Birmingham	Empire[67]	Brookins and Van join the cast[68]
15/10/1934	Dudley	Opera House[69]	
22/10/1934	West London	Chelsea Palace Theatre[70]	
29/10/1934	NE London	Walthamstow Palace[71]	
12/11/1934	Liverpool	Bootle Metropole[72]	
19/11/1934	Blackpool	Opera House[73]	
10/12/1934	Central London	Metropolitan[74]	'Janice Hart is presenting the show'[75]
17/12/1934 to 01/01/1935	Hull	Tivoli Theatre[76]	
6/02/1935	Southampton	Hippodrome Theatre[77]	
11/02/1935	Boscombe	Hippodrome Theatre[78]	
18/02/1935	South London (Suburbs)	Croydon Grand Theatre[79]	
25/03/1935	Belfast	Empire Theatre[80]	

01/04/1935	Birmingham	Aston Hippodrome[81]	
08/04/1935	Wigan	Hippodrome[82]	
12/04/1935	Derby	Grand Theatre[83]	(plays twice nightly)
22/04/1935	Manchester	Metropole[84]	
24/04/1935	Bradford	Palace[85]	
06/05/1935	Gateshead	Empire[86]	
13/05/1935	Preston	King's Palace[87]	Jack London enters the cast: 'he figures at the piano'[88]
20/05/1935	Oldham	Palace[89]	
03/06/1935	London (Suburbs)	Lewisham Hippodrome[90]	
06/06/1935	London	South London Palace[91]	
	(Break in tour)		
19/11/1935	Liverpool	Rotunda[92]	John Payne's Trio[93]

Whether British theatre critics and audiences were able to hear the musical influences is hard to assess, though one review of the production in Belfast noted the presence of folk songs with 'swaying rhythm' and 'scenes which indicate how the rumba tunes originated'.[94] It appears Manning performed his Harlem act 'Mr Squashie', a character he was so associated with that a report of his arrival in London actually read: 'The Honorable Sir Squashie of Jamaica, British West Indies, whom you will remember as no less a personage than the inimitable Sam Manning, is here.'[95] Manning directly incorporated this character as two reviews list him as an additional cast member: one at the beginning of the tour, in Poplar, 'Andy and Squashie also figure in the company'; and three months later in Hull, 'Squashie'.[96] Neither reviewer recognized that Manning was Squashie. The character/performer is not mentioned elsewhere, so it seems reasonable to assume that this was Manning.

Contemporaneous reviews of *Nightbirds* seem to support Rye's comment that there was nothing distinctively Caribbean in the revue; they noted its reliance 'on old-time plantation melodies' and the presence of the 'Afro-American Jubilee Singers'.[97] Like many of Garland's revues, *Nightbirds* included a generic African village and a Harlem Night Club. One local newspaper explained the revue's music comprised *both* 'modern hot rhythm numbers and oldtime plantation melodies so beloved of America's [Black] population'.[98] But the music was being mediated for a predominantly white audience; and this is where framing Manning's performance practice as in *and* between sites is so crucial. Manning wrote and directed the revue and presumably selected its musical numbers. He acted in many of its scenes and, as the compere, he 'keeps the acts closely knitted together'.[99] He also conducted the band in at least one number. In this role, he was able to negotiate racist stereotypes by stepping into different scenes as well as controlling the proceedings. One review noted: 'whether as a black faced comedian or an immaculately dressed musical director [Manning] is excellent.'[100] Perhaps the most complex sequence to understand is the one in which Manning played an African chief (in the village scene). Manning appeared along with a chorus of women playing slaves (presumably enslaved by him as Chief); promotional material reported that 'when the "Abolition of Slavery" is pronounced and you have the opportunity of hearing the famous "Afro-American Jubilee Singers," this at least will take you right out of your own environment'.[101]

Putnam's concept here of the ricocheting between, helps us to understand what on the surface seems deeply problematic. As we have noted, David Olusoga has considered how the British deployed ideas of the so-called 'civilising mission in Africa' to justify British colonization.[102] The image of freed African people clearly plays into this trope; yet the presence of the 'Jubilee Singers' clearly aurally refers listeners to the spirituals of the Fisk Jubilee choir. The second image powerfully supersedes the first, reinstating white people's enslavement of hundreds of thousands of Black people. Harvey Young positions the idea of reclaiming in his consideration of staging violence perpetuated against Black people:

> Re-claiming does not require that we erase the past and script a new one. The prefix tells us this. To reclaim is to take something back. It is to possess something in the present while knowing that it has only recently been back in your possession. It is to remain aware of its previous 'claims' even as you articulate your own. It is to know the past in the present as you work toward creating a future.[103]

If we acknowledge that Manning was consistently involved with activism and protests throughout his career, towards creating a future, *Nightbirds* becomes an important site to read what Putnam calls the travels of the 'Sly Mongoose' of jazz and to acknowledge a potential reclaiming.

Just as Manning 'ricocheted between' frames, so did *Nightbirds* through its music, Cyril Blake's Rhythm Five. Blake was born in Trinidad, and though he had mainly worked in the UK, he had extensive experience of US Black music practices. He was part of the reformed Southern Syncopated Orchestra, after the tragic death of thirty-one of its band members, alongside two other Caribbean players, his brother George 'Happy' Blake and 'the distinguished organist Wendell Bruce-James'.[104] Blake then moved to Paris in the mid-1920s and played with the group accompanying Florence Mills;

and in the early 1930s, he played with Leon Abbey in Paris. In 1933, he began a residency at London's Pavilion theatre with his brother.[105] His band's performance in *Nightbirds* was noted for its speed and rhythm. One review noted it 'caused something of riot, indicated by stamping and cheering'.[106] This is by no means a universal response – praise for musical skill valued very different qualities: the *Belfast Telegraph* praised Blake's band as 'a study in rhythmic restraint, and in there the drummer's work with the wire brushes is worth watching and hearing'.[107] Reviews of the music tend to refer to swing and jazz almost indistinguishably, noting their swing while commenting on the band's 'original arrangements of the two classics of jazz – "Dinah" and "Some of These Days"'.[108] (Shelton Brooks, an African Canadian composer wrote the latter song.)

The revue featured the work of other Black composers. W. C. Handy's 'St Louis Blues' was played by the ensemble.[109] It also included film musical songs, like 'Pettin' in the Park' from *42nd Street* (1933), pointing to Hollywood's influence on variety theatre.[110] The vocalist Pep Graham sang a variety of material, songs like 'River Blues'.[111] Alongside scat singing (for the popularity of this and Cab Calloway particularly, see Chapter 9), she sang 'My Kid's a Crooner', a song co-written by the British composer Reg Montgomery and a white American jazz singer Marion Harris:

> [in the song] she doubled the ordinary tempo and made a new tune of this popular number. Perhaps not sure of how much a Belfast audience would appreciate scat singing she did not travel too far into the realms of 'hi di ho,' but what she did scat had everything.[112]

Examining the professional backgrounds of the *Nightbirds'* cast demonstrates Will Garland's reach in British theatre in supporting Black practitioners' professional development. Garland's networks connected US and Caribbean performers while providing training routes for British performers of African descent.

Harlem Nightbirds: The cast

Little is known about Johnny 'Shorty' Mounsey, but the reviews of his work in *Nightbirds* point to his established presence in Britain: 'with his wide experience of British audiences [he] is probably as funny as anyone else in the company.'[113] Mounsey was a singer and comedian. Given his thirty-year association with Black cast shows run by Garland and others, it seems likely he was of African descent – coverage of the show would suggest he was also British or a Caribbean British subject. He first appears working with his long-time partner Andy Clarke with Will Garland's *Coloured Lights* (1925) and Mounsey's adverts for work.[114] Mounsey's big break came while he was understudying for Scott and Whaley's revue *Money Makers* (1927).[115] One night, he went on for Scott; he was so successful that the producer launched a second tour starring him in the leading role.[116] Mounsey would later return to work with Garland,[117] and in white-produced shows like Lew Leslie's *Blackberries* (1931) alongside Eddie Emmerson and Ike Hatch. Mounsey also performed alongside the John Payne Trio in variety.[118] Other cast members from *Harlem Nightbirds*, like the Five Black Flashes ('the original [*racial descriptor*] song and dance sensation')[119] had also played in variety alongside John Payne and Lewis Hardcastle.[120]

The *Gleaner* explained Sam Manning's tour in the UK as his plan 'to let my bucket down for local talent', noting 'one of his finds is Pep Graham, a "torch" singer from Liverpool'.[121] Adverts described Pep Graham as 'the Josephine Baker of England'.[122] Graham was born Phoebe Louisa Williams (b. 1899, Liverpool, UK; d. 1982, unknown). Her father was Jeremiah Macauley, who was from Freetown, Sierra Leone, and her mother was Esther Wilson, from Dublin, Ireland. Her father was a wheelwright, perhaps based at the nearby docks.[123] The 1911 census reports her father's death, and the family's subsequent change of address suggests the dire financial straits the family must have been in while she was growing up.[124] Currently, no further information emerges about Graham and her life until she married John Williams in 1924.

In 1928, Graham began touring with Will Garland's company in *Brown Birds*; she remained in *Swanee River* (1929). In 1931, Graham became a nightclub singer: 'Hutch and a Piano are at the Café Anglais, [...] Pep Graham, Parisian [Black] comedienne, has settled down at Romano's.'[125] Graham presented a range of material which showed the impact of Black US music on her repertoire, in 1931 singing Cab Calloway's 'You Can't Stop Me Loving You'.[126] She covered music from popular films; shortly after Al Jolson featured 'Rainbow Round My Shoulders' in *The Singing Fool* (1928), she brought it into her act.[127] Paris was not a fiction: Graham did perform at Monseigneur's nightclub there,[128] and further into Europe.[129] While she was at Romano's, Graham continued to perform in variety theatre. Newspapers frequently compared Graham to Janice Hart (see Chapter 2), and Graham maintained an active presence in British theatre until the 1950s.[130]

Reviews of her in *Nightbirds* describe her as 'a torch singer, with an American and a Continental reputation [that] adds a touch of brilliance. This very peppy person also appears as a dancer'.[131] Howard Rye notes that the Paris descriptor for Graham:

avoided the need to make definite statements about ancestry which would either be untrue or would disabuse audiences of their expectations of a performer with a more exotic origin than hers. It also no doubt reflects the status of Paris as the centre of European chic.[132]

As we have seen in the case of Hart/Cassie Walmer, Black performers were able to negotiate expectations around nationality and identity; in this case, newspapers portrayed Graham as American. Even the US entertainment magazine *Billboard* reported Graham as American in listing her under the 75 per cent of nightclub acts in London that were American.[133] In 1932, they again reported Graham as an American who had come to London 'from Paris'.[134] Sam Manning's publicity material for Graham suggested she was 'reminiscent of that great artist Florence Mills'.[135]

Almost uniquely, we know who was running the publicity material for *Harlem Nightbirds*: Eric Walrond, an important Caribbean novelist and writer of the Harlem Renaissance who had found himself out of work in the UK. Walrond's biographer, James Davis, explains that he had known Manning and Ashwood Garvey in New York, and seeing his struggle, they offered him the post of publicity manager, though it is unclear what exactly this entailed.[136] Walrond's presence allows us to know that the marketing material in some way correlated to Manning's aims, and publicity material for the show actually noted its British credentials: 'This is the only coloured revue touring in England at the present moment, and unlike most famous coloured revues, the artistes are all British.'[137] Walrond secured international coverage for the show. An article in the *Trinidad Guardian* reported that it was 'All Black and All-British', explaining that the company 'featured singers and musicians from Britain's old Black communities of Liverpool and Cardiff supplemented by more recent Caribbean arrivals'.[138] Walrond's connection to *Nightbirds* points to the complex professional networks around individual shows – and the persistence of transatlantic professional communities.

After the production: Leaving Britain

Manning's activities in the UK between June and the final extra performance of *Nightbirds* in November 1935 are unclear. The *New York Amsterdam News* reported that he was travelling to the Caribbean in search of 'talent for a big musical comedy show',[139] funded by Frances, Countess of Warwick (Frances Evelyn 'Daisy' Greville). They report Manning was hoping that 'by October it is hoped an entirely original musical show will be launched in England, something that will be a change from "Jaded Jazz".'[140] The *Gleaner* placed the Countess more centrally, as leading 'a search for new stage "stars"' through the Society of International Studies, with the support of Manning.[141] Manning returned to Britain in October and recorded Caribbean spirituals in the UK; reviews noted they were 'quite distinctive from the usual American spirituals'.[142] *Nightbirds* would give one more performance in November 1935;[143] but Manning did not produce anything else. Variations on the show continued to tour British theatre, presumably without Manning's involvement. In 1950, *Harlem Comes to Town* toured with several of the 1936 *Nightbirds* cast, including Pep Graham and Shorty Mounsey.[144]

Manning's next few years are hard to follow. He was clearly involved with the Florence Mills Social Parlour, which he opened in 1937. Newspapers reported that Rudolph Dunbar, Manning and Ashwood Garvey had opened the club as a 'sort of headquarters for [Black people] in the English Metropolis'.[145] Patrons might include 'Ike Hatch, Benny Carter, Reginald Forsythe, Ivan Anderson, John Payne [...] Leon Goodman, a white writer, dropped in for a visit'.[146] The *Negro Star* proudly detailed that, in 1936, the club hosted Jesse Owens after his Olympic triumph.[147] Manning next worked in British theatre in Lew Leslie's *Blackbirds of 1938* (though only appears in a few specific references).[148] He joined the cast of *The Sun Never Sets* at Drury Lane (Todd Duncan's British stage debut alongside Adelaide Hall).[149] In May 1939, Manning was again advertising in Jamaican newspapers for performers: 'See that you are in the show of shows that Sam Manning plans to take over to London in June.'[150]

Any plans Manning had were brought to an end when developments in Central Europe put a halt to his plans, and Manning returned to New York in March 1939. He listed his profession in the immigration reports as Actor-Producer (his relationship with Ashwood Garvey appears to have ended by this point).[151] Ashwood Garvey continued her activism and campaigning, touring newly independent countries in Africa and returning to the United States shortly before her death in 1969. Manning returned to US professional theatre in 1941.[152] He continued to record music,[153] and made two short Calypso musical films, *Quarry Road* and *Willie Willie*. In 1947, Manning directed the musical *Caribbean Carnival* on Broadway (Pearl Primus choreographed). This Broadway musical, while unsuccessful in any commercial sense, saw Manning again working as music director, composer, lyricist and sketch writer.[154] Manning also continued as an activist. In 1944, he was part of the committee for the 'League for the Freedom of Darker Peoples, and of all Oppressed Peoples, Africans and Those of African Descent Everywhere in the World'.[155] He died in 1960.

The impact Amy Ashwood Garvey had on British theatre is an intriguing one. Perhaps new documents will emerge to paint a clearer picture; we can certainly suggest that her having some kind of influence was likely. The contradictions that Sam Manning's performance practice presents may seem too great to rectify; the apparent taking on of a role which clearly can be seen to amplify anti-Caribbean sentiment seems baffling alongside his lengthy career and engagement with anti-colonialism and striving for racial equality. Without access to this character or any way of hearing Manning's perspective (though such a document may later emerge), we can only guess. We have established that Putnam's work on Manning provides a model for understanding him as ricocheting between spaces, as inhabiting at least in part the idea of the sly mongoose (a song he helped make popular). Understanding his work in Britain reveals *Harlem Nightbirds* as musical theatre which ricocheted between Harlem, the Caribbean and the UK, and Manning's role in that show as actively deploying resistant strategies.

9

Swing from Calloway to 'Snakehips' Johnson

Swing or jazz? This chapter involves an in-depth conversation about two figures who were instrumental to swing music. The term 'swing' is worth its own clarification – jazz music *can* swing, but not all jazz music *is* swing. Swing music itself is a subgenre of jazz as a whole. A product of the 1930s, it is generally defined as a dance music orchestrated by full big bands of trumpets, trombones, saxes and rhythm. It utilizes a heavy beat on all four beats of the bar (opposed to other forms of jazz that stress 2 and 4) and combines the improvisatory nature of solo work with charted instrumentation. Utilizing regional elements, it propelled jazz to the forefront of popular music through the decade and remained steadfast within popular consciousness into the mid-1940s. This definition will help the reader contextualize the interchangeability between the words 'jazz' and 'swing' in the context of the era we are exploring.

The chapter explores the work of Cab (Cabell) Calloway III (1907–94), who, though widely known as a performer and conductor, is rarely known for his work in the UK. It addresses Calloway's influence on, and the subsequent work of conductor, dancer and singer, Ken 'Snakehips' Johnson (Kenrick Reginald Hijmans Johnson) (b. 1914, Guyana; d. 1941, London).

The relationship of Britain to jazz is, to understate it, a complex one. Any survey of the existing literature reveals disquieted notions of how jazz culturally situates itself in Britishness, or as British. Various historical accounts of artists entering Britain to impart or deposit jazz in a proposed transitory nature are available, and notions of an established and localized sound are muddled by narratives from the other countries by which jazz seemingly arrived. It would seem that the identity of jazz as being British is as complex as some white British abilities to reckon with Black Britishness as also being a localized and palpable construct. Jason Toynbee, Catherine Tackley and Mark Doffman point to this elusiveness while they maintain that there is an incontestable origin of jazz in African American roots:

> African diasporic culture from which jazz emerged is a form of nurture, involving care and protection in the face of a racialized regime of social, symbolic and sometimes physical violence. But it is also a process of translation, adaptation and change in response to those same power relations.[1]

Toynbee, Tackley and Doffman also justify the need to explore jazz as British as well. This recontextualization affirms the value of the jazz practitioners' work while attending respectfully to the ethnological origins of their creations. In evoking Paul Gilroy, Toynbee, Tackley and Doffman suggest: 'if home and away, continuity and change, tradition and hybridity are opposed terms they nevertheless confront one another in a dialectic of productive tension.'[2] While they suggest there was only 'a relatively small African diasporic population in Britain' prior to the First World War,[3] their notions of exploring and celebrating the roots of their creators are crucial to understanding its importance.

Considering swing music within British theatre

This chapter finds itself in a unique position within a text primarily focused on theatre: why is the British swing band inconvenient within the history of Black British musical *theatre*? As in other sections of this book, this chapter does not exist within a vacuum. The practitioners' performance and working practices are as much a part of the narrative of artistry as they are of erasure and of recovery: every practitioner we have considered here existed within a broader scaffolding of interconnected networking across music and theatre industries. On the surface, Cab Calloway and Ken Johnson represent an 'otherness' to Britishness, both because of being Black and because the former was African American and the latter Afro-Guyanese (Guyana then a British subject). Upon further dissection, both of these artists have links to Britain that add to our narrative of theatre being a collection of sorts at this time: British audiences were enthusiastically hearing their work, and their influence was driving the sound of the genre that ultimately influenced aspects of theatre as well. Johnson was inspired by seeing Calloway perform in New York and developed his moniker via Earl 'Snakehips' Tucker.

By the time swing bands were a marked moment in mid-1930s Britain, it is worth noting that jazz had been establishing its underground presence in nightclubs from previously being in theatres in the early 1920s.[4] With even physical precedence, it is of the utmost importance to note the presence of swing bands in British variety theatre: the trumpeter Grenadian-born Leslie 'Jiver' Hutchinson played extensively in British variety – in 1932 playing 'Lawd You Made the Night Too Long' at Glasgow Empire Theatre.[5] Duke Ellington was billed as 'Harlem's aristocrat of jazz' in his visit to British variety theatres, for example at the Holborn Empire in July 1933.[6] Three months later, Louis Armstrong was playing the same theatre as part of his wider tour of British venues that had started with the Palladium in August 1933.[7] Armstrong was frequently billed as 'The World's Greatest Trumpeter'[8] – one advertisement for his performance in Sheffield specifically invited 'Bandsmen, Instrumentalists' to see the 'Sensational Bandmaster' perform.[9] Jack Hylton, the white band leader and music producer, led Armstrong's 1934 tour, where Armstrong's conducting skills were particularly commentated on: 'trumpet solos, and crooning, all delivered with tremendous energy, especially by the conductor himself.'[10] Armstrong was sometimes received in racialized terms. One review noted: 'the invasion of London by [...] artists by [of African descent].'[11]

Cab Calloway in the UK

Cab Calloway is undoubtedly one of the most famous practitioners explored in this book by music standards, but his work was also enjoyed in British theatre settings. As one of the most established figures of the swing era, his profile as an entertainer is immortalized largely through his time at Harlem's Cotton Club in the 1930s, as conductor of his self-titled orchestra, as well as a performer on stage and in film throughout his long career. It is almost impossible to mention Calloway's name without hearing the warm brassy line of 'Minnie the Moocher' (1931), from which his improvised 'hi-de-hi-de-hi' lyric would become the calling card of his career. Perhaps it is Calloway's rooting as a leading figure in the Harlem swing band that has footed him so deeply in the consciousness of Americana, but Calloway also played a significant part in shifting the sounds of popular music in the UK. Here, we consider Calloway's time in British theatres, and we suggest that he converted at least some of his audience into financially and artistically invested patrons – challenging the act of white consumption.

It is difficult to discuss Cab Calloway's career without wading into the waters of academia that support or contest his subversion of Black stereotyping. Scholars point to varying aspects of his work, in particular his association with the Cotton Club, as allowing Black labour to be consumed by exclusively white audiences (see the discussion of Clarence Robinson's work there in Chapter 7). Refusing to contextualize his career in a broader sense further undervalues the abilities of a practitioner that was clearly well aware of his facility and capacity. Calloway was well practised in acts of resistance before he visited the UK. The musicologist Nate Sloan

IMAGE 7 *Cab Calloway at the Trocedero, Elephant and Castle, South London, in 1934. (Photo by Fox Photos/Getty Images.)*

gives numerous examples of these in his aptly titled article 'Constructing Cab Calloway: Publicity, Race and Performance in 1930s Harlem Jazz'. Sloan challenges notions from scholars such as Kathy Ogren who put forth that Calloway's work contributed to a contrived tradition of jazz performance that 'may have trapped both blacks and whites in roles that were not "authentic" but staged'.[12] Sloan invokes reclamations from Jayna Brown: 'although the white gaze is always incorporated on some level' at segregated Harlem clubs, 'the scope, range and rhythm of their artistry is not limited to the expectations of white spectatorship'.[13] Sloan also points to the important work of Anne Cheng on Josephine Baker, where she noted that 'the boundaries of ownership and objecthood cannot be disciplined or controlled no matter how much ideology might wish them to be'.[14]

Sloan maintains that, 'In their quest to brand a Harlemaestro who could attract the spending money of both white and black audiences, Calloway, Mills [manager], and Williams upended racial stereotypes as much as they reinforced them'.[15] As a record producer and jazz promoter, Mills had key relationships with a number of Black musicians, including Duke Ellington. Sloan considers how Calloway's manager Irving Mills created a promotional manual that specifically addressed the unusual details of Calloway's performances:

Key branding points from the manual that were meant to exoticize the singer – his 'hi-de-ho' catch-phrase, his use of Harlem slang, and his singular vocal style – were also the exact performative traits that enabled Calloway to subvert his constructed persona and assert a self-fashioned identity even when performing in a segregated nightclub.[16]

A reconstructed or, as Sloan attests, a *constructed* view towards understanding how Calloway negotiated white audiences in the United States opens new understandings of what exactly he was doing in the UK. As in the United States, British theatre audiences surely knew of Calloway before his arrival. Having spent time in Chicago's Sunset Cafe in the late 1920s after taking over as leader of the Alabamians from Louis Armstrong, Calloway ended up in New York City at the famed Cotton Club which would act as his springboard to fame from 1931 to 1934. Calloway's records were released in the UK in 1932,[17] and in a short film *The Big Broadcast* intended for cine-variety, which played extensively in 1933.[18] The British newspaper the *Daily Herald* made reference to Calloway's signature eclectic style, writing in 1932: 'Cab Calloway's Band, a leading [Black] dance band which is directed by a dynamic personality who sings in a mode which one either admires beyond reason or hates to distraction.'[19] In January 1934, newspapers reported that Calloway was coming to the UK for a tour produced by Irving Mills – his manager Ned E. Williams had written to the *Era* the same month in advance, clearly concerned that the style might confuse a British audience:

I am anxious to learn whether gramophone records and the motion pictures have familiarised the British public with Calloway's style sufficiently to appreciate his unique performance and his personality. I am sure they will, if he is accepted as an individual entertainer, rather than as a mere band leader.[20]

Calloway also had to negotiate other barriers; the contemporary restrictions on American bands were a clear obstacle, something which he was famous enough to negotiate. Calloway received permission to play from the Ministry of Labour in February 1934, a decision white jazz bandleader Spike Hughes explained may have 'far-reaching effects':

[Calloway] has been granted a permit to play at the Kitcat Restaurant with his orchestra. There has been an unwritten agreement between British hotel and restaurant owners, band leaders and the Ministry of Labour during the past three years that no United States band should be allowed in England except to play in music-halls and public dance-halls. An official of the Ministry of Labour told me yesterday that the case of Cab Calloway was exceptional, but that it was a case 'considered on its merits'.[21]

In March 1934, *His Hi-de-Highness of Ho-de-ho* was in Britain and headlining at the London Palladium.[22] Reports of the Palladium concert note: 'Many dance band leaders were in the audience, which would have liked him to have gone on for hours.'[23] *The Stage* further describes what must have been a hit as English audiences became familiarized with his style in announcing the last week of his time there: 'capital audiences are enjoying their "scat" singing and "hot" syncopation'.[24] They note Elisabeth Welch 'joined the Calloway combination this week, and meets with great success for numerous songs, among them being the capital "Lullaby in Blue"'.[25] Welch, by then an established performer owing to her recent work in Cole Porter's *Nymph Errant*, operates at the cutting edge of Black musical performance practice to packed theatregoing audiences. Calloway's audiences were not limited to London; the *Wireless Portsmouth Evening News* advertised an accessible broadcast to a larger audience:

> Those listeners to whom the breathless enunciation of 'hotcha' and 'skiddyboddle' spells ecstasy will delight in the 'In Town To-night' supplement from the Daventry station at 7:30 tonight, for none other than the world-famous 'scat' singer, Cab Calloway, will appear before the microphone. As this American [obsolete racial descriptor] gentleman has been offered £400 to appear in a single West End variety programme, many radio fans will feel they are getting value for their licence money.[26]

Circling back to the previously explored notion that Calloway's work moved beyond being 'made for white consumption',[27] his time in the UK may also serve as evidence of this subversion. Biographer Alyn Shipton is one of few who discusses thoughts on his time in the UK and Calloway's remembrance of the 'lack of overt racial prejudice' he experienced while in Britain, which 'made him feel free [and that in London] he was living as a normal human being for the first time in his life'.[28]

This points to the fact that Calloway himself felt a lesser presence of prejudice over his time in the UK. His time spent there was marked by accommodation befitting a high-profile performer, and this felt intrinsically different from similar experiences in the United States. His presence in transatlantic jazz is concrete, and traces of his career and its successes in Britain are evidently resistant performance practice. He returned to the UK to play Sportin' Life in the 1952 British premiere of *Porgy and Bess*, and again several times subsequently to tour variety and music venues in the UK (his last visit was for a performance at the Barbican in 1991). Sloan notes: 'viewing Calloway, his ensemble, and his contemporary Harlem entertainers as laborers, artists, and politically engaged individuals operating in a racist superstructure makes manifest the different spaces of black America that they portrayed in their work.'[29] Working inside theatre spaces in the UK alongside Black theatre performers such as Welch indicates Calloway surely contributed towards opening pathways for artists of Colour.

Ken Johnson and the West Indian Dance Orchestra

'The war was a long way off. A second later it had crashed into their midst.'[30] When the theatres in London had closed in the face of the Blitz, the nightclubs remained open. Ken 'Snakehips' Johnson and his band were the star attraction at the Café de Paris, which had reduced its prices to appeal to a wider crowd of off-duty service personnel. In September 1940, as the Blitz began, one newspaper described Johnson's reassurance to his patrons when the air-raid sirens went off that 'Anyone can go still *further* down [...] But if they do, they'll miss the time of their lives.'[31] Even in January 1941, the British high society newspaper *Tatler* carried an advertisement for the club's 'luncheon, tea dansant, dinner and supper, always London's finest cabaret, enjoy yourself in safety 20 feet below ground'.[32] But the safety was to be short-lived, and on 8 March 1941, the Café de Paris was hit by a 50kg high-explosive bomb. Thirty-four people died, including Johnson and members of his band. Johnson died holding his baton, at the tragically young age of twenty-six.

Johnson is one of the most fascinating figures to emerge from this stage of swing music in Britain. Largely known by the nickname Ken 'Snakehips' Johnson, had he survived, Johnson's West Indian Dance Orchestra might have continued on the path to being the most sought-after ensemble and authority of swing music in Britain. The 'Snakehips' nickname points to a duality in his identity – since he picked it up in response to seeing American dancer Earl 'Snakehips' Tucker perform in 1934 in New York.[33] Though he is remembered principally for his work as a conductor and a singer, he started his career as a dancer; he even appeared in a small role in the British film *Oh Daddy* (1935). His dual career as conductor and as dancer is even more remarkable given the little formal training he received. The *West Middlesex Gazette* calls him the 'dynamic dancing conductor' in 1937, in this wonderful description of a young Black man:

> Tall, good-looking Ken Johnson shows his nickname of 'Snakehips' is no idle boast. Conducting his boys with energy, a streak of rippling rhythm, his sparkle and vitality are electrifying. His twinkling feet scarcely seem to touch the stage when he goes into a tap routine, while for thrills, his acrobatic tap dance on a miniature staircase wants some beating.[34]

The presence of the staircase suggests he knew enough about tap to reference Bill 'Bojangles' Robinson's routine. Ken Johnson's bands had a presence in British theatre, as Catherine Tackley notes: 'The first bookings that the West Indian Dance Orchestra achieved were on the variety circuit, playing in theatres and cinemas following the long tradition of black entertainment on the British stage.'[35]

Johnson arrived in the UK for schooling in his mid-teens, but it was quickly evident that he would pursue a path of entertainment rather than his family lineage in medicine. The formative event that seems to have sparked the addition of conducting to his artistic portfolio was his aforementioned trip to New York. Matera describes this trip as his 'opportunity to see the great Black swing bands of the day firsthand', and that Johnson would claim he had the opportunity to lead Fletcher Henderson's orchestra on one occasion, which ignited his musical spark.[36] Johnson's musical career took off largely after his return to the UK from the United States in early 1936: Johnson advertised himself as 'just returned from Hollywood [...] Hollywood's latest sensation' seeking offers for 'variety, production or cabaret and films'.[37]

The young pathfinder was returning to a unique landscape on the musical scene, as the Musicians' Union had prohibited US bands entering the year before; since Johnson was from Guyana, then British Guiana, he was a British subject and could circumvent such rules.[38] This vacuum would eventually inspire him to step in as frontman of a new musical ensemble of Black musicians. In 1936, Johnson and West End theatre musician and Jamaican trumpeter Leslie Thompson formed a band of their own. Thompson recalled that the band had no fixed name, though often featured Jamaican in the title, for example the Jamaican Emperors of Jazz – perhaps indicating his background over Johnson's.[39] Thompson recalled that 'Johnson was a stick wagger – he was no musician'.[40] The band split after a period over contract disputes, and Johnson took total control as conductor, then known as the West Indian Dance Orchestra. At time of its inception, Thompson and Johnson would work closely to bring together many of the most prolific Black musicians working in Britain at the time.

Catherine Tackley discusses the ensemble's unique situation, because Johnson's band was a product of what was otherwise assumed to be a largely American culture:

> Having stood in for missing African-American jazz musicians in the aftermath of the 1935 restrictions, black British musicians, including those who were citizens of the British Empire, had a complex dual insider/outsider status. On one hand, their particular cultural roots could be subsumed within an all-encompassing notion of Britishness from the jazz establishment which sought to legitimise and authenticate British jazz. On the other, both collectively and as individuals, they remained novelties.[41]

Tackley's suggestion that the ensemble were, collectively and individually, 'novelties' is problematic; it denotes that the ensemble were mystifyingly attempting to find their feet in Britain because jazz was an American unfamiliarity. There is, however, no notion that this was exclusively the case. Despite an obvious connection with American communities and a transatlantic understanding of what was transpiring musically, consider Matera's thoughts:

Thus, despite the differences in their backgrounds, black musicians often arrived in London with greater familiarity with jazz – and a whole range of black musical idioms – than their white contemporaries had. Many viewed these sounds as part of their musical heritage as people of African descent, rather than merely a foreign import from the United States.[42]

Like Tackley, Jason Toynbee maintains that the band was 'very much American in its derivation'.[43] However, this also denies a potentially much larger cultural connection that could understand how jazz could be reclaimed and fostered in respective pockets – it was not just a by-product of the Black US experience alone. Consider Matera, who writes that Leslie Thompson 'insisted that jazz was "an inherent trait" of Jamaican music and the island was swinging just like New Orleans in the 1920s. According to him, even if you did not play an instrument, you grew up with an attachment to jazz'.[44] US musicians were also able to listen to Johnson in reverse. One Pennsylvania paper notes in 1938 that 'American swing bands will do well to nip a page from the book of one Snakehips Johnson, British swingster who devotes a half hour each Monday over GSP Daventry [...] His swing rendition of "Swanee River" is really something and his version of "Memphis Blues" is slightly terrific.'[45] The deeper cultural connections these musicians harboured within their respective geographical access cannot be ignored.

Johnson's profile as a conductor gained momentum as the band became more established, eventually being dubbed the 'Jamaican Emperor of Jazz',[46] with his 'Ambassadors of Rhythm, from Jamaica'.[47] Their reach moved beyond London; in 1936, they performed in Liverpool: 'A new all-sepia act opened [...] Appearing are Ken "Snakehips" Johnson, the Jamaican Emperors [sic] of Jazz, Valaida Snow with her trumpet and singing and the team of Radcliffe and Rodgers.'[48] Snow's presence in the line-up is interesting and reveals the ways Black musicians made connections outside of traditionally accepted centres of jazz music. Johnson and his band, now billed as the Ambassadors of Jazz, toured widely in 1936;[49] by the end of that year, Johnson started to appear in US Black newspapers. The *Pittsburgh Courier* noted 'Europe's latest band sensation "Bowls 'Em Over" in London', making a comparison between Johnson's performance and that of Cab Calloway.[50]

Johnson's ensemble would certainly have been interpreted as a leading authority of how the developing form of swing jazz was being understood in the UK. In 1938, the Chiswick Empire advertised that 'until you have heard their exhilarating interpretations of modern jazz and swing your "hot" rhythm education cannot be considered complete'.[51] In 1938, the British jazz critic Leonard G. Feather noted that Johnson had 'fulfilled the promise' the columnist had placed in him, noting that they were at the forefront of the jazz scene.[52] By 1939, his band became known as the 'Emperors of Swing', and he told one interviewer that 'I've encouraged the American band complex, and I get more co-operation than is usual with bands over here. All the boys come from the West Indies and round about.'[53]

In the short years he was active, Johnson's ensemble was heralded as the leading purveyor of swing dance music in Britain. The ensemble and Johnson's career are worth further dissection in British music and theatre scholarship for numerous reasons. He demonstrates multiple kinds of overlapping resistant practices: in addition to being Black, he was also a gay man. He was a conductor, who was really a dancer. Tom Cullen's biography of Johnson's partner, Gerald Hamilton (some twenty-four years Johnson's senior), notes their living arrangements. Hamilton, a critic and internationalist, is immortalized as the real-life inspiration for Christopher Isherwood's *Mr Norris Changes Trains* and was infamously penned 'the wickedest man in Europe'.[54] Stephen Bourne, in his work recovering LGBTQ histories, notes that Johnson referred to Hamilton as his husband.[55]

With all this, it appears that Johnson's interest may have lay more in establishing an ensemble and network for Black musicians as a conductor than in being a maestro from the beginning. In October 1940, the British Jamaican radio broadcaster Una Marson (see 'The 1940s in context') interviewed Johnson on BBC's *Calling The West Indies* about his transition from dancing to conducting. Johnson sets out the formation of the band as one of the key elements of his success and ability to transition:

UM: So you left London a tap dancer, and returned a band conductor?

KJ: Well, Una, I first had to convince them that I could conduct as well as I could dance.

UM: And how did you set about it?

KJ: Well, when I got over here, I got a band together, nearly all Jamaicans. We were billed as the Jamaican Emperors of Jazz, and we got stage engagements in various cinemas in the country.

UM: Yes?

KJ: And then after a year, I reorganized the band with West Indians from all the important islands in the West Indies; a real West Indian band.

UM: And this new venture led you where?

KJ: Well, again, we were very lucky: we got a contract to play at a smart West End club: the Florida. We stayed there for two years, and made some very good contacts.[56]

Johnson's maintenance of an all-Black, or even an all-Black-appearing, ensemble demonstrates remarkable conviction at this time. Some histories may maintain that being a Black ensemble was a by-product of the racist exclusionary practices of the UK government and Musicians' Union at this time. Toynbee notes: 'the formation of black ensembles was also prompted by the need for solidarity to cope with an entrenched colour bar, which could affect musicians as well as those in more traditional working-class occupations.'[57] There may be some truth in this; however, an oversimplification of the rationale behind developing this as only exclusionary is problematic. Toynbee remarks that the West Indian Dance Orchestra 'were understood in a very general sense as authentic purveyors of African-American swing, although none were African Americans', and that 'although the musicians originated from various different parts of the Caribbean, [...] some, indeed, had been born and bred in the UK'.[58] Johnson's conviction even in his interview with Marson suggests no hesitancy in identifying the group with strong links to its identity both as Black British and as influenced via island roots. Consider further that the press was continually focused on their origination, but not for being American. Clearly, their success did not depend on being depicted as falsifying American identity as argued. Even when having arrived from outside Britain, a simplified identification of their musical contribution as 'American' detracts from the cultural resonance these musicians felt with their respective countries, and how this shaped their product.

Upon his takeover of the ensemble from Leslie Thompson, Johnson was clearly continually interested in it being a Black group: 'West Indian' would remain in the name as a reclaimed equivalent for 'good', and the group's success seemed to only benefit, not disadvantage, from Black identifiers, a fact well known to Johnson. This reclaims a narrative that the band was functioning as 'Jamaican', 'West Indian' or 'coloured' as 'an exoticist dimension and a marketing of blackness to majority white audiences'.[59] Johnson, after being unable to secure the Black trombonist Frank Williams for a tour, hired two white musicians instead – both of whom played in blackface while with the ensemble.[60] There was a need here to keep the ensemble appearing exclusively Black – one that would incontestably lead towards its continued success. Later in the interview with Marson, they discuss the later move into recording and radio work: after touring through 1936, the group would land residencies in clubs. Starting in the West End Old Florida Club in 1937, which would result in Leslie Thompson's eventual recusal from the band and the shift towards Johnson's leadership and its new name, the group eventually made the move to the Café de Paris, which led to further recording opportunities. Its location made it an ideal place to record in early evening and to continue on to other clubs at night.

It is clear these recordings were also internally motivated. Johnson and the group seemingly must have known that being recorded would afford them the opportunity to be heard not only in London and Britain but also further across the Atlantic and beyond, establishing a further comprehension of a network of Black internationalism. Matera notes: 'the Johnson band's sound circulated farther afield and that – even while performing for white, largely upper- and middle-class patrons and, via the radio, a wider British listening audience – its members continued to have other publics in mind.'[61] It is no question then why the band continued to record even when external clubs would favour the albums over their live performances, as their popularity still remained high, as well as their ability to further network in Black circles; they also recorded with Una Mae Carlisle and Fats Waller, being two examples of recording sessions that would emerge from this time.[62]

Regardless of these inconsistencies, there is still validity in exploring Johnson's life and career in greater detail. Inconsistent narratives ranging from his 'known lack of musical ability'[63] to his possession of a musical doctorate[64] all point to a greater curiosity to recover and recontextualize the groundwork laid by this tragically lost artist. Toynbee, Tackley and Doffman note that 'Johnson's band is an important example of Black British musicians producing jazz which achieved commercial success by addressing the expectations of British audiences, but which also expressed, in various ways, the musicians experiences as Black British'.[65] Even in this prefatory unearthing of these artists' work, it is evident that their experiences point to a larger deficiency in the British conception of what the Black contribution truly meant at this time; and further, how it is non-viable to separate their work from being the seeds of a web of performance practice with connective tissue still alive today. Berendt and Huesmann point to a beautiful parallel spirit in consideration of revisionary performance practice, perhaps unknowingly, at the conclusion of *The Jazz Book*:

> But it is above all jazz, as a music of revolt against all that is too convenient, which can demand of its listeners that they revise standards valid years ago and be prepared to discover new norms. [...] Nearly one hundred years after it began, jazz is still what it was then: a music of protest; that, too, contributes to its aliveness. It cries out against social and racial and spiritual discrimination, against the clichés of picayune bourgeois mortality, against the functional organization of modern mass society, against the depersonalization inherent in this society, and against that categorization of standards that leads to the automatic passing of judgments wherever these standards are not met.[66]

The 1940s in context

During the Second World War, many people from across the countries Britain had colonized came to the UK to contribute to the war effort: 2.5 million men from Britain's Empire served across the world – soldiers from five different continents (Europe, North America, Australasia, Africa and Asia). The majority did not serve in Britain itself; instead fighting in theatres of war abroad. David Olusoga notes that of these, 'more than twelve thousand West Indians served in the British forces during the war, many of them highly skilled specialists'.[1]

Radio broadcasts attempted to promote inclusion and gratefulness to those who had come to serve 'the motherland'; Black performers were frequently part of these efforts. In 1942, Una Marson began hosting *Calling the West Indies*, a BBC radio series (see 'The 1930s in context'). The Ministry of Information created films of the radio broadcasts of *Hello! West Indies* (1943) and *West Indies Calling* (1944), featuring Marson and, from Trinidad, Ulric Cross and Learie Constantine. Cross (1917–2013) was a decorated RAF squadron leader who would go on to be a lawyer and judge. Constantine (1901–71) was an international cricketer who was working at the time with the Ministry of Labour and National Service to support Caribbean war workers. In 1944, he successfully sued a London hotel for turning him away. Constantine eventually became the first Black person to become a peer (a sitting Lord in the UK's House of Lords) and was influential in the passing of the 1965 Race Relations Act.[2]

As the United States entered the Second World War in 1941, the mobilization of American troops caused a surge in the existing Black population of Britain: 'On the eve of D-Day, in June 1944, there were a hundred and thirty thousand African American GIs, both army and air force, stationed in Britain.'[3] The United States racially segregated its troops until 1948.

In Hull, in February 1944, a Black US military band gave a concert at the Regal Concert Cinema called *Rhapsody in OD* (olive drab being the colour of their uniforms), which featured 'Lift Ev'ry Voice and Sing' – now regarded as the African American National Anthem.[4] The song was composed by J. Rosamond Johnson, with lyrics by his brother, James Weldon Johnson (for further discussion on the importance of this song, see the Epilogue).

In March and again in May 1944, Langston Hughes' ballad opera *The Man who Went to War* was broadcast on BBC radio. It was recorded in New York with key African American performers Josh White, a guitarist and singer; Ethel Waters, a jazz singer and actor; and the much beloved singer Paul Robeson. Hughes was unable to find a US broadcaster as a result of the production's explicit political and anti-racist content.[5] Its final lines speak to the *Pittsburgh Courier*'s Double V campaign, launched in February 1942, a fight for victory against fascism *and* racism. The opera closes with the rousing words:

> To break the power of Hitlerism and Jim Crowism all over the earth, folks – for this we fight! To make a world – including America – where everybody's free – for this we fight.
> Freedom of worship, freedom of press, freedom from want, freedom from fear. For this we fight.[6]

After the war, despite the vast labour shortages in the UK, 'the Ministry of Labour remained stridently opposed to recruitment in the West Indies';[7] but nonetheless hundreds of British subjects from the Caribbean began to arrive to seek work in the UK. The arrival of the *Empire Windrush* on 21 June 1948 is celebrated as a starting point for this mass migration to the UK, though Olusoga notes that 'between 1945 and 1950 only five thousand migrants from the West Indies arrived in Britain'; a larger period of migration took place in the next decade.[8]

Clearly Caribbean practitioners had long established the presence of Pan-Caribbean music and dance cultures in theatre in the UK. It remains notable that one month before the arrival of HMT *Empire Windrush*, there was already a Caribbean-inspired musical in the West End, *Calypso* (May 1948). The show brought together Caribbean performers with Black British radio stars Edric Connor and Evelyn Dove (see Chapter 10). Connor (b. 1913, Trinidad; d. 1968, London) arrived in the UK in 1944 and became a key figure in British theatre and cultural life. He was both a singer and folklorist and an expert in Calypso music. Dove (b. 1902, London; d. 1987, Epsom) established a career as one of Britain's foremost cabaret singers.

Social and political contexts of the Second World War

The Second World War had a massive impact on all aspects of daily life in the UK. The Blitz in London led to the closure of theatres from August 1940 to June 1941, and V1 and V2 rocket raids in 1944 saw theatres close again. During the war, Black troops (whether US or British citizens and 'colonial' subjects) received a hostile welcome. There were a number of assaults in nightclubs on GIs and on Black British subjects. In 1943, the LCP held their twelfth annual meeting in Liverpool 'as a gesture of solidarity both with the [Black population] and the West Indian technicians [drafted to help with the war effort]'.[9] Liverpool faced further racially motivated violence when 'organized attacks on the homes and clubs of black people' took place in 1948.[10]

Britain's control of India was increasingly challenged, notably by Gandhi's 'Quit India' movement in 1942, which led to his subsequent arrest. The CAA supported the Indian fight for independence and particularly 'the uncompromising refusal of Indian leaders to support the Allies'.[11] The Pan-African Federation was founded in 1944, and the fifth Pan-African Conference was held in Manchester in 1945. This particular conference is seen as vitally important and, as 'a precursor of the independence of Africa, is considered the most important. Interestingly two of the main organizers of this conference were diasporic Caribbean people: George Padmore and Amy Ashwood Garvey'.[12]

In 1947, Britain conceded its control of India through the partition (which split India and Pakistan). The partitioning led to mass population movements of around 15 million people and subsequent brutal violence and civil unrest. Gandhi was assassinated in 1948. In the Caribbean, Britain did not concede colonial control until much later: in 1962, to countries including Jamaica and Trinidad and Tobago; and in 1966, Barbados and Guyana. In Africa, Britain only started to award countries independence from the mid-to-late 1960s and beyond.

US contexts and British connections

Throughout the 1940s, Paul Robeson continued to play a major role in fighting anti-Black racism in the United States, setting up an anti-lynching organization in 1946, the American Crusade Against Lynching (ACAL), to protest the government's inaction. Fifty-six Black people had been murdered in the summer of 1946 alone. Though the NAACP did not involve itself with ACAL, W. E. B. Du Bois did.[13] Robeson also had a continuing role in British anti-racism and labour movements, and he repurposed musical theatre songs to do so. In 1949, a regional UK newspaper reported that, at the Assembly Hall in front of 300 delegates to the Electrical Trades Union Conference, he recited Langston Hughes's 'The Freedom Train' before singing:

Finally, came the song which has been linked with his name for the last 15 years, Old Man River. But with a difference he brought in a substitution for the last few lines. Instead of 'get a little drunk and land in gaol' it was 'show a little grit ...'[14]

Paul Robeson's visit and performance for Scottish miners in the same year was documented in the newsreel 'A Star Drops In'.[15] In 1950, Paul Robeson was denied a US passport because he had been 'extremely active in [*sic*] behalf of the independence for the colonial peoples of Africa'.[16]

On stage

The Second World War impacted West End theatre in many ways. Practically, theatres closed twice in London due to bombing – for a period in August 1940 to 25 June 1941 and during the V2 bombing in 1944–5. As noted in Chapter 9, losses included Ken 'Snakehips' Johnson in March 1941.

Many important Black practitioners performed or worked in the UK during this time. Rudolph Dunbar (b. 1907, Guiana; d. 1988, London) conducted the London Philharmonic Orchestra playing William Grant Still's 'Afro-American Symphony'. This was broadcast live on radio in April 1942. The African American Todd Duncan (1903–98) performed recitals in the UK in 1947. Duncan also played across Scotland and England, singing pieces by Handel, Brahms and Strauss alongside 'Ol' Man River' and an unnamed number from *Porgy and Bess*.[17]

Key African American choreographer Katherine Dunham (1909–2006) also worked in the UK. Dunham directed and choreographed the musical show *A Caribbean Rhapsody* (1948) in the West End, alongside delivering anthropology lectures.[18] One review suggested she was 'seeking new works to conquer, she invaded Britain this summer'.[19] The Nicholas Brothers also performed in the West End and in regional British variety theatre.

Several plays transferred from Broadway which explicitly tackled Black US experience (though rarely written by writers of African descent). Two white writers, Arnaud d'Usseau and James Gow, wrote *Deep are the Roots* (in the UK, 1947 and 1950), a play about racism in the Southern US states which opened on Broadway in 1945. It toured with the African American performers Gordon Heath and later Connie Smith (for a biography of Smith, see Key Figure 8).[20]

Robert Adams (b. 1902, Guyana; d. 1965, Guyana) worked extensively in UK theatre in the 1940s. Adams had appeared alongside Paul Robeson in several plays in the 1930s, including the British premiere of Lillian Hellman's play *The Little Foxes* (1942).[21] Hellman was a white US playwright who was politically active and later blacklisted during the McCarthy era. When Adams was left playing servant roles, critics' reviews of plays noted he was a fine actor who had been 'badly wasted' in such a part.[22]

In 1944, Adams proposed and established the Negro Repertory Arts Theatre in the UK. They produced a series of plays which showcased Black performers in the UK, including Eugene O'Neill's *All God's Chillun Got Wings* (1944). They also planned to produce 'the operetta Porgy and Bess' which would have been the British premiere of Gershwin's opera, but the show did not come to pass.[23] The company became linked to – perhaps subsumed into – the Unity Theatre, where Adams and Ida Shepley staged *All God's Chillun* in 1946. Shepley (b. 1908, Nantwich, UK; d. 1975, London) had Caribbean heritage and worked on TV as a presenter and later as an actor. Adams continued as an activist, giving lectures to Equity with the African American actor Hilda Simms on the Black experience in theatre.[24]

When *Anna Lucasta* (1947) transferred from the United States to the West End, its lead, Frederick O'Neal, then chair of the US Negro Theatre Group, was reported to be involved in a new attempt to set up the UK equivalent. In fact, though O'Neal supported it, *Anna Lucasta*'s understudies established the Negro Theatre Company in June 1948. One report suggested that the group had forty members and rehearsed at the Caribbean Club in Denman Street.[25] Its founding members included two Trinidadians, Edric Connor and Ulric Cross; as well as Ida Shepley; Neville Crabbe; and Pauline Henriques. Ida Shepley (born in Nantwich) had, like Marian Anderson, also trained as a singer with Amanda Aldridge. Shepley broadcast extensively on BBC radio as a contralto from 1938 onwards, sometimes alongside Elisabeth Welch (who by then was based in the UK). Pauline Henriques (b. 1914, Jamaica; d. 1998, Brighton, UK) was an actor and performer in the UK and the first Black British woman to perform on BBC TV in the live broadcast of the Unity's *All God's Chillun* (1946). Later, she was a counsellor and activist for women's rights. Neville Crabbe was an actor and later married Henriques. He worked in the UK because 'there is far more opportunity for serious theatre work here than in the United States'.[26]

Pauline Henriques had a significant impact on the Negro Theatre Company. She directed the musical revue *Something Different* for them, which also starred African American performers Emmett 'Babe' Wallace (an actor, singer and composer) and Mabel (alt. Mable) Lee. Lee recalled performing at the Palladium for eighteen months around this time: 'I represented Harlem and Africa.' She also taught 'the Suzie Q and all those jive numbers' with Buddy Bradley.[27] At the curtain of *Something Different*, Frederick O'Neal said that 'the group should be encouraged in the hope that it will reflect Negro culture at its best and show us a side of the theatre where [Black] artists have the advantage over others'.[28] By March 1949, Edric Connor and other representatives from the group met with Paul Robeson as he arrived to give a series of concerts in the UK.[29] Though the group seems to have closed by the end of the decade, Henriques went on to perform in the British premiere of Noël Coward's *Point Valaine* and Eugene O'Neill's *SS Glencairn* (in the latter alongside Connie Smith).[30]

In this period, the breadth of the African diaspora can be seen on Britain's stages. The Jamaican comedian Lionel Trim appeared in the London premiere of *Sunny River* (1943, Romberg and Hammerstein). Touring orchestras and bands presented shows that moved between theatres and dance halls, bands like 'Al Jennings and His All Star All Coloured Caribbean Orchestra',[31] and Don Leonardo and His Calypso Orchestra. Many musicians came from Trinidad, including the pianist Winifred Atwell and the singer Jan Muzurus. Atwell (c.1910–83), the celebrated boogie-woogie pianist, arrived in London in 1946 to further her music training and played widely in British theatres from 1947 onwards. She went on to broadcast regularly with the singer Evelyn Dove on the BBC. Muzurus (no clear details) was an operatic baritone who appeared in the Buddy Bradley choreographed *Sauce Tartare* alongside the white movie star Audrey Hepburn, the African American singer and dancer Muriel Smith (1923–85) and the Jamaican dancer Dudley Heslop (1924–2011).[32] One reviewer noted that Muzurus had 'deservedly found a niche for himself in West End revue'.[33] Muzurus also played Lun Thah, a Thai character, in the London premiere of *The King and I* (1953), something which reveals contemporaneous conflations of racial identities beyond 'not white'.

Calypsonians were quick to engage in theatre work where it was possible. Lord Beginner (Egbert Moore) (1904–81) and Lord Kitchener (Aldwyn Roberts) (1922–2000), who had both travelled on the *Windrush*, recorded with Cyril Blake in 1950.[34] Lord Woodbine (Harold Adolphus Philips) (1929–2000) and Lord Caresser (Rufus Callender) (1910–76) were also all from Trinidad, and all had various engagements with British theatre. Lord Caresser, for example, appeared in variety from October 1948.[35]

Ray Ellington (b. 1916, London; d. 1985), the jazz drummer and bandleader, also worked in variety theatre in the late 1940s.[36] Ellington's father was African American and his mother was Russian Orthodox Jewish. He had a strict religious upbringing before turning to the stage from the age of twelve.

Throughout the 1940s, revues continued to highlight Black performers in the West End and across the UK. Chris Gill (possibly African American but his background is unclear) featured in shows like *Why Go to Paris?* (1941) and *Harlem to Kentucky* (1944).[37] Elisabeth Welch continued to perform in shows like *Tuppence Coloured* (1948) and *Oranges and Lemons* (1949), as well as in variety with the Black British pianist and composer Reginald Foresythe. Reviews of Irving Berlin's revue *This Is the Army* (1943) at the London Palladium note that the show featured dancers of colour, though there are no names.[38] Buddy Bradley's influence continued in the 1940s. He tended to choreograph shows alongside white ballet choreographers, including *Wednesday After the War* (1941), which featured a ballet choreographed by Pauline Grant, and *Here Come the Boys* (1946), with choreography credits split between himself, Lydia Sokolova and Jack Hulbert.

Black dancers continued to feature in revues. In 1948, two Black tap dancers, L. D. Jackson (possibly African American) and the African American tap pioneer Cornell Lyons went into the revue *Here, There and Everywhere* (1948). The two had previously performed alongside Dizzy Gillespie and Duke Ellington.[39] Individual acts continued to excel – performers like Ike Hatch (see Key Figure 8) and the African American

IMAGE 8 *Elisabeth Welch, December 1945, performing at a concert held to raise funds for the Newsvendors' Benevolent Institution in the London Palladium. (Photo by Kurt Hutton/Picture Post/Hulton Archive/Getty Images.)*

singer Adelaide Hall, who was often accompanied by Fela Sowande on the piano and organ (sometimes listed as Aircraftman Sowande in the *Radio Times*). Sowande also accompanied Evelyn Dove, and he conducted the BBC Orchestra in 1944, playing his own composition. The *Radio Times* noted Sowande was 'now musical director of the Colonial Film Unit attached to the Ministry of Information and organist of the Kingsway Hall, Holborn'.[40]

On film

Paul Robeson continued to experience fame and adoration in the UK. In 1940, the drama *Proud Valley* featured him as a miner accepted into a Welsh village, telling the powerful story of a Black man's heroic sacrifice. Elisabeth Welch appeared and sang in *Fiddlers Three* (1946). Perhaps the most important Black British film was unfinished: *A World is Turning* (1948) aimed to showcase Black British communities and included the African American Adelaide Hall in performance (Hall was born in the United States but came to live full-time in the UK). Only the rushes of the film survive. Perhaps the most significant film featuring Black performers was *Stormy Weather* (1943); the film brought together Black US stars like Cab Calloway, Fats Waller, Bill Robinson, Lena Horne and Ada Brown and was widely screened.

IMAGE 9 *Paul Robeson (1898–1976) during a visit to London, February 1949. (Photo by George Konig/Keystone Features/Getty Images.)*

On television: The post-war switch-on, June 1946

When British TV was switched back on after the war, television programming featured a range of Black performance. Buddy Bradley again broadcast on television in shows like *Cafe Continental* (broadcast on 8 November 1947) and as choreographer and possibly even performer in Ike Hatch's *Kentucky Minstrels* (broadcast on 19 June 1948). Stage revues were broadcast, including *Sauce Tartare* (4 September 1949); and other variety TV shows included the Black British performers Ida Shepley alongside African Americans Ike Hatch and Johnny Nit. Berto Pasuka's Les Ballets Nègres was broadcast on 8 June 1949. Many important plays were broadcast live during this period. Pauline Henriques recalled the importance of the BBC's broadcasting of plays, 'giving black actors like Robert Adams, Edric Connor and myself, a play of that stature to act in'.[41]

10

Calypso and Black resistance

In Chapter 9, we explored how swing and Calypso music were an established presence in British theatre long before the passengers of the *Empire Windrush* disembarked at Tilbury docks on 21 June 1948 and brought musicians like Lord Kitchener to the UK. In this chapter, we gesture towards the scale of the work of Caribbean Black practitioners in theatre in the late 1940s by addressing the work of key figures such as Berto Pasuka, born Wilbert Passerley (b. 1911, Jamaica; d. 1963, London), Edric Connor and Pauline Henriques. This period saw West End musicals represent the Caribbean experience (or attempt to), as well as a continued wider presence in variety and in other forms of broadcasting. The chapter explores the formation of key Black theatre organizations in the 1940s, often led by people from the Caribbean, in partnership with other practitioners of African descent. Groups like Les Ballets Nègres and the Negro Theatre Company strengthened and formalized Black creative activism in the UK. Amanda Biddell notes that, after the Second World War, artist-settlers from the Caribbean 'worked within British cultural institutions and trends and used their position to espouse a positive vision of national belonging that was multiracial, anti-racist, and that emphasized Britain's historic connection to its West Indian colonies'.[1]

As we have established in Chapter 9, there was an ongoing presence of Caribbean music in theatres in the UK; this presence sometimes confused boundaries between South American and Caribbean sounds. At the London Palladium in 1942, within the revue *Best Bib and Tucker*,

Edmund Ros and 'his Cuban band' performed 'Caribbean Rhapsody'.[2] Ros (b. 1910, Trinidad; d. 2011, Spain) was a Venezuelan bandleader who later performed as Edmundo Ros. Ros's mother was a Black Venezuelan woman, and his father was a white Scottish man. He had trained at the Royal Academic of Music from 1937 to 1942, before establishing his own band in 1940.[3] Ros continued to play in nightclubs and variety theatre throughout the 1940s, working at the Coconut Grove club before settling at the Mayfair restaurant, the Bagatelle. There, and through his many recordings, he popularized sambo, rhumba and mambo music for high society audiences, including Princess Elizabeth (shortly before she became Queen). Musicals and revues in the 1940s clumsily gestured towards musical multiplicities: the revue *A Day in Trinidad* (1947) specifically featured 'The West African Tribes';[4] and *Some Song and Dances of Spain and the Caribbean* (the Torch Theatre, London, 1949) blended Latin American musical cultures with Trinidadian Calypsonian singer Lord Beginner.[5] The blurriness between these popular music styles, in their public dissemination and reception in the UK, to some extent reflects the legacy of the African diaspora. However, it is also a product of the commercial popularity of these new music styles in the UK and a desire to quickly repackage and present them in front of audiences.

Calypso (1948)

Hedley Briggs, a white actor and writer, was perhaps aware of Katherine Dunham's work in *Carib Song* (1945) and *Bal Negre* (1946) when he produced the musical *Calypso* (1948), a month before the arrival of the *Windrush*. Briggs, a theatrical jack-of-all-trades 'devised, designed and directed' the musical.[6] Briggs' career had already intersected with important Black creative practitioners, and he had danced in Buddy Bradley's and Frederick Ashton's *High Yellow* (1933). *Calypso*'s cast included Black and white performers, but the performers of African descent were the stars. One advertisement noted: 'A new West Indian Musical with the famous Radio Stars Edric Connor, Evelyn Dove, Mabel Lee, Don Leonardo and His Calypso Orchestra.'[7] Edric Connor's influence is explored later in the chapter (see also Key Figure 12).

Though the musical ran for only thirty-two performances, it demonstrates the widespread influence of Caribbean performers in the UK, even in the context of a white authored piece. Intriguingly, *Calypso*'s short run tallies with Sam Manning's similarly titled Broadway musical *Caribbean Carnival* (1947), which did not see anything like Dunham's longevity.

Edric (Esclus) Connor (b. 1913, Trinidad; d. 1968, London) originally studied to become a mechanical and structural engineer. He was also a folk song expert (in Trinidadian Calypso songs) and a singer himself as well as a journalist. In January 1945, the *New York Amsterdam News* reported that Connor was passing through the United States on his way to the UK, to 'join the fight against Hitler by making munitions in English war factories'.[8] Connor quickly became a major part of British music and theatrical life and an established broadcaster in BBC radio programs like *Songs of the West Indies* and *Travellers' Tales*. Much of his work involved performing Trinidadian folk songs – something he did in live performance, for example at the International Arts Centre in 1945, and in numerous lectures.[9] Best known for songs like the 'Manchester United Calypso', Connor faced considerable racism that prevented his career developing further; his work as an ethnomusicologist led to several publications of sheet music. He was the first Black actor to appear at the Royal Shakespeare Company, and, with his wife Pearl, he ran the Edric Connor Agency.

KEY FIGURE 12 *Edric Connor, a short biography.*

Before they worked on *Calypso*, Don Leonardo and his orchestra had played in variety and in dance halls. Leonardo arrived in the UK from the Caribbean in July 1947; the *New Musical Express* reported that Gino Arbib, a manager, had funded their travels and arranged for them to audition 'within an hour of their arrival' for the BBC. They were assembled of 'Two guitars, trumpet, flute doubling clarinet, two bongos, two graters, chocio, marracas. Also featured with the band are two Mentor [*sic*] Calypso dancers, Carlos and Cherry.'[10] Cherry is presumably Cherry Adele, who became part of the *Calypso* company and a later key member of Les Ballets Nègres; Adele originally toured with Al Shaw and his Blue Hawaiians in 1946.[11]

The critics description of *Calypso* points to a lack of nuance in responses:

A cheerful team of [Caribbean] players dance and sing in gay dresses and Trinidad settings. They deserve a much better musical play than this infantile nonsense, with an incredibly sugary plot. Only once do we get a genuine Calypso song in doggerel, about Lincoln's Gettysburg speech. The music has a tom-tom touch, but it is fidgety and unimpressive and the local dances, officially described as traditional, are mostly boring.[12]

Given the dates, it is possible that this number was the unrecorded Calypso 'Abraham Lincoln Speech at Gettysburg' by the Calypsonian Growling Tiger – or at least inspired by it. Spencer Mawby notes: 'Calypso was a style that was often overtly political and widely influential.'[13] White reviewers were clearly uncomfortable with the form in the musical. The right-wing periodical *Truth* noted:

> Near the end of the show came a sample of the quaint doggerel songs written locally on topical subjects and exploited by dance-band leaders. It was on Lincoln's Gettysburg speech, and to me the happiest moment of the evening. [...] The white members of the Calypso cast were singularly ineffective. Mixed casts, I fear, are unworkable.[14]

Contemporary reviews of the show reveal the continuing racism faced by Black performers on West End stages, even when disguised as half-hearted essentialist flattery. Reviews of Edric Connor's performance note he sang a Calypso called 'Democracy', which is presumably the same number.[15] The possibility of a protest Calypso in a West End musical around the 'all men are created equal' is thrilling – whether or not it was Growling Tiger's song.

Black theatre companies: Early formations

While the writer of *Calypso*, Briggs, was white, the musical's Black cast were part of an established network of Black practitioners who led developments in the UK. During the 1940s, there were two attempts to establish a Black theatre company, notably Paul Robeson had suggested such a group in 1936.[16] In 1944, Robert Adams, a Guyanese actor (and British subject), set up the Negro Repertory Arts Theatre; Peter Noble, writing in *The Stage*, praised the company as an important endeavour:

> At present many [performers of colour] engage themselves in other jobs rather than spend their time playing servile parts [...] But offer them real-life characters in new and classic Black plays and Londoners will be truly astonished to realise what a wealth of [Black] talent we possess in this country.[17]

One account suggests that Peter Noble, a white writer and journalist, was part of this project, but no supporting information can be found to confirm this, though Noble was involved with the Unity Theatre.[18] It seems that the Negro Repertory Arts Theatre was then possibly part of the Colchester production of *All God's Chillun Got Wings* (1944), but nothing more seems to have come of Adams' plans. One account suggests that the theatre company produced *Calypso*, but again, no corroboration can be found.[19] The company seems to disappear from the records.

In November 1947, Robert Adams wrote an essay in *New Theatre*, through the Equity Page, which invited union members to contribute about the problems Black actors experienced as 'something contributory to the support of the white artists'.[20] Adams poses the question, 'Why is the British Negro artist so considered in the theatre? Why is there always the argument either that he has not the talent or that he will not be "box office"?'[21] He describes the double discrimination Black British subjects received from white producers who assumed only Black Americans 'had any talent. The African or West Indian was called second-rate'.[22] He closes the essay by making the plea for Black actors, particularly Black British actors, to be considered as equals: 'ours will be a dynamic contribution.'[23] At the same time as he was pursuing his performance career and fighting for the status of Black performers, Adams completed his legal training and became a lawyer. In 1952, Richie Riley (co-founder of Les Ballets Nègres) and Edric Connor both wrote to *The Stage* to explain the situation of Black British performers and echoing Adams' earlier commentary. Riley wrote that 'no encouragement whatsoever is given by theatrical circles to British Negroes'.[24] Connor wrote: 'the public will never know the extent to which we are humiliated by our American brothers.'[25] Connor made clear that the biggest problem facing Black British theatre practitioners was 'finding a place at a reasonable rental, within easy reach of theatregoers, where we could put on shows on a professional basis'.[26]

In 1948, the Negro Theatre Company was formed – it was falsely reported that the Black American actor Frederick O'Neal, who was performing in *Anna Lucasta* in London, was involved; something which Edric Connor would later blame for being partly responsible for the British company's ultimate failure.[27] O'Neal had previously founded the American Negro Theatre company. The Negro Theatre Company distanced themselves by noting they were not a branch of the American Negro Theatre company 'or in any way connected with it'.[28] Asserting their British connection was clearly necessary and important (not least because they were either British subjects or British citizens). The company formed and quickly produced work, a musical concert called *Something Different*: 'under the direction of Pauline Henriques, they will be seen in Thornton Wilder's one-act play *The Happy Journey to Trenton and Camden* and in a scene from *Golden Boy* at the Maccabi House [...] Some variety items will be given.'[29] The founding company members, as recorded by *The Stage*, were Ulric Cross, Edric Connor, Neville Crabbe, George Brown, Ida Shepley and Pauline Henriques.[30]

The Negro Theatre Company clearly had the support of Robeson, as the *Manchester Guardian* reported: 'More than a hundred artists attended the Caribbean Club, Denman Street, London, W.1. yesterday for auditions conducted by Edric Connor, the West Indian singer. The guests included Paul Robeson, who promised his support for the gesture.'[31] The Caribbean Club was an important part of Black life in the UK; the Florence Mills Social Parlour had long since closed down. The club faced racist violence; for example, there were reports of American Air Force and RAF officers beating up two Black men leaving the premises in March 1945.[32] The Negro Theatre

IMAGE 10 *Edric Connor (on the far right) addresses the company. The women are unnamed in the caption; however, Ida Shepley is clearly identifiable as the last seated woman to the left of Connor. (Photo by KEYSTONE-FRANCE/Gamma-Rapho via Getty Images.)*

Company did not continue beyond 1949, though they gave a further concert with the Welsh brothers of African descent, born in Cardiff, known as the Hermanos Deniz Cuban Rhythm Band (who played alongside the Ray Ellington Quarter) at Poplar Town Hall.[33] The company was an attempt to formalize the performance networks that reached across performers of African descent working in the UK and across all kinds of musical and theatrical life.

Edric Connor

Reviews of *Calypso* noted Connor's performance, or rather, the lack of it: 'it is a pity that this fine artist gets so few opportunities.'[34] He was already an established performer in the UK, and in regards to musicals, had played Joe in a radio adaptation of Hammerstein and Kern's *Show Boat* in 1944. He sang extensively with Evelyn Dove in a weekly radio program called *Serenade in Sepia* – which later transitioned to TV when it was switched back on after the war. He also performed in important live television plays, alongside Henriques and Shepley. Connor continued this mixture of acting, presenting and performance: *Variety in Sepia* (1947) saw him perform alongside Winifred Atwell, Cyril Blake and Buddy Bradley. In 1949, Connor was playing in variety theatre as 'an experiment'; however, he was successful and repeated songs he had made popular on his radio broadcasts.[35]

The Connor and Evelyn Dove pairing in *Calypso* clearly built on both of their name recognition as radio stars.[36] One April 1949 notice in *The Stage* remarked that Connor was performing in the music hall only two nights before he was giving a recital at the Wigmore Hall in April 1949, where he would be singing a range of songs, from 'West Indian calypsos to spirituals and classical songs'.[37] His repertoire in variety included spirituals like 'Weepin' Mary' – he movingly recalled performing this in 1944 to a West End audience who were enduring the losses of war. After he stopped singing, his audience was silent: 'I thought I had failed, but the lights went up, to reveal a theatre audience dressed in black, with white handkerchiefs pressed against their faces and mouths.'[38] He recalled that 'Ol' Man River' was something of an anti-climax, but he was still performing that song in variety in 1949 – it was clearly closely associated with Black concert singers of his stature, as part of his repertoire.[39] In 1947, Connor recorded *Serenade in Sepia* (1947). Footage remains of his extraordinary performance of 'Water Boy', preserving his range and vocal presence. In his biography, he notes that, when he tried to train, he was unwelcome at the Royal Academy of Dramatic Art – the principal wanted him to take only 'private lessons from one his teachers'.[40] He ended up being supported by Rose Bruford, then Head of Drama at the Royal Academy of Music. He performed as 'De Lawd' in their student production of *Green Pastures* – the rest of the cast were white women students in black make-up.[41] He received vocal lessons from Julius Guttman, an exiled Jewish singer, to help build his technique and repertoire.[42]

In the 1950s, Connor had an expansive career across musicals, music recording, plays and films – but one which was stymied by anti-Black racism. He starred in the British movie *Cry the Beloved Country* (1951), based on the Alan Paton novel, alongside Sidney Poitier. He went on to appear in the somewhat unlikely Antonín Dvořák musical *Summer Song* (1955) and was the first Black performer with the Royal Shakespeare Company as Gower in *Pericles* in 1958.[43] He also published collections of Caribbean and specifically Trinidadian folk songs and produced steel drum bands tour from the Caribbean to the UK. He recorded numerous songs, including the 'Manchester United Calypso' in 1957, and was clearly involved with disseminating Calypso music to a wider audience in the UK. He successfully trained as a TV producer but was never commissioned to make any work. Connor was closely involved in anti-racist activism and in building the Black theatrical community in the UK. Though much of this work took place outside of the period of this book, it is worth noting that, with his wife, Pearl, he formed a theatrical agency in 1957 specifically for Black artists. Pearl and

Edric Connor opened their house in Notting Hill as a meeting place for Caribbean students. The Connors knew and worked with intellectuals like C. L. R. James and George Padmore and hosted visitors like the West Indian Cricket team.[44] Edric Connor invited his friend Paul Robeson to their home in 1949, a decision which Connor later believed led to his application for a US visa to be refused.[45] Pearl, an important activist in her own right, recalled after his death that 'Edric paid the price for his conviction and belief in the liberation of black people'.[46] When Berto Pasuka's Les Ballets Nègres made their first TV appearance in June 1946, Edric Connor introduced them.

Berto Pasuka and Les Ballets Nègres

Wilbert 'Bertie' Passley arrived in the UK from Jamaica in 1939; he styled himself as Berto Pasuka throughout his professional life. In 1946, he formed the first Black dance company in the UK with Richie Riley, a company which ran until 1953. In 1997, Riley recalled the legacy of the company as 'in every shape and form, ballet in a black idiom'.[47] Les Ballets Nègres staged numerous important pieces that presented Caribbean and African themes and stories in theatres across the UK, on TV (in June 1946, June 1949 and January 1950) and in discussion on radio in July 1947. Until recently, Pasuka's work had been largely forgotten in histories of British dance, until the important recovery and preservation work that Leon Robinson, Thea Barnes and Keith Watson have conducted. Both Riley and Pasuka were gay men; their experience in the UK was clearly shaped by this double discrimination ('homosexual acts' were not legal in the UK until 1967 and are still not legal in Jamaica at the time of writing).

Though the Arts Council denied the company funding in the 1950s, a decision which in part led to its demise, in the 1980s they funded Stephen Dwoskin's important documentary film *Ballet Black* (1985), which preserved the dance work and oral histories of those involved with Ballets Nègres. Subsequently, in the late 1990s, Robinson worked with Riley to stage a celebration of the company's work, which took place in 1999 at the London South Bank, though Riley did not live to see it. The event restaged some of Pasuka's choreography. Black dancer Darren Panton who performed in the company noted: 'I can't believe we weren't taught about them during our training. To know what they achieved so long ago is an inspiration for all black artists working today.'[48]

Thea Barnes, who has critically addressed the importance of Pasuka's work, notes: 'Pasuka chose alternative, subaltern narratives and movement vocabularies and situated them within a European theatrical frame.'[49] In her approach, she considers how, having located their work, there is a need to move on from the myth that Pasuka and the company was 'an anomaly situated outside legitimized renditions of British dance history'.[50] This section brings new information to Pasuka's biography – and in particular considers the company's broadcasting and their widespread presence in British creative industries. Les Ballets Nègres were part of the contemporary modern dance scene; their first composer was Leonard Salzedo, an Anglo-Spanish composer and music director for Ballet Rambert. The company staged numerous important work which explicitly staged Caribbean and African themes and stories.

A 'culturally diverse company of approximately 25 members (dancers, musicians, and other support staff), performers came from Jamaica, Liverpool, Ghana, Nigeria, England, and Trinidad'.[51] Their ballets included *De Prophet* (1946); *They Came* (1946); *Market Day* (1946); *Aggrey* (1946); *Blood* (1946); *De Bride Cry* (1948); *Nine Nights* (1950); and *Cabaret 1920* (1950, with music by the white composer Geoffrey Russell Smith). Their work played in London and in repertoire in Birmingham, Nottingham and

IMAGE 11 *Arrival of Berto Pasuka's Les Ballets Nègres in Basel, Switzerland 1947. (Photo by ATP/RDB/ullstein bild via Getty Images.)*

Manchester, along with smaller tour dates across the UK and in Europe. The company included Cherry Adele (who also appeared in *Calypso*), John Lagey (later known as the wrestler Johnny Kwango), Joseph Layode, Roy Carr, Ben E. and Pearl Johnson, Marjorie Blackman, Lander Moore, Brenda Davies and Doris Bah. Leon Cassel-Gerrard, a white producer and agent, represented the company; Cassel-Gerrard also managed Ken Johnson.[52] The ballets were composed for piano, with tom-tom and maraca accompaniment. Pasuka originally worked with the Nigerian guitarist Ambrose Campbell, who led six other musicians in the West African Rhythm Brothers.[53] He later worked with Korley Martey's African Ensemble.

Thea Barnes notes Marcus Garvey Jr's ideas had been 'a key influence' on Berto Pasuka and Richie Riley as young performers in Jamaica – where they had been part of a theatrical production Garvey was involved in.[54] Pasuka was the first to leave; having arrived in the UK, he trained in classical ballet 'to give himself a wider range of movement and more control, but he realized that it was not a suitable idiom or system for his black dancers or relevant to the themes he wished to express'.[55] Pasuka first advertised for work in June 1941 as a 'native dancer';[56] by the following year, he was playing in variety in a 'Battle of the Bands'-style event as a dancer for Edmundo Ros and his rhumba band. In June 1944, Pasuka advertised himself as 'the world's only male coloured dancer with a Ballet Technique: repertoire includes Jungle Dance, Dance de L'Orient, Manhattan Serenade, Vacant for Revue'.[57]

Pasuka performed in *Men of Two Worlds* (1946), a problematic film starring Robert Adams (the two worlds are Africa and Europe). The film funded the ballet company's formation and introduced Pasuka to a wider circle of Black performers in the UK. By the time Riley arrived in the UK, Val Wilmer notes that Pasuka was an established part of the Bloomsbury intellectual circles; not only was his lover 'a man of Fabian family connections' but in addition George Bernard Shaw also supported the formation of the company.[58] *The Stage* reported in 1947 that Pasuka had been 'encouraged by Dame Sybil Thorndike [to recruit a company of] Jamaican dancers from talent already hidden in London'.[59] This connection with literary and artistic societies was extensive. Angus McBean photographed the company and Pasuka himself – these images were widely reproduced; and the artist Benno Schotz sculpted a bronze of Pasuka. It led to the company forming the Ballets Nègres Society – to support the company's activities.

Pasuka rehearsed with the company before they began to tour, noting in 1948: 'I was glad that hardly any of the company had been dancers. That meant that they were not spoiled for me before I could train them.'[60] Theatre and dance critics' response to the company's work is often one of shock at the strangeness and an attempt to describe its powerful effect for their readers. In 1946, a *The Stage* critic described Pasuka's work, saying that the choreographer knew 'the value of a stage-picture and knows how to impress it indelibly upon the mind. His prophet, quivering in the throes of despair, haunts the memory as vividly as Robeson's desolate cry rings in the ear, years after hearing him sing a spiritual.'[61] The company, and Pasuka, were highly praised for their work which challenged expectations of what dance could achieve. The ballet dancer and critic Beryl de Zoete wrote in the *New Statesman*: 'There is no doubt that [...] Berto Pasuka has discovered a new art form.'[62] There is clearly a relationship between the choreographic practice of Pasuka and Dunham, and the two were aware of one another's work. In 1948, Dunham brought her own piece, *A Caribbean Rhapsody*, to London and for a national tour.

> The third act saw the quietening of the native drums for it was the orchestra's turn under its conductor Daniel Mendelssohn, together with the star, Katherine Dunham, to steal the show with their rendering of the 'blues' which Katherine Dunham sang in her inimitable husky voice, captivating the audience.[63]

Barnes notes Dunham was 'acquainted with Pasuka, corresponded with him and, when she was in London, attended the same performances'.[64]

The company broadcast on television three times during their existence – in June 1946, June 1949 and in January 1950. In July 1946, Pasuka broadcast in a special radio program about his company with Ambrose Campbell and Leonard Salzedo.[65] Though the 1950 broadcast could have reached less than 1 per cent of the population, since very few people had a TV set at this time, one critic reported that 'the strong rhythm, the gusto and the strangeness would charm viewers who might be afraid to like ordinary ballet because it is known to be a highbrow taste'.[66] Sadly, it appears that this final broadcast was never made, owing to a broadcasting fault.[67] The sense of a wider audience than 'ordinary ballet' though is interesting, because there was clearly a civic importance and funding of the work at local levels – if only briefly. The *Worthing Herald* discusses the company's appearance at the Pier Pavilion in January 1949 and notes: 'the Corporation Entertainments Department is co-operating with the Ballets Nègres Society to make the presentation possible here.'[68] This kind of co-production might have been followed elsewhere, as there was clearly a sense of civic occasion in Manchester where three of the women from the cast had tea with the Lady Mayoress.[69] Similarly, in Nottingham, heads of the co-operative movement 'and many other distinguished figures' as well as the Mayor and his wife attended.[70]

Members of the company discussed the importance of their work as activism. Marjorie Blackman, a Guyanese dancer and early member of the company, was also a committee member of the LCP. When she was interviewed in 1949, Blackman explained her views on racism: 'I believe it is just ignorance, and that the way to dispel it is to meet as many people as possible. The Ballet Nègres are doing good work that way.'[71] *Nine Nights* explicitly staged the Black Caribbean experience in presenting mourning rituals and spirituality:

The ballet shows the first and ninth night ceremonies in the house of a mother who has lost her own. On the ninth night the ghost of the dead appears, and a feast of rum, rice and fish is spread for it. After he has made his appearance the spirit is sent back to the land of the dead, and the food, flowers and bed are destroyed. Then the final candle is extinguished.[72]

Though Ballets Nègres did not produce a musical, Pasuka was clearly involved in expanding possibilities for dance on British stages. He also was involved in plans for 'a spectacular musical show in the West End in which he and the members of his Ballets Nègres will appear'.[73] Nothing came of the plans, though *Cabaret 1920* (1950) was clearly an extensive production – set in a Harlem nightclub during prohibition.[74]

Musical theatre clearly framed responses to Black performers on British stages in the late 1950s. One *The Stage* article complained in 1951 that, 'at a recent theatre visited by the Ballets Nègres, the resident orchestra insisted upon playing *No, No, Nanette*, between the first two ballets'.[75] Pasuka influenced contemporary ballet choreographers such as Andrée Howard (who had also worked alongside Buddy Bradley in the 1940s).[76] After the company folded in 1953, the absence of Pasuka in the UK was noted in the press. One article in 1955 berated the lack of audience for more experimental performances: 'Pasuka, whose hands were likened to [Alicia] Markova's now ekes out an existence in the poor quarter of Paris.'[77] After the closure of the company he acted in Sean O'Casey's *Cock-O-Doodle Dandy* (1959). He died in 1963, penniless, so his friends and the Jamaican and wider Black community raised funds for his funeral. Arthur Coddling, who led the appeal, explained that, after the company broke up, Pasuka 'went to dance in clubs and musicals in Paris and London'.[78]

George Padmore wrote in 1946 that, through Pasuka's work, the Black performer 'had taken his rightful place in the London theatre and in the history of ballet'.[79] *Aggrey* (1946) stages the clearest anti-racist activism. The ballet was based on 'an idea by the African philosopher',[80] the writings and ideas of Dr James Emman Kwegyir Aggrey, an educationalist, activist and philosopher, born in what is now Ghana. Aggrey used the image of the piano keys to promote interracial harmony. Reviewers for the ballet explained to their readers: 'As on a piano keyboard, real harmony is only achieved by the blending of black and white notes.'[81] Aggrey influenced many Black thinkers, including Kwame Nkrumah (who was part of the Amy Ashwood Garvey and C. L. R. James circle in London in the 1930s, and the first president of Ghana).[82] Though the metaphor might seem somewhat trite, or even accommodationist, Pasuka stages the piece in a way that retains his agency: the ballet physically staged a piano, the men played the black keys, the women played the white – Pasuko played the pianist playing the keys. The music of the work was said to have been 'inspired by Tin Pan Ally [*sic*]'[83] – a different aesthetic from the more explicitly West African percussion. In her consideration of Pasuka's work, Anita Gonzalez reflects on Thea Barnes' recognition of the complexity of his identity, which connected him to Black and Southeast Asian traditions: 'Pasuka dances through the British world named as a Black artist, but in the United States he might align himself with other communities. The point is, Pasuka's identity is multifaceted, allowing him to represent diversity that extends beyond the Black label.'[84] Pasuka advocated for multiracial possibility, as George Padmore suggested at the beginning of the company's work. Pasuka explained: 'I hope that what the politicians have failed to do, Art will accomplish in bringing the black and white races closer together in understanding.'[85] Pasuka's dance practice is rooted in a Black activism which enacts interracial possibility. Edric Connor's remarkable achievements and determination were limited by white supremacist thinking and anti-Black racism, thinking which could not tolerate the redistribution of material resources required to permit him to fulfil his potential. Yet, despite this, his career made a material impact on the development of the British stage.

In each chapter, we have pointed to the discrepancies, the hampering of and the marginalizing of practitioners of African descent, but also the many significant achievements of Black practitioners which shaped musical theatre practices, and which shaped audience experience of the form. In this book, we have consistently argued that the history of British musical theatre is hardly even a history of musicals; it is certainly not a history of white people. It is a story that relies on Black artistry and activism, and of Black-led interracial possibility, despite white people's continuing appropriation and minimization of the power of Black practitioners, of Black community and of Black theatre making. The community building and creative generosity of Black performers – of their skill and training, artistic vision and achievement – that is the story. For us to move towards what is not just an inclusive historiography but an *accurate* one, we need to deal with the inconvenient, yet brilliant, reality.

EPILOGUE

Sean

At the time of writing it is mid-August 2020. By this point, millions of people have taken to the streets across the world to affirm the value of what it means when a single mouth promises that 'Black Lives Matter'. To affirm that in order to say 'Black Lives Matter' it means that the bearer of those words must believe that they matter not only in this moment but in the previous moment, and in each moment to come. To affirm that sometimes in the moments that have passed they have not rung as true, or that if those words were ringing, they may have been unreceived or unsolicited, and that although this has not weakened their resolve, it has dampened their impact.

At the start of Chapter 1 on Will Marion Cook, we note Cedric Robinson's positioning of several key early Black practitioners and their contributions. Two of these people are J. Rosamond Johnson and James Weldon Johnson, the American composer and writer-activist, respectively, who were responsible for the creation of what has now been immortalized as the Black National Anthem, 'Lift Ev'ry Voice and Sing'. The collaboration of this piece by these two brothers is momentous for numerous reasons: James Weldon penned the poem to read at a celebration of Abraham Lincoln's birthday, an almost fitting setup in itself. The words written by one of the first Black attorneys admitted to the bar in the American South would soon be set to music by his brother John Rosamond, and in doing so, would manifest one of the staunchest anthems of pride, courage and perseverance that Black culture has claimed to date. How fitting that this anthem, for our purposes, was written in 1900 – the very year our historiographical journey in this text begins.

The text is full of promise and vision, and its composition shakes rafters in its anticipatory melodic and harmonic styling, the truest call to peaceful arms and steadfast onwardness:

> Lift ev'ry voice and sing
> 'Til earth and heaven ring
> Ring with the harmonies of Liberty
> Let our rejoicing rise
> High as the list'ning skies
> Let it resound loud as the rolling sea
>
> Sing a song full of the faith that the dark past has taught us
> Sing a song full of the hope that the present has brought us

Facing the rising sun of our new day begun
Let us march on 'til victory is won

I have been reflecting on this piece, considering what it means that these
authors, who were not only activists and the truest renaissance men of their
own right but also at a later point in their career were actively dedicated
to creating material for New York theatre audiences, were also in circles
with many of the very people we have mentioned in this text. I have
been reflecting also that they were writing these words at and from the
very beginning and that their words were being spoken and sung by their
Black sisters and brothers, young and wise, across the United States, and
undoubtedly, in Britain as well – for as we have seen, the extent of Black
sister and brotherhood, of Black family, knows no bounds.

My musical background is grounded firmly in the liturgical world of
church music, not unlike many of my Black musical colleagues, and I became
an organist through my studies. I consider the times I've played this hymn,
and the voices that have sung it with me. I also consider the times that I
have not played it, the communities in which I have engaged musically that
have never and to this day still know not of its existence, and of the length
of time it took until I did finally know it: embarrassingly, much too late in
a lifetime surrounded by music. I can see the Black faces of the choristers
who have recited the text vocally with eyes shut; so confident of its words
that they read as an external engraving upon their own hearts, eternally
etched and readable by the world: collective, subconscious and subjacent
in its ability to speak the unspeakable between Black minds who harbour a
mutual understanding and resolve.

The words themselves pull at me: we 'lift *every* voice and sing', when
we say that *every single* voice matters and is worthy of listening to. Its
duality does not escape me either: we '*lift every voice* and sing' when
we talk collectively; it takes all of our voices, Black, white and all others
inclusive, to proclaim these truths. The middle of this hymn has always
struck me musically: those who know its composition are familiar with the
developmental music accompanying the text 'Sing a song full of the faith
that the dark past has taught us, sing a song full of the hope that the present
has brought us' is sung in unison, a seismic shift from the rest of this chordal
piece. The two lines differentiate greatly in their melodic contour: the first
one outlines a largely major modal journey, whereas the second one moves
to a minor, more tense line that resolves into a huge harmonic shift back to
the recapitulatory end of the verse.

I find this so telling of the anthem's journey, as well as of ours as a collective
people. Compare with the words: the contrapuntal nature of major and
minor existing together, of 'faith of the dark past' sung just before the 'hope
that the present has brought us'. This oppositional nature is telling, in my
opinion: yes, we exist in a world that has silenced Black voices, Black bodies,
Black spirit. Yes, we are now inheritors of dark histories, of paths watered

by tears and stained by blood. Yet, there is hope. We amplify Black voices increasingly and become more aware of how much our ears need them. We march in the same streets that have been literally stained by the blood of those who have reached the pinnacle of sacrifice to one day 'face the rising sun of the new day' we look to begin.

And so, it is now up to us to lift every voice and sing. In both realms: lift our own voices *and* lift the voices of others that have been unheard. The practitioners we have laid out here have committed their labour in lifting their own voices. Many of them did so literally in their art, most of them did so actively in their cause, and all of them did so by virtue of who they were. Many of their voices we did not know, even a short time ago. Many of their voices you have not known. But now you do. One of the most beautiful parts of the journey of this anthem is that it has been sung and adopted by people and nations alike across the world, of all colours and walks – likely by at least as many millions of people who still march for those freedoms today. Textually, you will notice upon examination of all of its stanzas that it speaks to the Black experience, but never explicitly: therefore, there is a collectively inherited responsibility in its words which affirms that, yes, this is Black experience, but no, it is not the Black experience singularly to bear and shift.

When we consider the alternative histories that these practitioners have layed down not as fringe but as mainstream, we lift every voice. When we learn their names, we lift every voice. When we celebrate not the works that they created but further the fact that they did them, we lift every voice. When we support the archivists, historians, writers who unearth their stories, we lift every voice. Black lives *do* matter. And they matter for so many reasons, but most importantly, they matter because we, as collective human consciousness, have not realized they mattered fully in moments of our complicated past. We can right them.

Let us in the theatre be the ones who march forward and insist that our histories are not only equitable but simply also comprehensive and fully inclusive. Let us say now, that in standing as allies, in learning our own histories and refusing to be taught fragmentedly unfinished ones, that in saying 'Black lives *matter*', that we refuse to allow any of these names to go unheard again. Let us say now, that in reflecting on the past, these names will be a learned part of our consciousness, and that in that consciousness we can decide what kind of future for the theatre we want our students to create, we want our practitioners to mould, we want our audiences to reflect. There is so much work to be done beyond the pages of this book, and the work is not exclusive. With your help, let us 'march on 'til victory is won'.

APPENDIX A

In Dahomey's UK touring

Drawing on digitized local newspapers, this appendix lays out the tour of *In Dahomey* in two sections: first, with the Williams and Walker company (see Table 5); and second, with the Charles Avery and Dan Hart tours (Table 6). The theatre capacity information has been sourced from a range of locations, including *The Era* and *The Stage* as well as the extraordinary work at the Arthur Lloyd Music Halls and Theatres site (http://www.arthurlloyd.co.uk/index.html). An asterisk denotes an estimated seat capacity based on other touring venues the show visited. Note, that these are *absolute maximum capacities*, which it is unlikely were met – however, the show's habit of returning to venues suggests it did at least good business.

TABLE 5 In Dahomey *tour with Williams and Walker.*

Date	City	Theatre Name	Seat Capacity	Total Number of Available Seats (potential capacity audience)
01/05/1903	London	Shaftesbury Theatre (200 performances)	1,800	360,000
25/01/1904	London	Woolwich Grand Theatre	1,680	11,760
01/02/1904	Hull	Theatre Royal	1,200	8,400
08/02/1904	London	Stoke Newington Alexandra Theatre	2,025	14,175
15/02/1904	London	Richmond Prince of Wales	1,370	9,590
22/02/1904	London	Islington Marlborough Theatre	2,612	18,284

29/02/1904	Brighton	Theatre Royal	952	6,664
10/03/1904	London	Kennington Theatre	1,347	9,429
14/03/1904	London	Hammersmith King's Theatre	3,000	21,000
21/03/1904	Bristol	Prince's Theatre	2,154	15,078
04/04/1904	London	Peckham Crown Theatre	2,000	14,000
11/04/1904	Newcastle upon Tyne	Royal	1,249	8,743
18/04/1904	Sheffield	Lyceum	1,068	7,476
02/05/1904	Edinburgh	Lyceum	658	4,606
09/05/1904	Glasgow	Royalty	1,314	9,198
16/05/1904	Manchester	Prince's Theatre	1,890	13,230
23/05/1904	London	Borough Theatre	1,500	10,500
				542,133

TABLE 6 In Dahomey *tour with Avery and Hart.*

Date	City	Theatre	Seat Capacity	Total Number of Available Seats (potential capacity audience)
18/07/1904	Blackpool	Grand Theatre	1,100	7,700
01/08/1904	Southport	Opera House	1,492	10,444
15/08/1904	Hull	Grand Theatre	2,500	17,500
29/08/1904	Sheffield	Lyceum	1,068	7,476
08/09/1904	Oldham	(Unknown)	1,000*	7,000*
12/09/1904	London	Fulham Grand Theatre	2,239	15,673
19/09/1904	London	Ealing Theatre	2,000	14,000
26/09/1904	Southampton	Grand Theatre	1,800	12,600
03/10/1904	Portsmouth	New Theatre Royal	667	4,669
10/10/1904	Bournemouth	Theatre Royal	800	5,600

17/10/1904	London	Coronet Theatre	1,143	8,001
24/10/1904	Dublin	Theatre Royal	2,011	14,077
31/10/1904	Cork	Opera House	1,000	7,000
07/11/1904	Belfast	Theatre Royal	1,000*	7,000*
14/11/1904	Manchester	New Queen's Theatre	2,800	19,600
18/11/1904	London	Peckham Crown Theatre	2,000	14,000
28/11/1904	Birmingham	Grand	2,200	15,400
06/12/1904	Bradford	Theatre Royal	1,800	12,600
13/12/1904	Leeds	Grand Theatre	1,550	10,850
09/01/1905	Great Yarmouth	Aquarium Theatre	1,500	10,500
23/01/1905	London	The Dalston	2,000	16,000
30/01/1905	Swansea	Grand Theatre	2,500	17,500
06/02/1905	Newport	Lyceum	1,250	8,750
01/08/1905	Keighley	New Queen's Theatre	1,800	12,600
07/08/1905	Aldershot	Theatre Royal	881	6,167
14/08/1905	Yarmouth	Theatre Royal	1,000*	7,000*
21/08/1905	Keighley	New Queen's Theatre	1,800	12,600
28/08/1905	York	Theatre Royal	1,300	9,100
04/09/1905	Sunderland	Avenue	2,500	17,500
11/09/1905	Leicester	Opera House	2,550	17,850
23/09/1905	Douglas	Theatre Royal	1,100	7,700
25/09/1905	Bolton	Theatre Royal	1,800	12,600
02/10/1905	London	Marlborough Theatre	2,612	18,284
				385,341

APPENDIX B

Will Garland's touring works

Table 7 presents Will Garland's touring productions in the UK. Note that these shows often visited Ireland or, after 1920, both Northern Ireland and Ireland.

TABLE 7 *A list of Will Garland's touring productions in the UK.*

Date	Show Name	Garland's Role or Position in Company	Details
1905–6	*Darktown Entertainers*	Vocalist (trio act)	Performs with Douglas and Bauman as a variety act on music hall billings
1906–15	*A Trip to C–ntown* (NB this is unredacted and written in full during the period)	Performer, Producer	A short revue originally featuring Garland, Douglas and Bauman, initially co-produced with Douglas and Garland. Originally billed with (*In Dahomey*) after the main title: once listed as *A Trip to Chinatown*;[1] it is referenced as *In Dohomay* [*sic*] in Manchester[2]
1908	*Pullman Porters*	Performer, producer	'A musical melange' featuring Garland, Douglas and company and 18 singers[3]
1909	*The Bogus Prince*[4]	Performer, producer	'a burlesque [...] operetta'[5] 'the vocalism is pleasing, the dancing smart, and the comedy clever'[6]
1909	*Darkest America*	Producer, performer	A short revue within a variety billing[7]
1910	*Some Revue – All Black*[8]	Producer, performer	(Sometimes known as *Some Revue*)
1910	*Black America*[9]	Producer, performer	(Possibly interchangeable name with *Darkest America*)

1915–22	*Coloured Society* (also performed as *All Black*; sometimes *All Black!*)	Performer (vocalist); *c.*1917 onwards Producer, comedian	Originally produced by George Sax, Garland takes control of the production around 1917. Garland's shift being named as producer comes after the point Eddie Emmerson starts working on the tour in October 1917.[10] It was originally a mini-revue within a variety billing. By 1922, *All Black* is a whole billing[11]
1922–4	*Down South*	Performer, producer	'a varied programme of songs and dances, which are interspersed with comic episodes'[12]
1925–7	*Coloured Lights*	Performer, producer	Featured 'a cabaret jazzband'[13]
1927	*Creole Carols*	Performer, producer	'later on there is a mirror display and an invasion of the auditorium by the songster principals'[14]
1927	*Coloured Birds*	Producer, performer	Possibly a test name for *Brown Birds*[15]
1927–37	*Brown Birds*	Producer, performer	'A riot of syncopation in twelve flights'[16]
1927–8	*Coloured Follies*[17]	Producer, performer	—
1929–30	*Swanee River* (aka *Swannee River*)	Producer, performer,	This revue is a whole variety bill;[18] a 'revue in twelve ripples'.[19] 'There is some good dancing of the whirlwind type, and jazz music by the Charleston syncopators'[20]
1931–7	*Brown Buddies* (aka 'the Creole Revue: *Brown Buddies*')	Producer, performer	Revue as whole bill.[21] Songs included 'River Stay' 'Way from My Door', 'You Can't Get to Heaven That Way', 'She's Got Something Ev'rybody Wants', 'Hawaiian Stars Are Gleaming', 'Oh, Rosalita', 'Songs I Heard at Mother's Knee' and 'Hullabaloo'[22]
1933	*Black Buddies*	Producer, performer	—
1933	*Plantation Pleasures*	Co-producer, performer	Co-produced with John C. Payne
1933–6	*Rhapsody in Black*	Producer, performer	Revue as whole bill.[23]

NOTES

Prelims

1. Theresa Saxon, '*In Dahomey* in England: A (Negative) Transatlantic Performance Heritage', *Atlantic Studies* 13, no. 2 (2016), 265.

2. Since we wrote this preface, clear data have been released. In the United States, the APM Research Lab reported that, from 2020 to 5 January 2021, 55,580 of Black Americans have lost their lives to Covid-19, '16.8% of all deaths of known race, but represent 12.4%' of the US population.[1] See 'The Color of Coronavirus: Covid-19 Deaths by Race and Ethnicity in the US', APM Research Lab, https://www.apmresearchlab.org/covid/deaths-by-race#black. In the UK, official analysis in July 2020 found that men with Black African backgrounds had 'the highest rate of death involving Covid-19, 2.7 times higher than males of White ethnic background; females of Black Caribbean ethnic background had the highest rate, 2.0 times higher than females of White ethnic background.' See 'Updating Ethnic Contrasts in Deaths Involving the Coronavirus (COVID-19), England and Wales: Deaths Occurring 2 March to 28 July 2020', Office of National Statistics, last updated 16 October 2020, https://www.ons.gov.uk/peoplepopulationandcommunity/birthsdeathsandmarriages/deaths/articles/updatingethniccontrastsindeathsinvolvingthecoronaviruscovid19englandandwales/deathsoccurring2marchto28july2020#overview-of-ethnic-group-breakdowns. Though this may not seem relevant to a book about theatre history, this further evidence of structural racism has shaped the time of the book's writing.

3. C—n songs: we refer to them henceforth with our neologism faux-black vernacular (FBV) songs.

Introduction

1. Peter Fryer, *Black People in the British Empire* (London: Pluto Press, 1988), xi.

2. Ben Macpherson, *British Musical Theatre: Imperialism, Identity and Ideology 1890–1939* (London: Palgrave, 2018), 138.

3. David Olusoga, *Black and British: A Forgotten History* (London: Macmillan, 2016), xvi.

4. Kofi Agawu, *The African Imagination in Music* (Oxford: Oxford University Press, 2016), 308.

5. Macpherson, *British Musical Theatre*, 149, n. 24.

6. Stephen Banfield, 'Music, Text and Stage: The Tradition of Bourgeois Tonality to the Second World War', *The Cambridge History of Twentieth-Century*

Music, ed. Nicholas Cook and Anthony Pople (Cambridge: Cambridge University Press, 2004), 98.

7   Ben Macpherson, 'Some Yesterdays Always Remain: Black British and Anglo-Asian Musical Theatre', in *The Oxford Handbook of the British Musical*, ed. Robert Gordon and Olaf Jubin (Oxford: Oxford University Press, 2017), 676.

8   Robert Gordon, Olaf Jubin and Millie Taylor, *British Musical Theatre since 1950* (London: Bloomsbury Publishing, 2016), 27.

9   Gordon, Jubin and Taylor, *British Musical Theatre*, 98.

10   Ibid., 99.

11   Macpherson, 'Some Yesterdays', 688.

12   Fryer, *Black People*, xii.

13   Arianne Johnson Quinn, *British and American Musical Theatre Exchanges (1920–1970): The 'Americanization' of Drury Lane* (London: Palgrave, forthcoming).

14   Christopher Balme, 'The Bandmann Circuit: Theatrical Networks in the First Age of Globalization', *Theatre Research International* 40, no. 1 (2015), 20.

15   *Manchester Courier and Lancashire General Advertiser*, 10/11/1909, 1, https://www.britishnewspaperarchive.co.uk/viewer/bl/0000206/19091110/151/0001.

16   'The Lily of Bermuda', *Daily Gazette for Middlesbrough*, 12/11/1909, 3, https://www.britishnewspaperarchive.co.uk/viewer/bl/0000159/19091112/055/0003.

17   The work is listed in Kurt Gänzl, *British Musical Theatre* (Oxford: Oxford University Press, 1986), 1044. See Colin Chambers, *Black and Asian Theatre in Britain: A History* (London: Routledge, 2011), 69, 71.

18   Ryuko Kubota, 'Confronting Epistemological Racism, Decolonizing Scholarly Knowledge: Race and Gender in Applied Linguistics', *Applied Linguistics* 41, no. 5 (2020), https://doi.org/10.1093/applin/amz033.

19   Fryer, *Black People*, 118.

20   Stephanie Batiste, *Darkening Mirrors: Imperial Representation in Depression-era African American Performance* (Durham, NC: Duke University Press, 2011), 3.

21   Batiste, *Darkening Mirrors*, 4.

22   bell hooks, *Black Looks: Race and Representation* (Boston: South End Press, 1992), 21.

23   Priyamvada Gopal, *Insurgent Empire: Anticolonial Resistance and British Dissent* (London: Verso Books, 2019), 31. Emphasis in original.

24   Ifeoma Kiddoe Nwankwo, *Black Cosmopolitanism: Racial Consciousness and Transnational Identity in the Nineteenth-Century Americas* (Philadelphia: University of Pennsylvania Press, 2014), 9, 11.

25   Bennetta Jules-Rosette, *Josephine Baker in Art and Life: The Icon and the Image* (Urbana: University of Illinois Press, 2007), and Jo A. Tanner, *Dusky Maidens: The Odyssey of the Early Black Dramatic Actress* (Westport, CT: Greenwood Press, 1992).

26 Michael Omi and Howard Winant, 'Once More, with Feeling: Reflections on Racial Formation', *PMLA* 123, no. 5 (2008), 1570. They refer to Michael Omi and Howard Winant, *Racial Formation in the United States* (1986; repr. London: Routledge, 2014).

27 Tania Canas, 'Diversity Is a White Word', ArtsHub Australia, 01/09/2017, https://www.artshub.com.au/education/news-article/opinions-and-analysis/professional-development/tania-canas/diversity-is-a-white-word-252910.

28 Sara Ahmed, 'The Nonperformativity of Antiracism', *Meridians* 7, no. 1 (2006), 106–7.

29 Michalinos Zembylas, 'Affect, Race, and White Discomfort in Schooling: Decolonial Strategies for "Pedagogies of Discomfort"', *Ethics and Education* 13, no. 1 (2018), 87.

30 Jason Toynbee, Catherine Tackley and Mark Doffman, 'Another Place, Another Race? Thinking through Jazz, Ethnicity and Diaspora in Britain', in *Black British Jazz: Routes, Ownership and Performance*, ed. Jason Toynbee and Catherine Tackley (London: Routledge, 2014), 4.

31 Paul Gilroy, *The Black Atlantic: Modernity and Double Consciousness* (London: Verso Books, 1993), xi.

32 Annalisa Oboe and Anna Scacchi, 'Introduction', in *Recharting the Black Atlantic: Modern Cultures, Local Communities, Global Connections* (London: Routledge, 2008), 7.

33 Stuart Hall, 'What Is This "Black" in Black Popular Culture?', *Social Justice* 20, no. 1/2 (1993), 108.

34 Ibid., 113.

35 Gilroy, *Black Atlantic*, 36.

36 Ibid.

37 Fred Moten, *In the Break: The Aesthetics of the Black Radical Tradition* (Minneapolis: University of Minnesota Press, 2003), 26.

38 Ibid., 39.

39 Matthew D. Morrison, 'The Sound(s) of Subjection: Constructing American Popular Music and Racial Identity through Blacksound', *Women & Performance: A Journal of Feminist Theory* 27 no. 1 (2017), 22.

40 Paula Seniors, *Beyond Lift Every Voice and Sing: The Culture of Uplift, Identity, and Politics in Black Musical Theater* (Columbus: Ohio State University Press, 2009), 4.

41 Seniors, *Beyond Lift*, 6.

The 1900s in context

1 Saidiya Hartman, *Lose Your Mother: A Journey Along the Atlantic Slave Route* (New York: Farrar, Straus and Giroux, 2007), 136.

2 Duke University Data+ Group 3, 'Introduction', *Remembering the Middle Passage*, 30/07/2019, https://sites.duke.edu/middlepassage/.

3 Olusoga, *Black and British*, 404.

4   Ibid., 404.

5   Ibid., 406.

6   Jonathan Hyslop, 'The Invention of the Concentration Camp: Cuba, Southern Africa and the Philippines, 1896–1907', *South African Historical Journal* 63, no. 2 (2011), 259.

7   Ron Ramdin, *The Making of the Black Working Class in Britain*, updated edn (London: Verso, 2017), 53.

8   Jeffrey Green, 'The Jamaica Native Choir in Britain, 1906–1908'. *Black Music Research Journal* 13, no. 1 (1993), 15–29, doi:10.2307/779404.

9   Ibid.

10   Rainer Lotz, *Black People: Entertainers of African Descent in Europe and Germany* (Bonn: Birgit Lotz Verlag, 1997), 54.

11   Stephen Bourne, 'Whaley, Edward Peter [Eddie] (1877×80–1960), comedian and singer', *ODNB* (2013), https://www.oxforddnb.com/view/10.1093/ref:odnb/9780198614128.001.0001/odnb-9780198614128-e-101362.

12   'Stage Gossip', *Derby Daily Telegraph*, 18/01/1928, 5, https://www.britishnewspaperarchive.co.uk/viewer/bl/0000327/19280118/065/0005.

13   *MHTR*, 18/08/1905, 9, https://www.britishnewspaperarchive.co.uk/viewer/bl/0002237/19050818/110/0009.

Chapter 1

1   Cedric Robinson, *Forgeries of Memory and Meaning: Blacks and the Regimes of Race in American Theater and Film Before World War II* (Chapel Hill: University of North Carolina Press, 2007), 182.

2   Marva Griffin Carter, *Swing Along: The Musical Life of Will Marion Cook* (Oxford: Oxford University Press, 2008), 52.

3   Ibid.

4   Ibid.

5   Daphne Brooks, 'Open Channels: Some Thoughts on Blackness, the Body, and Sound(ing) Women in the (Summer) Time of Trayvon', *Performance Research* 19, no. 3, (2014), 62–8, http://dx.doi.org/10.1080/13528165.2014.935171.

6   Macpherson, *Cultural Identity in British Musical Theatre*, 140.

7   Saxon, *In Dahomey*, 265.

8   Daphne Brooks, *Bodies in Dissent: Spectacular Performances of Race and Freedom, 1850–1910* (Durham, NC: Duke University Press, 2006), 275.

9   W. E. B. Du Bois, *The Souls of Black Folk*, 1903. Project Gutenberg, http://www.gutenberg.org/files/408/408-h/408-h.htm.

10   Raymond Knapp, *The American Musical and the Formation of National Identity* (Princeton: Princeton University Press, 2006), 74.

11   'Dahomey On Broadway', *New York Times*, 19/02/1903, 9, ProQuest.

12   Ibid.

13 'The Drama: Negroes Win Favor – New-York Theatre', *New York Tribune*, 19/02/1903, 9, ProQuest.

14 Saxon, *In Dahomey*, 275.

15 'Theatre & Music Hall Mems.', *LPA*, 02/01/1904, 7, https://www. britishnewspaperarchive.co.uk/viewer/bl/0001516/19040102/024/0007.

16 'Things Theatrical', *Bournemouth Daily Echo*, 30/12/1903, 2, https://www. britishnewspaperarchive.co.uk/viewer/bl/0000638/19031230/038/0002.

17 *Greenock Telegraph and Clyde Shipping Gazette*, 23/06/1903, 3, https://www.britishnewspaperarchive.co.uk/viewer/ bl/0000472/19030623/067/0003.

18 Carter, *Swing Along*, 66.

19 *Greenock Telegraph and Clyde Shipping Gazette*, 3.

20 David Krasner, 'Rewriting the Body: Aida Overton Walker and the Social Formation of Cakewalking', *Theatre Survey* 37, no. 2 (1996), 67–92.

21 Robinson, *Forgeries*, 158.

22 'From the Green Room', *Birmingham Daily Gazette*, 22/06/1904, 9, https://www.britishnewspaperarchive.co.uk/viewer/ bl/0000668/19040622/181/0009.

23 *The Sporting Times*, 09/07/1904, 10, https://www.britishnewspaperarchive. co.uk/viewer/bl/0001682/19040709/091/0010.

24 'Before The Footlights: *In Dahomey* at the "Grand",' *Hull Daily Mail*, 16/08/1904, 4,https://www.britishnewspaperarchive.co.uk/viewer/ BL/0000324/19040816/027/0004.

25 Carter, *Swing Along*, 111.

26 Ibid., 124.

27 *The Music and Scripts of 'In Dahomey'*, ed. Thomas L. Riis (Middleton: A-R Editions, American Musicological Society, 1996), xiv.

28 Brooks, *Bodies*, 234.

29 Ibid., 238.

30 Ibid.

31 Ray Sapirstein, '"Original Rags": African American Secular Music and the Cultural Legacy of Paul Laurence Dunbar's Poetry', in *Black Music, Black Poetry: Genre, Performance and Authenticity*, ed. Gordon Thompson (Farnham: Ashgate Publishing, 2013), 21.

32 Paul Laurence Dunbar, 'We Wear the Mask' ([1893] 2020), [online], https:// www.poetryfoundation.org/poems/44203/we-wear-the-mask.

33 Brooks, *Bodies*, 222.

34 We have redacted the genre term/slur here. James Smethurst, 'Paul Laurence Dunbar and Turn-into-the-20th-Century African American Dualism' *African American Review* 41, no. 2 (2007), 378.

35 Catherine Parsonage, *The Evolution of Jazz in Britain, 1800–1935* (London: Routledge, 2017), 97.

36 Ibid.

37   Carter, *Swing Along*, 62.

38   'Written, Composed, and Played By Coloured C—ns', *The Tatler*,
      20/05/1903, 32, https://www.britishnewspaperarchive.co.uk/viewer/
      BL/0001852/19030520/036/0032.

39   Brooks, *Bodies*, 276.

40   Marva Griffin Carter, *Swing Along: The Songs of Will Marion Cook*, William
      Brown, Ann Sears. Albany, TROY 839/40, 2006, compact disc. Liner Notes.

41   Carter, *Swing Along*, 128.

Chapter 2

1   'United States Passport Applications, 1795–1925', database with images,
      FamilySearch (M1490) Passport Applications, 02/01/1906 to 31/03/1925 >
      Roll 317, 1916 July to August, certificate no 30501–31100 > image 203 of
      1324; citing NARA microfilm publications M1490 and M1372 (Washington,
      DC: National Archives and Records Administration, n.d.).

2   Paula Seniors, 'Ada Overton Walker, Abbie Mitchell, and the Gibson Girl:
      Reconstructing African American Womanhood', *International Journal of
      Africana Studies* 13, no. 1 (2007), 38–67, and Tanner, *Dusky Maidens*.

3   Thomas L. Riis, 'The Experience and Impact of Black Entertainers in
      England, 1895–1920', *American Music* 4 no. 1 (1986), 56.

4   Michael Pickering, *Blackface Minstrelsy in Britain* (Aldershot: Routledge,
      2008); and in reference to (white) performer Eugene Stratton, see Michael
      Pickering, 'Eugene Stratton and Early Ragtime in Britain', *Black Music
      Research Journal* 20 no. 2 (2000), 151–80.

5   Pickering, *Blackface Minstrelsy*, 17.

6   Robinson, *Forgeries*, 148.

7   Annemarie Bean, 'Black Minstrelsy and Double Inversion, Circa 1890', in
      African American Performance and Theater History: A Critical Reader, ed.
      David Krasner and Henry J. Elam (Oxford: Oxford University Press, 2001),
      188–9.

8   Her catchphrase on billing information was 'Yours In Ragtime'.

9   Jeffrey Green and Rainer E. Lotz, 'Davis, Belle (b. 1874, d. in or after 1938),
      Dancer and Singer', *ODNB*, 23 September 2004, https://doi.org/10.1093/
      ref:odnb/64723.

10   Rainer Lotz, 'Black Women Recording Pioneers', *IAJRC Journal* 40, no. 2
      (2007), 34.

11   Lotz, *Black People*, 66.

12   Green and Lotz, 'Davis, Belle'.

13   Lotz, 'Black Women', 34.

14   Jayna Brown, *Babylon Girls: Black Women Performers and the Shaping of
      the Modern* (Durham, NC: Duke University Press, 2009), 41.

15   'Stoke on Trent', *The Era*, 26/03/1898, 23, https://www.
     britishnewspaperarchive.co.uk/viewer/bl/0000053/18980326/111/0023;
     'Amusements in St Helens', *The Era*, 08/05/1897, 20, https://www.
     britishnewspaperarchive.co.uk/viewer/bl/0000053/18970508/043/0020.

16   'Amusements in St Helens', *The Era*, 08/05/1897, 20, https://www.
     britishnewspaperarchive.co.uk/viewer/bl/0000053/18970508/043/0020.

17   'St Helen's New Royal and Opera House', *The Stage*, 06/05/1897,
     7, https://www.britishnewspaperarchive.co.uk/viewer/
     bl/0001179/18970506/098/0007.

18   *MHTR*, 04/10/1901, 4, https://www.britishnewspaperarchive.co.uk/viewer/
     bl/0002237/19011004/058/0004.

19   'The Stage', *Freeman* (Indianapolis, IN) 11, no. 37, 10/09/1898, 5, Readex.

20   *MHTR*, 16/08/1901, 5, https://www.britishnewspaperarchive.co.uk/
     viewer/bl/0002237/19010816/068/0005; and 'One Good Song Brings On
     Another', *The Era*, 24/08/1901, 28, https://www.britishnewspaperarchive.
     co.uk/viewer/bl/0000053/19010824/294/0028; 'The Palace', *West London
     Observer*, 21/03/1902, 6, https://www.britishnewspaperarchive.co.uk/viewer/
     bl/0000437/19020321/142/0006.

21   *The Era*, 05/07/1902, https://www.britishnewspaperarchive.co.uk/viewer/
     bl/0000053/19020705/292/0031.

22   'The Stage', *Freeman* (Indianapolis, IN) 11, no. 37, 10/09/1898, 5. Readex.

23   'Extra Cards', *MHTR*, 16/08/1901, 4, https://www.britishnewspaperarchive.
     co.uk/viewer/bl/0002237/19010816/061/0004.

24   Sapirstein, 'Original Rags', 34.

25   'The Stage', *Freeman* (Indianapolis, IN) 8, no. 45, 07/11/1896. 6. Readex.

26   'c–n shouting', Arnold Shaw, *Black Popular Music in America: The Singers,
     Songwriters and Musicians Who Pioneered the Sounds of American Music*
     (New York: Schirmer Books, 1986), 44.

27   'Route', *Freeman* (Indianapolis, IN) XIV, no. 24, 15/06/1901, 5, Readex.

28   'grotesques', 'The Empress Brixton', *MHTR*, 21/06/1901, 7, https://www.
     britishnewspaperarchive.co.uk/viewer/bl/0002237/19010621/120/0007.

29   'The Metropolitan', *The Era*, 20/07/1901, 17, https://www.
     britishnewspaperarchive.co.uk/viewer/bl/0000053/19010720/199/0017.

30   'Collins', Music Hall', *Islington Gazette*, 18/06/1901, 5, https://www.
     britishnewspaperarchive.co.uk/viewer/bl/0000438/19010618/069/0005.

31   'The Metropolitan', *MHTR*, 23/08/1901, 7, https://www.
     britishnewspaperarchive.co.uk/viewer/bl/0002237/19010823/118/0007.

32   'The Empire Palace', *Sheffield Daily Telegraph*, 07/10/1902, 7,https://www.
     britishnewspaperarchive.co.uk/viewer/bl/0000250/19021007/079/0007.

33   'p----------s' - notably in African American newspapers they are
     usually referred to as the picks or pics. 'Extra Cards', *MHTR*,
     23/08/1901, 4, https://www.britishnewspaperarchive.co.uk/viewer/
     bl/0002237/19010823/076/0004.

34 'America's Greatest C–n Cantatrice', 'Collins, Islington', *Tottenham and Edmonton Weekly Herald*, 07/06/1901, 5, https://www.britishnewspaperarchive.co.uk/viewer/bl/0001716/19010607/078/0005.

35 *MHTR*, 06/09/1901, 4, https://www.britishnewspaperarchive.co.uk/viewer/bl/0002237/19010906/090/0004.

36 'The Empire Theatre Bradford', *Yorkshire Evening Post*, 01/10/1902, 1, https://www.britishnewspaperarchive.co.uk/viewer/bl/0000273/19021001/017/0001.

37 'The London', and 'The Middlesex', *The Stage*, 09/01/1902, 20, https://www.britishnewspaperarchive.co.uk/viewer/bl/0001179/19020109/023/0020.

38 Burgoyne appears to have worked in the UK briefly in Manchester during April 1907, for example 'Tivoli Theatre', *Manchester Courier and Lancashire General Advertiser*, 23/04/1907, 1, https://www.britishnewspaperarchive.co.uk/viewer/bl/0000206/19070423/215/0001, though no further locations or dates have yet been found under this name.

39 Jeanne Klein, 'The Cake Walk Photo Girl and Other Footnotes in African American Musical Theatre', *Theatre Survey* 60, no. 1 (2019), 70.

40 Ibid. 69.

41 'The Negro Comedian', *Plaindealer* (Topeka, Kansas) I. no. 6, 10/02/1899, *Readex*.

42 UK, Incoming Passenger Lists, 1878–1960 New York, New York, United States, ARRIVAL DATE: 05/06/190, PORT OF ARRIVAL: Southampton, England, SHIP NAME: St Paul, SHIPPING LINE: American Line, OFFICIAL NUMBER: 116693, ancestry.co.uk

43 'Bringing Harlem to Broadway', *Daily News* (New York), 10/07/1927, 95, ProQuest.

44 *MHTR*, 19/05/1905, 10, https://www.britishnewspaperarchive.co.uk/viewer/bl/0002237/19050519/128/0010.

45 'Electric Theatre', *Journal Gazette* (Mattoon, IL), 09/08/1907, 4.

46 'The Gotham', *Times Union* (Brooklyn, NY), 11/01/1908, 8;'Majestic Theater, Chicago', *The Daily Herald* (Arlington Heights, IL), 28/02/1908, 5;'Majestic Theater', *The Inter Ocean* (Chicago, IL), 01/03/1908, 44;'New Theatre', *Marengo Republican-News* (Marengo, IL), 08/05/1908, 2.

47 For a two-week tour: 'Theatrical Jottings', *The New York Age*, 28/10/1909, 6.

48 'New Orpheum', *The San Francisco Examiner*, 02/01/1910, 66;'Orpheum', *The Daily Telegram* (Long Beach, CA) 29/01/1910, 3; 'Theatrical Jottings', *The New York Age*, 10 Feb 1910, 6; 'Orpheum', *The Morning Examiner* (Ogden, UT) 27/02/1910, 5; 'Orpheum', *The Lincoln Star* (Lincoln, NE), 13/03/1910, 14; 'Theatrical Jottings', *The New York Age*, 24/03/1910, 6; 'Theatrical Jottings', *The New York Age*, 14/04/1910, 6; 'Majestic: Always Novelty Vaudeville', *Chicago Tribune*, 21/04/1910, 7;[Gossip], *The New York Age*, 05/05/1910, 6; 'Theatrical Jottings', *The New York Age*, 02/06/1910, 6; 'Theatrical Jottings', *The New York Age*, 16/06/1910, 6; 'Theatrical Jottings', *The New York Age*, 14/07/1910, 6.

49 'The Gallery God Sees Miss Belle Davis and "Picks"', *Freeman* (Indianapolis, IN), 14/05/1910, 6, Readex.

50 *The New York Age*, 15/09/1910, 6, Readex.

51 *New York Age*, 31/10/1912, 6, Readex.'Eastern Theatrical Notes', *Freeman* (Indianapolis, IN), 14/01/1913, 5.

52 Year: 1915; Arrival: New York, New York; Microfilm Serial: T715, 1897–1957; Microfilm Roll: Roll 2395; Line: 9; Page Number: 34, Source Information, Ancestry.com. New York, Passenger and Crew Lists (including Castle Garden and Ellis Island), 1820–1957 [database on-line]. Provo, UT, USA: Ancestry.com Operations, Inc., 2010.

53 National Archives and Records Administration (NARA); Washington, DC; Roll #: 238; Volume #: Roll 0238 – Certificates: 51581–52400, 24 February 1915 to 6 March 1915. Volume: Roll 0238 – Certificates: 51581–52400, 24 February 1915 to 6 March 1915. Ancestry.com. U.S. Passport Applications, 1795–1925 [database online]. Lehi, UT, USA: Ancestry.com Operations.

54 'The Lovely Limit', *The Era*, 10/03/1915, 7, https://www.britishnewspaperarchive.co.uk/viewer/bl/0000053/19150310/069/0007.

55 'The Theatre Royal', *Dublin Evening Telegraph*, 20/03/1915, 8, https://www.britishnewspaperarchive.co.uk/viewer/bl/0002093/19150320/162/0008.

56 Green and Lotz, 'Davis, Belle'.

57 'Attractions for Next Week', *Sheffield Independent*, 28/02/1919, 2, https://www.britishnewspaperarchive.co.uk/viewer/bl/0001464/19190228/047/0002; 'Cardiff Empire', *The Stage*, 13/11/1919, 10, https://www.britishnewspaperarchive.co.uk/viewer/bl/0001179/19191113/021/0010; *The Stage*, 15/01/1920, 14, https://www.britishnewspaperarchive.co.uk/viewer/bl/0001179/19200115/055/0014.

58 'South London', *The Stage*, 11/05/1928, 11, https://www.britishnewspaperarchive.co.uk/viewer/bl/0001179/19281011/039/0011.

59 'Hackney Empire', *The Stage*, 22/05/1930, 4, https://www.britishnewspaperarchive.co.uk/viewer/bl/0001179/19300522/019/0004.

60 *The Stage*, 27/05/1926, 29, https://www.britishnewspaperarchive.co.uk/viewer/bl/0001179/19260527/089/0029.

61 *Inter-State Tattler* (New York), 12/07/1929: 9, Readex.

62 'Swansea', *The Stage*, 03/04/1930, 4, https://www.britishnewspaperarchive.co.uk/viewer/bl/0001179/19300403/014/0004.

63 'Wanted', *The Stage*, 09/09/1937, 14, https://www.britishnewspaperarchive.co.uk/viewer/bl/0001179/19370909/071/0014.

64 Howard Rye, 'Southern Syncopated Orchestra: The Roster', *Black Music Research Journal* 30, no. 1 (2010), 39.

65 Ibid., 38.

66 Rainer Lotz, 'Cross Cultural Links, Black Minstrels, Cakewalks and Ragtime', in *EuroJazzLand: Jazz and European Sources, Dynamics and Contexts*, ed. Luca Cerchiari, Laurent Cugny and Franz Kerschbaumer (Lebanon, NH: Northeastern University Press, 2012), 143–66, 162.

67   'Opera House Northampton', *Northampton Chronicle and Echo*, 18/06/1892, 2, https://www.britishnewspaperarchive.co.uk/viewer/bl/0002127/18920618/084/0002.

68   'Uncle Tom's Cabin at Kilburn Town Hall', *Kilburn Times* 19/08/1892, 5, https://www.britishnewspaperarchive.co.uk/viewer/bl/0001813/18920819/090/0005.

69   'Distressing Suicide in Wigan', *Wigan Observer and District Advertiser*, 04/07/1902, 5, https://www.britishnewspaperarchive.co.uk/viewer/bl/0001974/19020704/139/0005.

70   'The Home of Melody and Song', *The Era*, 10/01/1903, 31, https://www.britishnewspaperarchive.co.uk/viewer/bl/0000053/19030110/301/0031.

71   *The Era*, 10/01/1903, 22, https://www.britishnewspaperarchive.co.uk/viewer/bl/0000053/19030110/181/0022.

72   'Gossip', *The Stage*, 15/01/1903, 21, https://www.britishnewspaperarchive.co.uk/viewer/bl/0001179/19030115/163/0021.

73   'Tivoli', *Irish Independent*, 06/02/1903, 4, https://www.britishnewspaperarchive.co.uk/viewer/bl/0001019/19030320/067/0003.

74   'New Cross Empire', *Woolwich Gazette*, 20/03/1903, 3, https://www.britishnewspaperarchive.co.uk/viewer/bl/0001019/19030320/067/0003.

75   'Gossip', *The Stage*, 16/02/1905, 15, https://www.britishnewspaperarchive.co.uk/viewer/bl/0001179/19050216/129/0015.

76   The correct term *excentrique* is notable because, while performing in Germany, she also uses 'excentric', in German – only this time in announcing herself as Australian. *LPE*, 17/12/1904, 6, https://www.britishnewspaperarchive.co.uk/viewer/bl/0001516/19041217/019/0006.

77   'The Zoo Hippodrome', *Scottish Referee*, 03/07/1905, 6, https://www.britishnewspaperarchive.co.uk/viewer/bl/0001876/19050703/096/0006.

78   *The Era,* 10/06/1905, 10, as a single page, demonstrates how the variety industry worked: producers who ran a series of theatres moving performers around their venues or individual theatres or small conglomerates. Morcashani is listed as part of the Barrasford tour; elsewhere on the same page 'Livermore Tour company' instructs its acts to 'Address all communications, Billing Matter &c […] two clear weeks in advance of opening', https://www.britishnewspaperarchive.co.uk/viewer/bl/0000053/19050610/281/0028.

79   *Berliner Tageblatt*, 13/02/1913, 11; 'Australian eccentric', in *Berliner Tageblatt*, 10/02/1913, 6, http://data.theeuropeanlibrary.org/BibliographicResource/3000098457721.

80   Jeff Bowersox, 'Mapping African-American Entertainers Before The Jazz Age' [online], https://blackcentraleurope.com/interactive-maps/mapping-entertainers/.

81   Lotz, 'Black Women', 39.

82   Estado de Sao Paulo (Sao Paulo, Brazil), 15/07/1909, 10, Readex: World Newspaper Archive.

83   'London Syndicate Halls', *The Era*, 10/12/1913, 35, https://www.
      britishnewspaperarchive.co.uk/viewer/bl/0000053/19131210/392/0035.

84   'Violation of the Public Amusements Act', *Blyth News*
      23/01/1892, 7, https://www.britishnewspaperarchive.co.uk/viewer/
      bl/0002840/18920123/109/0007.

85   'copper coloured c—n artiste', 'What a Hit', *MHTR*, 14/09/1900,
      4, https://www.britishnewspaperarchive.co.uk/viewer/
      bl/0002237/19000914/035/0004.

86   'The Cardiff Empire', *Evening Express* (Wales), 24/02/1902, 1.

87   'Manchester Hippodrome', *MHTR*, 23/09/1909, 15, https://www.
      britishnewspaperarchive.co.uk/viewer/BL/0002237/19090923/201/0015.

88   'THE THEATRES', *The Manchester Guardian*, 28/04/1903, 7, ProQuest.

89   'Fortune and Granville', *The Era*, 14/01/1905, 38, https://www.
      britishnewspaperarchive.co.uk/viewer/bl/0000053/19050114/384/0038;
      'Hull: Royal', *The Stage*, 26/01/1905, 7, https://www.
      britishnewspaperarchive.co.uk/viewer/bl/0001179/19050126/008/0007.

90   *The Era*, 11/02/1905, 36, https://www.britishnewspaperarchive.co.uk/
      viewer/bl/0000053/19050211/325/0036. 'Aladdin', *Todmorden & District
      News*, 17/02/1905, 5, https://www.britishnewspaperarchive.co.uk/viewer/
      bl/0001940/19050217/096/0005; *The Era*, 18/02/1905, 36, https://www.
      britishnewspaperarchive.co.uk/viewer/bl/0000053/19050218/306/0036.

91   'Bolton', *MHTR*, 24/03/1905, 13, https://www.britishnewspaperarchive.
      co.uk/viewer/bl/0002237/19050324/172/0013; *LPE*, 25/03/1905,
      3, https://www.britishnewspaperarchive.co.uk/viewer/
      bl/0001516/19050325/022/0003; *The Era* 25/03/1905, 36, https://www.
      britishnewspaperarchive.co.uk/viewer/bl/0000053/19050325/328/0036.

92   'Paragon', *MHTR*, 07/04/0905, 5, https://www.britishnewspaperarchive.
      co.uk/viewer/bl/0002237/19050407/058/0005; 'Palace', *The Era*,
      22/04/1905, 27, https://www.britishnewspaperarchive.co.uk/viewer/
      bl/0000053/19050422/207/0027.

93   'Music Halls', *Leeds Mercury*, 30/05/1905, 8, https://www.
      britishnewspaperarchive.co.uk/viewer/bl/0000747/19050530/139/0008.

94   'Birmingham', *The Stage*, 08/06/1905, 3, https://www.
      britishnewspaperarchive.co.uk/viewer/bl/0001179/19050608/022/0003;
      'Collins's', *MHTR*, 09/06/1905, 8, https://www.britishnewspaperarchive.
      co.uk/viewer/bl/0002237/19050609/111/0008; 'Miss Cassie Walmer',
      The Era, 17/06/1905, 32, https://www.britishnewspaperarchive.co.uk/
      viewer/bl/0000053/19050617/276/0032; 'Duchess Palace, Balham',
      MHTR, 23/06/1905, 5, https://www.britishnewspaperarchive.co.uk/viewer/
      bl/0002237/19050623/052/0005.

95   'The Metropolitan', *MHTR*, 30/06/1905, 5, https://www.
      britishnewspaperarchive.co.uk/viewer/bl/0002237/19050630/053/0005;
      'The Hippodrome', *Eastbourne Gazette*, 19/07/1905, 8, https://www.
      britishnewspaperarchive.co.uk/viewer/bl/0001928/19050719/206/0008;
      'Miss Cassie Walmer', *The Era*, 22/07/1905, 32, https://www.
      britishnewspaperarchive.co.uk/viewer/bl/0000053/19050722/309/0032;

'Music Halls', *MHTR* 28/07/1905, 8, https://www.britishnewspaperarchive.co.uk/viewer/bl/0002237/19050728/099/0008.

96 'Margate', *The Era* 05/08/1905, 8, https://www.britishnewspaperarchive.co.uk/viewer/bl/0000053/19050805/069/0008.

97 'Stoll', *MHTR*, 08/09/1905, 4, https://www.britishnewspaperarchive.co.uk/viewer/bl/0002237/19050908/045/0004;'Portsmouth', *The Era*, 09/09/1905, 17, https://www.britishnewspaperarchive.co.uk/viewer/bl/0000053/19050909/105/0017; 'Bradford', *The Era*, 16/09/1905, 8, https://www.britishnewspaperarchive.co.uk/viewer/bl/0000053/19050916/115/0008; 'Blackpool', *MHTR*, 29/09/1905, 14, https://www.britishnewspaperarchive.co.uk/viewer/bl/0002237/19050929/207/0014.

98 'North Shields', *The Era*, 21/10/1905, 15, https://www.britishnewspaperarchive.co.uk/viewer/bl/0000053/19051021/134/0015; 'Stockton', *LPE*, 28/10/1905, 12, https://www.britishnewspaperarchive.co.uk/viewer/bl/0001516/19051028/065/0012.

99 'West Hartlepool', *The Era*, 04/11/1905, 12, https://www.britishnewspaperarchive.co.uk/viewer/bl/0000053/19051104/096/0012; 'Oldham', *The Era*, 18/11/1905, 13, https://www.britishnewspaperarchive.co.uk/viewer/bl/0000053/19051118/094/0013; 'The Palace Theatre', *Dundee Evening Telegraph*, 28/11/1905, 5, https://www.britishnewspaperarchive.co.uk/viewer/bl/0000563/19051128/133/0005.

100 'Dundee', *MHTR*, 01/12/1905, 14, https://www.britishnewspaperarchive.co.uk/viewer/bl/0002237/19051201/171/0014; 'Palace', *Aberdeen Press and Journal*, 04/12/1905, 1, https://www.britishnewspaperarchive.co.uk/viewer/bl/0000576/19051204/123/0001; 'Leeds', *MHTR* 15/12/1905 https://www.britishnewspaperarchive.co.uk/viewer/bl/0002237/19051215/217/0017.

101 She was billed as 'The Dusky Princess': 'Palace Theatre', *Hull Daily Mail*, 10/05/1905, 2, https://www.britishnewspaperarchive.co.uk/viewer/bl/0000324/19050510/079/0002; 'Empire Palace, South Shields', *MHTR* 12/05/1905, 4, https://www.britishnewspaperarchive.co.uk/viewer/bl/0002237/19050512/046/0004; 'Miss Cassie Walmer', *The Era*, 29/04/1905, 36, https://www.britishnewspaperarchive.co.uk/viewer/bl/0000053/19050429/325/0036; 'AMUSEMENTS', *The Scotsman*, 13/10/1903, ProQuest.

102 Bill Egan, *African American Entertainers in Australia and New Zealand: A History, 1788–1941* (Jefferson, NC: McFarland, 2019), 116.

103 Egan, *African American Entertainers*, 122.

104 Theresa Runstedtler, *Jack Johnson, Rebel Sojourner: Boxing in the Shadow of the Global Color Line* (Berkeley: University of California Press, 2013), 53.

105 Egan, *African American Entertainers*, 118–19.

106 'New Empire', *Burnley News* 03/03/1920, 1, https://www.britishnewspaperarchive.co.uk/viewer/bl/0000699/19200303/014/0001.

107 'The Alhambra', *The Era* 28/03/1923, 15, https://www.britishnewspaperarchive.co.uk/viewer/bl/0000053/19230328/199/0015.

108   'Stratford Empire', *The Era* 11/04/1923, 15, https://www.
      britishnewspaperarchive.co.uk/viewer/bl/0000053/19230411/168/0015;
      Louise Peacock, 'Grock "Genius Among Clowns"', in *Popular Performance*,
      ed. Adam Ainsworth, Oliver Double and Louise Peacock (London:
      Bloomsbury, 2017) 118–36, 120.

109   *Lancashire Evening Post*, 31/05/1924, 1, https://www.
      britishnewspaperarchive.co.uk/viewer/bl/0000711/19240531/002/0001.

110   Egan, *African American Entertainers*, 177.

111   Egan, *African American Entertainers*, 182.

112   'Birds of the Night', *West Middlesex Gazette*, 03/06/1933, 14, https://www.
      britishnewspaperarchive.co.uk/viewer/bl/0002564/19330603/280/0014.

113   'Women of the World', *West London Observer*, 16/02/1934, 4, https://www.
      britishnewspaperarchive.co.uk/viewer/bl/0000437/19340216/042/0004.

114   'Palace Theatre Burnley', *Barnoldswick & Earby Times*,
      24/07/1942, 2, https://www.britishnewspaperarchive.co.uk/viewer/
      bl/0001529/19420724/039/0002.

115   'Palace of Varieties', *Radio Times*, 1471, 18/01/1952, 35, https://genome.
      ch.bbc.co.uk/2b948c85ec9243b7b08ce0ab4f9f3d00.

116   Klein, 'The Cake Walk', 69.

117   Nadine George-Graves, 'Spreading the Sand: Understanding the Economic
      and Creative Impetus for the Black Vaudeville Industry', *CONTINUUM:
      The Journal of African Diaspora Drama, Theatre and Performance* 1, no. 1
      (2014), http://continuumjournal.org/index.php/spreading-the-sand.

The 1910s in context

1   'Nigeria', in *A Dictionary of World History*, ed. A. Kerr and E. Wright
    (Oxford: Oxford University Press 2006), www.oxfordreference.com.

2   Marc Matera, 'Pan-Africanism', in *New Dictionary of the History of Ideas*,
    ed. Maryanne Cline Horowitz, vol. 4 (New York: Charles Scribner's Sons,
    2005), 1701–7. Gale eBooks.

3   For more on this, see Stephen Bourne, *Black Poppies: Britain's Black
    Community and the Great War* (Cheltenham: The History Press, 2019)
    which documents this period through individual case studies and interviews
    set in a wider context.

4   Fryer, *Staying Power,* 475

5   Fryer, *Staying Power*, 506.

6   Bourne, *Black Poppies*, 220.

7   On Cardiff, see Fryer, *Staying Power*, 487; and for Liverpool in the same
    book, 485.

8   Ibid., 506.

9   Susan Cook, 'Flirting with the Vernacular: America in Europe, 1900–45', in
    The Cambridge History of Twentieth-Century Music, ed. Nicholas Cook and
    Anthony Pople (Cambridge, Cambridge University Press, 2004), 167.

10 Hilary Moore, *Inside British Jazz: Crossing Borders of Race, Nation and Class* (Farnham: Ashgate, 2007), 19.

11 They are listed as C. Foster, Herbert Sutton, W. Hilliard, R. M. Cooper and C. A. Hawkes. See 'The Palace', *The Era*, 01/03/1913, 24,https://www.britishnewspaperarchive.co.uk/viewer/bl/0000053/19130301/274/0024; the quartet's names and a blurry photo appear in an advert for the group in *The Era*, 19/03/1913, 11, https://www.britishnewspaperarchive.co.uk/viewer/bl/0000053/19130319/106/0011.

12 Howard Rye, 'Mitchell, Louis (A.)', in *Grove Music Online* (2003), https://www.oxfordmusiconline.com.

13 'Portsmouth', *The Stage*, 12/04/1917, 11, https://www.britishnewspaperarchive.co.uk/viewer/bl/0001179/19170412/144/0011.

14 'Black Lightning', *Weekly Dispatch* (London), 02/05/1915, 4, https://www.britishnewspaperarchive.co.uk/viewer/bl/0003358/19150502/061/0004.

15 Chambers, *Black and Asian Theatre*, 71.

16 'Ragtime Revue', *The Era*, 19/03/1913, 8,https://www.britishnewspaperarchive.co.uk/viewer/bl/0000053/19130319/077/0008.

17 'Moss Empire's New Revue', *The Era*, 07/06/1913, 20,https://www.britishnewspaperarchive.co.uk/viewer/bl/0000053/19130607/237/0020.

18 *The Era*, 05/11/1913, 25, https://www.britishnewspaperarchive.co.uk/viewer/bl/0000053/19131105/267/0025.

19 'W. H. DORSEY DEAD: Famous Musician and Arranger Passes Out After Long Illness', *The Chicago Defender* 31/03/1920, 7, Proquest.

20 'New York Negro Sends London Jazz Mad', *Los Angeles Herald*, 44, no. 150, 25/04/1919, 1.

21 'Jazz Inventor Dead', *Hull Daily Mail*, 15/06/1919, 3, https://www.britishnewspaperarchive.co.uk/viewer/bl/0000324/19190515/013/0003.

Chapter 3

1 'World's Greatest Fighter at the King's Theatre', *Dundee Courier*, 04/01/1916, https://www.britishnewspaperarchive.co.uk/viewer/bl/0000164/19160104/152/0008.

2 *Dublin Daily Express* 22/10/1915, 6,https://www.britishnewspaperarchive.co.uk/viewer/bl/0001384/19151022/167/0006.

3 Jack Johnson, *Jack Johnson in the Ring and Out* (Auckland: Papamoa Press, 2017), 103. (Originally published in 1927.)

4 Keith Gregson and Mike Huggins, 'Sport, Music-Hall Culture and Popular Song in Nineteenth-Century England', *Culture, Sport, Society* 2, no. 2 (2007), 82–102, doi:10.1080/14610989908721840.

5 'World's Greatest Fighter at the King's Theatre', *Dundee Courier*, 04/01/1916, 8, https://www.britishnewspaperarchive.co.uk/viewer/bl/0000164/19160104/152/0008.

6   'Jack Johnson in Dundee' *Dundee Evening Telegraph*, 03/01/1916,
    3, https://www.britishnewspaperarchive.co.uk/viewer/
    bl/0000563/19160103/040/0003.

7   *Hull Daily Mail*, 30/11/1915, 3, https://www.britishnewspaperarchive.co.uk/
    viewer/bl/0000324/19151130/017/0003.

8   'World's Greatest Fighter'.

9   'Because Johnson won', *Dundee Courier*, 7/07/1910, 4,https://www.
    britishnewspaperarchive.co.uk/viewer/bl/0000164/19100707/073/0004;
    Bexhill-on-Sea Observer, 09/07/1910, 11, https://www.
    britishnewspaperarchive.co.uk/viewer/bl/0001530/19100709/126/0011.

10 Paula Marie Seniors, 'Jack Johnson, Paul Robeson and the Hypermasculine
    African American *Übermensch*', in *The Harlem Renaissance Revisited:
    Politics, Arts and Letters*, ed. Jeffrey O. G. Ogbar (Baltimore, MD: Johns
    Hopkins University Press, 2010), 155.

11 'Pugilism and the Palladium', *MHTR*, 05/10/1911, 9.

12 *Cheltenham Looker-On*, 29/04/1916, 11, https://www.
    britishnewspaperarchive.co.uk/viewer/bl/0000506/19160429/011/0011.

13 *Dundee Courier*, 04/07/1916, 4, https://www.britishnewspaperarchive.co.uk/
    viewer/bl/0000164/19160704/046/0004.

14 Henry T. Sampson, *Blacks in Blackface: A Sourcebook on Early Black
    Musical Shows*, 2nd edn (Lanham, MD: Scarecrow Press, 2013), 385.

15 'Why Johnson faked his fight with Willard', *Dundee People's Journal*,
    08/01/1916, 6, https://www.britishnewspaperarchive.co.uk/viewer/
    BL/0000698/19160108/079/0006.

16 Edward A. Robinson, 'The Pekin: The Genesis of American Black Theater',
    Black American Literature Forum 16, no. 4 (1982), 138.

17 Charles J. Johnson, 'The Short, Sad Story of Cafe de Champion – Jack
    Johnson's Mixed-Race Nightclub on Chicago's South Side', *Chicago Tribune*,
    25/05/2018, https://www.chicagotribune.com/history/ct-met-cafe-de-
    champion-jack-johnson-chicago-20180525-story.html.

18 William Benbow, 'Down Memory Lane', *Indianapolis Recorder*,
    15/04/1950, 13, https://newspapers.library.in.gov/cgi-bin/indiana?a=d&d=I
    NR19500415-01.1.13.

19 Seniors, *Beyond Lift*, 47.

20 'Advert', *Norwood News*, 13/08/1915, 4, https://www.
    britishnewspaperarchive.co.uk/viewer/BL/0002308/19150813/140/0004.

21 Richard Zimmerman and Tim Smolko, 'Jordan, Joe', in *The Grove
    Dictionary of American Music*, Oxford Reference Online, 2013.

22 Rick Benjamin, 'From Barrell house to Broadway: The Musical Odyssey
    of Joe Jordan', https://web.archive.org/web/20200324034732/http://www.
    dramonline.org/albums/from-barrelhouse-to-broadway-the-musical-odyssey-
    of-joe-jordan/notes.

23 Emmett G. Price, 'Joe Jordan', *Encyclopedia of the Harlem Renaissance: A–J*,
    ed. Cary D. Wintz and Paul Finkelman (New York: Routledge, 2004), 648–9,
    648.

24 'Manchester', *The Stage*, 22/12/1910, 23, https://www.
   britishnewspaperarchive.co.uk/viewer/bl/0001179/19101222/077/0023;
   'Reading', *MHTR*, 23/02/1911, 15, https://www.britishnewspaperarchive.
   co.uk/viewer/bl/0002237/19110223/195/0015.

25 *Edinburgh Evening News*, 29/05/1915, 7, https://www.
   britishnewspaperarchive.co.uk/viewer/BL/0000452/19150529/150/0007.

26 *Dublin Daily Express*, 22/10/1915, 6,https://www.britishnewspaperarchive.
   co.uk/viewer/bl/0001384/19151022/167/0006.

27 W. H. Dorsey, *The Long Lost Blues* (Sheet Music, Chicago: Will Rossiter,
   1915).

28 Sampson, *Blacks in Blackface*, 320.

29 Catherine Parsonage, 'A Critical Reassessment of the Reception of Early Jazz
   in Britain', *Popular Music 39*, no. 2 (2003), 318.

30 *Pall Mall Gazette*, 09/04/1913, 16, https://www.britishnewspaperarchive.
   co.uk/viewer/bl/0000098/19130409/211/0016.

31 Michael Brocken and Jeff Daniels, *Gordon Stretton, Black British
   Transoceanic Jazz Pioneer: A New Jazz Chronicle* (Lanham, MD: Lexington
   Press, 2018), see also Jeff Daniels and Howard Rye, 'Gordon Stretton: A
   Study in Multiple Identities', *Popular Music History 4*, no. 1 (2009), 77–90.

32 Daniels and Rye, 'Gordon Stretton', 80–1.

33 'Darktown Jingles', *The Era* 31/05/1916, 22,https://www.
   britishnewspaperarchive.co.uk/viewer/bl/0000053/19160531/273/0022.

34 Ibid.

35 Howard Rye, 'Fearsome Means of Discord: Early Encounters with Black
   Jazz', in *Black Music in Britain: Essays on the Afro-Asian Contribution to
   Popular Music, Popular Music in Britain*, ed. Paul Oliver (Milton Keynes,
   Open University Press, 1990), 47.

36 'Theatres Wanted', *The Era*, 28/06/1916, 3, https://www.
   britishnewspaperarchive.co.uk/viewer/bl/0000053/19160628/060/0003.

37 *The Era*, 24/05/1916, 18, https://www.britishnewspaperarchive.co.uk/viewer/
   bl/0000053/19160524/338/0018.

38 Ibid.

39 Ibid.

40 *The Era*, 08/11/1916, 3, https://www.britishnewspaperarchive.co.uk/viewer/
   bl/0000053/19161108/409/0003.

41 Brocken and Daniels, *Gordon Stretton*, 113.

42 *The Era*, 23/08/1916, 17, https://www.britishnewspaperarchive.co.uk/viewer/
   bl/0000053/19160823/255/0017.

43 *Derby Daily Telegraph*, 15/08/1916, 2,https://www.britishnewspaperarchive.
   co.uk/viewer/bl/0000327/19160815/009/0002.

44 Ibid.

45 'Local Entertainments', *Airdrie & Coatbridge Advertiser*,
   02/12/1916, 4, https://www.britishnewspaperarchive.co.uk/viewer/
   bl/0002391/19161202/068/0004.

46   *The Era*, 23/08/1916, 3, https://www.britishnewspaperarchive.co.uk/viewer/
bl/0000053/19160823/068/0003.

47   *Yarmouth Independent*, 18/11/1916, 8,https://www.britishnewspaperarchive.
co.uk/viewer/bl/0001943/19161118/104/0008.

48   'Tivoli', *The Era*, 20/12/1916, 21,https://www.britishnewspaperarchive.
co.uk/viewer/BL/0000053/19161220/347/0021.

49   'Stockton Hippodrome' *Hartlepool Northern Daily Mail*,
26/09/1916, 1, https://www.britishnewspaperarchive.co.uk/viewer/
bl/0000377/19160926/016/0001.

50   *Evening Despatch*, 04/04/1916, 2, https://www.britishnewspaperarchive.
co.uk/viewer/bl/0000671/19160404/041/0002.

51   Sax advertises as an agent for revue show acts in 1915: 'If you have
the goods, we can place you at once'; see 'George Sax Ltd', *The Era*,
22/09/1915, 23, https://www.britishnewspaperarchive.co.uk/viewer/
bl/0000053/19150922/334/0023.

52   *The Stage*, 17/07/1919, 4, https://www.britishnewspaperarchive.co.uk/
viewer/bl/0001179/19190717/009/0004.

53   *Evening Despatch*, 04/04/1916, 2, https://www.britishnewspaperarchive.
co.uk/viewer/bl/0000671/19160404/041/0002.

54   'The Pavilion', *Newcastle Journal*, 14/03/1916, 8, https://www.
britishnewspaperarchive.co.uk/viewer/bl/0000569/19160314/083/0008.

55   'The Stage', *Newcastle Journal*, 11/03/1916, 7, https://www.
britishnewspaperarchive.co.uk/viewer/bl/0000569/19160311/033/0007.

56   'The Pavilion', *Newcastle Journal*, 14/03/1916, 8, https://www.
britishnewspaperarchive.co.uk/viewer/bl/0000569/19160314/083/0008.

57   *The Pavilion Newcastle Journal*, 14/03/1916, 8, https://www.
britishnewspaperarchive.co.uk/viewer/bl/0000569/19160314/083/0008.

58   'The Hippodrome', *Preston Herald*, 15/07/1916, 4, https://www.
britishnewspaperarchive.co.uk/viewer/bl/0001667/19160715/077/0004.

59   Craig Martin Gibbs, *Black Recording Artists, 1877–1926: An Annotated
Discography* (Jefferson, NC: McFarland, 2012), 34. Rainer Lotz also traces
him in *Black People*, 277–8.

60   *Evening Despatch*, 04/04/1916, 2, https://www.britishnewspaperarchive.
co.uk/viewer/bl/0000671/19160404/041/0002.

61   'Important Announcement', *The Era*, 21/07/1915, 7, https://www.
britishnewspaperarchive.co.uk/viewer/bl/0000053/19150721/063/0007.

62   *Jarrow Express*, 28/07/1916, 6, https://www.britishnewspaperarchive.co.uk/
viewer/bl/0001610/19160728/090/0006.

63   Ibid.

64   'Derby Entertainments Grand Theatre', *Derbyshire Advertiser and Journal*,
29/04/1916, 3, https://www.britishnewspaperarchive.co.uk/viewer/
bl/0001084/19160429/056/0003.

65   Ibid.

66   'Stage Gossip', *Derby Daily Telegraph*, 19/10/1927, 5, https://www.
britishnewspaperarchive.co.uk/viewer/bl/0000327/19271019/077/0005.

67   'Pot-Pourri', *The Era*, 17/06/1899, 13, https://www.britishnewspaperarchive.
      co.uk/viewer/bl/0000053/18990617/039/0013.

68   A. Simons, 'Black British Swing. (Cover story)', *IAJRC Journal* 41, no. 3
      (2008), 35–44.

69   David Gilbert, *The Product of Our Souls: Ragtime, Race, and the Birth
      of the Manhattan Musical Marketplace* (Chapel Hill: University of North
      Carolina Press, 2015), 154.

70   Tim Brooks, *Lost Sounds: Blacks and the Birth of the Recording Industry,
      1890–1919* (Chicago: University of Illinois Press, 2010), 301.

71   Brooks, *Lost Sounds*, 301–13.

72   *Pall Mall Gazette*, 5/12/1916, 5, https://www.britishnewspaperarchive.co.uk/
      viewer/bl/0000098/19161205/059/0005.

73   Ibid.

74   Specifically referring to the band see 'The Letters of Eve', *The Tatler*,
      02/08/1916,https://www.britishnewspaperarchive.co.uk/viewer/
      bl/0001852/19160802/009/0006. For the trial, 'Champagne and N—
      Band at Ciro's', *Aberdeen Evening Express*, 10/11/1916, 5, https://www.
      britishnewspaperarchive.co.uk/viewer/bl/0000445/19161110/073/0005.

75   Amy Absher, *The Black Musician and the White City: Race and Music in
      Chicago 1900–1967* (Ann Arbor: University of Michigan Press, 2014), 22.
      Ultimately, the club closed after Johnson's then wife killed herself in their shared
      upstairs rooms, amid accusations of domestic abuse perpetrated by Johnson.

76   'Watch Your Step', *The Stage*, 23/03/1916, 14, https://www.
      britishnewspaperarchive.co.uk/viewer/bl/0001179/19160323/064/0014.

77   'In the Limelight', *Liverpool Echo*, 24/12/15, 3, https://www.
      britishnewspaperarchive.co.uk/viewer/bl/0000271/19151224/010/0003.

78   'The Grand: Watch Your Step', *Birmingham Daily Post*,
      25/04/1916, 4, https://www.britishnewspaperarchive.co.uk/viewer/
      bl/0000033/19160425/086/0004.

79   Pollard also is found in *Special Mixtures* in Edinburgh; see *The Scotsman*,
      04/12/1916, 1,https://www.britishnewspaperarchive.co.uk/viewer/
      bl/0000540/19161204/016/0001; in 'an effective drum solo', in *Any
      Complaints* in Bristol, 'The Empire and Hippodrome', *Western Daily
      Press*, 14/11/1916, 1, https://www.britishnewspaperarchive.co.uk/viewer/
      bl/0000104/19160711/047/0001.

80   'Watch Your Step at Finsbury Park', *The Era*, 22/03/1916, 21, https://www.
      britishnewspaperarchive.co.uk/viewer/bl/0000053/19160322/198/0021.

81   *Irish Independent*, 19/09/1916, 2, https://www.britishnewspaperarchive.
      co.uk/viewer/bl/0001715/19160919/189/0002.

82   *The Era*, 16/02/1916, 19, https://www.britishnewspaperarchive.co.uk/viewer/
      bl/0000053/19160216/437/0019.

83   Suyin Hayes, 'Transatlantic Stardom: African American Trailblazers in British
      Film', *British Film Institute* (2016) [online], https://www.bfi.org.uk/news-
      opinion/news-bfi/features/african-american-stars-british-film.

84   Stephen Bourne, *Black in the British Frame: Black People in British Film and
      Television* (Cheltenham: The History Press, 2005), 2.

85 'Stage Gossip', *Derby Daily Telegraph*, 18/01/1928, 5, https://www.britishnewspaperarchive.co.uk/viewer/bl/0000327/19280118/065/0005.

86 'Obituary: Duncan Whaley', *The Telegraph*, 22/07/2000, https://www.telegraph.co.uk/news/obituaries/1349751/Duncan-Whaley.html.

87 'Dalston Theatre', *The Era*, 19/04/1916, 13, https://www.britishnewspaperarchive.co.uk/viewer/bl/0000053/19160419/181/0013.

88 Bourne, *Black Poppies*, 165.

89 'Tivoli, New Brighton', *Liverpool Daily Post,* 6/06/1916, 8, https://www.britishnewspaperarchive.co.uk/viewer/bl/0000648/19160606/162/0008.

90 *The Era*, 23/08/1916, 3, https://www.britishnewspaperarchive.co.uk/viewer/bl/0000053/19160823/068/0003.

91 'Falkirk Grand Theatre', *Falkirk Herald*, 22/11/1916, 2, https://www.britishnewspaperarchive.co.uk/viewer/bl/0000733/19161122/055/0002.

92 'Stockport', *The Era* 14/06/1916, 11, https://www.britishnewspaperarchive.co.uk/viewer/bl/0000053/19160614/117/0011.

93 'In Palace Revue', *Thanet Advertiser*, 10/03/1916, 6, https://www.britishnewspaperarchive.co.uk/viewer/bl/0001697/19170310/115/0006.

94 'Liverpool', *The Era* 19/07/1916, 15, https://www.britishnewspaperarchive.co.uk/viewer/bl/0000053/19160719/195/0015.

95 'Wanted Feb 7', *The Stage*, 03/02/1916, 33, https://www.britishnewspaperarchive.co.uk/viewer/bl/0001179/19160203/035/0033.

96 'Wanted May 8', *The Era*, 19/04/1916, 22, https://www.britishnewspaperarchive.co.uk/viewer/bl/0000053/19160419/305/0022.

97 *The Era,* 23/08/1916, 3, https://www.britishnewspaperarchive.co.uk/viewer/bl/0000053/19160823/068/0003.

98 'Salford', *The Era* 23/08/1907, 17, https://www.britishnewspaperarchive.co.uk/viewer/bl/0000053/19160823/260/0017.

99 'Birmingham', *The Era*, 26/04/1916, 20, https://www.britishnewspaperarchive.co.uk/viewer/bl/0000053/19160426/242/0020.

100 *The Era* 23/08/1916, 3, https://www.britishnewspaperarchive.co.uk/viewer/bl/0000053/19160823/068/0003.

101 'Gloucester Palace', *The Era* 28/09/1907, 10, https://www.britishnewspaperarchive.co.uk/viewer/bl/0000053/19070928/103/0010. 'Palace Playhouse of Varieties', *Dundee Evening Telegraph*, 24/02/1916, 2, https://www.britishnewspaperarchive.co.uk/viewer/bl/0000563/19160224/128/0002.

102 'Wanted, Dec 4', *The Era*, 29/11/1916, 22, https://www.britishnewspaperarchive.co.uk/viewer/bl/0000053/19161129/327/0022.

103 'Theatre Royal', *Irish Independent*, 21/03/1916, 4, https://www.britishnewspaperarchive.co.uk/viewer/bl/0001715/19160321/101/0004.

104 'Palace Playhouse', *The Era*, 26/01/1916, 8, https://www.britishnewspaperarchive.co.uk/viewer/bl/0000053/19160126/103/0008; and 'Accrington', *The Era* 14/05/1910, 5, https://www.britishnewspaperarchive.co.uk/viewer/bl/0000053/19100514/226/0005.

105   *The Era*, 21/08/1909, 26, https://www.britishnewspaperarchive.co.uk/viewer/
       bl/0000053/19090821/202/0026.

106   *The Era*, 23/08/1916, 3, https://www.britishnewspaperarchive.co.uk/viewer/
       bl/0000053/19160823/068/0003.

107   *The Era*, 26/01/1916, 22, https://www.britishnewspaperarchive.co.uk/viewer/
       bl/0000053/19160126/307/0022.

108   *Manchester Evening News*, 25/01/1916, 3, https://www.
       britishnewspaperarchive.co.uk/viewer/bl/0000272/19160125/013/0003.

109   'Blackburn', *The Era*, 09/02/1916, 8, https://www.britishnewspaperarchive.
       co.uk/viewer/bl/0000053/19160209/091/0008.

110   There is a photograph of the performance in: *The Sketch*,
       19/01/1916, 24, https://www.britishnewspaperarchive.co.uk/viewer/
       BL/0001860/19160119/025/0024; for details of the previous
       year's ice-skating sequence, see 'London Variety Stage', *The Stage,*
       09/09/1915, 15, https://www.britishnewspaperarchive.co.uk/viewer/
       bl/0001179/19150909/214/0015.

111   'Uncle Tom's Cabin', *The Era*, 23/02/1916, 3, https://www.
       britishnewspaperarchive.co.uk/viewer/bl/0000053/19160223/045/0003.

112   'Dalston Theatre', *The Era*, 19/04/1916, 13, https://www.
       britishnewspaperarchive.co.uk/viewer/bl/0000053/19160419/181/0013.

113   'Concert and Stage', *Bournemouth Graphic*, 23/06/1916, 4, https://www.
       britishnewspaperarchive.co.uk/viewer/bl/0002173/19160623/015/0004.

114   Ibid.

115   'Bordesley Palace Theatre', *Evening Despatch,* 22/02/1916, 3, https://www.
       britishnewspaperarchive.co.uk/viewer/bl/0000671/19160222/051/0003.

116   Nadine George-Graves, 'Identity Politics and Political Will: Jeni LeGon
       Living in a Great Big Way', in *The Oxford Handbook of Dance and Politics*,
       ed. Rebekah J. Kowal, Gerald Siegmund and Randy Martin (Oxford: Oxford
       University Press, 2017), 529, doi:10.1093/oxfordhb/9780199928187.013.47,
       529.

117   Ibid., 530.

Chapter 4

1   Lotz in *Black People* updates his earlier chapter: Rainer E Lotz, 'Will Garland
     and His Negro Operetta Company', in *Under the Imperial Carpet: Essays in
     Black History 1780–1950*, ed. Rainer E. Lotz and Ian Pegg (Crawley, Rabbit
     Press: 1986), 130–44. More recently the extraordinary collection with more
     than forty-five CDs of early recorded music also discusses Garland at length:
     Jeffrey P. Green, Rainer E. Lotz, Horst Bergmeier, Holger Stoecker, Hans-
     Jürgen Mahrenholz, Susanne Ziegler, Konrad Nowakowski and Howard
     Rye, *Black Europe: The Sounds and Images of Black People in Europe Pre-
     1927* (Osterholz: Bear Family Productions, 2013).

2   'The Stage', *Freeman* 13, no. 8, 24/02/1900, 5, Readex.

3   Registration State: Iowa; Registration County: Lee; Roll: 1643178, Ancestry. com. U.S., World War I Draft Registration Cards, 1917–1918 [database online], Provo, UT, USA: Ancestry.com, 2005.

4   Robinson, *Forgeries*, 128.

5   Howard Rye and Jeffrey Green, 'Black Musical Internationalism in England in the 1920s', *Black Music Research Journal* 15, no. 1 (1995), 105, https:// www.jstor.org/stable/779323.

6   'Stage Gossip', *Derby Daily Telegraph*, 19/10/1927, 5, https://www. britishnewspaperarchive.co.uk/viewer/bl/0000327/19271019/077/0005; 'Stage Gossip', *Derby Daily Telegraph*, 18/01/1928, 5, https://www. britishnewspaperarchive.co.uk/viewer/bl/0000327/19280118/065/0005.

7   Ibid.

8   Paul Oliver, 'Introduction', in *Black Music in Britain: Essays on the Afro-Asian Contribution to Popular Music, Popular Music in Britain*, ed. Paul Oliver (Milton Keynes: Open University Press, 1990), 12.

9   Rye and Green, 'Black Musical Internationalism', 105. Fela Sowande (Chief Olufela Obafunmilayo 'Fela' Sowande, b. 1905, near Lagos; d. 1987 Ohio) was a Nigerian pianist, organist and composer who had a long association with British theatre.

10 Robinson, *Forgeries*, 182.

11 'Moss Empires Ltd', *The Stage*, 18/08/1927, 10, https://www. britishnewspaperarchive.co.uk/viewer/bl/0001179/19270818/032/0010.

12 *Birmingham Daily Gazette*, 10/03/1936, 6, https://www. britishnewspaperarchive.co.uk/viewer/bl/0000669/19360310/104/0006.

13 Mario A. Charles, 'The Age of a Jazzwoman: Valada Snow, 1900–1956', *The Journal of Negro History* 80, no. 4 (1995), 188.

14 'Publisher's Song Notes', *The Stage*, 27/05/1937, 6, https://www. britishnewspaperarchive.co.uk/viewer/bl/0001179/19370527/024/0006.

15 Personal communication between John Schumann and the authors, August 2020. His great aunt's name is spelt variously but usually singularly with an 'n'.

16 Oral history of Jazz in Britain – Leslie Thompson, 1901–87 (speaker, male; interviewee), 1987-08-11, 1987-11-13, British Library Collection. Rosie Garland was a producer in her own right: 'Mrs Will Garland, wife of the well-known producer, is rehearsing an act for the moving picture houses in London, and it seems like only a matter of time now before the English managers will be trying the American method of pictures and variety.' Ivan H. Browning, 'Across the Pond', *The Chicago Defender,* 09/04/1927, 6, ProQuest.

17 'J. A. Jackson's Page: From "Dear Old London"', *The Billboard*, 08/07/1922, 42, ProQuest.

18 Ivan H. Browning, 'European Notes', *The New York Amsterdam News*, 28/11/1928, 8, ProQuest.

19 'Queen's Poplar', *The Stage,* 06/04/1933, 5, https://www. britishnewspaperarchive.co.uk/viewer/bl/0001179/19330406/022/0005.

20 'Newcastle-Upon-Tyne', *The Stage,* 25/08/1927, 15, https://www. britishnewspaperarchive.co.uk/viewer/bl/0001179/19270825/045/0015.

21 'Uncle Tom's Pilgrimage', *The Bioscope*, 16/02/1928, 40, https://www.britishnewspaperarchive.co.uk/viewer/BL/0002396/19280216/163/0040.

22 Randye Jones, 'John C. Payne', *Afrocentric Voices in Classical Music* (2019), http://www.afrovoices.com/wp/john-c-payne-biography.

23 Ivan H. Browning, 'Across the Pond', *The Chicago Defender*, 26/01/1929, 6, ProQuest.

24 A. A. Haston, 'With our Performers in Europe', *The New York Amsterdam News*, 23/12/1925, 5, ProQuest.

25 Fannie Cotton, 'Fannie Cotton Writes from London', *Philadelphia Tribune*, 31/01/1929, 6.

26 Ivan H. Browning, 'Across the Pond', *The Chicago Defender*, 03/12/1927, 8, ProQuest.

27 Ivan H. Browning, 'News of London', *The New York Amsterdam News*, 01/08/1928, 6, ProQuest.

28 Ivan H. Browning, 'Across the Pond', *The Chicago Defender*, 03/12/1927, 8, ProQuest.

29 Ivan H. Browning, 'Across the Pond', *The Chicago Defender*, 01/10/1928, 9, ProQuest.

30 Ivan H. Browning, 'Our Performers in Europe', *The New York Amsterdam News*, 02/10/1929, 9, ProQuest.

31 'JOHN PAYNE'S PARTY', *The Chicago Defender*, 03/11/1928, 7, ProQuest.

32 Louis Drysdale, 'La Scienza Della Voce: Just a Few Explanations on My Method of Teaching this Beautiful Art', *The New York Amsterdam News*, 18/05/1927, 13, ProQuest.

33 Ivan H. Browning, 'Browning's London Letter', *The Chicago Defender*, 18/02/1928, 7, ProQuest.

34 Rachel Gillett, 'Jazz and the Evolution of Black American Cosmopolitanism in Interwar Paris', *Journal of World History* 21, no. 3 (2010), 478.

35 05/04/1914 Year: 1914; Arrival: New York, New York, USA; Microfilm Serial: T715, 1897–1957; Line: 6; Page Number: 23 Source Information Ancestry.com. New York, Passenger and Crew Lists (including Castle Garden and Ellis Island), 1820–1957 [database online]. Provo, UT: Ancestry.com Operations, Inc., 2010.31/10/1914; Arrival: New York, New York, USA; Microfilm Serial: T715, 1897–1957; Line: 6; Page Number: 62 Source Information Ancestry.com. New York, Passenger and Crew Lists (including Castle Garden and Ellis Island), 1820–1957 [database online]. Provo, UT: Ancestry.com Operations, Inc., 2010.

36 *New York Age*, 07/01/1915, 6, *Readex AllSearch*,

37 'Collins', *LPE*, 02/11/1906, 2, https://www.britishnewspaperarchive.co.uk/viewer/bl/0001516/19061102/003/0002.

38 'Hippodrome', *Scottish Referee*, 30/10/1908, 4, https://www.britishnewspaperarchive.co.uk/viewer/bl/0001876/19081030/097/0004.

39 Lotz, *Black People*, 662.

40 'Next Week at the Empire', *Northern Whig*, 14/05/1915, 3, https://www.britishnewspaperarchive.co.uk/viewer/bl/0000434/19150514/086/0003.

41   Ibid.

42   'Birmingham', *The Stage,* 01/04/1920, 23, https://www.britishnewspaperarchive.co.uk/viewer/bl/0001179/19200401/091/0023.

43   'Birmingham', *The Stage,* 11/05/1922, 2, https://www.britishnewspaperarchive.co.uk/viewer/bl/0001179/19220511/010/0002.

44   *Western Daily Press,* 31/05/1927, 4,https://www.britishnewspaperarchive.co.uk/viewer/bl/0000264/19270531/005/0004.

45   'The Grand', *Staffordshire Sentinel,* 22/06/1929, 2, https://www.britishnewspaperarchive.co.uk/viewer/bl/0000525/19290622/032/0002.

46   'The Coliseum Theatre', *Gloucestershire Echo,* 09/03/1926, 3, https://www.britishnewspaperarchive.co.uk/viewer/bl/0000320/19260309/080/0003.

47   Howard Rye, 'Showgirls and Stars: Black-Cast Revues and Female Performers in Britain 1903–1939', *Popular Music History* 1, no. 2 (2006), 169.

48   'Hippodrome', *Leeds Mercury,* 19/06/1928, 9, https://www.britishnewspaperarchive.co.uk/viewer/BL/0000748/19280619/201/0009.

49   Ivan H. Browning, 'Stage News: Across the Pond', *The Chicago Defender,* 02/04/1927, 10, ProQuest.

50   'Empire', *Shields Daily News,* 13/09/1927, 4, https://www.britishnewspaperarchive.co.uk/viewer/bl/0001168/19270913/099/0004.

51   'Stage Gossip', *Derby Daily Telegraph,* 19/10/1927, 5, https://www.britishnewspaperarchive.co.uk/viewer/bl/0000327/19271019/077/0005.

52   *Yorkshire Post and Leeds Intelligencer,* 02/07/1929, 5, https://www.britishnewspaperarchive.co.uk/viewer/bl/0000250/19290521/150/0005.

53   Ward, 'Music, Musical Theater', 40.

54   Ibid., 71.

55   'American Dances', *Nottingham Journal,* 20/08/1927, 7, https://www.britishnewspaperarchive.co.uk/viewer/BL/0001898/19270820/130/0007.

56   'A Riot of Syncopation', *Western Daily Press,* 12/10/1928, 13, https://www.britishnewspaperarchive.co.uk/viewer/bl/0000264/19281012/110/0013.

57   'Tivoli Theatre', *Aberdeen Press and Journal,* 15/12/1925, 3, https://www.britishnewspaperarchive.co.uk/viewer/bl/0000577/19251215/020/0003.

58   Swannee River: 'Ripples of Laughter at the Opera House', *Kent & Sussex Courier,* 5/04/1929, 2, https://www.britishnewspaperarchive.co.uk/viewer/BL/0000483/19290405/059/0002.

59   *The Era,* 27/01/1926, 16, https://www.britishnewspaperarchive.co.uk/viewer/bl/0000053/19260127/239/0016.

60   William Livingstone, 'Mabel Mercer: William Livingstone Visits with the Singers' Singer', *American Stereo Review* 34 no. 2 (1975), 61.

61   Renee Lapp Norris, 'Opera and the Mainstreaming of Blackface Minstrelsy', *Journal of the Society for American Music* 1, no. 3 (2007), 341.

62   'A Riot of Syncopation', *Western Daily Press,* 12/10/1928, 13, https://www.britishnewspaperarchive.co.uk/viewer/bl/0000264/19281012/110/0013.

63   'Negro Melodies', *West Middlesex Gazette,* 02/06/1928, 6, https://www.britishnewspaperarchive.co.uk/viewer/bl/0002564/19280602/083/0006.

64   David P. Johnson, 'Golden Stool, The,' *Encyclopedia of Africa* (Oxford
      Reference Online, 2010), https://www-oxfordreference-com.i.ezproxy.
      nypl.org/view/10.1093/acref/9780195337709.001.0001/acref-
      9780195337709-e-1666.

65   David P. Johnson, 'Asante', *Encyclopedia of Africa* (Oxford Reference Online,
      2010), https://www-oxfordreference-com.i.ezproxy.nypl.org/view/10.1093/
      acref/9780195337709.001.0001/acref-9780195337709-e-0262.

66   Robinson, *Forgeries*, 182.

The 1920s in context

1   David Krasner, *A Beautiful Pageant: African American Theatre, Drama and
      Performance in the Harlem Renaissance 1910–1927* (New York: Palgrave
      Macmillan, 2002), 170.

2   Howard Rye and Jeffrey Green, 'Black Music Internationalism in England in
      the 1920s', *Black Music Journal* 15, no. 1 (1995), 96.

3   Babacar M'Baye, 'Pan-Africanism, Transnationalism, and Cosmopolitanism
      in Langston Hughes's Involvement in the First World Festival of Black Arts',
      South Atlantic Review 82, no. 4 (2017), 148–9.

4   'What's in the Magazines', *Newcastle Daily Chronicle*,
      06/05/1921, 8, https://www.britishnewspaperarchive.co.uk/viewer/
      bl/0001634/19210506/146/0008.

5   'Among the Books and Authors', *Daily Herald* 06/04/1927, 9, https://www.
      britishnewspaperarchive.co.uk/viewer/bl/0000681/19270406/166/0009;
      'The Poet of his Race', *The Sphere* 07/05/1927, 38, https://www.
      britishnewspaperarchive.co.uk/viewer/bl/0001861/19270507/041/0038.

6   Eric Walrond, 'The Negro Renaissance', *Clarion*, 01/07/1929,
      15, https://www.britishnewspaperarchive.co.uk/viewer/
      bl/0002732/19290701/059/0015.

7   Lindsey R. Swindall, *The Politics of Paul Robeson's Othello* (Jackson:
      University of Mississippi Press, 2010), 32.

8   Fryer, *Staying Power*, 514–16.

9   Ibid., 518.

10   Hakim Adi and Marika Sherwood, *Pan-African History: Political Figures from
      Africa and the Diaspora Since 1787* (Abingdon: Taylor & Francis, 2003), 70.

11   'Claim of the Negroes', *West London Observer*, 06/07/1928, 5, https://www.
      britishnewspaperarchive.co.uk/viewer/bl/0000437/19280706/058/0005.

12   'Prince and the Jazz Band', *Western Mail*, 08/09/1924, 7, https://www.
      britishnewspaperarchive.co.uk/viewer/bl/0000104/19240908/178/0007.

13   Ivan Browning, 'Across the Pond', *The Chicago Defender*, 17/07/1926, 6,
      ProQuest.

14   Romeo L. Dougherty, 'Europe Fair to Negro Actors: Feels Negro Papers
      Should Get Behind Equity for Robeson Affair', *The New York Amsterdam
      News* 24/10/1928, 7, ProQuest.

15 'Negro Spirituals', *The Era*, 06/07/1927, 8,https://www.britishnewspaperarchive.co.uk/viewer/bl/0000053/19270706/107/0008.

16 'Broadcasting', *Western Morning News*, 10/09/1927, 8, https://www.britishnewspaperarchive.co.uk/viewer/bl/0000329/19270910/061/0008; 'A Social Titbit', *Belfast Telegraph*, 18/07/1827, 8, https://www.britishnewspaperarchive.co.uk/viewer/bl/0002318/19270718/125/0008.

17 'Concerts', *Pall Mall Gazette* 28/05/1920, 8, https://www.britishnewspaperarchive.co.uk/viewer/bl/0000098/19200528/097/0008; 'Maurice Piena', *The Era*, 25/05/1920, 7, https://www.britishnewspaperarchive.co.uk/viewer/bl/0000053/19210525/135/0007; 'Concerts', *Westminster Gazette*, 19/11/1920, 5, https://www.britishnewspaperarchive.co.uk/viewer/bl/0002947/19201119/030/0005.

18 'Guildhall, Plymouth', *Western Morning News*, 19/01/1921, 4, https://www.britishnewspaperarchive.co.uk/viewer/bl/0000329/19210119/151/0004.

19 'Contralto, Coming Here on 18th, Enjoyed Europe', *The Pittsburgh Courier*, 01/12/1928, 5; 'Prom 05 20:00 16 Aug 1928, Queen's Hall' [online], https://www.bbc.co.uk/events/eqg8q9.

20 'The Realm of Music', *The Era*, 21/02/1925, 10, https://www.britishnewspaperarchive.co.uk/viewer/bl/0000053/19250221/101/0010; Jordan Goodman, *Paul Robeson: A Watched Man* (London: Verso Books 2013), 8.

21 Floyd, *The Power of Black Music*, 107.

22 E.g., Ivan H. Browning, 'Across the Pond', *The Chicago Defender*, 16/04/1927, 7, ProQuest.

23 Rye and Green, 'Black Music Internationalism', 101.

24 'The Strand', *The Stage,* 09/06/1927, 16, https://www.britishnewspaperarchive.co.uk/viewer/bl/0001179/19270609/052/0016.

25 David Linton and Len Platt, 'Dover Street to Dixie and the Politics of Cultural Transfer and Exchange', in *Popular Musical Theatre in London and Berlin 1890–1939*, ed. Len Platt, Tobias Becker and David Linton (Cambridge: Cambridge University Press, 2014), 182.

26 B. Maine, 'Rhythm: Black and White', *Northern Whig*, Belfast, 11/08/1923, 10, https://www.britishnewspaperarchive.co.uk/viewer/bl/0001542/19230811/263/0010.

27 *The Sketch*, 13/06/1923, 32,https://www.britishnewspaperarchive.co.uk/viewer/bl/0001860/19230613/034/0032.

28 Ivan H. Browning, 'Our European Letter', *The New York Amsterdam News*, 10/08/1927, 10, ProQuest.

29 'Aston Hippodrome', *The Stage*, 18/02/1926, 22, https://www.britishnewspaperarchive.co.uk/viewer/bl/0001179/19260218/073/0022.

30 'Our Acts a Sensation', *The Chicago Defender*, 31/07/1926, 7, ProQuest.

31 'Sissle and Blake to Go to Europe', *The Pittsburgh Courier*, 22/08/1925, 10, ProQuest.

32 'Blake and Sissle Capture Londoners', *Afro-American,* 19/12/1925, 5, ProQuest.

33 'Sissle and Blake Going Abroad After Present Tour', *Afro-American,* 22/08/1925, A4, Proquest.

34 'Sissle and Blake, Hailed in England as "Ambassadors of Syncopation"', *The Pittsburgh Courier*, 19/12/1925, 9, ProQuest.

35 Ibid.

36 'Coloured Revue Artistes', *The Era*, 15/06/1927, 5, www. britishnewspaperarchive.co.uk/viewer/bl/0000053/19270615/062/0005.

37 Ibid.

38 Ivan H. Browning, 'Across the Pond', *The Chicago Defender*, 13/10/1928, 6, ProQuest. Using relative labour value: 'Five Ways to Compute the Relative Value of a UK Pound Amount, 1270 to Present,' MeasuringWorth, 2020, www.measuringworth.com/ukcompare/.

39 *Hull Daily Mail*, 10/09/1929, 2, https://www.britishnewspaperarchive.co.uk/viewer/bl/0000324/19290910/013/0002.

40 'Independence Day', *Genome: Radio Times 1923–2009* [online], https://genome.ch.bbc.co.uk/25ed2f94beed47638e556ef38fd368ee.

Chapter 5

1   Ivan H. Browning, 'Browning's London Letter', *The Chicago Defender*, 18/02/1928, 7, ProQuest.

2   'Backstage with Stagestruck', *Inter-State Tattler*, 02/03/1928, 13, Readex. Eddie Emmerson was often spelled Emerson; Emmerson is used generally in the rest of the book for consistency.

3   'London Taken by Storm by Our Own', *The New York Amsterdam News*, 22/02/1928, 8, ProQuest.

4   George McKay, *Circular Breathing: The Cultural Politics of Jazz in Britain* (Durham, NC: Duke University Press, 2005), 3.

5   'Stage Stars Aid Relief Fund', *The Chicago Defender,* 18/02/1928, 1, ProQuest.

6   'London Taken by Storm by Our Own'. Images survive of Baker's travels; see Debbie Challis, *Croydon Airport Calling* (blog), 12 October 2015, http://croydonairportcalling.blogspot.com/2015/10/why-josephine-baker-flew-in-and-out-of.html.

7   'Stage Stars Aid Relief Fund: Jo Baker Is Acclaimed in London Show Artists Make Brilliant Performance', *The Chicago Defender,* 18/02/1928, 1, ProQuest.

8   'Sissle and Blake, Hailed in England as "Ambassadors of Syncopation"', *The Pittsburgh Courier*, 19/12/1925, 9, ProQuest.

9   *The Era*, 05/12/1923, 20, https://www.britishnewspaperarchive.co.uk/viewer/bl/0000053/19231205/278/0020.

10 *Yorkshire Post and Leeds Intelligencer*, 29/12/1921, 3, https://www.britishnewspaperarchive.co.uk/viewer/bl/0000687/19211229/071/0003.

11 'Still Dancing', *The Era*, 18/11/1925, 8, https://www. britishnewspaperarchive.co.uk/viewer/bl/0000053/19251118/076/0008.

12 Arianne Johnson Quinn, '"Don't Fence Me In": Culture, Style, and Identity in Cole Porter's London Works (1918–1954)', PhD thesis, Princeton University, 2019.

13 'Noble Sissle Earns $20,000 He Testifies', *Afro-American*, 15/01/1927, 8, ProQuest. The figure here is based on income value (multiple of average income which would be needed to reach that); see Samuel H. Williamson, 'Seven Ways to Compute the Relative Value of a U.S. Dollar Amount, 1790 to present,' MeasuringWorth, 2020, https://www.measuringworth.com/.

14 'Chiswick Empire Programme', *Middlesex County Times*, 21/11/1925, 13, https://www.britishnewspaperarchive.co.uk/viewer/bl/0002464/19251121/173/0013.

15 Noble Sissle, 'Why Jazz Has Conquered All Over: Noble Sissle Tells Europeans Reasons for Success of New Departure', *The New York Amsterdam News*, 06/02/1929, 8, ProQuest.

16 A. A. Haston, 'With our Performers in Europe', *The New York Amsterdam News*, 23/12/1925, 5, ProQuest.

17 'Vaudeville: Sissle-Blake Split', *Variety*, 21/09/1927, 28, ProQuest.

18 'Blackpool Opera House', *The Stage*, 24/11/1927, 6, https://www. britishnewspaperarchive.co.uk/viewer/bl/0001179/19271124/018/0006; 'Glasgow Pavilion', *The Stage*, 01/12/1927, 4, https://www. britishnewspaperarchive.co.uk/viewer/bl/0001179/19271201/014/0004; 'Legitimate: In London for Sissle', *Variety*, 29/02/1928, 53, ProQuest.

19 'Sissle May Import Revue', *Afro-American*, 26/11/1927, 8, ProQuest.

20 'Orchestra and Cabaret: Sissle Importing Revue', *The Billboard* 19/11/1927, 22, ProQuest.

21 'Vaudeville: Noble Sissle, Alone', *Variety*, 07/12/1927, 27, ProQuest.

22 *The Stage*, 16/02/1928, 13, https://www.britishnewspaperarchive.co.uk/viewer/bl/0001179/19280216/033/0013.

23 'Land'o Melody: Sissle Placing Songs Abroad', *The Billboard* 10/03/1928, 22, ProQuest.

24 Other cast members had already performed in the UK before *Shuffle Along*, including Lottie Gee, Aubrey Lyles, Flournoy Miller and Mattie Wilks.

25 'Choosing Between Jazz and Classical Dancing', *Dundee Evening Telegraph*, 19/11/1925, 3, https://www.britishnewspaperarchive.co.uk/viewer/bl/0000563/19251119/034/0003.

26 Stephen Bourne, 'Mills, Florence [real name Florence Winfrey; married name Florence Thompson] (1895–1927), Singer and Dancer,' *ODNB*, 23/10/2004, https://www-oxforddnb-com.i.ezproxy.nypl.org/view/10.1093/ref:odnb/9780198614128.001.0001/odnb-9780198614128-e–65972.

27 Zakiya R. Adair, 'Respectable Vamp: A Black Feminist Analysis of Florence Mills' Career in Early Vaudeville Theater', *Journal of African American Studies* 17, no. 1 (2013), 8.

28   Caroline Bressey and Gemma Romain, 'Staging Race: Florence Mills, Celebrity, Identity and Performance in 1920s Britain', *Women's History Review* 28 no. 3 (2019), n.p., doi:10.1080/09612025.2018.1493119.

29   Ibid.

30   For a typical example, see 'Florence Mills', *Birmingham Daily Gazette*, 07/11/1927, 1, https://www.britishnewspaperarchive.co.uk/viewer/bl/0000669/19271107/018/0001.

31   Ivan Browning, 'Across the Pond', *The Chicago Defender* 01/10/1927, 9, ProQuest.

32   'Sunday Concert at Chiswick Empire', *Acton Gazette*, 17/02/1928, 7, https://www.britishnewspaperarchive.co.uk/viewer/bl/0002462/19280217/100/0007.

33   Noble Sissle, 'Two hundred Dollars Sent to George Walker's Mother', *The Chicago Defender*, 12/06/1926, 7, ProQuest.

34   'Sissle Planning Show for London Engagements', *The Billboard,* 04/02/1928, 7, ProQuest.

35   Ivan H. Browning, 'Across the Pond', *The Chicago Defender*, 11/02/1928, 7, ProQuest.

36   'Sissle & Blake's "*In Bamville*" the Best Show in Chicago Illinois Theater', *The Chicago Defender*, 05/04/1925, 6, ProQuest.

37   'Suite in Syncopated Music', *Dundee Evening Telegraph*, 01/12/1925, 5, https://www.britishnewspaperarchive.co.uk/viewer/bl/0000563/19251201/049/0005.

38   'Four Harmony Kings Invade London Hall: English Church Goers Hear Spirituals', *The Chicago Defender*, 27/02/1926, 3, ProQuest.

39   Ivan H. Browning, 'Nora Holt Is Hostess in London's most Exclusive Café', *The Chicago Defender*, 07/09/1929, 7.

40   Ivan H. Browning, 'Across the Pond', *The Chicago Defender,* 12/10/1929, 6, ProQuest.

41   Ivan H. Browning, 'Ivan H. Browning Explains Spreading of Prejudice; Is Host to the R. S. Abbotts', *The Chicago Defender*, 14/09/1929, 6.

42   Ivan H. Browning, 'Browning's London Letter', *The Chicago Defender,* 18/02/1928, 7, ProQuest.

43   Ivan H. Browning, 'Across the Pond', *The Chicago Defender*, 09/04/1927, 6, *ProQuest.*

44   'FLO' MILLS BENEFITS TO BE STAGED ABROAD', *Afro-American*, 24/12/1927, 5, ProQuest.

45   Ivan H. Browning, 'News of London', *The New York Amsterdam News*, 21/03/1928, 9, ProQuest.

46   Gopal, *Insurgent Empire*, 19.

47   Hannen Swaffer, 'Queen of the Coloured Stars', *The People*, 01/09/1939, 5, https://www.britishnewspaperarchive.co.uk/viewer/BL/0000729/19390101/067/0005.

48   Ibid.

49   Ibid.

50   'Priscilla in Paris', *The Tatler*, 08/02/1928, 24, https://www.
      britishnewspaperarchive.co.uk/viewer/bl/0001852/19280208/025/0024.

51   'London Air Port Improvements', *Times*, 31/01/1928, 9; and for the movie
      release, see 'Picture Theatres', *Times*, 16/03/1928, 12. For both sources, see
      the *The Times Digital Archive*, Gale.com.

52   'For Flood Victims', *Westminster Gazette*, 30/01/1928, 7, https://www.
      britishnewspaperarchive.co.uk/viewer/bl/0002947/19280130/107/0007.

53   Frank C. Taylor and Gerald Cook, *Alberta Hunter: A Celebration in Blues*
      (New York: McGraw Hill, 1988), 97.

54   Ibid.

55   'London Taken By Storm By Our Own', *The New York Amsterdam News*,
      22/02/1928, 8, ProQuest.

56   Presumably they are the same artists mentioned here in an article
      encouraging aspiring actors to pursue high school diplomas: 'Facts! Not
      Bull', *Indianapolis Recorder*, 16/06/1928, 3, https://newspapers.library.
      in.gov/cgi-bin/indiana?a=d&d=INR19280616-01.1.3.

57   'Dublin', *The Stage*, 15/08/1929, 18, https://www.britishnewspaperarchive.
      co.uk/viewer/bl/0001179/19290815/068/0018.

58   'Feldman', *The Stage*, 8/08/1929, 3, https://www.britishnewspaperarchive.
      co.uk/viewer/bl/0001179/19290808/012/0003.

59   'First Class Music in Penzance', *Cornishman*, 18/04/1929, 5, https://www.
      britishnewspaperarchive.co.uk/viewer/bl/0000331/19290418/061/0005.

60   'Music in the West', *Western Morning News*, 14/11/1928, 11, https://www.
      britishnewspaperarchive.co.uk/viewer/bl/0000329/19281114/124/0011.

61   (2009) 'Rediscovering George Garner, March 5, 1939', *Los Angeles
      Times* [online], https://latimesblogs.latimes.com/thedailymirror/2009/03/
      rediscovering-g.html.

62   Advert 'London Theatre of Varieties Ltd', *The Era*, 26/09/1925,
      10, https://www.britishnewspaperarchive.co.uk/viewer/
      bl/0000053/19250926/137/0010.

63   'Newcastle-Upon-Tyne', *The Stage*, 25/08/1927, 15, https://www.
      britishnewspaperarchive.co.uk/viewer/bl/0001179/19270825/045/0015.

64   *Radio Times* listings 1927/8. For the full list, see https://genome.ch.bbc.co.uk
      /5a004c71bc024f57b961bdcc3f9993e3.

65   Rainer E. Lotz, 'Abbey, Leon', *Grove Music Online* (2003),
      https://www.oxfordmusiconline.com/grovemusic/view/10.1093/
      gmo/9781561592630.001.0001/omo-9781561592630-e-2000000600.

66   *Bombay Jazz*, 11:30 25/09/2014, BBC Radio 4, 30 mins, https://
      learningonscreen.ac.uk/ondemand/index.php/prog/06E3F358?bcast=114196695.

67   Arthur Badrock, 'Hatch and Carpenter in England', [online] http://www.vjm.
      biz/articles6.htm.

68   'Ike Hatch Issue Title – Airway 1938', British Pathé (1938), [online], https://
      www.britishpathe.com/video/ike-hatch-issue-title-airway.

69 'Stage Struck at the Hippo', *Portsmouth Evening News*, 12/01/1926, 4, https://www.britishnewspaperarchive.co.uk/viewer/bl/0000290/19260112/099/0004.

70 'Birmingham', The Stage, 03/06/1926, 21, https://www.britishnewspaperarchive.co.uk/viewer/bl/0001179/19260603/071/0021.

71 'Broadcasting', *Times*, 31/10/1929, 26. *The Times Digital Archive*.

72 Stephen Bourne, 'Heydays', *The Stage*, 01/07/1999, 11, https://www.britishnewspaperarchive.co.uk/viewer/bl/0001637/19990701/066/0011.

73 'Other 34 – no Title', *Afro-American*, 01/06/1929, 4.

74 Todd Decker, *Show Boat: Performing Race in An American Musical* (Oxford: Oxford University Press, 2013), 128.

75 Decker, *Show Boat*, 127.

76 Ivan H. Browning, 'Negro Entertainers in Europe', *The New York Amsterdam News*, 12/09/1928, 6, ProQuest.

77 Walter Balliett, *American Singers: Twenty-Seven Portraits in Song* (Mississippi: University Press of Mississippi, 2006), 23.

78 'Glasgow Program', *The Scotsman*, 02/01/1924, 3, https://www.britishnewspaperarchive.co.uk/viewer/bl/0000540/19240102/173/0003; and 'Catchy Tunes for the Party', *Dundee Courier*, 14/12/1923, 7, https://www.britishnewspaperarchive.co.uk/viewer/bl/0000164/19231214/135/0007.

79 'Alberta Hunter', *The Era*, 22/02/1928, 13, https://www.britishnewspaperarchive.co.uk/viewer/bl/0000053/19280222/168/0013.

80 Hunter quoted in Balliett, *American Singers*, 24.

81 J Rogers. '"N——" in "Show Boat" Stirs Rogers', *Philadelphia Tribune*, 04/10/1928, 9, ProQuest. (The slur in this article is not redacted in the catalogue.)

82 Ibid.

83 Ibid.

84 Ibid.

85 *The Bystander*, 30/05/1928, 18, https://www.britishnewspaperarchive.co.uk/viewer/bl/0001851/19280530/018/0018.

86 Decker, *Show Boat*, 129.

87 'Drury Lane Show Boat', *The Stage*, 10/05/1928, 16, https://www.britishnewspaperarchive.co.uk/viewer/bl/0001179/19280510/056/0016.

88 Taylor and Cook, *Alberta Hunter*, 102.

89 Decker, *Show Boat*, 129.

Chapter 6

1 Stephen Bourne's three books *Elisabeth Welch: Soft Lights and Sweet Music* (Lanham, MD: The Scarecrow Press, 2006); *Evelyn Dove: Britain's Black Cabaret Queen* (London: Jacaranda, 2006); and *Nina Mae McKinney: The Black Garbo* (Duncan, OK: Bear Manor Media, 2012).

2   G. Schuyler, 'Actress Wept on Seeing Statue of Liberty, on Return to
     U.S.: Alberta Hunter Compares American Reception with Unprejudiced
     Appreciation Received Abroad', *Afro-American*, 20/12/1930, 8, ProQuest.

3   G. S. Schuyler, 'Europe Gives Race Actors Better Chance than U. S.' *The
     Chicago Defender*, 20/12/1930, 5, ProQuest.

4   'Music Halls', *Birmingham Daily Gazette*, 13/03/1928, 3, https://www.
     britishnewspaperarchive.co.uk/viewer/bl/0000669/19280313/042/0003.

5   Marvel Cooke, 'Alberta Hunter Is No Cinderella, but Her Storm Is Just About
     As Romantic!', *New York Amsterdam News*, 05/11/1938, 21, ProQuest.

6   'Noble Sissle Lauds Duke of Windsor's Aid to our Actors', *Philadelphia
     Tribune*, 18/11/1937, 14, ProQuest.

7   Ivan H. Browning, 'European Notes', *New York Amsterdam News*,
     26/12/1928, 7, ProQuest

8   Ivan H. Browning, 'European Notes', *New York Amsterdam News*,
     10/04/1929, 13, ProQuest.

9   'Montmartre', *Philadelphia Tribune*, 01/02/1934, 5, ProQuest.

10   See K. T. Ewing, 'What Kind of Woman? Alberta Hunter and Expressions
     of Black Female Sexuality in the Twentieth Century', in *Black Female
     Sexualities*, ed. Trimiko Melancon and Joanna M. Braxton (New Brunswick,
     NJ: Rutgers University Press, 2015), 100–12.

11   William Barlow, '*Looking Up at Down*': The Emergence of Blues Culture
     (Philadelphia: Temple University Press, 1989), 154.

12   'Argyle Birkenhead', *Liverpool Echo* 22/02/1928, 1, https://www.
     britishnewspaperarchive.co.uk/viewer/bl/0000271/19280222/014/0001.

13   Frank C. Taylor and Gerald Cook, *Alberta Hunter: A Celebration in the
     Blues* (New York: McGraw Hill, 1988), 104.

14   'Items', *The Stage*, 08/03/1928, 23, https://www.britishnewspaperarchive.
     co.uk/viewer/bl/0001179/19280308/078/0023.

15   'Alberta Hunter Gets Extension', *New York Amsterdam News*, 11/07/1928,
     10, ProQuest.

16   See 'Edith Day in Show Boat', *The Radio Times: Genome* [online], https://
     genome.ch.bbc.co.uk/2d09de437eab49c5ae127f72bfad4951.

17   Balliett, *American Singers*, 27.

18   E. A. Wiggins, 'Across the Pond', The Chicago Defender, 24/06/1933, 5,
     ProQuest.

19   'Alberta Hunter Gets Paris Job: American Singer to Replace Josephine Baker
     at the Casino October 1', *New York Amsterdam News,* 13/09/1933, 7,
     ProQuest.

20   For a description of her continental European activities in this period, see
     Taylor and Cook, *Alberta Hunter*, 118–40.

21   'Alberta Hunter Still Going Big in England: Sponsors of Ellington Still Hope
     to Take Duke and His Band to London,' *New York Amsterdam News*,
     17/11/1934, 10, ProQuest.

22   'HMV Notes', *Cornishman*, 01/11/1934, 8, https://www.
     britishnewspaperarchive.co.uk/viewer/bl/0000331/19341101/086/0008.

23 Anthony Fields, 'Hey Days', *The Stage*, 12/02/1998, 13, https://www. britishnewspaperarchive.co.uk/viewer/bl/0001637/19980212/083/0013.

24 Henry De La Tour, 'Negro Performers in Europe', *New York Amsterdam News*, 11/08/1934, 6, ProQuest.

25 'Hackney Empire', *The Stage*, 01/11/1934, 3, https://www. britishnewspaperarchive.co.uk/viewer/bl/0001179/19341101/018/0003.

26 'Publisher's Song Notes', *The Stage*, 11/10/1934, 6, https://www. britishnewspaperarchive.co.uk/viewer/bl/0001179/19341011/021/0006.

27 'Publisher's Song Notes', *The Stage*, 19/07/1934, 11, https://www. britishnewspaperarchive.co.uk/viewer/bl/0001179/19340719/053/0011.

28 *The Era*, 28/12/1934, 10, https://www.britishnewspaperarchive.co.uk/viewer/ bl/0000053/19341228/081/0010.

29 'Lewisham Hippodrome', *The Era*, 09/01/1935, 13, https://www. britishnewspaperarchive.co.uk/viewer/bl/0000053/19350109/137/0013.

30 Roy D. Coverley, 'Race Question Not in Existence in Denmark,' *The Chicago Defender*, 21/12/1935, 4. ProQuest.

31 'Singer Warns Against Nazis: Alberta Hunter Back from Triumphant London Season Scores Nazis', *New York Amsterdam News*, 09/02/1935, 1, ProQuest.

32 Allan McMillan, 'Theatre Chat: From Broadway To Harlem', *Afro-American*, 28/12/1935, 8, ProQuest.

33 'Alberta Hunter to Sing Coronation Swing Tunes', *Afro-American*, 08/05/1937, 8, ProQuest.

34 'Alberta Hunter Returns to London Music Halls', *Afro-American*, 12/02/1938, 11, ProQuest.

35 'Alberta Hunter Goes to London for Broadcast', *Afro-American*, 16/04/1938, 11, ProQuest.

36 Marvel Cooke, 'Alberta Hunter Is No Cinderella, but Her Storm Is Just About As Romantic!', *New York Amsterdam News*, 05/11/1938, 21. *ProQuest.*

37 Alberta Hunter, 'Alberta Hunter's Little Notebook', *Afro-American*, 03/10/1942, 10, *ProQuest.*

38 'Program Complete for Brilliant N. A. A. C. P. Theatrical Benefit', *Philadelphia Tribune*, 04/12/1930, 7. ProQuest.

39 'Stars to Appear at Benefit', *New York Herald Tribune*, 25/11/1929, 19, ProQuest.

40 'Alberta Hunter in Royal Celebration', *New York Amsterdam News*, 19/02/1938, 16, ProQuest.

41 Barlow, *Looking Up at Down*, 154.

42 Steve Cushing, *Blues Before Sunrise: The Radio Interviews* (Urbana: University of Illinois Press, 2010), 45.

43 See Anthea Kraut, *Choreographing Copyright: Race, Gender, and Intellectual Property Rights in American Dance* (Oxford: Oxford University Press, 2016), 144–155.

44 Ibid., 146.

45   Ibid., 149.

46   Ivan H. Browning, 'European Notes', *New York Amsterdam News*, 09/02/1927, 10.

47   Taylor and Cook, *Alberta Hunter*, 105.

48   Chappy Gardner, 'Lafayette Theatre in New York Accused of "Shaking Down Actors"', *The Pittsburgh Courier*, 09/05/1931, 1, ProQuest. Geraldyn Dismond, 'Alberta Hunter Goes to Bat', *Afro-American*, 18/10/1930, 9. ProQuest.

49   'Charles Doyle Wins Salary Suit: Actors' Equity Association Again Comes to Rescue of another Performer', *New York Amsterdam News*, 22/10/1930, 10, ProQuest.

50   'Miss Hunter on Keith Circuit', *New York Amsterdam News*, 07/08/1929, 13. ProQuest.

51   '"Perfidious Albion" Would Close Her Doors to all Visiting Negro Performers', *New York Amsterdam News*, 08/06/1935, 12, ProQuest.

52   'Alberta Hunter in Athens, Greece: Prejudices in Europe at a Minimum, She Discovers', *The Chicago Defender*, 09/05/1936, 24, ProQuest.

53   Albert Hunter, 'Italy Bars Race Performers', *The Chicago Defender*, 27/02/1937, 20, ProQuest.

54   Angela Y. Davis, *Blues Legacies and Black Feminism: Gertrude Ma Rainey, Bessie Smith, and Billie Holiday* (New York: Knopf Doubleday, 2011), 21.

55   Maria V. Johnson, '"Jelly Jelly Jellyroll": Lesbian Sexuality and Identity in Women's Blues', *Women & Music* 7 (2003), n.p. Gale Academic OneFile [online database].

56   David Román, *Performance in America: Contemporary U.S. Culture and the Performing Arts* (Durham, NC: Duke University Press, 2005), 208.

57   Ibid., 179.

58   Michael Feinstein, 'It Went a Little Something Like This: A Social History of the Great American Songbook Era', *New York Times*, 15/02/2015, SS3–11, ProQuest.

59   John S. Wilson, 'Mabel Mercer, Phraser of Songs, Dies', *New York Times*, 21/04/1984, 1, ProQuest.

60   On Cook: Stephen Holden, 'Benevolent Monarchs of the Songbook Realm', *New York Times*, 02/12/2011, 1, ProQuest. On Sinatra, King Cole and Holiday, see Wilson, 'Mabel Mercer', 1.

61   Elvis Costello, 'Joni's Last Waltz?', https://www.jonimitchell.com/library/view.cfm?id=1182.

62   Wilson, 'Mabel Mercer', 1.

63   J. Nickeson, 'Food News: A Novel Eggnog', *New York Times* 05/12/1955, 36, ProQuest.

64   'Southern Syncopated Orchestra', *Dundee Evening Telegraph*, 25/05/1920, 3, https://www.britishnewspaperarchive.co.uk/viewer/bl/0000563/19200525/042/0003.

65   'Ole Lunnon', *The Chicago Defender*, 21/08/1926, 7, ProQuest.

66   James Haskins, *Mabel Mercer: A Life* (New York: Macmillan, 1987), 28.

67   Jayna Brown, *Babylon Girls: Black Women Performers and the Shaping of the Modern* (Durham, NC: Duke University Press, 2008), 247.

68   Ivan Browning, 'Across the Pond', *The Chicago Defender*, 17/07/1926, 6, ProQuest.

69   Floyd G. Snelson, 'Harlem Negro Capitol of the Nation', *New York Age*, 1/11/1944, Readex.

70   Maya Cantu, 'Recovering Ada "Bricktop" Smith', in *Reframing the Musical: Race, Culture and Identity*, ed. Sarah Whitfield (London: Red Globe Press, 2019), 61.

71   Ibid., 62.

72   T. Denean Sharpley Whiting, *Bricktop's Paris: African American Women in Paris between the Two World Wars* (New York: Whiting Suny Press, 2015), 34.

73   Ivan H. Browning, 'European Notes', *New York Amsterdam News*, 11/09/1929, 8, ProQuest.

74   J. Rogers, 'Give Big Show for the Gold Star Mothers', *Afro-American*, 29/07/1933, 15, ProQuest.

75   Edgar Wiggins, 'Across the Pond', *The Chicago Defender*, 26/02/1938, 19, ProQuest.

76   Haskins, *Mabel Mercer*, 14.

77   Ibid., 11.

78   Howard Rye, 'Southern Syncopated Orchestra: The Roster', *Black Music Research Journal* 30, no. 1 (2010), 61.

79   Ivan H. Browning, 'Across the Pond', *The Chicago Defender*, 25/02/1933, 5, ProQuest.

80   Floyd Snelson, 'Harlem', *New York Age*, 01/11/1941, 10, Readex.

81   'Southern Syncopated Orchestra', *Dundee Courier*, 11/05/1920, 5, https://www.britishnewspaperarchive.co.uk/viewer/bl/0000164/19200511/053/0005.

82   Ward, 'Music, Musical Theater', 53.

83   Haskins, *Mabel Mercer*, 15–16.

84   Ibid.,16.

85   'The Halls', *Evening Dispatch*, Birmingham, UK, 14/12/1918, 2, https://www.britishnewspaperarchive.co.uk/viewer/bl/0000671/19181214/045/0002.

86   'Olympia Theatre', *The Irish Times* 21/10/1924, ProQuest Historical Newspapers.

87   Cantu, 'Recovering Ada', 70.

The 1930s in context

1   Matera, 'Pan-Africanism'.

2   Susan D. Pennybacker, *From Scottsboro to Munich: Race and Political Culture in 1930s Britain* (Princeton: Princeton University Press, 2009), 25.

3   Ibid.

4   *Negro Anthology 1931–1933*, ed. Nancy Cunard (London: Wishart and Co, 1934), https://digitalcollections.nypl.org/items/294108d0-4abd-0134-e9a7-00505686a51c.

5   Gopal, *Insurgent Empire*, 305.

6   Pennybacker, *From Scottsboro*, 52.

7   There is a comprehensive history of Moody in Stephen Bourne, *Mother Country: Britain's Black Community on the Home Front, 1939–45* (New York: The History Press, 2013), 22.

8   Deborah J. Rossum, '"A Vision of Black Englishness": Black Intellectuals in London, 1910–1940', *Stanford Electronic Humanities Review 5*, no. 2 (1997) [online], https://web.stanford.edu/group/SHR/5-2/rossum.html#53.

9   Fryer, *Staying Power*, 524.

10   Ibid., 564.

11   Spike Hughes, 'All-Coloured Play of Many Accents Written by West Indian Girl', *Daily Herald*, 16/01/1934, https://www.britishnewspaperarchive.co.uk/viewer/bl/0000681/19340116/055/0003.

12   Denise de Caires Narain, 'Marson, Una Maud Victoria (1905–1965), Writer and Feminist' in *Oxford Dictionary of National Biography* (23 September 2004), https://www-oxforddnb-com.i.ezproxy.nypl.org/view/10.1093/ref:odnb/9780198614128.001.0001/odnb-9780198614128-e-69624.

13   'Ban on Foreign Artists: More Notices to Leave American Variety Performers,' *The Manchester Guardian*, 09/01/1932, 11, ProQuest.

14   Matera, *Sound of Black London*, 150.

15   See, e.g., 'Britain Bars American Negro Entertainers; Denies General Exclusion of Foreign Artists', *New York Times*, 08/01/1932, 26, ProQuest.

16   'Vaudeville: Harmony Kings Back in England', *The Billboard*, 03/09/1932, 8, ProQuest

17   Ivan H. Browning, 'Europeans "Across The Pond": The Palladium', *The Pittsburgh Courier*, 26/11/1932, 5, ProQuest.

18   Ivan H. Browning, 'Browning's Inside', *The Pittsburgh Courier*, 09/09/1939, 20, ProQuest.

19   'Hull Variety' *Hull Daily Mail*, 10, https://www.britishnewspaperarchive.co.uk/viewer/bl/0000324/19300828/117/0010.

20   'The London Stage', *Graphic*, 22/03/1930, 19 https://www.britishnewspaperarchive.co.uk/viewer/bl/0000057/19300322/031/0019.

21   'Looking Around', *The Era*, 25/06/1930, 9, https://www.britishnewspaperarchive.co.uk/viewer/bl/0000053/19300625/163/0009.

22   'London Theatre', *The Stage*, 15/10/1931, 14 https://www.britishnewspaperarchive.co.uk/viewer/bl/0001179/19311015/054/0014.

23   'Gramophone Notes', *Montrose Standard*, 19/08/1938, 6, https://www.britishnewspaperarchive.co.uk/viewer/bl/0002751/19380819/146/0006.

24   Floyd G. Snelson. 'Where the Color Line Fades', *The Pittsburgh Courier*, 25/06/1932, 11, ProQuest.

25   Goodman, *Paul Robeson*, 27.

26   Penny M. Von Eschen, *Race Against Empire: Black Americans and Anticolonialism* 1937–1957 (Ithaca, NY: Cornell University Press, 1997), 37.

27   'Troxy', *The Era*, 08/01/1936, 12, https://www.britishnewspaperarchive. co.uk/viewer/bl/0000053/19360108/114/0012.

28   'There is No Charge', *Airdrie & Coatbridge Advertiser*, 18/07/1936, 7, https://www.britishnewspaperarchive.co.uk/viewer/ bl/0002391/19360718/170/0007.

29   *The Era*, 12/08/1937, 4, https://www.britishnewspaperarchive.co.uk/viewer/ bl/0000053/19370812/036/0004.

30   'Adelaide Hall', *The Stage,* 08/06/1939, 6, https://www. britishnewspaperarchive.co.uk/viewer/bl/0001179/19390608/015/0006.

31   'Won Stage Contest', *Coventry Evening Telegraph*, 30/08/1939, 2, https:// www.britishnewspaperarchive.co.uk/viewer/bl/0000337/19390830/057/0002.

32   'That Harlem Rhythm', *The Bystander*, 15/03/1933, 24, https://www. britishnewspaperarchive.co.uk/viewer/BL/0001851/19330315/024/0024.

33   'Frank Woolf's Variety Gossip', *The Era* 08/06/1939, 11, https://www. britishnewspaperarchive.co.uk/viewer/bl/0000053/19390608/122/0011;'N ew Hippodrome Coventry', *Market Harborough Advertiser and Midland Mail*, 07/07/1939, 7, https://www.britishnewspaperarchive.co.uk/viewer/ bl/0002026/19390707/111/0007.

34   Ivan H. Browning, 'Across the Pond', *The Chicago Defender,* 24/05/1930, 10, ProQuest.

35   'West End Stars', *Kensington Post,* 15/07/1932, 4, https://www. britishnewspaperarchive.co.uk/viewer/bl/0002498/19320715/106/0004.

36   'Negro Dance Band', *Derby Daily Telegraph*, 13/07/1933, 5 https://www. britishnewspaperarchive.co.uk/viewer/bl/0000520/19330713/039/0005.

37   'Clarinet Recital in Bristol', *Western Daily Press*, 15/10/1932, 13 https://www.britishnewspaperarchive.co.uk/viewer/ bl/0000513/19321015/114/0013.

38   https://www.britishnewspaperarchive.co.uk/viewer/ bl/0000053/19380818/014/0002.

39   'Duke Ellington', *Worthing Gazette*, 14/06/1933, 3, https://www. britishnewspaperarchive.co.uk/viewer/bl/0002167/19330614/082/0003.

40   'Hippodrome', *Sussex Agricultural Express*, 05/05/1939, 13, https://www. britishnewspaperarchive.co.uk/viewer/bl/0000656/19390505/299/0013.

41   McKaye's identity is clarified in later advertisements in the United States; see 'Radio: HEAR … DE LLOYD McKAYE', *The Billboard,* 02/12/1939, 11, ProQuest.

42   Bourne, *Evelyn Dove*, 77.

Chapter 7

1   A. E. Wilson, 'A Principal Boy Gets Ready', *Picture Post*, 26/12/1942, 19,
     Picture Post Historical Archive, 1938–1957, https://link.gale.com/apps/doc/
     EL1800015337/GDCS?u=blibrary&sid=GDCS&xid=8bd27bac.

2   Gottschild, *Waltzing*, 102.

3   Brenda Dixon Gottschild, 'Bradley, Buddy', in *The International
     Encyclopedia of Dance* (Oxford: Oxford University Press, 1998),
     https://www-oxfordreference-com.i.ezproxy.nypl.org/view/10.1093/
     acref/9780195173697.001.0001/acref-9780195173697-e-0281.

4   Constance Valis Hill, 'Buddy Bradley: The Invisible Man of Broadway
     brings Jazz Tap to London', in *Proceedings of the Society of Dance History
     Scholars, Fifteenth Annual Conference*, ed. Christena L. Schlundt (Riverside:
     University of California, Riverside, 1992), 79.

5   Ibid.

6   Brian Seibert, *What the Eye Hears: A History of Tap Dancing* (New York:
     Farrar, Straus and Giroux, 2015), 163.

7   The National Archives in St. Louis, Missouri; St. Louis, Missouri; WWII
     Draft Registration Cards for District of Columbia, 10/16/1940-03/31/1947;
     Record Group: Records of the Selective Service System, 147; Box: 70,
     Ancestry.com. U.S. WWII Draft Cards Young Men, 1940–1947 [database
     online]. Lehi, UT: Ancestry.com Operations, Inc., 2011.

8   'Buddy Bradley, Director And Choreographer, Dead', *The New York Times*,
     25/07/1972, 32, ProQuest.

9   Henry Monaghan, 'Obituary: Henry LeTang', *The Guardian*, 09/05/2007,
     https://www.theguardian.com/news/2007/may/09/guardianobituaries.usa.

10   'The Lindy Hop', *Daily Mail*, 08/03/1932, 9. *Daily Mail Historical Archive,
     1896–2004*.

11   'Dance and Theatre Clubs', *The Times*, 6/11/1933, The Times Digital
     Archive.

12   'Kings', *The Stage*, 10/09/1931, 2, https://www.britishnewspaperarchive.
     co.uk/viewer/bl/0001179/19310910/008/0002.

13   'Brighton Entertainments', *West Sussex Gazette*, 20/06/1940, 8, https://www.
     britishnewspaperarchive.co.uk/viewer/bl/0002166/19400620/241/0008.

14   Ivan Patrick Gore, 'Cabaret', *The Stage*, 26/03/1931, 5, https://www.
     britishnewspaperarchive.co.uk/viewer/bl/0001179/19310326/027/0005.

15   'The Palladium', *The Stage*, 30/04/1931, 3, https://www.
     britishnewspaperarchive.co.uk/viewer/bl/0001179/19310430/020/0003.

16   *ISDN*, 19/09/1941, 30, https://www.britishnewspaperarchive.co.uk/viewer/
     bl/0001857/19410919/036/0030.

17   'The Palladium', *The Stage*, 30/04/1931, 3, https://www.
     britishnewspaperarchive.co.uk/viewer/bl/0001179/19310430/020/0003.

18   'American Musical Comedy', *The Scotsman*, 02/09/1931, 7, https://www.
     britishnewspaperarchive.co.uk/viewer/bl/0000540/19310902/356/0007.

19 'Buchanan Show will be a Hit', *Manchester Evening News*, 21/03/1943, 3, https://www.britishnewspaperarchive.co.uk/viewer/bl/0000272/19430421/030/0003.

20 'In the Limelight', *Liverpool Echo*, 14/05/1943, 2, https://www.britishnewspaperarchive.co.uk/viewer/bl/0000271/19430514/043/0002.

21 'Grieg and Grieg', *Daily Record*, 12/06/1943, 2, https://www.britishnewspaperarchive.co.uk/viewer/bl/0000728/19430612/019/0002.

22 W. Randy Dixon, 'Off the Cuff', *The Pittsburgh Courier*, 23/10/1943, Newspapers.com.

23 'Court Circular', *Times*, 09/12/1932, 17, The Times Digital Archive.

24 'Calls for Next Week', *The Era*, 02/11/1932, 19, https://www.britishnewspaperarchive.co.uk/viewer/bl/0000053/19321102/180/0019; 'Calls for Next Week', 13/10/1932, 8, https://www.britishnewspaperarchive.co.uk/viewer/bl/0001179/19321013/031/0008.

25 'The Cambridge', *The Stage*, 26/05/1949, 7, https://www.britishnewspaperarchive.co.uk/viewer/bl/0001179/19490526/027/0007.

26 'Sauce Tartare', *The Stage*, 14/04/1949, 3, https://www.britishnewspaperarchive.co.uk/viewer/bl/0001179/19490414/009/0003.

27 'Sauce Piquante', *The Stage*, 23/02/1950, 3, https://www.britishnewspaperarchive.co.uk/viewer/bl/0001179/19500223/009/0003.

28 'Blackbirds Wing North', *The Stage*, 14/05/1964, 1, https://www.britishnewspaperarchive.co.uk/viewer/bl/0001180/19640514/014/0001.

29 'Dancing Classifieds', *The Sydney Morning Herald* (Australia), 29/03/1937, 2. [Newspapers.com].

30 'Vaudeville: Bradley's Doubling', *Variety*, 02/02/1927, 24, ProQuest.

31 Gottschild, *Waltzing*, 103.

32 Marshall Sterns and Jean Sterns, *Jazz Dance: The Story of American Vernacular Dance* (Boston: De Capo Press, 1994), 167. (Originally published in 1968.)

33 Ivan H. Browning, 'Across the Pond', *The Chicago Defender*, 11/01/1930, 6, ProQuest.

34 'Billy Pierce's Numbers Go Over Big in "Ever Green" England', *The New York Age*, 29/11/1930, 6, ProQuest.

35 'Assemble Brown Skin Revue to Play in Big Paris Club', *The Pittsburgh Courier* (Pittsburgh), 08/11/1924, 17; 'Calls Browns for New Berlin Review', *Afro-American*, 15/11/1924, 6. (Both sources via ProQuest.)

36 Floyd Snelson, 'Theatrical Comment', *The Pittsburgh Courier*, 14/02/1925, 10, ProQuest.

37 Sterns and Sterns, *Jazz Dance*, 163.

38 Ibid., 164.

39 Ibid.

40 'Billy Pierce Opens Elaborate Dance Studio', *Afro-American*, 28/05/1927, 8, ProQuest.

41 'New York Tattler', *Tattler*, 08/06/1928, 10, Readex.

42 Constance Valis Hill, *Tap Dancing America: A Cultural History* (Oxford: Oxford University Press, 2010), 86.

43 'Legitimate: New Numbers in "G. V." By Colored Dance Stager', *Variety*, 10/03/1926, 23, ProQuest.

44 'Legitimate: Dances in New Musical Staged by Colored Men.' *Variety*, 16/06/1926, 37, ProQuest.

45 'Legitimate: Dances in *Show Boat*', *Variety*, 08/12/1926, 45, ProQuest.

46 'Buddy's "Sugar Foot Strut" on New $2,100 Floor', *Variety*, 26/10/1927, 30, ProQuest.

47 'New York Tattler: Wanted', *Inter-State Tattler*, 02/01/1927, 9, Readex.

48 'Legitimate', *Variety*, 14/11/1928, 51, ProQuest.

49 Jeffrey Spivak, *Buzz The Life and Art of Busby Berkeley* (Kentucky: University Press of Kentucky, 2011), 40.

50 Shelley C. Berg, 'The Sense of the Past: Historiography and Dance', in *Researching Dance: Evolving Modes of Inquiry*, ed. Sondra Horton Fraleigh and Penelope Hanstein (Pittsburgh: University of Pittsburgh Press, 1994), 227.

51 'Foreign Show News: Cochran Wants Colored Stagers from New York, and Likely Getting 'Em', *Variety*, 23/07/1930, 53.

52 Bourne, *Black in the British Frame*, 70. The stage musical's title was *Ever Green*, whereas the film's title was styled *Evergreen*.

53 'Billy Pierce Shaved by White Barber in Glasgow – He Likes It', *Variety*, 19/11/1930, 40, ProQuest.

54 'Cochran Edits New Revue', *Daily Herald*, 31/01/1931, 2, https://www.britishnewspaperarchive.co.uk/viewer/bl/0000681/19310113/032/0002.

55 'Vaudeville: Colored Boys Sent for in London's New Revue', *Variety*, 28/01/1931, 48, ProQuest.

56 'The Genius of Noël Coward', *Northern Whig*, 18/07/1932, 6, https://www.britishnewspaperarchive.co.uk/viewer/bl/0001542/19320718/157/0006.

57 *The Era*, 08/06/1932, 22, https://www.britishnewspaperarchive.co.uk/viewer/bl/0000053/19320608/258/0022.

58 This sum is taken from the comparative income value, the multiple value of the average income that would be needed to buy the commodity: 'Five Ways to Compute the Relative Value of a UK Pound Amount, 1270 to Present', Measuringworth.com, 2020.

59 The sum is again taken from the comparative income value: Samuel H. Williamson, 'Seven Ways to Compute the Relative Value of a U.S. Dollar Amount, 1790 to present,' MeasuringWorth.com, 2020.

60 Spike Hughes, *Second Movement: Continuing the Autobiography of Spike Hughes* (London: Museum Press, 1951), 106–7.

61 Ibid., 119.

62 Transcribed by authors: Leslie Thompson, *Oral Histories of Jazz in Britain*, interviewed by Val Wilmer 11/08/1987 to 13/11/1987, British Library.

63   Bradley quoted in Sterns and Sterns, *Jazz Dance*, 166.

64   Ibid.

65   Catherine Tackley, 'Jazz Dance and Black British Identities', in *Bodies of Sound: Studies Across Popular Music and Dance*, ed. Sherril Dodds and Susan C. Cook (Farnham: Ashgate, 2013), 198.

66   Jill Flanders Crosby and Michèle Moss, 'Jazz Dance from Emancipation to 1970', in *Jazz Dance: A History of the Roots and Branches*, ed. Lindsay Guarino and Wendy Oliver (Gainesville: University Press of Florida, 2014), 49.

67   Hill, 'Buddy Bradley', 80.

68   Tina Sutton, *The Making of Markova: Diaghilev's Baby Ballerina to Groundbreaking Icon* (New York: Pegasus, 2013), 294.

69   'Music', *Truth*, 15/06/1932, 20, https://www.britishnewspaperarchive.co.uk/viewer/bl/0002961/19320615/072/0020.

70   'Sunday 27 Nov 1932', https://www.rambert.org.uk/performance-database/performances/mercury-theatre-27-11-1932-evening/desperate-blues/.

71   'After Dark', *The Stage*, 28/06/1933, 9, https://www.britishnewspaperarchive.co.uk/viewer/bl/0000053/19330628/080/0009.

72   'Follow the Sun', *The Stage*, 02/01/1936, 19, https://www.britishnewspaperarchive.co.uk/viewer/bl/0001179/19360102/078/0019.

73   'Floodlight', *The Stage*, 27/05/1937, 8, https://www.britishnewspaperarchive.co.uk/viewer/bl/0001179/19370527/039/0008.

74   'Frances Day's Triumph', *The Era*, 01/07/1937, 19, https://www.britishnewspaperarchive.co.uk/viewer/bl/0000053/19370701/198/0019.

75   Leonard G. Feather, 'Signature Tune', *Radio Times*, 17/02/1939, 15.

76   Ivan H. Browning, 'Across the Pond', *The Chicago Defender*, 13/10/1928, 6, ProQuest.

77   'John Burk Attending Dance Congress in NY', *Binghamton Press*, 10/07/1934, 8, ProQuest.

78   Constance Valis Hill, *Brotherhood in Rhythm: the Jazz Tap Dancing of the Nicholas Brothers* (New York: Oxford University Press, 2000), 269.

79   James Haskins, *The Cotton Club* (New York: New York American Library, 1984), 162.

80   'Cabaret', *The Chicago Defender*, 12/10/1929, 7, ProQuest.

81   James Gavin, *Stormy Weather: The Life of Lena Horne* (New York: Atria Books, 2009), 35.

82   Walter Wincheli, 'Duke Ellington Is Hit in Blackberries of 1930', *New Journal and Guide* (1916–2003), 05/04/1930, 8.

83   'New Harlem Club', *The Chicago Defender*, 20/12/1930, 5, ProQuest.

84   Edward Perry, 'Manhattan Madness', *Afro-American*, 14/02/1931, 9, ProQuest.

85   Floyd Snelson Jr, 'No Depression for Harl'm Show Folk, Cars Show', *Afro-American*, 03/10/1931, 9, ProQuest.

86   William Forsythe, '"Shuffle Along", and Sissle at Howard', *The Pittsburgh Courier*, 11/02/1933, 1, ProQuest.

87 'More *Dark Doings* at Leicester Square', *The Era*, 19/07/1933, 16, https://www.britishnewspaperarchive.co.uk/viewer/ bl/0000053/19330719/107/0016.

88 'In the Limelight', *Liverpool Echo*, 25/08/1933, 10, https://www. britishnewspaperarchive.co.uk/viewer/bl/0000271/19330825/349/0010.

89 'Variety News', *The Era*, 02/08/1933, 17, https://www. britishnewspaperarchive.co.uk/viewer/bl/0000053/19330802/119/0017.

90 'Gossip from the Halls', *The Era*, 09/08/1933, 5, https://www. britishnewspaperarchive.co.uk/viewer/bl/0000053/19330809/047/0005.

91 'The Palladium', *The Stage*, 27/07/1933, 3, https://www. britishnewspaperarchive.co.uk/viewer/bl/0001179/19330727/022/0003.

92 'Nottingham', *The Stage*, 14/09/1933, 2, https://www. britishnewspaperarchive.co.uk/viewer/bl/0001179/19330914/009/0002.

93 'Liverpool', *The Stage,* 31/08/1934, 9, https://www.britishnewspaperarchive. co.uk/viewer/bl/0001179/19330831/038/0009.

94 'Leicester Square', *The Stage,* 14/10/1933, 3, https://www. britishnewspaperarchive.co.uk/viewer/bl/0001179/19330914/014/0003.

95 'The March of Time', *The Stage,* 05/10/1933, 5, https://www. britishnewspaperarchive.co.uk/viewer/bl/0001179/19331005/018/0005.

96 'Empire Theatre', *The Scotsman*, 07/11/1933, 10, https://www. britishnewspaperarchive.co.uk/viewer/bl/0000540/19331107/062/0010.

97 'Clarence Robinson's Revue Opens Apollo', *The New York Amsterdam News*, 24/01/1934, 14, ProQuest.

98 'Apollo Revue Much Better', *The New York Amsterdam News*, 21/02/1934, 8, ProQuest.

99 'Mixed Bathing', *Hull Daily Mail*, 23/02/1934, 11, https://www. britishnewspaperarchive.co.uk/viewer/bl/0000324/19340223/077/0011.

100 'Touch of Old "Sunny Spain"', *The New York Amsterdam News*, 21/04/1934, 6, ProQuest.

101 'Robinson's Stay in Europe a Short One', *The New York Amsterdam News*, 07/07/1934, 6, ProQuest.'All Birmingham Theatres in Full Swing Next Week', *Birmingham Daily Gazette*, 18/08/1934, 8. https://www. britishnewspaperarchive.co.uk/viewer/bl/0000669/19340818/179/0008.

102 Henri de La Tour, 'An Opportunity for the Apollo Theatre', *The New York Amsterdam News*, 08/09/1934, 6, ProQuest.

103 *The Era,* 12/08/1937, 4, https://www.britishnewspaperarchive.co.uk/viewer/ bl/0000053/19370812/036/0004.

104 'One D—n Noise After Another', *Illustrated Sporting and Dramatic News*, 06/09/1937, 26, https://www.britishnewspaperarchive.co.uk/viewer/ bl/0001857/19370806/030/0026.

105 Beswick Goodgame, 'Nicholas Brothers at Holborn', *The Era*, 13/01/1937, 5, https://www.britishnewspaperarchive.co.uk/viewer/ bl/0000053/19370113/050/0005.

106 Rudolph Dunbar, 'Adelaide Hall Is Returning', *New York Amsterdam News*, 23/10/1948, 1, ProQuest.

107 Brown, *Babylon Girls*, 239.

108 'Jazz Concerts', *Birmingham Daily Gazette*, 26/08/1947, 2, https://www.britishnewspaperarchive.co.uk/viewer/bl/0000669/19470826/037/0002.

Chapter 8

1 'New York, New York Passenger and Crew Lists, 1909, 1925–1957', database with images, FamilySearch, https://familysearch.org/ark:/61903/3:1:33SQ-G5C6-8LS?cc=1923888&wc=MFKM-2P8%3A1029950901; 21/05/2014, 4944 – vols. 10690–10691, 14 April, 1931, image 570 of 860; citing NARA microfilm publication T715 (Washington, DC: National Archives and Records Administration, n.d.).

2 The original advert specifies 'coloured' in both removed words. *The Stage*, 06/09/1934, 13, https://www.britishnewspaperarchive.co.uk/viewer/bl/0001179/19340906/055/0013.

3 Donald R Hill, *Calypso Calaloo: Early Carnival Music in Trinidad* (Gainesville: University Press of Florida, 1993), 218.

4 John Cowley, 'West Indies Blues: An Historical Overview, 1920s–1950s – Blues and Music from the English-Speaking West Indies', in *Nobody Knows Where the Blues Come from: Lyrics and History*, ed. Robert Springer (Jackson: University Press of Mississippi, 2006), 263.

5 Lara Putnam, *Radical Moves: Caribbean Migrants and the Politics of Race in the Jazz Age* (Raleigh: University of North Carolina Press, 2013), 161.

6 Marc Matera, *Black London: The Imperial Metropolis and Decolonization in the Twentieth Century* (California: University of California Press, 2015), 148.

7 Minkah Makalani, *In the Cause of Freedom: Radical Black Internationalism From Harlem to London, 1917–1939* (Raleigh: University of North Carolina Press, 2011), 202.

8 Kevin Parker, 'Garvey, Amy Ashwood', in *Encyclopedia of African-American Culture and History*, ed. Colin A. Palmer, 2nd edn(Macmillan Reference USA, 2006), 902–3. Gale eBooks.

9 Matera, *Black London*, 146.

10 James, *Holding Aloft*, 12.

11 Ibid., 51.

12 Von Eschen, *Race Against Empire*, 24.

13 Rhoda Reddock, 'The First Mrs Garvey: Pan-Africanism and Feminism in the Early 20th Century British Colonial Caribbean', *Feminist Africa* 19 (2014), 64.

14 Ibid., 65.

15 'Sam Manning and Syd Perrin Are Now with Us', *The Gleaner*, 01/05/1929, 7, https://gleaner.newspaperarchive.com/kingston-gleaner/1929-05-01/page-7/.

16 Cowley, 'West Indian Blues', 202.

17 'Around Harlem with Jackson', *Afro-American*, 31/01/1925, 4, ProQuest.

18 Cowley, 'West Indian Blues', 206.

19   'Clarence Williams Stages Revue at the New Douglas', *New York Age*, 5/06/1926, 6, Readex.

20   Cowley, 'West Indian Blues', 203.

21   Ibid., 204.

22   Ibid., 205.

23   *Negro World*, 13/12/1924, 10, Readex.

24   Rhoda Reddock, 'Radical Caribbean Social Thought: Race, Class Identity and the Postcolonial Nation', *Current Sociology* 62, no. 4 (July 2014), 505.

25   Kevin Parker, 'Garvey, Amy Ashwood'.

26   'At The Alhambra', *Inter-State Tattler*, 01/11/1929, 10, Readex.

27   'Parody on Rise and Fall of Marcus Garvey Plot', *The Pittsburgh Courier*, 11/12/1926, 10, ProQuest.

28   Sampson, *Blacks in Blackface*, 963.

29   'Lafayette Theatre', *Inter-State Tattler*, 12/08/1927, 4, Readex.

30   'Mrs Garvey's "Brown Sugar" Scores Big', *New York Age*, 20/08/1927, 6, Readex.

31   Reddock, 'Radical Caribbean', 505.

32   'Sam Manning and Syd Perrin Are Now with Us', *The Gleaner*, 01/05/1929, 7, https://gleaner.newspaperarchive.com/kingston-gleaner/1929-05-01/page-7/.

33   Bennie Butler, 'Theatre', *Inter-State Tattler*, 16/11/1928, 8, Readex.

34   Cowley, 'West Indian Blues', 215.

35   'At The Alhambra', *Inter-State Tattler*, 01/11/1929, 10, Readex.

36   Cowley, 'West Indian Blues', 215.

37   Michael Eldridge, 'There Goes the Transnational Neighbourhood: Calypso Buys a Bungalow', in *Music Power and Politics*, ed. Annie Janeiro Randall (New York: Routledge, 2002), 178.

38   Putnam, *Radical Moves*, 195.

39   Robinson, *Forgeries*, 182.

40   'Manning Scores At Lafayette Theatre', *New York Age*, 11/08/1928, 6, Readex.

41   *New York Age*, 05/10/1929, 6, Readex.

42   'New Theatrical Agency Formed in New York', *Afro-American*, 19/10/1929, 13, ProQuest.

43   'Theatrical Combine', *Inter-State Tattler*, 11/10/1929, 9, Readex; and *Inter-State Tattler*, 27/12/1929, 13, Readex.

44   'Harlem Nite Life', *Inter-State Tattler*, 30/05/1930, 11, Readex.

45   *Asbury Park Evening Press*, 17/08/1933, 2, ProQuest.

46   'Activities Among Union Musicians', *The New York Age*, 02/02/1929, 7, Newspapers.com.

47   'Sam Manning Pays Visit to British Guiana', *The Gleaner*, 20/08/1929, https://gleaner.newspaperarchive.com/kingston-gleaner/1929-08-20/page-14/.

48 'Sam Manning, the Celebrated Comedian', *The Workman* (Panama), 11/05/1929, 2. Digital Library of the Caribbean, Florida State University.

49 'The Palace', *The Gleaner*, 07/05/1929, 10, https://gleaner.newspaperarchive. com/kingston-gleaner/1929-05-07/page-10/.

50 'Atlantic Side Notes', *The Workman*, 01/06/1929, 5, Digital Library of the Caribbean, Florida State University.

51 Katherine A. Zien, *Sovereign Acts : Performing Race, Space, and Belonging in Panama and the Canal Zone*, Critical Caribbean Studies (New Brunswick, NJ: Rutgers University Press, 2017), 80.

52 'Manning to Continue Suit Against Garvey', *Afro-American*, 26/10/1929, 1, ProQuest.

53 'New York, New York Passenger and Crew Lists, 1909, 1925–1957', database with images, FamilySearch, (https://familysearch.org/ark:/61903/3:1:33S7-954J-WJ?cc=1923888&wc=MFV1-R68%3A1029914701: 2/10/2015), 4579 – vols. 10018–10019, 12 September 1929 > image 26 of 1016; citing NARA microfilm publication T715 (Washington, DC: National Archives and Records Administration, n.d.).

54 'New York, New York Passenger and Crew Lists, 1909, 1925–1957', database with images, FamilySearch, (https://familysearch. org/ark:/61903/3:1:33SQ-G5C6-8LS?cc=1923888&wc=MFKM-2P8%3A1029950901: 21/05/2014), 4944 – vols. 10690–10691, 14 April 1931 > image 570 of 860; citing NARA microfilm publication T715 (Washington, DC: National Archives and Records Administration, n.d.).

55 'Sam Manning Has Theatre in Harlem', *The Pittsburgh Courier*, 25/03/1933, 20, Newspapers.com.

56 'My Observations: Ethel Waters Walks; Sam Manning Runs', *The New York Amsterdam News*, 05/04/1933, 8, ProQuest.

57 John Cowley, 'London Is the Place: Caribbean Music in the Context of Empire 1900–60' in *Black Music In Britain: Essays on the Afro Asian Contribution to Popular Music*, ed. Paul Oliver (Milton Keynes: Open University Press, 1990), 62.

58 Reddock, 'The First Mrs Garvey', 67.

59 Hakim Adi and Marika Sherwood, *Pan-African History: Political Figures from Africa and the Diaspora since 1787* (Abingdon: Taylor & Francis, 2003), 70.

60 H. H. Head, 'New Coloured Show at the Poplar', *The Era* 26/09/1934, 19, https://www.britishnewspaperarchive.co.uk/viewer/bl/0000053/19340926/179/0019.

61 John Cowley, 'Cultural 'Fusions': Aspects of British West Indian Music in the USA and Britain 1918–51, *Popular Music 5* (1985), 81–96.

62 Howard Rye, 'Towards a Black British Jazz: Studies in Acculturation, 1860–1935', in *Black British Jazz: Routes, Ownership and Performance*, ed. Jason Toynbee and Catherine Tackley (London: Routledge 2014), 32.

63 'Belfast', *The Stage*, 21/03/1935, 7, https://www.britishnewspaperarchive. co.uk/viewer/bl/0001179/19350321/038/0007.

64 'Sam Manning Forms British Negro Revue', *The Daily Gleaner*, 19/03/1935, 21, https://gleaner.newspaperarchive.com/kingston-gleaner/1935-03-19/page-21/.

65 *Bournemouth Graphic*, 09/02/1935, 14, https://www.britishnewspaperarchive.co.uk/viewer/bl/0002174/19350209/096/0014.

66 H.H. Head, 'New Coloured Show at the Poplar', *The Era* 26/09/1934, 19, https://www.britishnewspaperarchive.co.uk/viewer/bl/0000053/19340926/179/0019.

67 'Comedies from Repertory Theatres', *Birmingham Daily Gazette*, 06/10/1934, 8, https://www.britishnewspaperarchive.co.uk/viewer/bl/0000669/19341006/141/0008.

68 'Here and there with variety', *The Era*, 10/10/1934, 16, https://www.britishnewspaperarchive.co.uk/viewer/bl/0000053/19341010/154/0016.

69 *Dudley Chronicle*, 18/10/1934, 1, https://www.britishnewspaperarchive.co.uk/viewer/bl/0002934/19341018/023/0001.

70 'London Syndicate Halls', *The Era*, 17/10/1934, 14, https://www.britishnewspaperarchive.co.uk/viewer/bl/0000053/19341017/111/0014.

71 'On the Road', *The Era*, 31/10/1934, 17, https://www.britishnewspaperarchive.co.uk/viewer/bl/0000053/19341031/178/0017.

72 'On Stage', *The Stage,* 08/11/1934, 1, https://www.britishnewspaperarchive.co.uk/viewer/bl/0001179/19341108/005/0001.

73 'On the Road', *The Era*, 21/11/1934, 15, https://www.britishnewspaperarchive.co.uk/viewer/bl/0000053/19341121/161/0015.

74 'London Syndicate Halls', *The Era*, 05/12/1934, 16, https://www.britishnewspaperarchive.co.uk/viewer/bl/0000053/19341205/132/0016.

75 'At the Met', *Kensington Post*, 07/12/1934, 4, https://www.britishnewspaperarchive.co.uk/viewer/bl/0002498/19341207/093/0004.

76 'Harlem Nightbirds', *Hull Daily Mail*, 14/12/1934, 18, https://www.britishnewspaperarchive.co.uk/viewer/bl/0000324/19341214/141/0018.

77 'Revue's Success at Southhampton', *The Era*, 06/02/1935, 8, https://www.britishnewspaperarchive.co.uk/viewer/bl/0000053/19350206/075/0008.

78 *Bournemouth Graphic*, 16/02/1935, 12, https://www.britishnewspaperarchive.co.uk/viewer/bl/0002174/19350216/083/0012.

79 *The Era*, 06/02/1935, 14, https://www.britishnewspaperarchive.co.uk/viewer/bl/0000053/19350206/233/0014.

80 'Empire Theatre', *Northern Whig* 19/03/1935, 11, https://www.britishnewspaperarchive.co.uk/viewer/bl/0001542/19350319/239/0011.

81 'Birmingham', *The Stage*, 28/03/1935, 11, https://www.britishnewspaperarchive.co.uk/viewer/bl/0001179/19350328/060/0011.

82 *The Stage*, 04/04/1935, 4, https://www.britishnewspaperarchive.co.uk/viewer/bl/0001179/19350404/018/0004.

83 'Grand Theatre, Derby', *Long Eaton Advertiser*, 12/04/1935, 6, https://www.britishnewspaperarchive.co.uk/viewer/bl/0002506/19350412/208/0006.

84 'Next Monday's Calls', *The Era*, 17/04/1935, 12, https://www.britishnewspaperarchive.co.uk/viewer/bl/0000053/19350417/105/0012.

85 *The Era*, 24/04/1935, 12, https://www.britishnewspaperarchive.co.uk/viewer/bl/0000053/19350424/118/0012.

86 'On Tour', *The Stage*, 09 May 1935, 1, https://www.britishnewspaperarchive.co.uk/viewer/bl/0001179/19350509/008/0001.

87 *Lancashire Evening Post*, 17/05/1935, 1, https://www.britishnewspaperarchive.co.uk/viewer/bl/0000711/19350517/018/0001.

88 'Harlem Nightbirds', *Lancashire Evening Post*, 14/05/1935, 3, https://www.britishnewspaperarchive.co.uk/viewer/bl/0000711/19350514/193/0003.

89 'On Tour', *The Stage*, 16/05/1935, 1, https://www.britishnewspaperarchive.co.uk/viewer/bl/0001179/19350516/005/0001.

90 'Revues', *The Stage*, 06/06/1935, 1, https://www.britishnewspaperarchive.co.uk/viewer/bl/0001179/19350606/004/0001.

91 'South London Palace', *The Stage*, 06/06/1935, 3, https://www.britishnewspaperarchive.co.uk/viewer/bl/0001179/19350606/017/0003.

92 *Liverpool Echo*, 19/11/1935, 10, https://www.britishnewspaperarchive.co.uk/viewer/bl/0000271/19351119/265/0010.

93 Ibid.

94 'The Empire Theatre', *Belfast News Letter*, 16/03/1935, 12, https://www.britishnewspaperarchive.co.uk/viewer/bl/0000038/19350316/235/0012.

95 Henry De La Tour, 'Negro Performers in Europe', *The New York Amsterdam News*, 11/08/1934, 6. ProQuest.

96 'Tivoli', *Hull Daily Mail*, 18/12/1934, 8, https://www.britishnewspaperarchive.co.uk/viewer/bl/0000324/19341218/054/0008.

97 'Birmingham Hippodrome', *Birmingham Daily Gazette*, 26/03/1935, 3, https://www.britishnewspaperarchive.co.uk/viewer/bl/0000669/19350326/052/0003.

98 'Where to go at Derby', *Derby Daily Telegraph* 16/04/1935, 9, https://www.britishnewspaperarchive.co.uk/viewer/bl/0000521/19350416/075/0009.

99 'Revue's Success at Southampton', *The Era*, 06/02/1935, 8, https://www.britishnewspaperarchive.co.uk/viewer/bl/0000053/19350206/075/0008.

100 'The Palace', *The Stage*, 02/05/1935, 6, https://www.britishnewspaperarchive.co.uk/viewer/bl/0001179/19350502/028/0006.

101 *Bournemouth Graphic*, 09/02/1935, 3, https://www.britishnewspaperarchive.co.uk/viewer/bl/0002174/19350209/017/0003.

102 Olusoga, *Black and British*, 406.

103 Harvey Young, *Embodying Black Experience: Stillness, Critical Memory, and the Black Body* (Ann Arbor: University of Michigan Press, 2010), 135.

104 Amon Saba Saakana, 'Culture, Concept, Aesthetics: The Phenomenon of the African Musical Universe in Western Musical Culture', *African American Review* 29, no. 2 (1995), n.p., Gale Academic OneFile, https://link-gale-com.i.ezproxy.nypl.org/apps/doc/A17534811/AONE?u=nypl&sid=AONE&xid=d14ce4da.

105 For more details on this, see Cowley, 'Cultural "Fusions"'.

106 H. H. Head, 'New Coloured Show at the Poplar', *The Era* 26/09/1934, 19, https://www.britishnewspaperarchive.co.uk/viewer/ bl/0000053/19340926/179/0019.

107 'Harlem Nightbirds', *Belfast Telegraph*, 19/03/1935, 2, https://www. britishnewspaperarchive.co.uk/viewer/bl/0002318/19350319/030/0002.

108 'The Empire Theatre', *Northern Whig*, 19/03/1935, 11, https://www. britishnewspaperarchive.co.uk/viewer/bl/0001542/19350319/238/0011.

109 Ibid.

110 *The Stage,* 15/11/1934, 11, https://www.britishnewspaperarchive.co.uk/ viewer/bl/0001179/19341115/057/0011.

111 'The Empire Theatre', *Northern Whig*, 19/03/1935, 11, https://www. britishnewspaperarchive.co.uk/viewer/bl/0001542/19350319/239/0011.

112 *Belfast Telegraph*, 19/03/1935, 2, https://www.britishnewspaperarchive. co.uk/viewer/bl/0002318/19350319/030/0002.

113 'Queen's, Poplar', *The Stage*, 27/09/1934, 3, https://www. britishnewspaperarchive.co.uk/viewer/bl/0001179/19340927/016/0003.

114 'Advertisement: Artistes Vacancies', *Kinematograph Weekly* (Archive: 1919–1959), 96.932 (1925), 72, ProQuest.

115 'The Money Makers', *The Stage*, 28/04/1927, 14, https://www. britishnewspaperarchive.co.uk/viewer/bl/0001179/19270428/041/0014.

116 'Harry Norris's Enterprises', 28/04/1927, 14, https://www. britishnewspaperarchive.co.uk/viewer/bl/0001179/19270428/041/0014.

117 'Newcastle-Upon-Tyne', *The Stage,* 23/08/1928, 25, https://www. britishnewspaperarchive.co.uk/viewer/bl/0001179/19280823/073/0025.

118 'Aston Hippodrome', *Birmingham Daily Gazette*, 09/05/1933, 5, https://www.britishnewspaperarchive.co.uk/viewer/ bl/0000669/19330509/176/0005.

119 'The Regent', *Hendon & Finchley Times*, 10/03/1933, 20, https://www. britishnewspaperarchive.co.uk/viewer/bl/0001600/19330310/330/0020.

120 'Stoll Tour', *The Era*, 08/02/1933, 17, https://www.britishnewspaperarchive. co.uk/viewer/bl/0000053/19330208/143/0017.

121 'Sam Manning Forms British Negro Revue', *The Daily Gleaner*, 19/03/1935, 21, https://gleaner.newspaperarchive.com/kingston-gleaner/1935-03-19/page-21/.

122 'Deepdane Hotel', *Surrey Mirror*, 15/01/1932, 12, https://www. britishnewspaperarchive.co.uk/viewer/bl/0000335/19320115/205/0012.

123 Class: RG13; Piece: 3476; Folio: 118; Page: 45, Ancestry.com. 1901 England Census [database on-line]. Provo, UT, USA: Ancestry.com Operations Inc, 2005.

124 Class: RG14; Piece: 22215, Ancestry.com. 1911 England Census [database on-line]. Provo, UT, USA: Ancestry.com Operations, Inc., 2011.

125 'Items', *The Stage,* 10/09/1931, 10, https://www.britishnewspaperarchive. co.uk/viewer/bl/0001179/19310910/045/0010.

126 'Publishers Notes', *The Stage*, 08/10/1931, 10, https://www. britishnewspaperarchive.co.uk/viewer/bl/0001179/19311008/041/0010.

127 'Swanee River at the Empire', *Sheffield Daily Telegraph*, 21/05/1929, 5, https://www.britishnewspaperarchive.co.uk/viewer/bl/0000250/19290521/150/0005.

128 'Times Square: CHATTER – Paris', *Variety* 102, no. 3, 01/04/1931, 44, ProQuest.

129 'Variety Items', *The Stage*, 18/04/1932, 5, https://www.britishnewspaperarchive.co.uk/viewer/bl/0001179/19320818/020/0005.

130 *Hull Daily Mail*, 14/12/1934, 18, https://www.britishnewspaperarchive.co.uk/viewer/bl/0000324/19341214/141/0018.

131 *The Era*, 26/09/1934, 19, https://www.britishnewspaperarchive.co.uk/viewer/bl/0000053/19340926/179/0019.

132 Rye, 'Towards a Black British Jazz', 32.

133 'MUSIC RADIO: London Cabaret Acts 75 Per Cent American', *The Billboard* 49 no. 43, 05/12/1931, 30. ProQuest.

134 "Vaudeville: London Colored Unit', *The Billboard* 44 no. 4, 23/01/1932, 8, ProQuest.

135 *Coventry Herald*, 29/05/1937, 11, https://www.britishnewspaperarchive.co.uk/viewer/bl/0000384/19370529/233/0011.

136 James C. Davis, *Eric Walrond: A Life in the Harlem Renaissance and the Transatlantic Caribbean* (New York: Columbia University Press, 2015), 264–5.

137 *Bournemouth Graphic*, 09/02/1935, 3, https://www.britishnewspaperarchive.co.uk/viewer/bl/0002174/19350209/017/0003.

138 Davis, *Eric Walrond*, 269.

139 'Sam Manning', *The New York Amsterdam News*, 06/07/1935, 11, ProQuest.

140 'Manning Is Tired of "Jaded Jazz" Abroad: On Way to West Indies for New Talent – Backed by Lady Warwick'. *The New York Amsterdam News*, 06/07/1935, 11, ProQuest.

141 'Mr Sam Manning is Coming Here Soon to Seek Local Talent', *The Gleaner*, 03/07/1935, 4, https://gleaner.newspaperarchive.com/kingston-gleaner/1935-07-03/page-4/.

142 'Parlaphone', *Central Somerset Gazette*, 18/10/1935, 3 https://www.britishnewspaperarchive.co.uk/viewer/bl/0002470/19351018/053/0003.

143 *Liverpool Echo*, 19/11/1935, 10, https://www.britishnewspaperarchive.co.uk/viewer/bl/0000271/19351119/265/0010.

144 *Nottingham Evening Post*. 28/11/1950. 3. https://www.britishnewspaperarchive.co.uk/viewer/bl/0000321/19501128/026/0003.

145 'Things Theatrical Florence Mills Club Opens in London', *Plaindealer*, 24/07/1936, 3, Readex.

146 Ibid.

147 Rudolph Dunbar, 'Colored Olympians Entertained at Florence Mills Social Parlor in London', *Negro Star*, 18/09/1936, 3, Readex: NewsBank.

148 Currently the only reference to this can be found in radio broadcast listings, which is curious because Manning was relatively well known in British theatrical circles. 'Regional', *Nottingham Journal*, 15/10/1938, https://www.britishnewspaperarchive.co.uk/viewer/bl/0001898/19381015/078/0004.

149 'Afro-West Indian Show', *The Stage,* 16/04/1959, 4, https://www. britishnewspaperarchive.co.uk/viewer/bl/0001180/19590416/039/0004.

150 'Calling All Stars', *The Daily Gleaner*, 08/05/1939, 16, https://gleaner. newspaperarchive.com/kingston-gleaner/1939-05-08/page-16/.

151 'New York, New York Passenger and Crew Lists, 1909, 1925–1957,' database with images, FamilySearch (https://familysearch. org/ark:/61903/3:1:33SQ-G5NH-9SS4?cc=1923888&wc=MFK7-V38%3A1030086501: 2/10/2015), 6296 – vols. 13555–13556, 15 March 1939 > image 80 of 713; citing NARA microfilm publication T715 (Washington, DC: National Archives and Records Administration, n.d.).

152 *New York Age*, 22/11/1941, 10, Readex.

153 'Disc Data', *People's Voice*, 6/06/1942, 28, Readex.

154 *The Stage*, 02/05/1935, 6, https://www.britishnewspaperarchive.co.uk/viewer/bl/0001179/19350502/028/0006; *The Era*, 06/02/1935, 8, https://www. britishnewspaperarchive.co.uk/viewer/bl/0000053/19350206/075/0008.

155 35. 'L'. 1944. MS African America, Communists, and the National Negro Congress, 1933–1947: Papers of the National Negro Congress. New York Public Library. Archives Unbound, https://link-gale-com.i.ezproxy.nypl.org/apps/doc/SC5105454734/GDSC?u=nypl&sid=GDSC&xid=c79ae8c2.

Chapter 9

1 Toynbee, Tackley and Doffman, 'Another Place', 3.

2 Ibid.

3 Ibid., 4.

4 Ibid., 4.

5 'Publisher's Notes', *The Stage*, 12/05/1932, 15, https://www. britishnewspaperarchive.co.uk/viewer/bl/0001179/19320512/058/0015.

6 'Holborn Empire', *The Stage*, 13/07/1933, 3, https://www. britishnewspaperarchive.co.uk/viewer/bl/0001179/19330713/024/0003.

7 'Holborn Empire', *The Stage,* 14/09/1933, 3, https://www. britishnewspaperarchive.co.uk/viewer/bl/0001179/19330914/014/0003.

8 *The Era*, 16/08/1933, 4, https://www.britishnewspaperarchive.co.uk/viewer/bl/0000053/19330816/033/0004.

9 *Sheffield Daily Telegraph*, 24/09/1932, 5, https://www. britishnewspaperarchive.co.uk/viewer/bl/0000250/19320924/290/0005.

10 'Empire', *The Stage,* 29/03/1934, 6, https://www.britishnewspaperarchive. co.uk/viewer/bl/0001179/19340329/024/0006.

11 'The invasion of London by Negro artists continues' – while we note negro is not a racial slur, in this example it is being used as one. 'Too Many Antics and High Cs', *Daily Herald*, 01/08/1933, 1, https://www. britishnewspaperarchive.co.uk/viewer/bl/0000681/19330801/013/0001.

12 Kathy Ogren, *The Jazz Revolution: Twenties America and the Meaning of Jazz* (New York: Oxford University Press, 1994), 75.

13 Brown, *Babylon Girls*, 6.

14 Anne Cheng, *Second Skin: Josephine Baker and the Modern Surface* (New York: Oxford University Press, 2010), 4.

15 Nate Sloan, 'Constructing Cab Calloway: Publicity, Race and Performance in 1930s Harlem Jazz', *Journal of Musicology* 36, no. 3 (2019), 372.

16 Ibid.

17 'Dance', *Daily Herald*, 02/02/1932, 12, https://www.britishnewspaperarchive. co.uk/viewer/bl/0000681/19320202/227/0012.

18 *The Era*, 21/12/1932, 22, https://www.britishnewspaperarchive.co.uk/viewer/ bl/0000053/19321221/239/0022.

19 'Dance', *Daily Herald*, 21/12/1932, 13, https://www.britishnewspaperarchive. co.uk/viewer/bl/0000681/19321221/377/0013.

20 S R Nelson, 'Cab Calloway Comes to Town', *The Era* 17/01/1934.

21 Spike Hughes, 'Cab Calloway: Surprise Permit', *Daily Herald*, 16/02/1934, 11, https://www.britishnewspaperarchive.co.uk/viewer/ bl/0000681/19340216/199/0011.

22 *The Era*, 14/03/1934, 4, https://www.britishnewspaperarchive.co.uk/viewer/ bl/0000053/19340314/046/0004.

23 Londoner, 'Cab Calloway', *Daily Gazette for Middlesbrough*, 07/03/1934.

24 *The Stage*, 22/03/1934, https://www.britishnewspaperarchive.co.uk/viewer/ bl/0001179/19340322/018/0003.

25 'The Palladium', *The Stage*, 22/03/1934, 3, https://www. britishnewspaperarchive.co.uk/viewer/bl/0001179/19340322/018/0003.

26 *Wireless Portsmouth Evening News*, 03/03/1934, 5, https://www. britishnewspaperarchive.co.uk/viewer/bl/0000290/19340303/125/0005.

27 Gunther Schuller, *The Swing Era: The Development of Jazz 1930–1945* (New York: Oxford University Press, 1991), 34.

28 Alyn Shipton, *Hi-de-Ho: The Life of Cab Calloway* (Oxford: Oxford University Press, 2013), 86.

29 Sloan, 'Constructing Cab Calloway', 399.

30 'Death Came to the Dance', *Liverpool Echo* 05/04/1941, 3, https://www. britishnewspaperarchive.co.uk/viewer/bl/0000271/19410405/085/0003.

31 'After the Theatre', *ISDN*, 06/09/1940, 31, https://www. britishnewspaperarchive.co.uk/viewer/bl/0001857/19400906/033/0031.

32 *The Tatler*, 01/01/1941, 1, https://www.britishnewspaperarchive.co.uk/ viewer/bl/0001853/19410101/002/0001.

33 Matera, *Black London*, 264.

34 'Dynamic Dancing Conductor', *West Middlesex Gazette*, 02/10/1937, 14, https://www.britishnewspaperarchive.co.uk/viewer/ bl/0002564/19371002/246/0014.

35 Catherine Tackley, 'Race, Identity and the Meaning of Jazz in 1940s Britain', in *Black Popular Music in Britain since 1945*, ed. Jon Stratton and Nabeel Zuberi (Farnham: Ashgate Popular Music, 2014), 19.

36 Matera, *Black London*, 264.

37   *The Era*, 15/01/1936, 5, https://www.britishnewspaperarchive.co.uk/viewer/
      bl/0000053/19360115/072/0005.

38   Tackley, 'Race, Identity', 14.

39   Leslie Thompson, *Leslie Thompson: An Autobiography As Told to Jeffrey P.
      Green* (Crawley: Rabbit Press, 1985), 89–94.

40   Thompson, *Leslie Thompson*, 93.

41   Tackley, 'Race, Identity', 26.

42   Matera, *Black London*, 153.

43   Jason Toynbee, 'Race, History, and Black British Jazz', *Black Music Research
      Journal* 33, no. 1 (2013), n.p.

44   Matera, *Black London*, 153.

45   'Radio Around the Dial', *Altoona Tribune* (Altoona, Pennsylvania),
      08/02/1938, 19, Newspapers.com.

46   'Belfast Ritz', *The Era*, 18/11/1936, 16, https://www.britishnewspaperarchive.
      co.uk/viewer/bl/0000053/19361118/128/0016.

47   'Frank Looks at the News', *The Era*, 22/04/1936, 17, https://www.
      britishnewspaperarchive.co.uk/viewer/bl/0000053/19360422/149/0017.

48   'Stage Screen Night Spots', *The New Amsterdam News*, 10/10/1936, 10,
      ProQuest.

49   'Coventry & District', *Coventry Evening Telegraph*, 24/08/1936,
      5, https://www.britishnewspaperarchive.co.uk/viewer/
      bl/0000337/19360824/098/0005.

50   'Ken Snakehips Johnson Bowls Em Over in London', *The Pittsburgh Courier*,
      12/12/1936, 17, Newspapers.com.

51   'Chiswick Empire', *Uxbridge & W. Drayton Gazette*, 04/11/1938,
      19, https://www.britishnewspaperarchive.co.uk/viewer/
      bl/0002286/19381104/269/0019.

52   Leonard G. Feather, 'Swing Out the Old, Swing in the New', *The Era*,
      30/12/1938, 23, https://www.britishnewspaperarchive.co.uk/viewer/
      bl/0000053/19381230/199/0023.

53   'Gave up Medicine to Study Syncopation', *Aberdeen Evening Express*,
      08/08/1939, 5, https://www.britishnewspaperarchive.co.uk/viewer/
      bl/0000445/19390808/130/0005.

54   Tom Cullen, *The Man Who Was Norris: The Life of Gerald Hamilton*
      (Columbia: Daedalus, 2014).

55   Stephen Bourne, *Fighting Proud: The Untold Story of the Gay Men Who
      Fought in Two World Wars* (London: I.B.Tauris, 2017), 149.

56   BBC 'Ken "Snakehips" Johnson interviewed by Una Marson 10-10-1940',
      https://www.bbc.co.uk/programmes/p06bsp3f.

57   Toynbee, 'Race, History'.

58   Tackley, 'Race, Identity', 11–12.

59   Toynbee, 'Race, History', n.p.

60   Matera, *Black London*, 264.

61 Ibid., 267.

62 Ibid.

63 Bourne, *Fighting Proud*, 148.

64 Constantine Fitzgibbon, *The Winter of the Bombs: The Story of the Blitz in of London* (London: W.W. Norton, 1957).

65 Toynbee, Tackley and Doffman, 'Another Place', 9.

66 Joachim Berendt and Günther Huesmann, *The Jazz Book: From Ragtime to the 21st Century*, 7th edn (Chicago: Lawrence Hill Books, 2009), 667.

The 1940s in context

1   Olusoga, *Black and British*, 486.

2   Fryer, *Staying Power*, 577.

3   Olusoga, *Black and British*, 467.

4   'American Negro Music', *Hull Daily Mail*, 23/02/1944, 3, https://www.britishnewspaperarchive.co.uk/viewer/bl/0000324/19440223/041/0003.

5   Michele Hilmes, 'Missing from History: Langston Hughes' The Man Who Went To War' 12/06/2015, http://blog.commarts.wisc.edu/2015/06/12/missing-from-history-langston-hughes-the-man-who-went-to-war-2/.

6   Fol. 7. Unassorted Materials – 1936–46. 1936–46. MS African America, Communists, and the National Negro Congress, 1933–1947: Papers of the National Negro Congress. 'For This We Fight', by Langston Hughes New York Public Library. Archives Unbound, Gale, 33.

7   Olusoga, *Black and British*, 492.

8   Ibid., 497.

9   Fryer, *Staying Power*, 530.

10 Olusoga, *Black and British*, 496.

11 Von Eschen, *Race Against Empire*, 56.

12 Reddock, 'Radical Caribbean', 497.

13 David Levering Lewis, *W.E.B. Du Bois: The Fight for Equality and the American Century, 1919–1963* (New York: H. Holt, 2000), 522.

14 'This was the Other Paul Robeson', *Worthing Herald*, 27/05/1949, 2, https://www.britishnewspaperarchive.co.uk/viewer/bl/0001920/19490527/023/0002.

15 *Mining Review 2nd Year No. 11* (1949), film, directed by Peter Pickering, National Coal Board.

16 Von Eschen, *Race Against Empire*, 10.

17 'A Plebiscite', *Dundee Courier*, 30/10/1947, 3, https://www.britishnewspaperarchive.co.uk/viewer/bl/0000564/19471030/023/0003; 'Todd Duncan's Recital', *Birmingham Daily Gazette*, 15/12/1947, 2, https://www.britishnewspaperarchive.co.uk/viewer/bl/0000669/19471115/041/0002; 'Todd Duncan', *The Scotsman*,

09/09/1947, 4, https://www.britishnewspaperarchive.co.uk/viewer/
bl/0000540/19470909/110/0004.

18   *The Sphere*, 16/10/1948, 23, https://www.britishnewspaperarchive.co.uk/
      viewer/bl/0001861/19481016/022/0023.

19   'The Dancing Anthropologist', *Manchester Evening News*,
      23/10/1948, 2, https://www.britishnewspaperarchive.co.uk/viewer/
      bl/0000272/19481023/016/0002.

20   'Deep are the Roots: Hull New Theatre, April 1950', *African Stories in Hull
      and Yorkshire*, 2018,https://www.africansinyorkshireproject.com/deep-are-
      the-roots.html.

21   'The Little Foxes', *The Stage*, 15/10/1942, 4, https://www.
      britishnewspaperarchive.co.uk/viewer/bl/0001179/19421015/025/0004.

22   'The Whitehall', *The Stage*, 06/03/1947, 7, https://www.
      britishnewspaperarchive.co.uk/viewer/bl/0001179/19470306/034/0007.

23   Peter Noble, 'Negro Theatre: Robert Adams's New Plan for London', *The
      Stage*, 24/08/1944, 5, https://www.britishnewspaperarchive.co.uk/viewer/
      bl/0001179/19440824/029/0005.

24   'British Equity', *The Stage*, 08/01/1948, 4, https://www.
      britishnewspaperarchive.co.uk/viewer/bl/0001179/19480108/021/0004.

25   *The Stage*, 10/06/1948, https://www.britishnewspaperarchive.co.uk/viewer/
      bl/0001179/19480610/060/0009.

26   'West Indian Journal', *Nottingham Journal*, 29/04/1953, 4, https://www.
      britishnewspaperarchive.co.uk/viewer/bl/0001898/19530429/085/0004.

27   Brenda Bufalino, Interview with Mable Lee, 16 February 2017, Jerome
      Robbins Dance Division, Oral Histories, https://digitalcollections.nypl.org/
      items/5ac7f56e-50ba-40d5-bdb9-b154a971688c.

28   'Negro Theatre', *The Stage*, 15/07/1948, 6, https://www.
      britishnewspaperarchive.co.uk/viewer/bl/0001179/19480715/040/0005.

29   George Padmore, 'Natives of London Give Robeson Royal Welcome', *The
      Chicago Defender*, 19/03/1949, 7, ProQuest.

30   'Coloured Four', *Daily Herald*, 05/06/1947, 2, https://www.
      britishnewspaperarchive.co.uk/viewer/bl/0000681/19470605/034/0002.

31   *Nelson Leader*, 29/03/1946, 1, https://www.britishnewspaperarchive.co.uk/
      viewer/bl/0001805/19460329/011/0001.

32   'Oh Boy', *The Stage*, 19/06/1958, 8, https://www.britishnewspaperarchive.
      co.uk/viewer/bl/0001179/19580619/074/0008.

33   Robert Tredinnick, 'Disc Dissertations', *Lincolnshire Echo*,
      15/05/1950, 4, https://www.britishnewspaperarchive.co.uk/viewer/
      bl/0000332/19500515/136/0004.

34   'Calypso Fans', *Western Mail*, 14/04/1950, 4, https://www.
      britishnewspaperarchive.co.uk/viewer/bl/0000104/19500414/062/0004.

35   'Calypso', *The Stage*, 14/11/1948, 3, https://www.britishnewspaperarchive.
      co.uk/viewer/bl/0001179/19481014/008/0003.

36   'Hackney Empire', *The Stage*, 04/08/1949, 5, https://www.
      britishnewspaperarchive.co.uk/viewer/bl/0001179/19490804/015/0005.

37   *The Stage,* 30/03/1944, 6, https://www.britishnewspaperarchive.co.uk/viewer/bl/0001179/19440330/032/0006.

38   'The Palladium', *The Stage,* 18/11/1943, 3, https://www.britishnewspaperarchive.co.uk/viewer/bl/0001179/19431118/015/0003.

39   Kurt Albert and Klaus Bleis, 'A Tribute to Carnell Lyons', n.d., https://web.archive.org/web/20200709131353/http://www.tap-and-tray.de/pdf/Carnell%20Lyons%20Story.pdf.

40   Radio Times Listing, no. 1102; 10/11/1944, https://genome.ch.bbc.co.uk/page/dc55749bb8344b9f9becc521335ffe22.

41   Stephen Bourne, 'A Sort of Magic from This Chaos', *The Stage,* 14/12/1995, 19.

Chapter 10

1   Amanda Biddell, *The West Indian Generation: Remaking British Culture in London, 1945–1965* (Liverpool: Liverpool University Press, 2017), 2.

2   'The Palladium', *The Stage,* 12/11/1942, 1, https://www.britishnewspaperarchive.co.uk/viewer/bl/0001179/19421112/007/0001.

3   'Ros, Edmundo', *Grove Music Online,* 2001, doi:10.1093/gmo/9781561592630.article.23817.

4   *The Stage,* 17/04/1947, 8, https://www.britishnewspaperarchive.co.uk/viewer/bl/0001179/19470417/049/0008.

5   'The Torch', *The Stage,* 24/11/1949, 7, https://www.britishnewspaperarchive.co.uk/viewer/bl/0001179/19491124/031/0007.

6   Program for *Calypso,* digitized edition held at V&A Archive, digitized for TradingFaces project (*c.*2008), https://web.archive.org/web/20200707185949/http://www.tradingfacesonline.com/item-details.asp?id=TFRS181.

7   *Norwood News,* 07/04/1948, 4, https://www.britishnewspaperarchive.co.uk/viewer/bl/0002308/19480507/044/0004.

8   'From Trinidad', *New York Amsterdam News,* 22/01/1944, 3, ProQuest.

9   Unindexed Back Matter. *New Statesman and Nation*; London no. 743, 19/05/1945, 29, ProQuest.

10   'New Calypso Orchestra Here', *Accordion Times and Musical Express* 18/07/1947, 1, ProQuest.

11   'Palace of Varieties', *Broughty Ferry Guide and Advertiser* (Dundee), 06/07/1946, 7, https://www.britishnewspaperarchive.co.uk/viewer/bl/0002669/19460706/092/0007.

12   Playhouse 'Calypso', *Daily Herald,* 25/05/1948, 3, https://www.britishnewspaperarchive.co.uk/viewer/bl/0000681/19480525/049/0003.

13   Spencer Mawby, 'The Caribbean in an International and Regional Context', in *The Oxford Handbook of the Ends of Empire,* ed. Martin Thomas and Andrew S. Thompson (Oxford: Oxford University Press, 2017), 345.

14   *Truth,* 04/06/1948, 11, https://www.britishnewspaperarchive.co.uk/viewer/bl/0002961/19480604/025/0011.

15 'The Wimbledon', *The Stage*, 13/05/1948, 4, https://www. britishnewspaperarchive.co.uk/viewer/bl/0001179/19480513/027/0004.

16 'Negro Theatre', *Sheffield Independent*, 27/03/1936, 6, https://www. britishnewspaperarchive.co.uk/viewer/bl/0001465/19360327/155/0006.

17 Peter Noble, 'Negro Theatre', *The Stage*, 24/08/1944, 5, https://www. britishnewspaperarchive.co.uk/viewer/bl/0001179/19440824/029/0005.

18 Peter D. Fraser, 'Adams, Robert', in *Dictionary of Caribbean and Afro–Latin American Biography*, ed. Franklin W. Knight and Henry Louis GatesJr (Oxford: Oxford University Press, 2016).

19 Ibid.

20 Robert Adams, 'Problems of the Negro in the Theatre', *New Theatre* 4, no. 5 (November 1947), 11.

21 Ibid.

22 Ibid.

23 Ibid.

24 Richie Riley, 'To the Editor of the Stage', *The Stage*, 30/10/1952, 11, https://www.britishnewspaperarchive.co.uk/viewer/ bl/0001179/19521030/053/0011.

25 Edric Connor, 'To the Editor of the Stage', *The Stage*, 30/10/1952, 11, https://www.britishnewspaperarchive.co.uk/viewer/ bl/0001179/19521030/053/0011.

26 Ibid.

27 Ibid.

28 'Negro Theatre Company', *The Stage*, 29/07/1948, 6, https://www. britishnewspaperarchive.co.uk/viewer/bl/0001179/19480729/023/0006.

29 'Negro Group', *The Stage*, 24/06/1948, 4, https://www. britishnewspaperarchive.co.uk/viewer/bl/0001179/19480624/022/0004.

30 'Negro Theatre Company', *The Stage*, 29/07/1948, 6, https://www. britishnewspaperarchive.co.uk/viewer/bl/0001179/19480729/023/0006.

31 'Forming British Negro Theatre Company', *The Manchester Guardian*, 14/03/1949, 3, ProQuest.

32 George Padmore, 'Colonials', *The Pittsburgh Courier*, 24/03/1945, 11, ProQuest.

33 'Quick Return for Hermanos Deniz Outfit', *Musical Express*, 22/04/1949, 4, ProQuest.

34 'The Wimbledon', *The Stage*, 13/05/1948, 4, https://www. britishnewspaperarchive.co.uk/viewer/bl/0001179/19480513/027/0004.

35 'Edric Connor Goes into Variety', *Musical Express*, London, 145, 15/07/1949, 4, ProQuest.

36 Bourne, *Black in the British Frame*, 95.

37 'Personalia', *The Stage*, 31/03/1949, 5, https://www.britishnewspaperarchive. co.uk/viewer/bl/0001179/19490331/011/0005.

38 Edric Connor, *Horizons: The Life and Times of Edric Connor* (Kingston: Ian Randle Publishers, 2007), 63.

39   'Shepherd's Bush Empire', *The Stage*, 30/06/1949, 5, https://www.
     britishnewspaperarchive.co.uk/viewer/bl/0001179/19490630/024/0005.

40   Connor, *Horizons*, 66.

41   Ibid., 67.

42   Ibid., 68.

43   Errol Hill, *Shakespeare in Sable: A History of Black Shakespearean Actors*
     (Amherst: University of Massachusetts Press, 1984), 142.

44   Pearl Connor's recollections in Connor, *Horizons*, 149, 152.

45   Connor, *Horizons*, 75.

46   Ibid., 155.

47   Riley quoted in Ramsay Burt, 'Elroy Joseph and the Hidden History of
     Black British Dance', in *The Routledge Companion to Dance Studies*, ed.
     Helen Thomas and Stacey Prickett (Abingdon: Routledge, 2019), Routledge
     Handbooks Online.

48   Keith Watson, 'They Were Britain's First Black Dance Company: How Come
     No One's Ever Heard of Them?' *The Guardian*, 05/08/1999, https://www.
     theguardian.com/culture/1999/aug/05/artsfeatures1.

49   Thea Barnes, 'Presenting Berto Pasuka', in *British Dance: Black Routes*, ed.
     Christy Adair and Ramsay Burt (London: Routledge, 2017), 27.

50   Ibid., 32.

51   Bob Ramdhanie, 'Ballets Nègres, Les', in *The Oxford Companion to Black
     British History*, ed. David Dabydeen, John Gilmore and Cecily Jones
     (Oxford: Oxford University Press, 2007).

52   'Personal', *The Stage*, 25/07/1946, 4, https://www.britishnewspaperarchive.
     co.uk/viewer/bl/0001179/19460725/022/0004; 'Black British Swing: The
     African Diaspora's Contribution to England's Own Jazz of the 1930s and
     1940s', 22/12/2012, https://web.archive.org/web/20200808173244/https://
     blackbritishswing.wordpress.com/.

53   Ibid., 21.

54   Barnes, 'Presenting', 17.

55   Janet Rowson Davis, 'Ballet on British Television, 1946–1947: Starting
     Again', *Dance Chronicle* 13, no. 2 (1990), 134.

56   *The Stage*, 26/06/1941, 7, https://www.britishnewspaperarchive.co.uk/
     viewer/bl/0001179/19410626/082/0007.

57   *The Stage*, 15/06/1944, 5, https://www.britishnewspaperarchive.co.uk/
     viewer/bl/0001179/19440615/033/0005.

58   Val Wilmer, 'Obituary Letter: Richie Riley', *The Guardian*, 22/05/1997, 17,
     ProQuest.

59   'Negro', *The Stage*, 20/11/1947, 4, https://www.britishnewspaperarchive.
     co.uk/viewer/bl/0001179/19471120/019/0004.

60   *Manchester Evening News*, 27/07/1948, 2, https://www.
     britishnewspaperarchive.co.uk/viewer/bl/0000272/19480727/019/0002.

61   'The Playhouse', *The Stage*, 22/08/1946, 4, https://www.
     britishnewspaperarchive.co.uk/viewer/bl/0001179/19460822/024/0004.

62 Beryl de Zoete, 'BALLET ON THREE STAGES', *New Statesman and Nation*, 04/05/1946, 317, ProQuest.

63 'Colourful Show at the Prince of Wales', *Biggleswade Chronicle*, 11/06/1948, 10, https://www.britishnewspaperarchive.co.uk/viewer/bl/0000753/19480611/128/0010.

64 Barnes, 'Presenting', 30.

65 'Radio Rhythm Club', *Radio Times* 91 no. 1187, 28/06/1946, 19.

66 Frederick Laws, 'Television', *The Sketch*, 18/01/1950, 29, https://www.britishnewspaperarchive.co.uk/viewer/BL/0001860/19500118/031/0029.

67 'Restored at the End', *Birmingham Daily Gazette*, 01/11/1951, 1, https://www.britishnewspaperarchive.co.uk/viewer/bl/0000669/19511201/014/0001.

68 'Negro ballet at the pier', *Worthing Herald*, 14/01/1949, 7, https://www.britishnewspaperarchive.co.uk/viewer/bl/0001920/19490114/145/0007.

69 'Entertainers Entertained', *Manchester Evening News*, 06/07/1949, 7, https://www.britishnewspaperarchive.co.uk/viewer/bl/0000272/19490706/107/0007.

70 'Ballet Negres', *Nottingham Evening Post*, 27/09/1949, 3, https://www.britishnewspaperarchive.co.uk/viewer/bl/0000321/19490927/022/0003.

71 'Mr Manchester's Diary', *Manchester Evening News*, 07/07/1949, 3, https://www.britishnewspaperarchive.co.uk/viewer/bl/0000272/19490707/021/0003.

72 *Nottingham Evening Post*, 28/12/1950, 3, https://www.britishnewspaperarchive.co.uk/viewer/bl/0000321/19501228/042/0003.

73 'Items', *The Stage*, 09/02/1950, 8, https://www.britishnewspaperarchive.co.uk/viewer/bl/0001179/19500209/027/0008.

74 'Playhouse', *Nottingham Journal*, 4, https://www.britishnewspaperarchive.co.uk/viewer/bl/0001898/19501227/078/0004.

75 'Entr'acte', *The Stage*, 20/08/1951, 8, https://www.britishnewspaperarchive.co.uk/viewer/bl/0001179/19510830/026/0008.

76 Susan Jones, 'From Text to Dance: Andrée Howard's "The Sailor's Return"', *Dance Research: The Journal of the Society for Dance Research* 26, no. 1 (2008), 13.

77 'Brazilian Show Deserved Better Audience', *West London Observer*, 19/08/1955, 3, https://www.britishnewspaperarchive.co.uk/viewer/bl/0000437/19550819/026/0003.

78 Paula James, 'A Plea to the Friends of Berto', *Daily Mirror*, 01/05/1963, https://www.britishnewspaperarchive.co.uk/viewer/bl/0000560/19630501/010/0002

79 George Padmore, 'London Correspondent: First Negro Ballet in London', *The Chicago Defender*, 08/06/1946, 15, ProQuest.

80 'Les Ballets Negres', *Hastings and St Leonards Observer*, 17/09/1946, 3, https://www.britishnewspaperarchive.co.uk/viewer/bl/0000293/19490917/077/0003.

81 'Twentieth Century', *The Stage*, 09/05/1946, 4, https://www.britishnewspaperarchive.co.uk/viewer/bl/0001179/19460509/026/0004.

82 Sylvia M. Jacobs, 'James Emman Kwegyir Aggrey: An African Intellectual in the United States', *The Journal of Negro History* 81, no. 1/4 (1996), 50.

83 'Twentieth Century', *The Stage*, 09/05/1946, 4, https://www.britishnewspaperarchive.co.uk/viewer/bl/0001179/19460509/026/0004.

84 Anita Gonzalez, 'Framing and Naming Black British Dance', in *British Dance: Black Routes*, ed. Christy Adair and Ramsay Burt (London: Routledge, 2017), 168.

85 George Padmore, 'London Correspondent: First Negro Ballet in London', *The Chicago Defender*, 08/06/1946, 15, ProQuest.

Appendix B

1 'Liverpool', *The Stage*, 06/08/1908, 3, https://www.britishnewspaperarchive.co.uk/viewer/bl/0001179/19080806/126/0003.

2 'Manchester', *The Stage*, 04/11/1915, 18, https://www.britishnewspaperarchive.co.uk/viewer/bl/0001179/19151104/007/0018.

3 'Colchester', *The Era*, 30/05/1908, 7, https://www.britishnewspaperarchive.co.uk/viewer/bl/0000053/19080530/078/0007.

4 *The Era*, 19/06/1909, 8, https://www.britishnewspaperarchive.co.uk/viewer/bl/0000053/19090619/150/0008.

5 'Salford', *MHTR*, 08/07/1909, 15, https://www.britishnewspaperarchive.co.uk/viewer/bl/0002237/19090708/193/0015.

6 'Hippodrome', *MHTR*, 30/10/1908, 15, https://www.britishnewspaperarchive.co.uk/viewer/bl/0002237/19090708/193/0015.

7 'The New Bedford Palace of Varieties', *The Era*, 23/04/1910, 18, https://www.britishnewspaperarchive.co.uk/viewer/bl/0000053/19100423/131/0018.

8 'Hippodrome', *Derbyshire Courier*, 09/10/1915, 4, https://www.britishnewspaperarchive.co.uk/viewer/bl/0000395/19151009/061/0004.

9 'Empire', *Western Daily Press*, 18/04/1910, 7, https://www.britishnewspaperarchive.co.uk/viewer/bl/0000264/19100418/197/0007.

10 'The Royal Hippodrome', *Dover Express*, 26/10/1917, 8, https://www.britishnewspaperarchive.co.uk/viewer/bl/0000330/19171026/052/0008.

11 'All Black', *The Era*, 14/07/1922, 4, https://www.britishnewspaperarchive.co.uk/viewer/bl/0000053/19220614/035/0004.

12 'Brighton', *The Stage*, 16/11/1922, 4, https://www.britishnewspaperarchive.co.uk/viewer/bl/0001179/19221116/016/0004.

13 'Belfast', *The Stage*, 19/11/1925, 14, https://www.britishnewspaperarchive.co.uk/viewer/bl/0001179/19251119/038/0014.

14 'Empire', *Western Daily Press*, 31/05/1927, 4, https://www.britishnewspaperarchive.co.uk/viewer/bl/0000264/19270531/005/0004.

15 'Stage Gossip', *Derby Daily Telegraph* 19/10/1927, 5, https://www.
    britishnewspaperarchive.co.uk/viewer/bl/0000327/19271019/077/0005.

16 'Shepherds Bush Empire', *West London Observer*, 01/06/1928,
    4, https://www.britishnewspaperarchive.co.uk/viewer/
    bl/0000437/19280601/070/0004.

17 *The Stage*, 30/08/1928, 6, https://www.britishnewspaperarchive.co.uk/
    viewer/bl/0001179/19280830/015/0006.

18 'Nottingham: Empire', *The Stage*, 18/07/1929, 4, https://www.
    britishnewspaperarchive.co.uk/viewer/bl/0001179/19290718/019/0004.

19 'Swansea', *The Stage*, 25/07/1929, 22, https://www.britishnewspaperarchive.
    co.uk/viewer/bl/0001179/19290725/023/0022.

20 'Birmingham', *The Stage*, 02/05/1929, 13, https://www.
    britishnewspaperarchive.co.uk/viewer/bl/0001179/19290502/041/0013.

21 'Coliseum Revue', *Portsmouth Evening News*, 30/06/1931, 3, https://www.
    britishnewspaperarchive.co.uk/viewer/bl/0000290/19310630/049/0003.

22 'Feldman', *The Stage*, 14/05/1931, 21, https://www.britishnewspaperarchive.
    co.uk/viewer/bl/0001179/19310514/082/0021.

23 'Dublin', *The Stage,* 30/11/1933, 2, https://www.britishnewspaperarchive.
    co.uk/viewer/bl/0001179/19331130/011/0002.

SELECT BIBLIOGRAPHY

Absher, Amy. *The Black Musician and the White City: Race and Music in Chicago 1900–1967*. Ann Arbor: University of Michigan Press, 2014.

Adair, Zakiya R. 'Respectable Vamp: A Black Feminist Analysis of Florence Mills' Career in Early Vaudeville Theater'. *Journal of African American Studies* 17, no. 1 (2013): 7–21, doi:10.1007/S12111-012-9216-3.

Adams, Robert. 'Problems of the Negro in the Theatre'. *New Theatre* 4, no. 5 (1947): 11.

Adi, Hakim and Marika Sherwood. *Pan-African History: Political Figures from Africa and the Diaspora Since 1787*. Abingdon: Taylor & Francis, 2003.

Agawu, Kofi. *The African Imagination in Music*. Oxford: Oxford University Press, 2016.

Ahmed, Sara. 'The Nonperformativity of Antiracism'. *Meridians* 7, no. 1 (2006): 104–26.

Balliett, Whitney. *American Singers: Twenty-Seven Portraits in Song*. Mississippi: University Press of Mississippi, 2006.

Banfield, Stephen. 'Music, Text and Stage: The Tradition of Bourgeois Tonality to the Second World War'. In *The Cambridge History of Twentieth-Century Music*, edited by Nicholas Cook and Anthony Pople, 90–122. Cambridge: Cambridge University Press, 2004.

Barlow, William. *'Looking Up at Down': The Emergence of Blues Culture*. Philadelphia: Temple University Press, 1989.

Barnes, Thea. 'Presenting Berto Pasuka'. In *British Dance: Black Routes*, edited by Christy Adair and Ramsay Burt, 15–34. London: Routledge, 2017.

Batiste, Stephanie. *Darkening Mirrors: Imperial Representation in Depression-Era African American Performance*. Durham, NC: Duke University Press, 2011.

Bauman, Thomas. *The Pekin: The Rise and Fall of Chicago's First Black-Owned Theater*. Champaign: University of Illinois Press, 2014.

Bean, Annemarie. 'Black Minstrelsy and Double Inversion, Circa 1890'. In *African American Performance and Theater History: A Critical Reader*, edited by David Krasner and Henry J. Elam, 171–91. Oxford: Oxford University Press, 2001.

Benjamin, Rick, 'From Barrell house to Broadway: The Musical Odyssey of Joe Jordan', http://www.dramonline.org/albums/from-barrelhouse-to-broadway-the-musical-odyssey-of-joe-jordan/notes.

Berendt, Joachim and Günther Huesmann. *The Jazz Book: From Ragtime to the 21st Century*. 7th edn. Chicago: Lawrence Hill Books, 2009.

Berg, Shelley C. 'The Sense of the Past: Historiography and Dance'. In *Researching Dance: Evolving Modes of Inquiry*, edited by Sondra Horton Fraleigh and Penelope Hanstein, 225–48. Pittsburgh: University of Pittsburgh Press, 2006.

Biddell, Amanda. *The West Indian Generation: Remaking British Culture in London, 1945–1965*. Liverpool: Liverpool University Press, 2017.

Bourne, Stephen. *Black in the British Frame: Black People in British Film and Television*. Cheltenham: The History Press, 2005.

Bourne, Stephen. *Black Poppies: Britain's Black Community and the Great War*. Cheltenham: The History Press, 2019.

Bourne, Stephen. *Elisabeth Welch: Soft Lights and Sweet Music*. Lanham, MD: The Scarecrow Press, 2006.

Bourne, Stephen. *Evelyn Dove: Britain's Black Cabaret Queen*. London: Jacaranda, 2006.

Bourne, Stephen. *Fighting Proud: The Untold Story of the Gay Men who Fought in Two World Wars*. London: I.B.Tauris, 2017.

Bourne, Stephen. *Mother Country: Britain's Black Community on the Home Front, 1939–45*. Cheltenham: The History Press, 2013.

Bourne, Stephen. *Nina Mae McKinney: The Black Garbo*. Duncan, OK: Bear Manor Media, 2012.

Bressey, Caroline and Gemma Romain. 'Staging Race: Florence Mills, Celebrity, Identity and Performance in 1920s Britain'. *Women's History Review* 28, no. 3 (2019): n.p., doi:10.1080/09612025.2018.1493119.

Brocken, Michael and Jeff Daniels. *Gordon Stretton, Black British Transoceanic Jazz Pioneer: A New Jazz Chronicle*. Lanham, MD: Lexington Press, 2018.

Brooks, Daphne. *Bodies in Dissent: Spectacular Performances of Race and Freedom, 1850–1910*. Durham, NC: Duke University Press, 2006.

Brooks, Daphne. 'Open Channels: Some Thoughts on Blackness, the Body, and Sound(ing) Women in the (Summer) Time of Trayvon'. *Performance Research* 19, no. 3 (2014): 62–8, doi:10.1080/13528165.2014.935171.

Brooks, Tim. *Lost Sounds Blacks and the Birth of the Recording Industry, 1890–1919*. Chicago: University of Illinois Press, 2010.

Brown, Jayna. *Babylon Girls: Black Women Performers and the Shaping of the Modern*. Durham, NC: Duke University Press, 2009.

Burt, Ramsay. 'Elroy Josephs and the Hidden History of Black British Dance'. In *The Routledge Companion to Dance Studies*, edited by Helen Thomas and Stacey Prickett. Abingdon: Routledge, 2019. Routledge Handbooks Online.

Canas, Tania. 'Diversity Is a White Word.' ArtsHub Australia, 01/09/2017, https://www.artshub.com.au/education/news-article/opinions-and-analysis/professional-development/tania-canas/diversity-is-a-white-word-252910.

Cantu, Maya. 'Recovering Ada "Bricktop" Smith'. In *Reframing the Musical: Race, Culture and Identity*, edited by Sarah Whitfield, 52–74. London: Red Globe Press, 2019.

Carter Marva Griffin. *Swing Along: The Musical Life of Will Marion Cook*. Oxford: Oxford University Press, 2008.

Carter Marva Griffin. *Swing Along: The Songs of Will Marion Cook, William Brown, Ann Sears*. Albany, TROY 839/40, 2006, compact disc. Liner Notes.

Chambers, Colin. *Black and Asian Theatre in Britain: A History*. London: Routledge, 2011.

Charles, Mario A. 'The Age of a Jazzwoman: Valada Snow, 1900–1956'. *The Journal of Negro History* 80 no. 4 (1995): 183–91.

Connor, Edric. *Horizons: The Life and Times of Edric Connor*. Kingston: Ian Randle Publishers, 2007.

Cook, Susan. 'Flirting with the Vernacular: America in Europe, 1900–45'. In *The Cambridge History of Twentieth-Century Music*, edited by Nicholas Cook and Anthony Pople, 152–85. Cambridge: Cambridge University Press, 2004.

Cowley, John. 'Cultural "Fusions": Aspects of British West Indian Music in the USA and Britain 1918–51'. *Popular Music* 5 (1985): 81–96, http://www.jstor.com/stable/853284.

Cowley, John. 'London Is the Place: Caribbean Music in the Context of Empire 1900–60'. In *Black Music in Britain: Essays on the Afro Asian Contribution to Popular Music*, edited by Paul Oliver, 57–76. Milton Keynes: Open University Press, 1990.

Cowley, John. 'West Indies Blues: An Historical Overview, 1920s–1950s – Blues and Music from the English-speaking West Indies'. In *Nobody Knows Where the Blues Come from: Lyrics and History*, edited by Robert Springer, 187–263. Jackson: University Press of Mississippi, 2006.

Crosby, Jill Flanders and Michèle Moss. 'Jazz Dance from Emancipation to 1970'. In *Jazz Dance: A History of the Roots and Branches*, edited by Lindsay Guarino and Wendy Oliver, 24–31. Gainesville: University Press of Florida, 2014.

Cunard, Nancy ed. *Negro Anthology 1931–1933*. London: Wishart and Co, 1934.

Cushing, Steve. *Blues Before Sunrise: The Radio Interviews*. Urbana: University of Illinois Press, 2010.

Daniels, Jeff and Howard Rye, 'Gordon Stretton: A Study in Multiple Identities'. *Popular Music History* 4, no. 1 (2009): 77–90.

Davis, Angela Y. *Blues Legacies and Black Feminism: Gertrude Ma Rainey, Bessie Smith, and Billie Holiday*. New York: Knopf Doubleday, 2011.

Davis, James C. *Eric Walrond: A Life in the Harlem Renaissance and the Transatlantic Caribbean*. New York: Columbia University Press, 2015.

Decker, Todd. *Show Boat: Performing Race in an American Musical*. Oxford: Oxford University Press, 2013.

Du Bois, W. E. B. *The Souls of Black Folk*. 1903. *Project Gutenberg* [online],http://www.gutenberg.org/files/408/408-h/408-h.htm.

Egan, Bill. *African American Entertainers in Australia and New Zealand: A History, 1788–1941*. Jefferson, NC: McFarland 2019.

Eldridge, Michael. 'There goes the Transnational Neighbourhood: Calypso Buys a Bungalow'. In *Music Power and Politics*, edited by Annie Janeiro Randall, 173–93. New York: Routledge, 2002.

Ewing, K. T. 'What Kind of Woman? Alberta Hunter and Expressions of Black Female Sexuality in the Twentieth Century'. In *Black Female Sexualities*, edited by Trimiko Melancon and Joanne M. Braxton, 100–12. New Brunswick, NJ: Rutgers University Press, 2015.

Floyd, Samuel. *The Power of Black Music: Interpreting Its History from African to the United States*. Oxford: Oxford University Press, 1995.

Fryer, Peter. *Black People in the British Empire: An Introduction*. London: Pluto Classics, 1988.

Fryer, Peter. *Staying Power: The History of Black People in Britain*. 1984, rev. edn. London: Pluto Books, 2010.

Gavin, James. *Stormy Weather: The Life of Lena Horne*. New York: Atria Books, 2009.

George-Graves, Nadine. 'Identity Politics and Political Will: Jeni LeGon Living in a Great Big Way'. In *The Oxford Handbook of Dance and Politics*, edited by Rebekah J. Kowal, Gerald Siegmund and Randy Martin, 511–34. Oxford: Oxford University Press, 2017, doi:10.1093/oxfordhb/9780199928187.013.47.

George-Graves, Nadine. 'Spreading the Sand: Understanding the Economic and Creative Impetus for the Black Vaudeville Industry'. *CONTINUUM: The*

Journal of African Diaspora Drama, Theatre and Performance 1, no.1 (2014), http://continuumjournal.org/index.php/spreading-the-sand.

Gilbert, David. *The Product of Our Souls: Ragtime, Race, and the Birth of the Manhattan Musical Marketplace.* Chapel Hill: University of North Carolina Press, 2015.

Gillett, Rachel. 'Jazz and the Evolution of Black American Cosmopolitanism in Interwar Paris'. *Journal of World History* 21, no. 3 (September 2010): 471–95.

Gilroy, Paul. *The Black Atlantic: Modernity and Double Consciousness.* London: Verso Books, 1993.

Gonzalez, Anita. 'Framing and Naming Black British Dance'. In *British Dance: Black Routes,* edited by Christy Adair and Ramsay Burt, 167–76. London: Routledge, 2017.

Goodman, Jordan. *Paul Robeson: A Watched Man.* London: Verso Books, 2013.

Gopal, Priyamvada. *Insurgent Empire: Anticolonial Resistance and British Dissent.* London: Verso Books, 2019.

Gordon, Robert, Olaf Jubin and Millie Taylor. *British Musical Theatre since 1950.* London: Bloomsbury, 2018.

Gottschild, Brenda Dixon. *Waltzing in the Dark: African American Vaudeville and Race Politics in the Swing Era.* London, Palgrave Macmillan, 2000.

Green, Jeffrey. 'The Jamaica Native Choir in Britain, 1906–1908'. *Black Music Research Journal* 13, no. 1 (1993): 15–29, doi:10.2307/779404.

Green, Jeffrey and Rainer E. Lotz, 'Davis, Belle (b.1874, d.in or after 1938), dancer and singer'. *Oxford Dictionary of National Biography,* 23 September 2004.

Green, Jeffrey P., Rainer E. Lotz, Horst Bergmeier, Holger Stoecker, Hans-Jürgen Mahrenholz, Susanne Ziegler, Konrad Nowakowski and Howard Rye. *Black Europe: The Sounds and Images of Black People in Europe Pre-1927.* 2 vols, 1 case of 44 sound discs (digital, mono. 4 3/4 in.). Osterholz: Bear Family Productions Ltd, 2013.

Gregson, Keith and Mike Huggins. 'Sport, Music-Hall Culture and Popular Song in Nineteenth-Century England'. *Culture, Sport Society* 2, no. 2 (1992): 82–102, doi:10.1080/14610989908721840.

Hall, Stuart. 'What Is This "Black" in Black Popular Culture?'. *Social Justice* 20, no. 1/2 (1993): 104–14.

Hartman, Saidiya. *Lose Your Mother: A Journey Along the Atlantic Slave Route.* New York: Farrar, Straus and Giroux, 2007.

Haskins, James. *The Cotton Club.* New York: New York American Library, 1984.

Haskins, James. *Mabel Mercer: A Life.* New York: Macmillan, 1987.

Hill, Constance Valis. *Brotherhood in Rhythm: The Jazz Tap Dancing of the Nicholas Brothers.* New York: Oxford University Press, 2000.

Hill, Constance Valis. 'Buddy Bradley: The Invisible Man of Broadway brings Jazz Tap to London'. In *Proceedings of the Society of Dance History Scholars, Fifteenth Annual Conference,* edited by Christena L Schlundt, 77–84. Riverside: University of California, Riverside, 1992.

Hill, Constance Valis. 'Jazz Modernism'. In *Moving Words: Re-writing Dance,* edited by Gay Morris, 198–212. London: Routledge, 2005.

Hill, Constance Valis. *Tap Dancing America: A Cultural History.* Oxford: Oxford University Press, 2010.

Hill, Donald. *Calypso Calaloo: Early Carnival Music in Trinidad.* Gainesville: University Press of Florida, 1993.

Hill, Errol. *Shakespeare in Sable: A History of Black Shakespearean Actors*. Amherst: University of Massachusetts Press, 1984.

hooks, bell. *Black Looks: Race and Representation*. Boston: South End Press, 1992.

Hughes, Spike. *Second Movement: Continuing the Autobiography of Spike Hughes*. London: Museum Press, 1951.

Hyslop, Jonathan. 'The Invention of the Concentration Camp: Cuba, Southern Africa and the Philippines, 1896–1907'. *South African Historical Journal* 63, no. 2 (2011): 251–76, doi: 10.1080/02582473.2011.567359.

Jacobs, Sylvia M. 'James Emman Kwegyir Aggrey: An African Intellectual in the United States'. *The Journal of Negro History* 81, no. 1/4 (1996): 47–61.

Johnson Quinn, Arianne. *British and American Musical Theatre Exchanges (1920–1970): The 'Americanization' of Drury Lane*. London: Palgrave, forthcoming.

Johnson, Jack. *Jack Johnson in the Ring and Out*. 1927. Auckland, NZ: Papamoa Press, 2017.

Johnson, Maria V. '"Jelly Jelly Jellyroll": Lesbian Sexuality and Identity in Women's Blues'. *Women & Music* 7 (2003): 31–52.

Jones, Susan. 'From Text to Dance: Andrée Howard's "The Sailor's Return"'. *Dance Research: The Journal of the Society for Dance Research* 26, no. 1 (2008): 1–17.

Jules-Rosette, Benneta. *Josephine Baker in Art and Life: The Icon and the Image*. Urbana: University of Illinois Press, 2007.

Klein, Jeanne. 'The Cake Walk Photo Girl and Other Footnotes in African American Musical Theatre.' *Theatre Survey* 60, no. 1 (2019): 67–90.

Knapp, Raymond. *The American Musical and the Formation of National Identity*. Princeton: Princeton University Press, 2006.

Krasner, David. *A Beautiful Pageant: African American Theatre, Drama and Performance in the Harlem Renaissance 1910–1927*. New York: Palgrave Macmillan, 2002.

Krasner, David. 'Rewriting the Body: Aida Overton Walker and the Social Formation of Cakewalking'. *Theatre Survey* 37, no. 2 (1996): 67–92.

Kraut, Anthea. *Choreographing Copyright: Race, Gender, and Intellectual Property Rights in American Dance*. Oxford: Oxford University Press, 2016.

Kubota, Ryuko. 'Confronting Epistemological Racism, Decolonizing Scholarly Knowledge: Race and Gender in Applied Linguistics'. *Applied Linguistics*, doi. org/10.1093/applin/amz033.

Lapp Norris, Renee. 'Opera and the Mainstreaming of Blackface Minstrelsy'. *Journal of the Society for American Music* 1, no. 3 (2007): 341–65, doi:10.1017.S1752196307070113.

Levering Lewis, David. *W.E.B. Du Bois: The Fight for Equality and the American Century, 1919–1963*. New York: H. Holt, 2000.

Linton, David and Len Platt. 'Dover Street to Dixie and the Politics of Cultural Transfer and Exchange'. In *Popular Musical Theatre in London and Berlin 1890–1939*, edited by Len Platt, Tobias Becker and David Linton, 170–86. Cambridge: Cambridge University Press, 2014.

Livingstone, William. 'Mabel Mercer: William Livingstone Visits with the Singers' Singer'. *American Stereo Review* 34, no. 2 (1975): 60–5.

Lotz, Rainer E. 'Black Diamonds Are Forever: A Glimpse of the Prehistory of Jazz in Europe'. *The Black Perspective in Music* 12, no. 2 (1984): 217–34, www.jstor. org/stable/1215023.

Lotz, Rainer E. 'Black Music Prior to the First World War: American Origins and German Perspectives'. In *Cross the Water Blues: African American Music in Europe*, edited by Neil A. Wynn, 66–88. Jackson: University Press of Mississippi, 2007.

Lotz, Rainer E. *Black People: Entertainers of African Descent in Europe, and Germany*. Bonn: Birgit Lotz Verlag, 1997.

Lotz, Rainer E. 'Black Women Recording Pioneers.' *IAJRC Journal* 40, no. 2 (2007): 32–41, ProQuest: Music and Performing Arts Collection.

Lotz, Rainer E. *German Ragtime and Prehistory of Jazz: The Sound Documents*. Essex: Storyville Publications, 1985.

Lotz, Rainer E. 'Will Garland and the Negro Operetta Company'. *The Black Perspective in Music* 14, no. 3 (1986): 291–302, doi:10.2307/1215068.

Lotz, Rainer E. 'Will Garland and His Negro Operetta Company'. In *Under the Imperial Carpet: Essays in Black History 1780–1950*, edited by Rainer E. Lotz and Ian Pegg, 130–44. Crawley: Rabbit Press 1986.

M'Baye, Babacar. 'Pan-Africanism, Transnationalism, and Cosmopolitanism in Langston Hughes's Involvement in the First World Festival of Black Arts'. *South Atlantic Review* 82, no. 4 (2017): 139–59.

McKay, George. *Circular Breathing: The Cultural Politics of Jazz in Britain*. Durham, NC: Duke University Press, 2005.

Macpherson, Ben. 'Some Yesterdays Always Remain: Black British and Anglo-Asian Musical Theatre'. In *The Oxford Handbook of the British Musical*, edited by Robert Gordon and Olaf Jubin. Oxford: Oxford University Press, 2017.

Macpherson, Ben. *British Musical Theatre: Imperialism, Identity and Ideology 1890–1939*. London: Palgrave, 2018.

Makalani, Minkah. *In the Cause of Freedom: Radical Black Internationalism From Harlem to London, 1917–1939*. Raleigh: University of North Carolina Press, 2011.

Matera, Marc. *Black London: The Imperial Metropolis and Decolonization in the Twentieth Century*. California: University of California Press, 2015.

Matera, Marc. 'Pan-Africanism'. In *New Dictionary of the History of Ideas*, Vol. 4, edited by Maryanne Cline Horowitz, 1701–7. New York: Charles Scribner's Sons, 2005.

Moore, Hilary. *Inside British Jazz: Crossing Borders of Race, Nation and Class*. Farnham: Ashgate, 2007.

Morrison, Matthew D. 'The Sound(s) of Subjection: Constructing American Popular Music and Racial Identity through Blacksound'. *Women & Performance: A Journal of Feminist Theory* 27, no. 1 (2017): 13–24, doi:10.1080/0740770X.2017.1282120.

Moten, Fred. *In the Break: The Aesthetics of the Black Radical Tradition*. Minneapolis: University of Minnesota Press, 2003.

Nwankwo, Ifeoma Kiddoe. *Black Cosmopolitanism: Racial Consciousness and Transnational Identity in the Nineteenth-Century Americas*. Philadelphia, University of Pennsylvania Press, 2005.

Oboe, Annalisa and Anna Scacchi. 'Introduction'. In *Recharting the Black Atlantic: Modern Cultures, Local Communities, Global Connections*, edited by Annalisa Oboe and Anna Scacchi, 1–10. London: Routledge, 2008.

Oliver, Paul. 'Introduction'. In *Black Music in Britain: Essays on the Afro-Asian Contribution to Popular Music, Popular Music in Britain*, edited by Paul Oliver. Milton Keynes: Open University Press, 1990.

Olusoga, David. *Black and British: A Forgotten History*. London: Macmillan, 2016.

Omi, Michael and Howard Winant. 'Once More, with Feeling: Reflections on Racial Formation'. *PMLA* 123, no. 5 (2008): 1565–72, www.jstor.org/stable/25501959.

Omi, Michael and Howard Winant. *Racial Formation in the United States*. London: Routledge, 2014. (Originally published in 1986.)

Parsonage, Catherine. 'A Critical Reassessment of the Reception of Early Jazz in Britain.' *Popular Music* 39, no. 2 (2003): 315–36.

Parsonage, Catherine. *The Evolution of Jazz in Britain, 1800–1935*. London: Routledge, 2017.

Pennybacker, Susan D. *From Scottsboro to Munich: Race and Political Culture in 1930s Britain*. Princeton: Princeton University Press, 2009.

Pickering, Michael. *Blackface Minstrelsy in Britain*. Aldershot: Routledge, 2008.

Pickering, Michael. 'Eugene Stratton and Early Ragtime in Britain'. *Black Music Research Journal* 20, no. 2 (2000): 151–80, https://www.jstor.org/stable/779465.

Pilgrim, David. 'The Tragic Mulatto Myth'. *Jim Crow Museum of Racial Memorabilia*, 2012 [online], https://www.ferris.edu/jimcrow/mulatto/.

Price, Emmett G. 'Joe Jordan'. In *Encyclopedia of the Harlem Renaissance: A–J*, edited by Cary D. Wintz and Paul Finkelman, 648–9. New York: Routledge, 2004.

Putnam, Lara. *Radical Moves: Caribbean Migrants and the Politics of Race in the Jazz Age*. Raleigh: University of North Carolina Press, 2013.

Ramdin, Ron. *The Making of the Black Working Class in Britain*, upd. edn. London: Verso, 2017.

Ramsen, Nancy. 'Alberta Hunter'. In *Contemporary Musicians: Profiles of the People in Music*, edited by Michael L. LaBlanc, 100–2. Detroit: Gale Research, 1992.

Reddock, Rhoda. 'The First Mrs Garvey: Pan-Africanism and Feminism in the Early 20th Century British colonial Caribbean'. *Feminist Africa* 19 (2014): 58–77.

Reddock, Rhoda. 'Radical Caribbean Social Thought: Race, Class Identity and the Postcolonial Nation'. *Current Sociology* 62, no. 4 (2014): 493–511, doi:10.1177/0011392114524507

Riis, Thomas L. 'The Experience and Impact of Black Entertainers in England, 1895–1920'. *American Music* 4, no. 1 (1986): 50–8, http://www.jstor.org/stable/3052184.

Riis, Thomas L. ed., *The Music and Scripts of* In Dahomey. Middleton: A-R Editions, American Musicological Society, 1996.

Robinson, Cedric J. *Forgeries of Memory and Meaning: Blacks and the Regimes of Race in American Theater and Film before World War II*. Chapel Hill: University of North Carolina Press, 2007.

Robinson, Edward A. 'The Pekin: The Genesis of American Black Theater'. *Black American Literature Forum* 16, no. 4 (1982): 136–8, https://doi.org/10.2307/2904220.

Román, David. *Performance in America: Contemporary U.S. Culture and the Performing Arts*. Durham, NC: Duke University Press, 2005.

Rossum, Deborah J. '"A Vision of Black Englishness": Black Intellectuals in London, 1910–1940'. *Stanford Electronic Humanities Review* 5, no. 2 (1997), https://web.stanford.edu/group/SHR/5-2/rossum.html#53.

Rowson Davis, Janet. 'Ballet on British Television, 1946–1947: Starting Again'. *Dance Chronicle* 13, no. 2 (1990): 103–53, www.jstor.org/stable/1567736.

Runstedtler, Theresa. *Jack Johnson, Rebel Sojourner: Boxing in the Shadow of the Global Color Line*. Berkeley: University of California Press, 2013.

Rye, Howard. 'Fearsome Means of Discord: Early Encounters with Black Jazz'. In *Black Music in Britain: Essays on the Afro-Asian Contribution to Popular Music*, edited by Paul Oliver, 45–57. Milton Keynes: Open University Press, 1990.

Rye, Howard. 'Mitchell, Louis (A.).' *Grove Music Online*, 2003, doi:10.1093/gmo/9781561592630.article.J304200.

Rye, Howard. 'Showgirls and Stars: Black-Cast Revues and Female Performers in Britain 1903–1939'. *Popular Music History* 1, no. 2 (2006): 167–88.

Rye, Howard. 'Southern Syncopated Orchestra: The Roster'. *Black Music Research Journal* 30, no. 1 (2010): 19–70.

Rye, Howard. 'Towards a Black British Jazz: Studies in Acculturation, 1860–1935'. In *Black British Jazz: Routes, Ownership and Performance*, edited by Jason Toynbee and Catherine Tackley, 23–42. London: Routledge, 2016.

Rye, Howard and Jeffrey Green. 'Black Musical Internationalism in England in the 1920s'. *Black Music Research Journal* 15, no. 1 (1995): 93–107, doi:10.2307/779323.

Saba Saakana, Amon. 'Culture, Concept, Aesthetics: The Phenomenon of the African Musical Universe in Western Musical Culture'. *African American Review* 29, no. 2 (1995): n.p,. Gale Academic OneFile.

Sampson, Henry T. *Blacks in Blackface: A Sourcebook on Early Black Musical Shows*, 2nd edn. Lanham, MD: The Scarecrow Press, 2013.

Sapirstein, Ray. '"Original Rags": African American Secular Music and the Cultural Legacy of Paul Laurence Dunbar's Poetry'. In *Black Music, Black Poetry: Genre, Performance and Authenticity*, edited by Gordon Thompson, 19–37. Farnham: Ashgate Publishing, 2013.

Saxon, Theresa. '*In Dahomey* in England: A (Negative) Transatlantic Performance Heritage'. *Atlantic Studies* 13, no. 2 (2016): 265–81, doi:10.1080/14788810.2015.1113373.

Seibert, Brian. *What the Eye Hears: A History of Tap Dancing*. New York: Farrar, Straus and Giroux, 2015.

Seniors, Paula. *Beyond Lift Every Voice and Sing: The Culture of Uplift, Identity, and Politics in Black Musical Theater*. Columbus: Ohio State University Press, 2009.

Seniors, Paula Marie. 'Jack Johnson, Paul Robeson and the Hypermasculine African American Übermensch.' In *The Harlem Renaissance Revisited: Politics, Arts and Letters*, edited by Jeffrey O. G. Ogbar, 155–76. Baltimore, MD: Johns Hopkins University Press, 2010.

Sharpley Whiting, T. Deaning. *Bricktop's Paris: African American Women in Paris between the Two World Wars*. New York: Whiting Suny Press, 2015.

Shaw, Arnold. *Black Popular Music in America: The Singers, Songwriters and Musicians Who Pioneered the Sounds of American Music*. New York, Schirmer Books, 1986.

Shipton, Alyn. *Hi-de-Ho: The Life of Cab Calloway*. Oxford: Oxford University Press, 2013.

Sloan, Nate. 'Constructing Cab Calloway: Publicity, Race and Performance in 1930s Harlem Jazz'. *Journal of Musicology* 36, no. 3 (2019): 372–400, https://doi.org/10.1525/jm.2019.36.3.370.

Smethurst, James. 'Paul Laurence Dunbar and Turn-into-the-20th-Century African American Dualism'. *African American Review* 41, no. 2 (2007): 377–86.

Sterns, Marshall and Jean Sterns. *Jazz Dance: The Story of American Vernacular Dance*. Boston: De Capo Press, 1994. (Originally published in 1968.)

Swindell, Lindsey R. *The Politics of Paul Robeson's Othello*. Jackson: University of Mississippi Press, 2010.

Tackley, Catherine. 'Jazz Dance and Black British Identities'. In *Bodies of Sound: Studies Across Popular Music and Dance*, edited by Sherril Dodds and Susan C. Cook, 193–208. Farnham: Ashgate, 2013.

Tackley, Catherine. 'Race, Identity and the Meaning of Jazz in 1940s Britain'. In *Black Popular Music in Britain Since 1945*, edited by Jon Stratton and Nabeel Zuberi, 11–26. Farnham: Ashgate Popular Music, 2014.

Tanner, Jo A. *Dusky Maidens: The Odyssey of the Early Black Dramatic Actress*. Westport, CT: Greenwood Press, 1992.

Taylor, Frank C. and Gerald Cook. *Alberta Hunter: A Celebration in Blues*. New York: McGraw Hill, 1988.

Thompson, Leslie. *Oral Histories of Jazz in Britain*, interviewed by Val Wilmer 11/08/1987 to 13/11/1987, British Library.

Thompson, Leslie and Jeffrey Green. *Leslie Thompson: An Autobiography As Told to Jeffrey P. Green*. Crawley: Rabbit Press, 1985.

Toynbee, Jason, Catherine Tackley and Mark Doffman. 'Another Place, Another Race? Thinking through Jazz, Ethnicity and Diaspora in Britain'. In *Black British Jazz: Routes, Ownership and Performance*, edited by Jason Toynbee, Catherine Tackley and Mark Doffman, 1–19. Farnham: Ashgate, 2014.

Toynbee, Jason. 'Race, History, and Black British Jazz'. *Black Music Research Journal* 33, no. 1 (2013): 1–25.

Von Eschen, Penny M. *Race Against Empire: Black Americans and Anticolonialism 1937–1957*. Ithaca, NY: Cornell University Press, 1997.

Ward, Brian. 'Music, Musical Theater, and the Imagined South in Interwar Britain'. *The Journal of Southern History* 80, no.1 (2014): 39–72, www.jstor.org/stable/23796843.

Young, Harvey. *Embodying Black Experience: Stillness, Critical Memory, and the Black Body*. Ann Arbor: University of Michigan Press, 2010.

Zembylas, Michalinos. 'Affect, Race, and White Discomfort in Schooling: Decolonial Strategies for "Pedagogies of Discomfort"'. *Ethics and Education* 13, no. 1 (2018): 86–104, doi:10.1080/17449642.2018.1428714.

Zien, Katherine A. *Sovereign Acts: Performing Race, Space, and Belonging in Panama and the Canal Zone*. Critical Caribbean Studies. New Brunswick, NJ: Rutgers University Press, 2017.

Zimmerman, Richard and Tim Smolko. 'Jordan, Joe.' In *The Grove Dictionary of American Music*. Oxford: Oxford University Press, 2013.

INDEX